the big red book of tomatoes

Lindsey Bareham

Grub Street • London

BY THE SAME AUTHOR

IN PRAISE OF THE POTATO
A CELEBRATION OF SOUP
ONIONS WITHOUT TEARS
THE LITTLE BOOK OF BIG SOUPS
SUPPER WON'T TAKE LONG
A WOLF IN THE KITCHEN
JUST ONE POT
DINNER IN A DASH
THE FISH STORE
PASTIES

With Simon Hopkinson

ROAST CHICKEN AND OTHER STORIES
THE PRAWN COCKTAIL YEARS

This new edition published 2011
by Grub Street,4 Rainham Close, London SW11 6SS
food@grubstreet.co.uk
www.grubstreet.co.uk

First published by Michael Joseph in 1999

Design and jacket design: Sarah Driver

A CIP catalogue for this book is available from the British Library

ISBN 978-1-908117-12-0

Printed and bound in by MPG Ltd, Bodmin, Cornwall
This book is printed on FSC (Forest Stewardship Council) paper

CONTENTS

ACKNOWLEDGEMENTS

Tomatoes, as this book became known in my house, lingered on so long, became so all-engrossing, that no one, least of all me, believed I would ever finish. So much so, in fact, that the phrase 'after tomato' is a code for 'I'll do it later, but I'll probably never get round to it.' There are so many fabulous ways of eating tomatoes, both raw and cooked, that I found it impossible to stop researching, cooking, and eating.

The best tomatoes we ate were grown in Italy, the south of France, and from gardens in Cornwall, Henley-on-Thames, and West London. Most were bought from my local greengrocers, Adamous & Sons, sadly now closed, and Andreas Fine Fruit and Vegetables, in Chiswick, and many more from street markets and greengrocers all over the place, from Marks & Spencer, Sainsbury, Safeway, Tesco, and the other multiples. Friends and colleagues have shared a wealth of knowledge, experience and recipes. Lynda Brown, who grows many varieties of tomatoes every year, was particularly helpful, so were Dottore Nino Squillacciotti, Emilio Regazzoni and Suzanna Gelmetti of Cirio Ricerche in Italy. Josa and Thoby Young, of the Fresh Food Company, Michael Michaud, of Peppers By Post, Alan Gear, of Ryton Organic Gardens, the staff at Books for Cooks, Antonio and Priscilla Carluccio, Roger de Freitas, Sandra Fairbank, Stan Hey, Giles Macdonagh, Emily Green and Sybil Kapoor filled in a few gaps. Many chef friends and other cookery writers helped consolidate ideas and recipes and particular recipes are credited throughout the book. However, special thanks to Simon Hopkinson, Ian Bates, Paul Merrony, Rose Gray, Alastair Little, Michel Roux and David Dorricott. The books I found particularly inspirational were: Michel Guérard's *Cuisine Gourmande* and *Cuisine Minceur,* translated by Caroline Conran, *The River Café Cook Book* and *The River Café Cook Book 2* by Rose Gray and Ruthie Rogers, Alastair Little's *Keep It Simple* and *Italian Kitchen*, Deborah Madison's *The Green's Cookbook*, Richard Olney's *A Provençal Table*, Franco and Ann Taruschio's *Leaves from the Walnut Tree*, and Jean and Pierre Troisgros' *Nouvelle Cuisine*. Also indispensable were Joanna Blythman's *The Food We Eat* and Lynda Brown's *The Shopper's Guide to Organic Food*. On a more personal level, special thanks to my sons Zach and Henry, to my agent Bruce Hunter, to my editor Jenny Dereham, copy-editor Hazel Orme, and Liz Moscrop and Jane Grofski.

Most importantly, again, thank you to Andrew Payne and HP, which could be getting its last vote of thanks.

introduction

'There is a little story from Romagna which goes as follows. There was once a priest who was always poking his nose into other people's affairs, not with malice – just simple nosiness. The parishioners who were nevertheless very fond of him nicknamed him Don Pomodoro (Mr Tomato) because, like the tomato, he was into everything.'

Franco Taruschio, *Leaves from the Walnut Tree*

It hardly seems possible that it is nearly twelve years since I first started writing the original edition of this book and I began after three years of cooking and researching the fruit we treat as a vegetable. Like all my single subject books – potatoes, soup and onions before this one – I could think of nothing else as I wrote. My love of cooking with tomatoes was the reason I started the book and I was obsessed with tomatoes. I am still surprised by the unusual recipes I find tucked away in the book and it's been a pleasure to be forced to re-read it from cover to cover looking for printers errors. I could easily fill another book with recipes revolving around tomatoes but although I have added a few, I didn't want to remove any. The biggest change in the last decade has been the quality of British tomatoes and their availability. In the late nineties we were in the throes of a so-called tomato revolution, when tomatoes were starting to be 'grown for flavour'. The British Tomato Growers Association had just been formed and they were determined to raise the profile of home-grown tomatoes and fight back against imports, particularly the long shelf-life varieties in classic sizes, from Spain, Holland and Poland, in particular. They also set about lengthening the tomato season from May to December. This is confusing for people who grow their own, who know that the native home grown season is late July, if you're lucky, through the autumn and the last green fruit that refuses to ripen. Many supermarkets, notably Waitrose and Marks & Spencer, now major on British tomatoes, particularly the intensely flavoured Isle of Wight fruit, and take pride in selling tomatoes that taste as good as they look. The range, particularly of cherry tomatoes, is immense. Increased fuel prices have had a huge effect on imports, particularly, ironically, from Jersey and Guernsey, and improved indoor growing technique has successfully extended the British commercial season. The biggest change, though, is the plethora of 'vine' tomatoes and other so-called speciality types with distinctive looks. 'Vine' and 'vine-ripened' is the ubiquitous new short hand for tomatoes with flavour. When tomatoes are sold with their calyx and vine intact we get a whiff of the smell of tomatoes. It makes their high price acceptable. It is worth noting, though, that the calyx is the first part of the plant to deteriorate, so for longer home shelf-life, it might be worth removing fruit from the vine. The tomato market has changed. We eat less but we are more discerning about the tomatoes we buy. Rarer varieties are becoming more popular and shoppers are asking for specific varieties grown in particular countries at particular times of the year. It is shocking, though, to learn, that 80% of the tomatoes we eat in the UK are unexciting cheap imports. Good news, though, is that there is now an educational website, www.thetomatozone.co.uk, aimed at school age children and www.britishtomatoes.co.uk has up to date information on every aspect of tomatoes, including the latest on tomatoes and health.

My greatest discovery since writing the book has been www.seedsofitaly.co.uk who sell the Franchi range of Italian tomato seeds, enabling me to grow my own San Marzano. I am lucky, too, to live near a greengrocer (www.andreasveg.co.uk) who delights in importing big craggy Italian varieties, the sort that inspired me to write this book in the first place.

This is a book about the pleasure of eating tomatoes.

Take a tomato that has been allowed to ripen on the vine: the plant will have sent its roots deep into the earth in search of food and water while the sun turns the skin of the fruit a deep, dark red. Slice this tomato, sprinkle it with salt, add cracked pepper and some good olive oil, then eat it. Pure pleasure. Or take the big, beefy tomatoes, which the French call Marmande. These are great for stuffing. Roast them until their skins split and their juices weep. Then there are plum tomatoes. The pointy crimson Italian varieties are particularly good. Their dense, fruity flesh makes them perfect for tomato sauces, preserves, and any recipe that requires diced tomatoes. And then there are those red and gold cherry tomatoes, which can be eaten like sweets. If any hang around long enough to wrinkle and lose their looks, they can be turned into the best ever tomato sauce.

After years of researching, cooking and writing, my enthusiasm for this versatile fruit is undiminished. The tomato is the heart and soul of so many soups, stews, sauces, ketchups and preserves that it deserves to be taken seriously. I hope this book will help you to enjoy cooking with tomatoes as much as I do.

Lindsey Bareham, May 2011

note on seasonings and health risks

'A world devoid of tomato soup, tomato sauce, tomato ketchup and tomato paste is hard to visualize.'

Elizabeth David, *Spices, Salts and Aromatics in the English Kitchen*

Unless otherwise specified, freshly ground black pepper should be used for pepper throughout. I also recommend the use of Maldon sea salt flakes. Fresh herbs should be used whenever possible, unless dried herbs are specified. Great care should be taken when preparing chilli peppers: always wash your hands thoroughly afterwards and be careful not to rub your eyes or to touch other sensitive parts of the body.

In some recipes, but not all, I have suggested that you disgorge aubergines to release any bitter juices. In practice I hardly ever bother to do this – the aubergines we can buy nowadays aren't usually bitter – so I leave it up to you to decide whether or not to disgorge!

The risks associated with salmonella mean that it is not advisable to serve soft-boiled and raw eggs to the very young, to pregnant women, to the elderly or anyone weakened by serious illness. To avoid possible health risks caused by pesticides and chemicals, carrots should always be peeled. Whenever possible, I would recommend choosing organic produce. Lemons should be unwaxed.

all you need to know about tomatoes

'The tomato imparts its delicious taste, at the same time acid and slightly sweet, to so many sauces and dishes that it can fairly be classed among the best of condiments. Happy are those who understand how to use it judiciously.'

Ernest Verdier, *Dissertations Gastronomiques*, 1928

HISTORY

'Thank goodness someone finally had the courage to eat one of those little golden-red globes and proclaim it for its delicious acidity and wondrous texture.'

James Beard, writing on the tomato in *Beard on Food*

The tomato has a colourful history. It is thought to have originated in South America, on the northern edge of the Andes, in Peru, Ecuador and Chile. There it grew wild, arriving as if by magic for its short season, the cherry-sized fruit picked by the ancient Peruvians but not regarded as sufficiently interesting to cultivate. It may have travelled to Central America through the centuries although, unlike its relative the potato, it is not recorded on pottery or other artefacts. It is unclear exactly who was first to cultivate *lycopersicon esculentum* ('edible wolf's peach') but by the time Cortes conquered Mexico in 1523, the tomato was ubiquitous, later to spread up the east coast of America. It is also unclear who brought the first tomatoes to Europe from the New World, but agreed among many that they were first cultivated in Spain. Perhaps it was Columbus, whose first explorations of the New World were in the late 1400s. It can't have been Cortes, although he usually gets the credit, along with introducing chocolate to Spain, because tomatoes had already reached Italy by 1522. Anyway, these early tomatoes were cherry-sized and yellow and, unthinkable though it now seems, they were viewed with suspicion, thought either poisonous or an aphrodisiac.

Although it is widely held that the Spanish introduced tomatoes to Naples in the sixteenth century, one story suggests that they came via Morocco, so acquiring the name *pomi de Morì* ('apples of the Moors'), subsequently translated by the French into *pommes d'amour*. They appeared in the second edition of *Gerard's Herball* in 1636 under the heading 'Apples of Love' but described as having a '... ranke and stinking savour'. The theory that tomatoes were an aphrodisiac also explains this particular name, but a more likely explanation is to do with their yellow colour. Hence 'golden apples', *pomme d'or* in France, *pomi d'oro* (which evolved into *pomodoro*) in Italy, and *goldapfel* in Germany. The English called them *tomata*, later tomato, from the Spanish *tomate*, which in turn came from the Aztec and Mexican, *tomata*. Most countries use an approximation of the original name: in Majorca *tomatiga*; in Malta, *tadam*; in India, *tamatar*, in Portugal *tomatada* and in Greece and Turkey, *domate*.

It wasn't until the arrival of a new strain of red tomato, developed from seeds brought to Italy from Mexico by two Jesuits, that tomatoes appeared on the culinary scene. The Neapolitans were quick to see the true potential of the new fruit. In the mid-1700s a chef called Francesco Leonardi was the first to match pasta with tomato, and meatballs with a tomato sauce. Others, particularly the British and Americans, remained cautious, regarding the tomato as an ornamental curiosity, but by the beginning of the nineteenth century tomatoes were creeping into cookery books. Colin

Spencer, in his exhaustively researched *Vegetable Book* (Conran Octopus), observes that, '. . . the fact that the tomato survived at all must be due to the enthusiasm that amateur gardeners had for the vegetable (and still have, for that matter), so that rural cookery of the nineteenth century was full of tomato chutneys, pickles and relishes'.

By the late nineteenth century the tomato had caught on big time. Today there is hardly a culture that doesn't embrace it, and it is one of the world's best-selling foods, grown as far afield as Iceland in the north and New Zealand in the south. However, it still has ground to cover. The tomato is little used throughout Asia, apart from in India, has no part in the Japanese diet, and has made no noticeable impact in China, where it wasn't introduced until the 1930s.

SO WHAT IS A TOMATO AND ARE THEY GOOD FOR YOU?

> 'Dear Albert, I have read in the past and heard from various people that tomatoes, grapes and wine are all extremely bad for arthritis. I know you are a chef and not a doctor, Albert, but have you heard this, and do you know why this could be?'
>
> L. Burnett, Fulham, SW 6
>
> 'How right you are! I am not a medical doctor, but I have heard this too, and the reason always given seems to be the acid content in these fruits. Everything in moderation, and a little of what you fancy does you good.'
>
> Albert Roux, 'Cher Albert', *ES Magazine*, 15 August 1996

The tomato is technically a berry, and therefore a fruit, but we use it as a vegetable. It takes forty to sixty days from flowering for a tomato to reach full ripening. A tomato is 93-95 per cent water. It is low in fat, contains 14 calories per 100 g and 1.5 per cent of total composition is fibre. Tomatoes are a good source of vitamins A and C and, when eaten raw, vitamin E. They also contain fructose and glucose (sugars), folic acid, potassium, calcium and mineral salts, including p-coumaric acid and chlorogenic acid, both claimed to 'flush out' carcinogens. Some vitamins are lost in cooking; raw and grilled tomatoes have the highest concentrations of nutrients.

Tomatoes get their red colour from lycopene, which is particularly dense in the skin, a natural carotenoid related to its better-known cousin beta-carotene. Lycopene is a powerful anti-oxidant, thought to combat the harmful effects of free radicals (rogue molecules), which are precursors of heart disease and cancer. Recent research from, among others, the American Association for Cancer

Research (April 1997) shows that people who eat more tomatoes, particularly processed tomatoes, are better protected against the growth of cancerous tumours. Lycopene is more readily absorbed into the bloodstream when the tomatoes are cooked with certain oils, such as olive oil but particularly corn oil, and the benefit of 40 g tomato paste is equal to that of 400 g whole, cooked tomatoes. The claims are particularly dramatic for men: eating tomatoes at least ten times a week reduces the risk of developing prostate cancer by 35 per cent, and halves the risk of heart disease.

Women will just have to make do with a face pack of tomato pulp mixed with yoghurt: tomato is good for the skin, refreshing, toning, aiding circulation and restoring acidity after cleansing. Well, that's what the British Tomato Growers' Association claim.

GROWN FOR FLAVOUR?

> **'... heirloom tomatoes outdo the modern kinds that most people eat, enthusiasts say, in flavour, tenderness and diversity. There are several thousand heirlooms in all. Some are tangy, some sweet; some as big as grapefruits, others as small as grapes. They come in zebra stripes, heart shapes, emerald green, deep purples, chocolate browns.'**
>
> Donna St George, 'The Tomato, Singing Its Siren Song',
> *New York Times*, 20 August 1997

When you bite into a tomato you want to taste a fruit that is juicy and tender, with the perfect balance of sweet and sour. You want to be able to smell the tomato, to get a whiff of that odd herby tang that always comes with home-grown ones. The shape and size should be irrelevant to quality. Tiny cherry tomatoes are the sweetest and the big, blowsy beef tomatoes are least likely to have much flavour. The ones in between – the so-called all-rounders, or salad tomatoes – are anyone's guess. Plum are supposed to be the best for cooking because, as a type, their flesh is denser and holds its form better.

The exact composition of any tomato is unique to its variety. The colour of the fruit, the thickness of the skin, the density of the flesh, the juiciness, the size of the pips and the amount of jellied juice around them is infinitely variable, but there are distinctive types of tomato.

Cherry and cocktail: Bite-sized and round, known as *pomodorini* in Italy. The flavour is sweet – they have the highest sugar content of all tomatoes – and concentrated. They are best eaten raw, and tend to be used for garnish or as a salad tomato, but are good when briefly grilled, barbecued or roasted with a smear of olive oil. Blitzed in a food-processor, they make intensely flavoured quick sauces and vinaigrettes.

All-purpose classic, slicing or salad: Medium-large, slightly squat and probably the most familiar, the shape is well suited to slicing. They tend to have a large seed cavity, sloppy textured flesh, and are often disappointing. Improve flavour by roasting or lengthy stewing.

Plum and baby plum: Plum or egg-shaped with a large core, tough skin and easy to peel. Also known as Roma, Italian tomato or, in the States, paste tomato. Available in various sizes, including cherry, mini and midi, but most often medium-size. Sometimes extremely elongated, particularly Italian varieties, most notably San Marzano from Naples, with a small nipple at the flower end. Dense, firm, meaty flesh and few seeds make it the chef's choice for cooking because it holds its form. Good flavour when properly ripened.

Beef or beefsteak, also called slicing: extra large and dark red, so-called because of their dense, beefy flesh. Usually imported from Holland and Spain, they tend to lack flavour and are best used for stuffing and baking. Look out for ridged and irregularly shaped large tomatoes – Marmande – from Provence and Morocco, occasionally Italy, Sicily, Greece and Cyprus, in particular. Look out for Jack Hawkins, an Isle of Wight variety.

Golden, yellow and pale orange: Yellow and pale orange tomatoes come in all shapes and sizes, from tiny cherry and pear shapes to salad size. They tend to have names that include 'gold' or 'sun' and taste much the same as equivalent red varieties. They are best eaten raw, with their skin left on. As with red tomatoes, their flesh is paler than the skin, but they tend to have small seeds.

Green: Either uniformly coloured or with distinctive stripes. Unless these tomatoes have been specially bred, green tomatoes are unripe. They are delicious cooked in all sorts of ways (see pages 407-419) and can be ripened (' . . . up to a point, Lord Copper . . .') singly in a warm spot. The process may be speeded up by placing one ripe tomato among a bowl of green ones.

Organic: Grown without pesticides. They must be free of chemicals and grown in soil that has not been treated with chemicals and has been managed to full organic standards for the past two years, as laid down by EU legislation. The chief hazard of organic tomato growing is early blight, which is conventionally controlled by spraying. For organic growers, harvesting early enough to beat the blight, and late enough for full flavour, is a race against time. Conventional industrial tomato-growing takes place under glass on an enormous scale, in what amounts to food-creating factories, using hydroponics, rarely soil. Industrially produced tomatoes are harvested under-ripe for resilience to transport, and arrive in the shops never having developed their flavour potential. Although supermarkets have caught up at last with the public's desire for flavour, and provide named varieties, the organic tomato can often deliver a better taste than a conventionally grown one. This is not only because they are cultivated in soil rich with natural potassium but because they are only grown in season and matured on the vine, hopefully with plenty of sun. The downside is that organic tomatoes are more fragile to transport and 20 to 50 per cent more expensive. Nevertheless, demand for organics has grown by

50 per cent every year for the last four years. Organic tomatoes should be eaten as soon as possible after harvesting: fast distribution from grower to consumer through box schemes is the best way to achieve this. Contact Organics Direct, tel. 020 7729 2828 and www.boxfreshorganics.co.uk .

Vine-ripened and 'grown for flavour': Supermarket hype. To give them their due, the supermarkets have taken heed of the plea that originated with Elizabeth David, probably in the fifties, later endorsed by Jane Grigson and perpetuated by every food writer, at some time or another, for tomatoes with flavour. To that effect they have spent huge resources in an attempt to find tomatoes that taste good. Because we love tomatoes so much, and we seem to want to buy them all year round (in 1997, £81.9 million worth of tomatoes were grown in Britain – in 2010 the retail value of UK produced tomatoes is £150 million – which is the second largest fruit and vegetable crop, second only to carrots, worth £83 million. Potatoes are categorized as an agricultural crop – we ate over £362 million worth of them), the supermarkets also want to supply us with tasty tomatoes outside the traditional tomato-growing season of July to October.

A solution, of sorts, is manifest in the term 'grown for flavour'. This, of course, begs the question, if tomatoes aren't grown for flavour, then what are they grown for? The answer, of course, is money.

However, attaching a label that says 'grown for flavour' to a bag of tomatoes is the customers' quasi-guarantee that the contents taste of something remotely resembling tomato. If, and this is the second part of the sting, the tomatoes are sold with part of their vine attached, they can be called 'vine-ripened' as well as 'grown for flavour'. This is a licence to ask exorbitant prices, and to compound the luxury image, the 'spray' or 'branch' of vine-attached tomatoes is sold laid out in a sculpted tray inside a plastic box. They certainly look attractive, particularly to city dwellers who like the idea of growing their own tomatoes, but don't always live up to expectations.

FRIDGE OR FRUIT BOWL?

> **'A number of rare or newly experienced foods have been claimed to be aphrodisiacs. At one time this quality was even ascribed to the tomato. Reflect on that when you are next preparing the family salad.'**
>
> **Jane Grigson, *The Mushroom Feast*, 1975**

The moment you get home with tomatoes, whether they are in a brown-paper bag, a plastic tray with clingfilm, or a plastic bag, take them out of their packaging. Place them in a bowl or basket, as you would any fruit, and leave them at room temperature. Remember, tomatoes are a sub-tropical fruit and dislike the cold: storing in the fridge impairs their flavour. Most of the tomatoes we buy in the supermarket – even those sold as grown for flavour and sun-ripened, *and* those on the vine – will improve their flavour if kept at room temperature for a few days. Their colour may deepen, and gradually, day by day, they will soften. Once the tomatoes have achieved their optimum state they should be eaten because they will quickly sag and wrinkle.

The life of soggy, over-ripe tomatoes will not be extended by putting them in the fridge – in fact, they will go soft even more quickly. Use them in sauces, stews, soups, and for the stockpot. If, and this is a big if, ripe tomatoes cannot be eaten and need to wait, they should be refrigerated in airtight, non-metal containers and used within a few days.

Blemished tomatoes – those with broken or bruised skin – will quickly turn bad. Organic tomatoes tend to have ripened longer on the vine than commercially grown tomatoes and therefore deteriorate faster. As a general rule, depth and consistency of colour, particularly with red tomatoes, is a fair indication of ripeness. If there are green patches or the tomatoes are very pale with a hint of greenness in the skin, or with 'green shoulders', they need to be 'brought on' or 'ripened'. Left somewhere warm, on top of the fridge or on a window-sill, preferably in direct sunlight, the tomato will turn deepest red. Even immature, pale green tomatoes – such as the rock-hard San Marzano I picked in Naples and left on the shelf in my study – turn from apple green through shades of yellow-orange to darkest tomato red in the right conditions. However, these tomatoes, which are officially known as 'mature green tomatoes', will never develop the delicious flavour they are supposed to have.

Direct sunlight and warmth are what tomatoes like best. Putting unripe tomatoes in a bowl of ripe ones may speed up the ripening process but will have no effect on the flavour. It is a fallacy to think that unripe tomatoes still attached to their vine will ripen with more flavour than those without.

POPULAR VARIETIES ON SALE

> **'I am sure the majority of people do not realise that for years tomatoes have been grown in rockwool (the same material used in our house walls) in glasshouses, and only grow through it when pumped full of fertiliser and nutrients. They look beautiful but, never having seen soil or the outside, it is no wonder that they are completely tasteless.'**
>
> **Mrs M. Chessman, Kent, quoted by Lynda Brown,**
> **in *The Shoppers Guide to Organic Food* (Fourth Estate, 1998)**

The choice of tomato varieties available to the British consumer has never been greater or better, and I'm not just talking about the selection on sale at the height of summer. Commercial growers, spurred by supermarket buyers who've been corralled by food writers, have invested in the search for tomatoes with flavour. New varieties, usually crossbred for good yield as well as taste, are coming thick and fast. Hence, a bewildering choice of varieties is now available at all times of the year. Many are British – British production is presently 80,000 tonnes, (this figure represents about a fifth of the total volume of tomatoes sold in the country through the year), in addition we import over 400,000 tonnes of fresh tomatoes.

In the UK the tomato is the fourth most popular fruit – after bananas, apples and oranges – and tomato production is big business. In traditional tomato-growing areas – the Mediterranean, for example – the seasonal nature of tomatoes is respected. No one *expects* to eat fresh tomatoes all year round. Instead they bottle, can and dry what is left over of the crop, and eat that when the fresh fruit has run out. Our tomato-growing season, however, has been extended from July to October to March until December, thanks to controlled glasshouse conditions with increased light. Until someone comes up with a tomato that has taste and that can be grown all year round, preferably in this country, the supermarkets are looking for suppliers to plug the three-month lull. Despite the difficulty of transportation, and the costs involved, one supermarket chain, at least, did look to South Africa. Watch the supermarket shelf for vine-ripened, 'grown for flavour' tomatoes to serve with your Christmas dinner. It will happen.

At the moment we eat approximately 7-8 kg of fresh tomatoes a year, which equates to 150 g per person per week. I don't know if I fit the national average or not. I doubt it. I eat fresh tomatoes every day, sometimes twice or three times a day, during the summer and autumn, but the rest of the time I rarely buy fresh. Instead, I use cans, bottles, tubes and packets.

When you are shopping for tomatoes, preferably during their natural season, choose them because they look and smell good, and decide what to do with them later. Don't forget, the tomatoes with unflawed skin, laid out so neatly on the supermarket shelf, have been harvested under-ripe for resilience to transport, prematurely ripened by exposure to ethylene gas and stored in coolers at precisely 38°F. Some are dipped in wax to make them shine. No wonder they never develop their flavour potential. Craggy, misshapen tomatoes, probably grown outside in earth in direct sunlight, will have deep red skin. Take a bite into one of those tomatoes – it will remind you of how a tomato should taste. Shop at your local greengrocer; encourage him to take trouble with his supplies. Tell him to chat up a few restaurant suppliers, who grow and import fabulous tomatoes, someone like Frances Smith of Appledore Salads (tel. 01233 758201) or Solstice (tel. 020 7498 7700), who supply London and the South East, or www.damhead.co.uk (tel. 0131 445 7425), in Scotland. If you are lucky you might get to taste some heritage tomatoes (see A Grower's Guide, page 23) or heirlooms, as they're called in America.

The following varieties, all commercially grown and widely available, are the best of what I've sampled recently. Read the labels carefully. 'Organic' and 'sun-ripened on the vine' are the words you are looking for. Isle of Wight tomatoes generally deliver the best flavour of the commercially produced British tomatoes currently available in our supermarkets.

Amaroso: Sweet medium-sized vine tomato, good all-rounder.

Angelle and Bon Bon: baby plum with strong, dark red colour and glossy finish. Intensely sweet yet plumy flavour, firm, crisp and fairly juicy.

Capri: organic, vine-ripened cocktail tomato with bright red colour and a good balance of sweetness and acidity.

Cheramy: medium-sized cherry tomato with dark red skin and rich fruit flavour with a hint of raspberries. Good firm texture.

Claret: vine-ripened with sweet and juicy flavour and just-picked aroma. Versatile all-rounder, good for salads and sauces.

Jack Hawkins: large beefsteak with deep red colour throughout the tomato. Irregular, lobed shape, sweet flavour and low acidity. Very juicy and tender skin. Perfect for slicing or stuffing.

Jester: Distinctive jester's hat-shaped tomato with sweet, full flavour. Grown for M&S in Lancashire for 10 years.

Marmande: Large, knobbly and ridged French variety. Excellent for salads. Look for dark red fruit, usually sold loose rather than on the vine.

Piccolini: immensely popular cherry vine tomato originally from Sicily and grown in various countries, some with a 'sun-ripened on the vine' tag. Some are organic. Super sweet from Lancashire but stronger more intense flavour from Portugal and Isle of Wight.

Reterno: organic large vine tomato with slightly boxy shape and good flavour. Usually sold as a truss rather than boxed.

Santini: Reliably sweet and fruity medium-sized tomato harvested when fully ripe and grown on the Isle of Wight. Red or yellow.

Sultan's Jewel: Distinctively pointy-shaped medium-small organic vine tomato with dark red skin and rich flavour.

Tamarillo: otherwise known as a tree tomato, large and elongated, about the size of a duck egg. Deep red glossy skin, which is thicker than that of regular tomatoes, orange-red flesh with black seeds. Cooking advised. Very tart. Australia, New Zealand and other semi-tropical countries.

Tomalini: Grown all year round in Kent specially for M&S. Sweet and juicy midi-plum with consistently good flavour.

RARE VARIETIES

Coeur de Boeuf (bull's heart): big, craggy variety with unusual, irregular shape. Indigenous to the South of France and many areas of Italy. Dense texture, delicious flavour.

Camone: small variety grown in the salty soil of Sardinia. Sweet enough to eat as a fruit but transforms tomato sauces.

Datterini: Sicilian cherry tomato, often described as the finest cherry variety with a superb flavour and good sweet-sour balance.

Marinda: distinctive green ribbed tomato with fabulous flavour and perfect for any of the green dessert recipes mentioned in the book. Grown in salty Sardinian soil.

San Marzano: the most prized plum tomato grown in volcanic sun-drenched soil around Naples. Sea salt air naturally seasons the plants. Distinctive long shape with a little nipple at the end.

TINS, BOTTLES, TUBES AND PACKETS: TOMATO PRODUCTS

> **'Do you remember those American Express ads which focused on drawings of restaurant celebrities? There was one of Nico Ladenis accompanied by the memorable words: "I have never used a sun-dried tomato in my life."**
>
> **There is nothing inherently wrong with sun-dried tomatoes, not if you like tomato-flavoured toffee, that is.'**
>
> Joe Hyam, 'Viewpoint', *Caterer & Hotelkeeper*, 15 June 1995

Some people are tinned-tomato snobs, thinking, incorrectly, that fresh is always best. Others, like me, use them all the time, even at the height of summer. The vast range of processed tomato products seems to be increasing in exact proportion to the number of new tomato varieties that appear daily on the supermarket shelf. Like fresh tomatoes, these processed tomato products are surprisingly variable. A comparative tasting is quite shocking. Some brands of so-called whole peeled tomatoes contain only three or four large overcooked tomatoes with fragments of skin in a watery juice. Others are literally jam-packed with even-sized tomatoes in a thick juice. Some taste acidic, leaving a bitter, metallic taste in the mouth. Others taste remarkably fresh and clean with a good balance of acidity and sweetness.

It is difficult to single out particular brands because quality varies from season to season. As a general rule go for Italian products. In Italy manufacturers stipulate varieties to their growers, and they cultivate a staggering selection of wonderful elongated (Roma) plum tomatoes. Do read labels carefully: Napolina, for example, which you would expect to be an Italian brand, isn't. Of all the supermarket own-brands, Tesco, in my opinion, is by far the best. Organic versions of most processed tomato products are available. Look out for Whole Earth (ketchup), Campo and Muir Glen (for diced and whole tomatoes, passata), Rapunzel and Cereal Terra (for sun-dried in olive oil), La Selva (bottled tomatoes from Tuscany). Kallo make organic stocks with a tomato base; one of the best is Tomato and Peppers.

Whole peeled tomatoes: known as *pomodori pelati* in Italy, and traditionally tinned or bottled in their own juice for use during the winter when fresh ones are not available. East of Naples the volcanic ash from successive eruptions of Mount Vesuvius has settled to create immensely fertile land ideally suited to the cultivation of tomatoes. Here they grow special elongated varieties for tinning and squashing into puree. San Marzano, which was almost wiped out by a virus and is now protected by the European Community, is a speciality of Naples, the Rolls-Royce, so to speak, of Italian plum tomatoes.

Bottled unpeeled tomatoes: occasionally available commercially but most often made at home by those who grow sufficient tomatoes. Treated properly (see page 394), using the best of the crop, these tomatoes will be full of summer flavour. In some Italian grocers they are sold as *pomodori nella bottiglia*, *filetti de pomodoro* and *pomodori pelati*. Once opened, store in the fridge and consume within a few days.

Chopped peeled tomatoes: chunks of tomato with seeds and core, in watery or thick tomato juice. Usually sold canned and often with additional flavourings such as basil, oregano or mixed herbs.

Crushed tomatoes, tomato pulp, or sugocasa: Known as *polpa di pomodoro* in Italy, it consists of small chunks of (mainly) seeded tomato in its own juice. Rustica by Cirio is, in my opinion, the best.

Chair de tomate: finely chopped Provence tomatoes in a thick tomato puree thickened with corn starch.

Passata: sieved, uncooked tomato pulp, usually sold in bottles or tetra paks. Once opened, store in the fridge and use within a few days. Quality varies enormously and you get what you pay for. Look out for passata that hasn't separated in the bottle, this will have the best viscosity and flavour.

Creamed tomatoes: smooth, thick, sieved tomatoes, usually sold in tetra paks. Packed with preservatives, but once opened, store in the fridge and use within a few days. Concentrated tomato paste/puree: smooth tomato pulp cooked until thick, dark and dry. Sold as single or double concentrate; single has fresher, sweeter flavour. Usually made with leftover tomato trimmings. To be used sparingly for thickening tomato sauces, adding to stews, etc. Sold in tubes and small cans. Once opened, a can will keep indefinitely in the fridge if sealed with a layer of olive oil. Also available made with sun-dried tomatoes. Norway, apparently, buys enormous quantities of tomato puree, which is distilled to make into 60 per cent proof alcohol.

Estratto: very dark, six-times concentrated tomato pulp, made by leaving the pulp in the sun to dry and stirring daily for about a fortnight until all the liquid has evaporated. Mixed with salt, shaped into blocks and wrapped in basil leaves, estratto was the first attempt to preserve the flavour of Italian tomatoes. It is occasionally available commercially, mostly in Sicily, also in Greece, Cyprus and

Persia, but can be found at Carluccio's, www.carluccios.com

Asceptic tomatoes: could one day be the tomato product of the future. Tomatoes are peeled, halved and the juice separated from the flesh. The juice then goes through a reverse osmosis process and a high proportion of the liquid is concentrated to improve flavour and colour. The concentrated juice, which isn't heat-damaged, is added later to the chopped tomato or kept separate for use in sauces and soups. In effect, the end result is cooked tomato flesh with concentrated fresh tomato juice. The benefit of processing tomatoes is that lycopene becomes more bio-available. In 1998 Marks & Spencer and Northern Foods engaged in a joint project on a reverse-osmosis tomato product.

Sun-dried tomatoes: on the jacket of Antonio Carluccio's *Southern Italian Feast* (BBC Books, 1998), there is a photograph of tables spread with tomatoes drying in the sun for as far as the eye can see. In Italy, this happens every August and September. Halved Roma (plum) tomatoes are sprinkled with salt and left until they turn leathery and dry. The *pomodori secchi* will keep as they are, to be rehydrated with water and a little vinegar, or preserved in olive oil, perhaps with garlic or other seasonings to add extra flavour. An approximation of sun-dried tomatoes can be made in the oven (see page 395). Fortnum & Mason produce a range of English dried-tomato products. Their version of sun-dried tomatoes (oven-dried) is packed in extra virgin olive oil with capers. A paste from these tomatoes is mixed with herbes de Provence. Serve sun-dried tomatoes stored in olive oil straight from the jar as antipasto, or in cooked dishes and salads. Leathery sun-dried tomatoes need to be rehydrated in hot water and left for at least 5 minutes, often longer. They can be used whole, sliced or chopped in stewed dishes and are improved by marinating in oil with other flavourings if they are to be served uncooked.

Bush tomato and akudjura: akudjura is an Aboriginal name for the native desert tomatoes, grown principally 220 km north of Alice Springs. The ripe fruit looks like a yellowish cherry tomato with a green tinge and is traditionally left on the bush to dry and shrivel until it resembles a reddish-brown raisin (it is also known as desert raisin). It is then ground and mixed with water to make a thick paste and rolled into huge balls. Ground akudjura has a zingy Marmite-tomato flavour, and is used, like a spice, in sauces, savoury dishes, bread, soup, etc. It is sold in 90 g bottles and stocked by Sainsbury and other selected stores, imported from Australia by Bush Foods.

Mi-cuit Tomatoes: soft, succulent, semi-dried tomatoes from France. Intensely flavoured like sun-dried, but can be eaten from the pack for use in salads, stir-fries, pastas, etc. Sold in 100 g packs by Merchant Gourmet.

Sun-drenched, sun-blushed, sun-kissed and similar names: tends to be small partially cooked tomatoes in oil with herbs. Intense flavour, useful for pasta, bruschetta, antipasti and salads, or to add last-minute vivacity to stews.

A WORD ABOUT GENETICALLY MODIFIED TOMATO PRODUCTS

Responding to a photo published in the Daily Telegraph *of Dr Nigel Poole and colleagues munching on GM tomatoes:*

'Dr Poole told the newspaper that over the past 10 years about 40 staff at Zeneca (a British biotechnology company) have eaten fresh GM tomatoes, which have not been approved for sale in Britain except in a tomato puree where the seeds are destroyed in the process . . . Mr Best, business development manager of ICI Seeds, which became Zeneca, was asked in 1989 whether the GM tomatoes tasted nice. He replied that eating them was not allowed: "If people swallowed the tomato seeds the plants could end up growing in a sewage farm somewhere and this would be an unauthorised release of a genetically engineered organism."'

Scientists get the pip over GM tomatoes *Independent*, 20 February 1999

In February 1995, the European Novel Food Regulations gave the green light to the production of genetically modified tomato puree. In 1996 this was extended to tomato paste products, and in 1997 to chopped-tomato products. Why, one wonders, when there is no shortage of ordinarily produced tomato products, do we need them made with genetically engineered tomatoes? The answer is simple, and it is commercial. The buzzword for tomatoes and tomato products is flavour. Tomatoes allowed to ripen on the vine tend to have greater flavour, but the difficulty for commercial producers is that as the tomatoes ripen the fruit becomes squashy. Consumers, it is believed, won't buy soft tomatoes. With genetic engineering, it is possible to produce tomatoes that can ripen on the vine without going squashy and with better flavour. These tomatoes take less water, which means that less irrigation is required while they are growing and ripening. Irrigation costs money. Thus, say the producers, the reason we need genetically produced tomatoes is so that the customer can have what they want: cheaper, tastier tomatoes. However, people working in the tomato industry believe that: 'This is being achieved by development of new varieties and fruit types, improved systems of handling fruit and grading after harvest to allow fruit to ripen on the vine and understanding more about the basic biology of plant growth and fruit development.' British Tomato Growers' Association, 9 July 1997.

Iceland, the frozen-food chain, is not convinced that it is safe to eat genetically engineered food, and in March 1998, it was the first of the large multiples to ban it. Sainsbury and Safeway both sell tomato puree from genetically altered tomatoes, designed by a British biotechnology company and grown in California. The fruit ripens slowly, cutting out waste. Both products are clearly labelled and the shops say they are selling well. A US company has developed the non-squashy Flavr Savr tomato for sale in US supermarkets, and has permission to market it in the UK. Most other major companies have their own versions in the pipeline.

But perhaps genetic engineering isn't all bad. Scientists have created a tomato that has been altered to boost its production of lycopene, which has been found to reduce the risk of prostate cancer (see pages 12-13) of which there is a low incidence in some Mediterranean countries, including Greece and Spain.

A GROWER'S GUIDE

'... only two things
that money can't buy
and that's True Love
and Home Grown Tomatoes ...
True Love, and Home Grown Tomatoes ...'

song written and sung by Guy Clark

This is a book about eating tomatoes and in order to eat the best possible tomatoes you need to grow them yourself. The simplest way to do this is to buy some tomato plants. They are stocked by garden centres, and for anyone with limited space there are small bush or dwarf varieties, such as tumbling tom, small fry and toy boy (also see www.gardening.about.com), which have been developed for patios and window-boxes. Look out for short-jointed dark-green plants. Avoid elongated or 'leggy', pale green plants. Always check that the plant has been watered regularly by turning the pot upside down. If it looks dry or the roots are sticking out of the bottom, don't buy it. Tomato plants can also be bought by mail order and are available from all the major seed suppliers. They come carefully packed in pluglets with full directions for potting up and planting out. This can be done in pots or in Gro-bags. If you go Gro-bag, a good tip is to cut the bottom out of the bag so the water can drain out, and the roots grow directly into the soil. Despite what the bag might say, the plants will need extra feed. Any organic or non-organic proprietary tomato feed will do.

Once they get going tomato plants are sturdy, but they sulk if their roots get cold, particularly when they are young. They need tender loving care, so keep them happy in an even temperature. Don't over-water, and don't forget to water then over-compensate. Feed them regularly so they grow steadily. Never plant them outside until mid-June when the weather is warm.

The choice of seeds now available from tomato specialists and general suppliers is fantastic. Heritage seeds, unusual varieties, organics, and a wide range of other seeds and seedlings are available by mail from Simpson's Seeds tel 01985 845004 or via their immensely helpful webside www.simpsonsseeds.co.uk. Another good source of unusual and heirloom seed is www.seedparade.co.uk.

If you are new to tomato-growing choose seeds or plants from all the main types of tomato: cherry, all-purpose, beef (these are the most difficult to find with good flavour, although Donna is particularly recommended), together with a selection of heritage and/or organic varieties. If you really want to cut a dash, choose green and black-striped chocodel, or another of the black varieties. Bon appétit.

tomato technique

'Poulet Minerva (see page 365) was named after our cat (seen with Barbara on the dust-wrapper of the first edition of *A Very Private Eye*), who liked tomato skins. Minerva was a brindled tortoiseshell who came with us from London (with black-and-white Tom) to Finstock in 1972. She was very fond of her food, and we noticed that she showed interest whenever tomatoes were being peeled and would eat the skins quite daintily. If there happened to be any custard around, that was another of her favourites.'

Hilary Pym and Honor Wyatt, *Cooking à la Pym*, Prospect Books, 1996

Is it really necessary to tell you how to peel and core a tomato? Or how to chop it to make concassé? Yes, most definitely, yes. The variation in timing given by cookery writers on how long a tomato needs to be immersed in boiling water before its skin can be peeled away is extraordinary. Some say 5 seconds, many say a minute, and I have read more than one who suggested 30 minutes. The truth is that the time depends on many variables: the ripeness of the tomato, its size, its colour, the number of tomatoes being immersed together, and whether the tomatoes are being dropped into boiling water or covered with boiled water.

It is important to realize that tomato flesh is very delicate, and boiling water will soften it quickly. That is why some chefs insist on peeling tomatoes by scraping the flesh off the skin, rather in the same way as if they were skinning a fish. This technique, though fiddly and time-consuming, is invaluable for dishes or garnishes that require concassé with the original texture of the tomato intact. Realistically, though, it is a method you might use for the odd tomato or if you have aspirations to earning three Michelin stars.

What follows, then, is the distilled wisdom of preparing many more tomatoes than I can possibly recall.

HOW TO PEEL A TOMATO

The brilliant shiny skin of the tomato is the external defence of the fruit. It provides a barrier to infection and prevents lactic-acid changes, which alter the flavour of the tomato. The skin has a high concentration of pigment – the same lycopene that provides the red in watermelon – which is an anti-oxidant. The skin extends the shelf life of the tomato. When it is broken the game is up: enzymes attack and the fruit quickly deteriorates. The skin contains no sugar, no acids and no vitamins. It is edible but indigestible. It is usually a surprise to discover how red the skin is by comparison with the flesh underneath.

Depending on what you plan to do with the tomatoes, you may wish to peel away the thin, almost plastic skin. I wholeheartedly agree with Marcella Hazan when she writes on the subject of tomato skins in *Marcella Cucina* (1997) that, 'A tomato's skin is a veil which obscures the wonders of its flesh. If you leave it on, the tomatoes will eventually shed their skin as they cook, and later you will either have to spit it out or, since it is not pleasant to chew on, swallow it.'

The neatest way to peel tomatoes is to score the top of the tomato with a small cross at the blossom end (opposite to the stalk end). Next, cut out the core: use a small sharp knife and cutting at an angle around the beige core where the stalk was attached, loosen a small cone shape of flesh around the core, lift it out and discard – it is not good to eat. I find it easier to do this first, because once the tomato has been peeled it is slippery, more difficult to grip firmly and thus to core. Drop the tomatoes into a pan of boiling water until the skin of the cross curls back. This takes 5-15 seconds depending on the ripeness of the tomato. Yellow/orange varieties tend to take longest. Size and type of tomato don't generally affect how quickly the skin peels back. Don't bother attempting to peel cherry tomatoes: they are too fiddly and will collapse in the process.

To stop the tomatoes continuing to soften, plunge them immediately into cold water, and leave them for a few seconds. Then, starting at the cross cut in the base, catch the skin between your thumb and the knife blade and strip it off in sections, working towards the stem end where the skin adheres more firmly. If you have a large quantity of tomatoes to peel, do them in batches.

Another, simpler method is to place the tomatoes in a bowl, pour over boiling water and count to 20. Prick a tomato with the point of a sharp knife; if the skin splits and peels back, they are ready to be drained and peeled. If not, leave for a few more seconds and check again.

Some people swear by the rather old-fashioned method of spearing a tomato on a fork and holding it over a gas or charcoal flame, turning until the skin splits.

You can peel very big tomatoes with a potato peeler. The swivel type is best, the sort that can glide over the tomato without exerting pressure and is so sharp that it just lifts the skin. Another way to peel tomatoes without scalding is to cut them lengthways into quarters. Discard the pips and juices and place a piece of tomato on a work surface skin side down. Then, slip a small, sharp knife between skin and flesh, and run the blade down the length of the tomato keeping it as close to the skin as possible. The tomato quarters are now ready to be sliced or cut into concassé.

REMOVING THE SEEDS

You can get rid of some of the seeds in medium and large tomatoes by cutting out the core, poking a finger gently into the hole then giving the tomato a squeeze and shaking out the seeds over a bowl. For stuffed tomato dishes or if the tomatoes are round, halve the tomatoes horizontally. Taking each half in turn, squeeze it over a bowl, shaking out the seeds. A small teaspoon, or the end of a teaspoon, is also helpful.

To seed plum tomatoes, halve the tomato through the core (or where the core used to be) and use a small teaspoon to scrape the seeds out of their cavity. If the tomato has a single straight furrow on top where it was attached to the plant, slice the tomato lengthways at this point, cutting perpendicularly to the furrow. You will find that the tomato comes open exactly where its seeds lie, and you can then easily scoop them out.

A WORD ABOUT SEEDS

Many recipes require the seeds to be removed from the cavity. There are several reasons for this. Some people, particularly chefs, believe that the seeds, like skin, are unsightly. More importantly, the seeds are held in a jelly-like colourless substance that, when heated, liquefies and makes the dish watery. This 'water' is easily driven off by boiling but then you are left with lots of seeds and, anyway, it might not be appropriate to the dish to have to cook it long enough to evaporate the liquid. Tomatoes are watery anyway and it doesn't take long for them to melt into a slop.

It is short-sighted, however, to regard the seeds and their serum as a waste of space. Their 'water' is intensely favoured. In fact, it is often the tastiest part of the tomato because this is where most of the sugars are. It adds a fresh vitality to stocks, soups, consommés, sauces, vinaigrettes and pasta dishes, and there are recipes throughout this book that ask for just that. Chopped tomato, for example, left to stand with a seasoning of salt or sugar will draw out this liquid (and from the tomato flesh) which, when whisked with olive oil, becomes a sauce or vinaigrette. Equally, the seeds and their 'water' contain a lot of pectin so help to set jam and chutneys. This explains why, when such tomato stock is left overnight in the fridge, it might well have set by the morning. If you are preparing concassé for a dish, it is always worth tipping the seeds and tomato debris into a sieve and catching the tomato stock. It will add a last-minute tomato-fresh flavour to your cooking. It will keep, covered, in the fridge for several days and can be frozen.

TO MAKE PASSATA/RAW TOMATO PULP/ RAW TOMATO PUREE

Passata is, by definition, sieved, uncooked tomatoes. However, everything sold in bottles and cartons as passata will have been processed and thus 'cooked'. It ends up as a thick, almost smooth, pip-flecked, dark red sauce. It should not be confused with chopped or crushed tomatoes. It is used in cooked dishes and improves radically if it is simmered for at least 30 minutes to concentrate the flavours.

Some people make what they think of as passata by placing whole, unpeeled medium or small ripe tomatoes in the bowl of a food-processor and blitzing at high speed for several minutes. This results in a frothy, thick, skin-flecked juice-cum-puree, which can then be passed through a food mill or sieve to catch pips, pith and scraps of skin. The pulp can then be used in dishes that require passata or could be seasoned, for use raw, for example, with red wine vinegar or balsamic vinegar and a pinch of sugar, then enriched and emulsified with olive oil.

Real passata is made by peeling and roughly chopping the tomatoes, then passing the whole lot through a food mill or large-holed sieve. Some pips are held back but many go through. A more refined version of passata, which is sold as crushed tomatoes or premium chopped tomatoes, is made by peeling, coring and seeding the tomatoes before they are pressed through a food mill or large-holed sieve. Crushed tomatoes are less watery, have a denser texture and only the odd stray pip. The same cheat's technique of using a food-processor to blitz tomato concassé results in a thicker, less watery, but similarly frothy, puree.

It is worth noting that the colour of tomatoes that have been liquidized in a food-processor is always paler and more pinky-orange than you might expect. If the tomatoes have been peeled first it will be even paler. Consequently, to get the best of both worlds – dark colour, thick texture – a mixture of unpeeled, and peeled, seeded tomatoes is blitzed together. A small quantity of commercial tomato juice, single concentrate puree or ketchup will also improve colour and might be useful for flavour too.

If you have a small quantity of tomatoes to render into a pulp, a quick way of doing so is to grate them: halve the tomatoes through the core and rub the cut side vigorously against the large holes of a cheese grater, continuing until all you are left with is skin, which you discard. The pulp can now be used as it is, or sieved to catch the pips (see also page 433).

TO MAKE TOMATO CONCASSÉ/DICED TOMATO

Concassé is the French name for peeled and chopped, crushed or ground tomatoes but almost invariably refers to peeled, diced tomato. In restaurants it is always made with dense-textured, fleshy tomatoes, and plum tomatoes are the usual choice.

To make concassé, the tomatoes are cored and peeled, halved lengthways and seeded. Each half is then cut in half, or into more sections if the tomatoes are very large or you want tiny pieces, and sliced across the strips to make dice. Concassé is used in cooked dishes that require a thick texture and/or no seeds. Try it in one of the following ways: dressed with a little vinaigrette and served as a salsa on its own or with other ingredients (see pages 183-192); dressed with a lot of vinaigrette to become tomato vinaigrette (see page 179); stirred into seasoned olive oil to become Sauce Vierge (see page 333); stirred into hot cream sauces just before serving; stirred into soups as a last-minute garnish or flavouring (see pages 63-64); as a salad garnish, perhaps tumbled over hot potato salad or green beans; or stirred into scrambled egg with a spoonful of thick cream.

TO MAKE TOMATO SHEETS/PETALS

Large beef tomatoes can be turned into sheets to use in layered dishes. Core, peel and cut a slice from both ends of the tomato. Then cut it in half through its depth, scoop away the seeds and trim the cavity to tidy it up, so that you end up with the opened shell, as it were, of the tomato. It is now ready for use or can be halved if smaller sheets are required.

TO MAKE TOMATO ROSES

> **'While we made tomato petals as a decoration, we never make tomato roses.'**
>
> **Nico Ladenis, *My Gastronomy*, Ebury, 1987**

Select firm tomatoes and, using a very sharp knife, peel off the skin from the top in one piece as though you were peeling an apple. Roll the strip of skin into a tight coil. Turn the coil over and you should have a tomato rose. Use for decoration.

tomatoes alone

'One August, years ago, I was wandering around the spacious property of a chateau up in Normandy, trying to work up a proper appetite for lunch. The land doubled as a horse farm, and a vicious brood mare had tried to bite me, an act rewarded with a stone sharply thrown against her ass. Two old men I hadn't seen laughed beneath a tree. I walked over and sat with them around a small fire. They were gardeners and it was their lunch hour, and on the flat stone they had made a circle of hot coals. They had cored a half-dozen big red tomatoes, stuffed them with softening cloves of garlic, and added a sprig of thyme, a basil leaf, and a couple of tablespoons of soft cheese. They roasted the tomatoes until they were soft and the cheese melted. I ate one with a chunk of bread and healthy-sized swigs from a jug of red wine. When we finished eating, and since this was Normandy, we had a sip or two of Calvados from the flask. A simple snack but indescribably delicious.'

Jim Harrison, *Hunger, Real and Unreal*

There are only so many ways to cook tomatoes and as all of them recur repeatedly throughout the book it seemed sensible to collect everything together to save unnecessary repetition. The recipes here demonstrate the basic techniques for roasting, grilling, stewing and frying, which can be adapted, embellished and quantities adjusted according to what you have to hand and what you require. Basil, for example, is indisputably the tomato's favourite herb, and pops up frequently. Other herbs, however, such as parsley, mint, coriander, thyme, marjoram and oregano, not forgetting chives, chervil, tarragon, savory, celery and sorrel, are all excellent alternatives.

ROAST TOMATO HALVES

SERVES 4-6

I tend to make a tray or two of these at a time because they are so delicious and so useful. I serve them on their own, on toast, with cheese and cold cuts of meat. I add them to salads, fold them into hot pasta and layer them with other grilled Mediterranean vegetables, such as red pepper, aubergine and courgette. An excellent way of serving them, for example, as a side vegetable or canapé (on bruschetta or similar), is to remove the skins before the tomatoes are roasted and scoop out the seeds. Then, when the tomatoes are ready, fill the cavities with a spoonful of tapenade or pesto.

Roast tomatoes are delicious pureed, juices and all, to make instant sauces that will liven up a potentially dull supper of poached chicken or boiled cauliflower. They are excellent in sandwiches and, rolled in a thin sheet of puff pastry with, for example, a slice of mozzarella, they make terrific canapés.

I ring the changes whenever I make them. Sometimes I season the unpeeled tomato halves with salt, pepper and a little sugar, then add a dribble of olive oil. At other times, I add a few drops of balsamic vinegar too. I quite often lay branches of thyme or rosemary over them. This has a surprisingly powerful effect on the final result. Similarly, slices of garlic, either posted between the seed cavities or wiped across the cut tomato halves, scent the flesh hauntingly.

Any medium-sized tomato can be prepared like this, but the most successful are plum tomatoes or another dense-fleshed variety. It is a good way to add interest and intensify the flavour of dull supermarket tomatoes. The juices should not be wasted.

- 10 medium tomatoes, peeled (or not)
- salt and pepper
- 2 tbsp olive oil
- 1 small bunch thyme (optional)

Pre-heat the oven to 300°F/150°C/gas mark 2.

Halve the tomatoes, cutting through the core if using plum tomatoes and through the circumference if using round tomatoes. If you wish, scoop out the seeds and central filaments (which can be used; see page 28). I rarely bother. Lay the tomato halves, cut side up, on a lightly oiled baking tray or tray lined with baking foil. Sprinkle them with salt, and pepper, then dribble with a little olive oil, just a few drops for each tomato. If you wish to flavour them with thyme, or another herb, lay the thyme twigs across the tomatoes.

Cook in the oven for at least 45 minutes or until the tomatoes have softened and collapsed, and the surfaces are lightly caramelized. Remove from the oven and leave to cool. The tomatoes will keep for a couple of days in the fridge if they are covered with clingfilm. When serving, don't forget the delicious juices, which should be scraped from the baking tray/s.

IN THE OVEN

ROAST TOMATOES

SERVES 4-6

These roast tomatoes are 'planted' core end down on a roasting tray, then cut with a cross in the style of restaurant-baked potatoes. A lump of butter and some fresh herbs are pushed into the cuts, and as they roast the tomatoes open like flowers. Plum tomatoes are best for this but any variety will do. Serve them hot and don't waste any of the buttery juices.

- 30 g butter
- 6 (or more) plum tomatoes
- salt and pepper
- basil or thyme or rosemary or oregano

Pre-heat the oven to 350°F/180°C/gas mark 4.

Place a sheet of kitchen foil on a baking tray. Smear it lightly with butter. Stand the tomatoes on the buttered foil and cut a deep cross in their pointed ends, almost to the base. Season with salt and pepper, press a knob of butter and a couple of leaves of basil or sprigs of one of the other herbs into the middle. Cook until the tomatoes are soft and very juicy, the 'petals' opening slightly, but still keeping their shape. This takes at least 20 minutes but up to 35, depending on the texture of the tomato and the quantity cooked at any one time.

SLOW-ROAST TOMATOES

SERVES 4-6

I discovered by accident that if you leave a tray of seasoned tomato halves in a very low oven for a couple of hours you end up with the best ever roast tomatoes. Their colour and flavour are deepened and their texture becomes moist and slippery but not the least bit dry. Serve them on their own or with simply cooked fish and grilled meat. Their flavour is at its best when they are eaten tepid. They will keep, covered, laid out on a plate in the fridge for a couple of days. In Morocco, where tomatoes grow sweet and tender, they cook them in this way with flavourings usually associated with desserts (see pages 422-423).

- 10 medium tomatoes
- salt and pepper
- 2 tbsp olive oil

Pre-heat the oven to 275°F/140°C/gas mark 1.

Halve the tomatoes – plum tomatoes lengthways, round tomatoes through their middles. Season with salt and pepper, and lay out, cut side uppermost, on a lightly oiled baking tray. Dribble olive oil over them, then place in the bottom of the oven and leave for 2 hours. Remove from the oven and allow to cool before serving.

ROAST BEEF TOMATOES

SERVES 2-4

Butter melts into the tomato halves as they roast, bake and poach simultaneously in their own juices. The tomatoes should be soft, blistered and puffy. Serve hot, lukewarm or cold, as a garnish, a vegetable or as part of a salad. The flesh, scraped out of the skin, can be passed through a sieve to make an intensely flavoured puree.

- 2 ripe beef tomatoes
- salt and pepper
- 25 g hard butter
- caster sugar

Pre-heat the oven to 350°F/180°C/gas mark 4.

Lay a sheet of kitchen foil on a flat baking sheet. Halve the tomatoes through their circumference. Arrange them on the foil. Season with salt and pepper and cover the cut surfaces with slices of butter. Sprinkle with sugar so that the butter is covered lightly. Cook for about 30 minutes, possibly longer, until the tomatoes are completely tender and the tops burnished.

ROAST VINE TOMATOES

SERVES 4

Serve these as a smart garnish with simply cooked fish, or squashed against garlicky bruschetta spread with black olive tapenade.

- 24 tomatoes on the vine
- 4 tbsp olive oil
- salt and pepper

Pre-heat the oven to 400°F/200°C/gas mark 6.

Use sharp scissors to snip the vine, aiming to end up with four sprays of 6 tomatoes. Plunge each bunch into boiling water for about 15 seconds then immediately into very cold water. Carefully peel away the skins. Pat the tomatoes dry on absorbent kitchen paper then lay out on an oven tray lined with foil. Dribble the olive oil over the tomatoes, season with salt and pepper, then place the tray on a shelf at the top of the oven. Cook for about 15 minutes, basting a couple of times, or until the tomatoes are tender but not overly squashy.

SEARED AND ROASTED TOMATOES

SERVES 4

Searing the cut surface of tomato halves in a frying pan before they are roasted results in a dark, almost caramelized surface. These are excellent eaten hot, warm or cold, and are always welcome, be it on their own or with grilled fish or meat – particularly lamb. To serve them as an appetizer or as the starting point for a vegetarian main dish, do as Gary Rhodes does: press a couple of the roasted tomatoes through a sieve and mix with the juices left in the pan to make a dressing for the remaining tomatoes. This simple but excellent dish is finished with a few basil leaves scattered over the top.

2-4 tbsp olive oil

6-8 firm, medium-sized tomatoes, cored and halved (across if round, lengthways if plum)

salt and pepper

1 tsp thyme or oregano leaves

a handful of basil leaves

Pre-heat the oven to 400°F/200°C/gas mark 6.

Heat 1 tablespoon of the olive oil in a non-stick frying-pan. When hot, arrange the tomatoes, cut side down, in the pan. Sear, without moving the tomatoes, for several minutes until a thin crust has formed. Transfer to a lightly oiled or foil-lined roasting tin and arrange cut side uppermost. Pour any cooking juices from the frying-pan over the tomatoes. Season with salt and pepper and sprinkle with the thyme or oregano.

Cook in the oven for 15 minutes or until the tomatoes are soft and juicy. Serve immediately or eat when warm or cold. To dress the tomatoes to serve as a starter, place 2 halves in the (unwashed) frying-pan with the remaining olive oil over a medium heat and crush the tomatoes into the oil with the back of a fork. Pass the mixture through a sieve. Arrange the tomatoes on a serving dish, sprinkle with torn basil leaves and spoon the dressing over the top. Serve with crusty bread and butter.

BAKED TOMATOES WITH OREGANO

These tomatoes are cored, peeled, salted and drained before they are cooked in the oven with a dribble of olive oil and a pinch of oregano or thyme. They are ready when they are charred and very soft and juicy. Serve them warm or cold on bruschetta or in salads, or hot with grilled meats.

- 8 medium round tomatoes, scalded and skinned
- 1 scant tsp caster sugar
- salt and pepper
- 2 tbsp olive oil
- 1 tsp chopped oregano leaves

Cut off a quarter of the tomato at the core end. Use a teaspoon to remove the seeds. Season the insides of the peeled tomatoes with sugar, salt and pepper. Place them upside down on a cake rack to drain, leaving them for at least 1 hour.

Meanwhile, pre-heat the oven to 400°F/200°C/gas mark 6. Line a baking tray with kitchen foil and smear with a little of the olive oil. Place the drained tomatoes the right way up on the foil. Sprinkle a share of the oregano leaves inside the tomatoes and dribble over a little oil. Bake for 20-40 minutes, until the tomatoes are charred at the edges and very soft. Carefully lift them on to a serving dish, taking care that they don't collapse. Pour any juices over the top.

BAKED TOMATOES WITH SOUR CREAM

SERVES 4

A simple and delicious idea: the tomatoes end up with the intensity of flavour brought about by roasting and the freshness of uncooked ones. The recipe comes from a favourite book, Arabella Boxer's *Garden Cookbook* (Weidenfeld and Nicolson, 1974).

- 750 g tomatoes
- 25 g butter, plus an extra knob
- salt and pepper
- 150 g sour cream

Pre-heat the oven to 350°F/180°C/gas mark 4.

Cut 500 g of the tomatoes in half horizontally. Butter a shallow fireproof dish and arrange the tomatoes in it. Dot with the rest of the butter and season with salt and pepper. Bake for 20 minutes.

Meanwhile, skin the remaining tomatoes and put them in the blender with the sour cream. Season with salt and pepper, then heat until boiling in a small pan. When the tomatoes are cooked, pour over the sauce and serve.

TOMATO TOMATOES

SERVES 4-6

Nino Squillacciotti, a chemist and food scientist who heads up new product development at Cirio's research centre just outside Naples, once told me that Cirio used to sell canned stuffed tomatoes. Plum tomatoes were cored, peeled, seeded and processed. The cavity was then stuffed with tomato pulp. Sadly, the labour involved meant the tomatoes weren't cost-effective but it occurred to me, as I contemplated making up a recipe for such a dish, that the perfect name for this way of preparing tomatoes would have been Tomato Tomatoes. The Troisgros brothers, in their book *The Nouvelle Cuisine of Jean and Pierre Troisgros* (Macmillan, 1980) have already nabbed this name for their dish Tomates à la Tomate. In it, peeled tomato halves are sautéd, then baked, simmered in cream, then stuffed with diced tomato mixed with a minute amount of onion, garlic and herbs. These Tomato Tomatoes are incredibly luxurious and richly flavoured. Serve them on their own or with simply cooked fish or chicken. They would also be excellent with fresh peas.

12 tomatoes, weighing about 1.5 kg
1 sprig of thyme
1 bay leaf
a few parsley stalks
2 onions, peeled and finely chopped
15 g butter
1 garlic clove, peeled and crushed
salt and pepper
5 tbsp vegetable oil
300 ml double cream

Peel 8 of the tomatoes, remove their seeds and cut them into small, even dice. Halve the remaining 4 unpeeled tomatoes horizontally. Squeeze them gently in the palm of your hand to remove the pips.

Tie the thyme, bay leaf and parsley stalks together to make a bouquet garni. Soften the onions in 10 g of the butter in a small sauté pan without browning. Add the diced tomatoes, the garlic, the bouquet garni and a little salt. Bring to the boil, cover the pan and cook for 25 minutes. Remove the bouquet garni, stir in the remaining butter and taste for seasoning.

Pre-heat the oven to 350°F/180°C/gas mark 4.

Season the tomato halves and sauté them in the hot oil in a round gratin dish, skin side up, for 5 minutes. Turn them over and finish cooking them in the oven for 10 minutes. Remove the tomatoes from the oven, cover with the cream and simmer for a few minutes over a low heat.

Arrange the tomato halves on a serving dish, coat them lightly with the hot cream and fill them with the pureed tomatoes.

TOMATO DISCS

Cutting discs out of sheets of tomato (see page 30) is a painstaking occupation. Setting aside the wastefulness of it – although the trimmings, seeds and juices have plenty of uses – what is the point?

The point is that they look wonderful. I once went to a lunch organized by the British branch of the Academie Culinaire where the chef remade tomatoes using sheets or discs of peeled tomato. Between each layer was a thin smear of tapenade. If it sounds elaborate, it was. But the little tomatoes looked and tasted stunning. At home, the discs might be used in elaborate stacked salads such as a refined Insalata Tricolore (see page 166). Alternatively, for a special occasion, they would make a marvellous appetizer with fresh pasta and scoops of soured cream topped with little dollops of caviare. However, I'm getting carried away here because, generally speaking, this *haute cuisine* treatment ranks along with 'turned' vegetables and 'carved' mushrooms. It is the preserve of classy gourmet restaurants and not something one would generally bother to do at home. However, when faced, one summer, with a glut of tomatoes and time on my hands, I made some, which I then poached and roasted in the oven in olive oil flavoured with garlic and herbs. The cooking is long and gentle so that the flavour of the tomatoes is intense but the flesh isn't broken down. They will keep for a few days, covered, in the fridge or could be bottled in olive oil for longer. They are so precious and so delicious that they tend to be served as a garnish, for example, with poached fish. (See also Tomatoes Stewed in Olive Oil, page 46)

6 large ripe plum tomatoes, cored and peeled

10 tbsp olive oil

2 new season garlic cloves, thinly sliced in rounds

1 tbsp thyme leaves

freshly ground black pepper

Pre-heat the oven to its lowest setting.

Halve the tomatoes lengthways. Cut out the inner ribs and scrape out the seeds. Using a round or oval pastry cutter, about 3 cm or 4 cm in diameter, cut out one shape from each tomato half. Coat the base of a metal baking-dish with some of the olive oil. Lay out the tomato discs, peeled side up, in a single layer. Scatter over the garlic slices and sprinkle the thyme leaves over the top. Dribble over more olive oil so that the tomatoes are partially immersed.

Place in the warm oven and leave for 1 hour. Baste the tomatoes a couple of times during 'cooking'. The idea is to soften them but not to break down the fibres: they should keep their form but the flavour will be intensified. Season with black pepper, and leave to cool in the dish. Transfer to a wide-rimmed jar or bowl, cover and store in the fridge for up to a week.

TOMATO CRISPS

Several years ago when Jean Christophe Novelli was cooking at the Four Seasons at Hyde Park Corner in London he invited me to lunch. He knew that I was working on a book about tomatoes and they featured throughout the meal. The idea that impressed me most was glassy, crisp sheets of tomato used as decoration for one of his elaborate preparations. When pressed, then and more recently, he was vague about how to make them. Then, when I was coming close to finishing the book, I thought about them again – and while I was leafing through Gordon Ramsay's *Passion For Flavour* (Conran Octopus, 1996), I saw a photograph of dried strawberries. 'If other fruits can be dried, why not strawberries?' he wonders. That was good enough for me. It is vital to use firm, ripe tomatoes, and the best results come from dense varieties, not those with seed cavities that bag open leaving huge gaps. Also, you are most likely to get a complete crisp if the tomato is sliced down the fruit, with the core at the top. Extraordinary though it might seem, you end up with a perfect cross section of tomato. The seeds are held in a wafer-thin sheet of glossy transparent orange. The skin forms a red halo.

The result is stunning to look at: the 'veins' make wonderful patterns and the seeds are held in place as if by magic. The taste is remarkably intense. This is why it is worth going to the bother of making tomato crisps. A pile of them looks magnificent. Use them as a garnish with creamy foods, soups and salads. They are also a surprising addition with pasta.

firm, ripe tomatoes
a little olive oil

Thinly slice the tomatoes lengthways. Discard the end slices and lay out the large middle slices on baking-sheets lined with non-stick silicon baking paper (from www.lakeland.co.uk tel. 015394 88100) or kitchen foil lightly greased with olive oil. Make sure the slices don't touch each other.

Turn the oven on to its lowest setting: ideally 170°F/80°C – you want the merest heat. Put in the baking-sheets, and leave until the tomato slices are crisp and dry. Some of mine were ready after 5 hours, but Gordon recommends 14 to 18 hours. The slices must be brittle and quite dry but not scorched. 'Test one by snapping it in half.' The colour will have dulled slightly but the slices will be glossy.

If you laid them out on foil, use a metal spatula to lift them off carefully.

UNDER THE GRILL

The following two quotations say all there is to say about grilled tomatoes:

> 'Then there is the warmed red billiard ball with its skin slit round the middle, so oddly known as grilled tomato. (I believe the official name for this dish is dressed tomatoes.)'
>
> Elizabeth David, *Vogue*, January 1960

> 'At the moment of writing we are watching a new student preparing half a dozen tomatoes for the grill. He has halved them and then nicked north, south, east and west through the skin for a ¼″, so that it will not split and collapse but merely open out slightly under the heat like the early development of a flower. For the twelve halves he has worked up 2 oz of butter on a chopping board with as much finely snipped fresh chives from the garden as the butter will hold. Then he has mounded this paste equally over the twelve cut surfaces, sprinkled overall lightly with proper gros sel, or French kitchen salt and proper peppercorns ground in a mill, and tonight he will cook them slowly under the grill to accompany loin of pork.'
>
> Fanny and Johnnie Cradock, *The Cook Hostess' Book*, Collins, 1970

GRILLED TOMATO HALVES

SERVES 2-4

It takes far longer to grill tomatoes than you might expect. It is no good just showing the tomatoes the grill: you don't want them barely warm, you want them cooked. Equally, you don't want a complete mush. To get the desirable scorched edges and juicy succulence that goes all the way through the tomato you need to keep an eye on them and adjust the temperature. Done well, and it is far easier to achieve perfection by roasting, they are sublime. Nothing can beat the way the fierce heat of the grill seems to concentrate flavours.

- 4 medium tomatoes
- 1-2 tbsp olive oil or melted butter
- salt and freshly ground black pepper

Pre-heat the overhead grill to its highest setting.

Halve the tomatoes through their middles. Smear the cut surfaces with the oil or melted butter and season with salt and pepper. Arrange on the grill rack and cook close to the heat source for a couple of minutes until the surface is scorched in places and the juices are beginning to run. Lower the temperature and cook until the tomatoes are tender and squashy when their sides are gently prodded.

GRILLED CHERRY TOMATOES

SERVES 2-4

500 g cherry tomatoes, stalks removed
3 tbsp olive oil
salt and pepper

Place the tomatoes in a bowl, pour over the olive oil and use your hands to smear them thoroughly. Lay them on a sheet of foil placed on a grill-pan, season with salt and pepper and cook, shaking the pan every so often, until the skins begin to pop and the juices run. They are ready when they are just beginning to collapse.

Tip the tomatoes, juices and all, into a hot serving bowl or on to plates and eat immediately (with crisp bacon and eggs). Alternatively, allow them to cool in their juices and dress them with a splash of balsamic vinegar.

TOMATO COULIS

MAKES APPROX 300 ML

Tomato coulis was the darling of *nouvelle cuisine*. It was the red puddle that accompanied everything, from the famous Troisgros vegetable terrine to the fan of raw duck breast that was served garnished with kiwi. It was always served *under* the food, a splash of fresh sauce that was the very antithesis of the old guard *haute cuisine* with its flour-based, cream-rich sauces.

Tomato concassé is cooked briefly in olive oil, flavoured minimally with garlic or onion, and herbs such as thyme, basil or parsley, pureed then simmered to the right consistency. If the tomatoes are full of flavour it will need nothing else except a little salt and pepper. The coulis is served hot or cold. It will keep in the fridge for several days and freezes well in small quantities.

Inevitably, for such a fashion victim, tomato coulis has a tarnished reputation as an enduring cliché of *nouvelle cuisine*. In many classical restaurant kitchens, however, here and in France, it has never gone out of fashion. (For the ultimate version, which is more complex and takes longer to prepare, see Classic Tomato Coulis, page 242)

- a knob of butter
- 1 tbsp olive oil
- 1 garlic clove, peeled and finely chopped
- 750 g ripe tomatoes, preferably vine-ripened plum or another fleshy variety, cored, peeled, seeded and roughly chopped
- a pinch of sugar
- salt and freshly ground black pepper
- a sprig of thyme, or basil, or flat-leaf parsley

Melt the butter with the oil in a sauté pan over a medium heat. Add the garlic, stir as it releases its flavour but don't let it brown. Add the tomato to the pan. Season with sugar, salt and pepper, then add the thyme and cook gently for about 35 minutes or until the tomato has reduced to a thick puree. If necessary, press it through a sieve. Taste and adjust the seasoning. If it seems too wet, continue cooking to drive off the excess liquid.

TOMATO FONDUE

Tomato fondue is a refinement of tomato coulis. The flavours are enhanced with shallot and white wine or vermouth, together with a little chicken stock. Garlic, if you wish, and herbs, such as tarragon, basil or thyme, are added with some fresh parsley. It tends to be served as a garnish with steaks, chops, grilled chicken or fish, and egg dishes. It is a good thing to stir into the pan juices after roasting or sautéing poultry, to make a quick sauce. But you can do what you like with it: it is delicious.

- 2 tbsp finely chopped shallot
- a small knob of butter
- 4 tbsp white wine or vermouth
- 6 tbsp chicken stock
- 400 g tomato concassé (see page 29)
- 1 garlic clove, peeled and finely chopped
- 1 tsp finely chopped basil or tarragon
- salt and freshly ground black pepper
- 1 tsp finely chopped flat-leaf parsley

Gently sauté the shallot in the butter until it turns glassy. Add the wine or vermouth and chicken stock. Boil down rapidly until syrupy, then stir in the tomato, garlic and basil or tarragon. Sauté, stirring and folding, for 3-4 minutes, to cook the tomatoes. Taste for seasoning, fold in the parsley and turn into a warm bowl.

PAN-ROASTED TOMATOES

SERVES 4

'Pan-roasted' sounds so much more appealing than 'stewed'. But that's what this is, very slowly stewed whole peeled tomatoes. You need a heavy-bottomed pan, so that the tomatoes can cook away slowly without scorching. The slow cooking intensifies the flavour, and the juices of the tomatoes are scented with garlic and thyme, and thickened with a little olive oil. Serve them as a side dish or spooned on to bruschetta or toasted muffins.

- 1 garlic clove, sliced in wafer-thin rounds
- 2 tbsp olive oil
- 8 ripe plum tomatoes, cored and peeled
- 2 springs of thyme
- salt and freshly ground black pepper

Place the garlic and olive oil in a wide, shallow, heavy-bottomed pan that can take the tomatoes in one layer. 'Plant' the tomatoes, cored side down, resting them against each other. Slide the sprigs of thyme between the tomatoes and season with salt and pepper. Tuck a sheet of greaseproof paper over the tomatoes, so that they are snugly covered, and place a lid on the pan.

Cook very gently for at least 30 minutes until the tomatoes are very soft but holding their shape. Transfer them to a serving dish. Boil the juices hard for a few minutes until thick and jammy, then strain over the tomatoes and serve hot or cold.

FRIED TOMATO HALVES

SERVES 2-4

Fried tomatoes are very good for breakfast with fried eggs. They are particularly good, but you have to get your timing right, fried up in leftover bacon fat. If you're in a hurry and don't mind them breaking up into a slop, then tomato slices will be ready in moments. Far better, however, to fry tomato *halves* and take slightly longer about it. But do take your time – there are few things worse (undercooked *grilled* tomatoes being one) than unevenly cooked fried tomatoes. What you're after is total mush without total breakdown. (For the ultimate version see Edouard de Pomiane's Tomates à la Crème on page 48.)

- 4 medium tomatoes
- salt and freshly ground black pepper
- ½ clove garlic, if liked
- 25 g butter or bacon fat

Halve the tomatoes through their middles and season the cut side with salt and pepper. If liked, smear the surface with the cut side of the garlic.

Melt the butter or bacon fat in a frying-pan and arrange the tomatoes skin side down. Cook over a medium-low heat for several minutes before turning. Then cook until the juices begin to flow and the edges blur. Turn back so that the cut side is uppermost. Continue to cook until the tomato halves are very tender. Serve with the buttery juices.

TOMATOES STEWED IN OLIVE OIL SERVES 4

This recipe comes from the Albert and Michel Roux book *French Country Cooking* (Sidgwick & Jackson, 1989). They suggest using 'very large good-quality tomatoes that are bursting with flavour for this fresh-tasting southern dish'. The tomatoes are skinned and gently cooked in very garlicky, herby olive oil which they drink up as they cook. They are served straight from the pot, sprinkled with a huge mound of finely chopped flat-leaf parsley. Serve them alone or with other things. They are delicious hot, but very good warm or cold.

- 150 ml top-quality olive oil
- 1 bouquet garni, made with plenty of basil
- 4 garlic cloves, unpeeled
- 1 kg ripe but firm large tomatoes, preferably Marmande, peeled
- salt and freshly ground black pepper
- 2 tbsp finely chopped flat-leaf parsley

Put the olive oil, bouquet garni and garlic in a flameproof casserole or earthenware pot and heat gently for 2 minutes. Put in the whole peeled tomatoes, season lightly with salt and pepper, cover and cook gently for 30 minutes. Carefully turn each tomato separately, cover and cook for another 15 minutes. By now, the tomatoes should have absorbed most of the oil and still kept their shape but be very soft. Depending on how ripe they are, you may need to cook them for a little longer.

Discard the bouquet garni and garlic cloves, sprinkle the tomatoes with parsley and serve.

SAUTÉED CHERRY TOMATOES SERVES 4

Briefly frying cherry tomatoes – be they red, orange or yellow –accentuates their natural sweetness. Serve them hot from the pan as a side vegetable, or stir them into prepared couscous with a handful of fresh herbs. They are also very good crushed with a fork into bruschetta or other toasted bread.

- a knob of butter
- 1 tbsp olive oil
- 250 g cherry tomatoes, stalks removed
- shredded basil or tarragon (optional)
- salt and freshly ground black pepper

Melt the butter and olive oil in a frying-pan over a medium heat. Add the tomatoes and toss them constantly, coating them all over with the buttery oil, for 5 or 6 minutes. They should be glossy and heated through. Some skins will break but don't let them cook so long that they burst and turn mushy. If adding herbs, snip them over the top, season with salt and pepper, toss again and tip the tomatoes and their juices into a serving dish.

MARINATED FRIED TOMATOES

SERVES 4

Some of the best meals I've ever eaten have been at the hand of Franco Taruschio when he was cooking at the Walnut Tree Inn just outside Abergavenny. Pomodori Fritti in Carpione, the Italian translation of this dish, is a delicious example of how Franco goes one step further with something that is already divine. I could eat breadcrumbed fried tomatoes until the cows come home, but on the occasions when I don't want to eat them like pancakes hot from the pan, I copy Franco: I lay them out in a dish and pour over a little sauce made with tomato puree, sugar, lemon juice, red wine vinegar and a few salted capers. The tomatoes can be eaten at once or left to marinate for a couple of hours before serving. It is difficult to give exact quantities for the flour and breadcrumbs required for cooking the tomatoes. It is important that the breadcrumbs are very fine and dry: stale or dried bread is essential. If you can't find salted capers, use capers bottled in vinegar but squeeze them dry.

4 large tomatoes, cored and peeled

2 eggs

salt and freshly ground black pepper

fine dry breadcrumbs

flour

approximately 250 ml olive oil

½ tsp tomato puree

a pinch of sugar

juice of 1 lemon

2 tbsp red wine vinegar

50 g small salted capers, well rinsed in a sieve held under cold running water

Cut the tomatoes into slices 0.5 cm thick. Crack the eggs into a bowl, season with salt and beat with a fork. Place the breadcrumbs in a second bowl and the flour in a third. Dip the tomato slices first in flour, so they are lightly coated, then in beaten egg, and finally press them into the breadcrumbs so they are coated all over.

Half fill a deep frying-pan with olive oil and place it over a medium heat. When the oil is hot, fry the breadcrumbed tomato slices, a few at a time, until they are golden brown on both sides. Remove with a perforated spoon, drain on kitchen paper and arrange them on a plate or in a shallow serving-dish.

When all the slices have been fried, discard almost all the oil. In the remaining oil, fry 1 tablespoon of breadcrumbs until golden. Add the tomato puree, sugar, lemon juice, vinegar, capers and a ladle of water, and stir well. Leave to simmer for 5 minutes, then pour the mixture over the tomatoes. Serve immediately or leave to marinate for a couple of hours before serving.

BEURRE DE TOMATE

SERVES 4

A luscious, fresh-tasting, sweet tomato puree.

250 g cherry tomatoes
2 tsp olive oil
50 g butter
salt and pepper

Liquidize the cherry tomatoes then pass through a fine sieve into a small pan. Heat through without allowing to boil. Whisk in the olive oil, butter and seasoning to taste.

EDOUARD DE POMIANE'S TOMATES À LA CRÈME

SERVES 2

I like the sound of Edouard de Pomiane. He wrote a stunningly good book called *Cooking in Ten Minutes* over fifty years ago, with tips such as 'first put on the kettle' (think about it), and that one should keep a supply of cooked jacket potatoes in the fridge (perfect again after 10 minutes in a hot oven).

Tomates à la Crème is a masterful recipe that works with any half-way decent tomatoes. The result is gorgeously gooey tomatoes so intensely flavoured that you'll probably start dishing them up at every possible opportunity. I love them on their own with crusty bread to mop up the delicious creamy juices but they are excellent with eggs and simply cooked fish.

4 medium-sized ripe tomatoes
a large knob of butter
salt and freshly ground black pepper
3 heaped tbsp crème fraîche

Cut the tomatoes in half through the circumference. Heat a frying-pan over a medium heat, melt the butter in it and lay out the tomatoes, cut side down. Cook for 5 minutes during which time you puncture, here and there, the rounded sides with a sharply pointed knife.

Carefully turn the tomatoes with a palette knife and cook for a further 10 minutes. Turn them again, and after a couple of minutes, when their juices have started to run, turn them back so that the cut sides are uppermost. Season with salt and pepper. Spoon the cream between the tomatoes and mix it lightly with the juices. As soon as it bubbles, slip the tomatoes and their sauce on to hot plates. Serve immediately.

TOMATES À LA POLONAISE

SERVES 2

Polonaise means 'in the style of Poland', but this simple idea for frying tomato halves in buttery chopped onion then finishing them off with a scoop of thick cream isn't obviously Polish. In fact, it was devised by Edouard de Pomiane, himself a Pole, who taught at the Institut Pasteur in Paris in the 1940s and wrote about food with light-hearted insight and good taste. Delicious alone, these tomatoes are also very good served with buttery spinach or leeks.

- a large knob of butter
- 1 medium onion, very finely chopped
- 4 ripe tomatoes, halved through their middles
- salt and freshly ground black pepper
- 75 g crème fraîche or thick cream

Melt the butter in a frying-pan and gently soften the onion. Put the tomatoes face downwards in the pan, increase the heat and cook for 5 minutes. Turn them. Pierce the skins with a fork in a couple of places. Season with salt and pepper. Pour on the cream between the tomatoes. Let the creamy sauce come to the boil and serve.

YOGHURT WITH TOMATOES

SERVES 4

Something to serve with curries: cooling, soothing and very interesting.

- 1 tbsp cooking oil
- 1 tsp mustard seeds
- 4 tomatoes, cored and peeled, then thickly sliced
- 100 ml thick, strained yoghurt (Total or another Greek brand)
- salt and freshly ground black pepper
- a few coriander leaves for garnish

Heat the oil in a small frying-pan and toast the mustard seeds, tossing or stirring, for a few seconds until aromatic. Add the tomatoes and mix them in well with the mustard seeds. Cook for 5 or 6 minutes until they are beginning to soften. Stir in the yoghurt, season with salt and pepper, heat through and serve garnished with the coriander.

IN THE PAN

TOMATO CURRY

SERVES 4

This dish is adapted from the tomato curry served at Kastoori, a commendable vegetarian restaurant in Tooting, south London, and one of the first places where I ever ate Indian vegetarian food. It is unusual to see curried tomatoes on a menu. At Kastoori, they cut the tomatoes into quarters so that the juices run to make the sauce with the various spices and coriander leaves, which are added right at the end, and cooking takes less than 5 minutes. In my version, the tomatoes are peeled, cored and halved, and a little creamed coconut combines with less tomato juice to make the sauce. I prefer to cook the tomatoes slowly and gently until they are just tender. That way, the flavours of the chillies, cinnamon, mustard seeds and cumin seep into the tomatoes, making a fragrant, thick and subtly flavoured curry. I like it on its own with some basmati rice, and creamy natural yoghurt on the side, but it would be excellent with spinach in any shape or form.

- 4 tbsp vegetable oil
- 1 tbsp mustard seeds
- 1½ tbsp cumin seeds
- 1 small cinnamon stick
- 2 cloves
- 2-3 green chillies, seeded and finely sliced in rounds
- 6 curry leaves, finely shredded, stalk removed if necessary
- 75 g creamed coconut, dissolved in 6 tbsp boiling water
- 2 tbsp finely chopped coriander leaves
- 12 medium tomatoes, cored, scalded and peeled, then halved through the middle
- salt and freshly ground black pepper
- a squeeze of lime juice

Heat the oil in a frying-pan over a medium heat. Add the mustard seeds, and once they've jumped and spluttered in the pan, add the cumin, cinnamon, cloves, chillies and curry leaves. Turn up the heat for about 10 seconds then down again before the curry leaves change colour. Stir in the dissolved coconut cream, with ½ tablespoon of coriander. Now arrange the tomatoes, cut side uppermost, in the pan spooning some of the sauce over the top. Season lightly with salt and pepper. Cover loosely with foil, adjust the heat to very low and leave to cook gently for about 30 minutes. Squeeze the lime juice over the top, sprinkle over the remaining coriander leaves and serve.

TOMATOES WITH CAPER AND TARRAGON BUTTER

SERVES 4

Spices, Salt and Aromatics in the English Kitchen is, I think, the only Elizabeth David book I didn't own (I do now though, thanks to the new Grub Street edition). Fortunately Sophie Grigson does, and it is thanks to her that I discovered this recipe for gently cooking whole tomatoes in butter and finishing them with tarragon and capers. The combination of flavours and textures is a fine balance of contrasts. Serve it alone as a light lunch dish or as second fiddle to red meat. Incidentally, there will be lots of caper and tarragon butter left over from this dish but it can be stashed in the freezer and goes with all sorts of things: on baked potatoes, with steaks and lamb kebabs.

25 g butter
500 g firm but ripe plum tomatoes
a pinch of sugar
salt and pepper

FOR THE CAPER AND TARRAGON BUTTER
75 g butter, softened
2 tbsp small capers, squeezed
1½ tbsp very finely chopped fresh tarragon leaves
a squeeze of lemon or lime juice

Melt the butter in a pan that can hold the tomatoes comfortably without cramping them together. Put them in, season with a pinch of sugar, salt and pepper, and cook, covered, over a gentle heat for about 20 minutes, turning a couple of times, or until very tender.

While the tomatoes are cooking, prepare the caper and tarragon butter by mashing all the ingredients together. Roll it into a sausage, wrap it in foil and chill it in the fridge or freezer.

When the tomatoes are ready, add a tablespoon of the caper and tarragon butter to the pan. Turn up the heat, cook for a few seconds as the butter melts, then serve immediately.

GREEK TOMATO PATTIES

MAKES 4

Diced tomato mixed with finely chopped red onion, salt, pepper, sugar and flour doesn't sound a very complete recipe. Nevertheless, this is a delicious little snack. Eat them hot from the pan (scale up the quantities to suit) or let them cool to lukewarm. Their Greek name is *domatokeftedes*.

- **1 large ripe plum tomato, cored, peeled and diced**
- **½ small red onion, finely chopped**
- **salt and freshly ground black pepper**
- **sugar**
- **3 tbsp self-raising flour**
- **2 tbsp olive oil**
- **20 mint leaves**

Tip the diced tomato into a mixing bowl with the onion, a generous pinch of salt, pepper and sugar. Stir everything together as you sieve the flour over gradually, continuing until the mixture is vaguely cohesive yet still damp. Mould into 4 patties then dust again, this time lightly, with flour.

Heat the oil in a frying-pan and drop in the patties, pressing them down slightly. Adjust the heat so that they fry briskly, and turn after about 30 seconds. The aim is to form a very crisp, golden brown barrier but to allow sufficient heat to pass through each patty and cook the flour in the middle.

Serve seasoned with black pepper and covered with several mint leaves.

BLOODY MARY ASPIC TOMATO RING

SERVES 6

Before Jennifer Paterson became one half of the Two Fat Ladies, she was the resident cook at the *Spectator*. Recipes from her feisty column are collected in *Feast Days* and it was here that I came across this idea for livening up a classic tomato ring, as it used to be called when it was the darling of the dinner party set in the seventies. The liquid – a highly seasoned tomato juice-cum-soup – is perked up with vodka and sherry in the style of a jolly good Bloody Mary. Fill it with whatever you fancy, but choose something light and moist, such as salmon, chicken or tuna, that goes well with mayonnaise and looks pretty against the glassy tomato circle. Jennifer fills her tomato jelly with sea trout and green mayonnaise. I like the idea of prawns or crab with half-moons of peeled cucumber and tomato mayonnaise (see page 149). Cold scrambled egg mixed with a little cream and tomato concassé would also be good – or how about roast tomatoes with watercress or wild rocket, garnished with a tumble of concassé? Or a green salad made with peeled broad beans, French beans and watercress with a dressing of lemon juice and olive oil?

You can use any well-flavoured, sieved but thick tomato juice for this recipe. Ideally you want a liquid that ends up very red rather than pale orange and watery. Personally, I prefer not to add cream to the mixture, which makes it too rich (with a creamy filling) and spoils the vivid red colour. Any of the chilled soup recipes would work well as they are the perfect solution but the exact seasoning is up to you, or see the Tomato Terrine on page 57.

In the Deep South of America, they make Fresh Tomato Aspic with 1.2 kg fresh peeled and seeded tomatoes pureed with the juice saved from the seeds; 250 g tomato concassé is mixed with a grated onion, diced green bell pepper, 3 tablespoons each of Worcestershire sauce and lemon juice, a few drops of Tabasco, 1½ teaspoons of salt and ½ teaspoon of black pepper. The tomato puree is warmed, 3 leaves of gelatine, previously softened in cold water, are stirred in, then all the other ingredients are incorporated. The mixture is poured into a suitable mould, refrigerated until it sets, then turned out. The quantities given here are sufficient for 8 or more. Both recipes look particularly stunning when made in a *kugelhopf* mould and turned on to a glass cake stand.

1 litre fresh tomato juice (see page 431) or 1 quantity Iced Tomato and Basil Soup (see page 63) or Chilled Roast Tomato Soup (see page 61) diluted with stock or water

17 g gelatine

You will need a 1 litre ring mould for this, but if you haven't got one handy, use a loaf tin or whatever: you will just have to put the filling around it rather than in the centre. Pour about 150 ml of the tomato juice into a small saucepan, bring to the boil, then throw in the gelatine off the heat, stirring like mad until it is thoroughly dissolved. Don't let it boil or it will self-destruct and not gel. When it is totally smooth pour it into the rest of the juice waiting in a jug or bowl. Season with the celery salt, about 10

celery salt
Tabasco
Worcestershire sauce
1 tbsp fresh lemon juice
1 tbsp sherry
3 tbsp vodka
150 ml single cream, optional
fresh herbs, such as chives, parsley, coriander or dill, to garnish
mayonnaise

shakes of Tabasco, Worcestershire sauce to taste (1 dessertspoon?), the lemon juice, sherry and vodka and mix thoroughly; check that the taste is to your liking.

If you wish (I prefer not) drizzle cream into the mixture, just giving it the odd swirl, then pour the lot into the mould, which has been rinsed out in cold water. Chill in the refrigerator until set, which is speeded up if the juice was already chilled. Turn out the mould on to a large plate, fill the middle with whatever you fancy and cover with mayonnaise.

Decorate with fresh herbs and serve.

TOMATO ASPIC WITH SAFFRON CREAM

SERVES 8-10

This stunning idea comes from one of my favourite books, *The Savoury Way* by Brenda Madison. Who could resist a description like the one that follows?

> 'The tomato base of this gel is seasoned with lemon zest and herbes de Provence and then poured into a flat dish to set. It is served in the dish, covered with a layer of saffron-flavoured sour cream flecked with purple bracts and leaves of basil, chives, and their blossoms. Actually, the sour-cream covering serves as a blank piece of paper. There is no end to the fanciful designs and decorations that can be made with thinly sliced vegetables and delicate blossoms.
>
> In my experience a little aspic is cool and refreshing – more than that is suddenly tiresome. But small portions, combined with crisp and lively things like radishes, olives, and the inner leaves of romaine, can make a bright start to a summer meal. This aspic can be cut into squares, triangles, and diamonds with ease.'

These few words made me want to make this faery food immediately – the perfect accompaniment is some tomato crisps (see page 40).

FOR THE ASPIC

1 tsp herbes de Provence or 2 tbsp chopped fresh herbs such as parsley, marjoram and thyme

750 ml tomato juice

2 shallots, finely diced

3 level tbsp agar-agar (vegetarian gelatine)

grated zest and juice of 1 lemon

sugar

1 tbsp finely sliced chives

2 tbsp finely chopped parsley or chervil

FOR THE SAFFRON CREAM

6 tbsp sour cream

a generous pinch of saffron threads, soaked in 2 tsp hot water

GARNISHES, AS AVAILABLE:

small leaves and flower bracts of purple thyme; small leaves and blossoms of flowering thyme; a few chives sliced in narrow rounds, and chive blossoms

First, make the aspic. Crush the dried herbs a little or chop with a knife. Heat the tomato juice with the herbs and shallots and slowly bring it to the boil. Stir in the agar-agar, lower the heat and simmer for 10 minutes, stirring frequently. Remove from the heat, stir in the lemon zest, and add the lemon juice, sugar to taste and the chives and parsley or chervil.

Pour the aspic into a small, flat serving dish measuring approximately 15 cm x 23 cm, and put it in the fridge to set, about 2 hours.

When the aspic is ready, whisk the sour cream with the saffron until it is creamy and smooth. If it is too thick to spread easily, stir in a little milk but don't make it runny. Pour it on to the aspic and spread it evenly over the surface. Scatter the herbs over the top and refrigerate until needed.

TOMATO SORBET

SERVES 6

A clever and refreshing idea. To turn it into a Bloody Mary Sorbet, add a little Worcester sauce and celery salt to the mixture. Serve balls of sorbet in a chilled glass with a small stick of celery.

- 1 kg tomatoes, cored, peeled, seeded and diced
- 15 ml tomato puree
- ¼ tsp salt
- 15 g icing sugar
- 10 drops Tabasco
- 30 ml vodka, plus extra for sprinkling
- a squeeze of lemon juice
- fresh basil leaves to garnish

Chill a bowl in the freezer. Purée the tomatoes in a blender or food-processor. Add the tomato puree, ¼ teaspoon of salt, the icing sugar, Tabasco and vodka. Mix well. Taste and adjust the seasoning with salt and lemon juice. Pour into the ice-cream maker and freeze according to the manufacturer's instructions. Transfer to the chilled bowl and freeze for about an hour, until firm. Spoon into champagne glasses, or something similarly posh, and serve sprinkled with a little extra vodka and garnished with basil leaves.

VODKA-SOAKED CHERRY TOMATOES

A pick-me-up snack from Louisiana.

- 1 punnet cherry tomatoes (225 g)
- 150 ml vodka
- 1 tbsp lemon juice
- 1 tbsp dry sherry
- 6 drops Tabasco
- 1 tsp Worcestershire sauce
- 3 basil leaves
- celery salt to serve

Prick the tomatoes all over with a cocktail stick. Mix together all the other ingredients except the celery salt in a bowl. Add the tomatoes. Cover and chill for several hours. Serve with cocktail sticks and celery salt for dunking. The liquid can be drunk as 'shots' or used to make Bloody Mary.

TOMATO TERRINE

SERVES 8

In my wildest flights of fancy, after I had spent weeks on end thinking about nothing but tomatoes, I dreamed up all manner of elaborate tomato terrines. I imagined them in different-shaped containers with layers of different-sized tomatoes, held in tomato jelly made with tomato stock. I imagined different-coloured versions, some made with yellow tomatoes, others with golden, I even thought of a green version. These terrines, so spectacular to behold and elegant on the plate, never materialized. Why go to all that trouble, I thought, when there are so many other, simpler, ways to present tomatoes? Then, one day, I was leafing through Sophie Grigson's *Taste of the Times* and came across a recipe for tomato terrine with basil, which seemed so uncomplicated that I dropped what I was doing and made it immediately. No gelatine, no stock, no fussing, this recipe is just slices of peeled, seeded tomatoes layered with freshly made pesto. It is left, weighted, overnight, and is served in slices in the normal way of terrines. I have adapted it freely, using the juices that seep from the tomatoes to make the dressing. It occurred to me that it would be good too if it were layered with a thick Roast Tomato Sauce (see page 245) and a few whole basil leaves instead of the pesto.

- 1 quantity Pesto (see page 281)
- olive oil
- 3 kg large ripe tomatoes, cored and peeled
- salt and freshly ground black pepper
- sugar
- 1 tsp red wine vinegar
- 8, or more, sprigs of basil to garnish
- freshly grated Parmesan (optional)

Set aside 1 tablespoon of pesto in a small pot. Pour over 2 tablespoons of olive oil and cover with clingfilm.

Quarter the tomatoes. Place a sieve over a bowl and scrape the pips and tomato juice directly into the sieve. Continue until all the tomatoes are prepared. Trim the pieces, if necessary, to get rid of any ridges, bumps and lumps, and to leave flat sheets of tomato. Place a cake rack over the draining-board. Lay out the pieces of tomato, sprinkle lightly with salt and even more lightly with sugar. Leave to drain for 30 minutes.

Line a 500 g loaf tin with clingfilm, allowing plenty of film to trail over the sides and ends. Brush the inside lightly with olive oil. Pat the tomato pieces dry, then arrange a layer, tightly snuggled together, over the base. Spread with a little of the pesto. Repeat these layers until the tomato is all used up, finishing with a layer of tomato. Fold over the trailing clingfilm loosely. Sit another loaf tin of the same size on top and weight it down (use cans of food or bags of rice or whatever is handy and heavy). Stand on a dish and leave overnight in the fridge, draining off the pressed-out liquid whenever you dive into the fridge to get something out (you'll be amazed by how much oozes out). Save this liquid.

To make the dressing, whisk the vinegar with the reserved pesto and oil and stir in 3 tablespoons of the reserved tomato liquid. Gradually whisk in another 2 tablespoons of olive oil. Taste, and if you think it needs it, add more tomato water and a hint of sugar and black pepper. Set aside until needed.

To serve, carefully drain any remaining juice from the tomato terrine, then turn it out on to a chopping-board or serving-dish and carefully peel away the clingfilm. Either take it to the table as it is or slice it in the kitchen: using a razor-sharp, thin-bladed knife, cut it into 2.5 cm slices. Lay a slice on each plate and spoon some of the pesto vinaigrette around and over it. Garnish with basil sprigs and a dusting of Parmesan, if liked. Serve immediately.

ROAST TOMATO BUTTER

Tomato butter is a handy thing to have in the fridge or freezer. Try it spread on toast or bruschetta, to add interest to sandwiches and canapés. A slice or two in a jacket potato or melted into a steaming bowl of new potatoes makes a change and it is a good thing to stir into hot pasta, or a sauce or soup as a last-minute seasoning. It goes well with plainly cooked fish, or chicken. In fact, once you've made up a batch of this salmon-pink butter, you'll wonder how you got by without it. At its simplest, it is concentrated tomato paste mixed into soft, creamy butter, but it can be made with fresh, roasted or sun-dried tomatoes. Fresh herbs are a good addition, and so are chunks of pitted black olives. It looks good too. Keep it in a roll, wrapped in clingfilm or foil, in the freezer, to be sliced like a swiss roll or softened and worked into individual small serving dishes.

- 100 g soft unsalted butter
- 6 Roast Tomato Halves (see page 33)

OPTIONAL EXTRAS

- 6 finely snipped basil leaves
- 3 finely chopped black olives
- 2 sun-dried tomatoes in olive oil
- a few drops of balsamic vinegar

Beat the soft butter until light and fluffy; this is quickly done in a blender. Press the tomatoes through a sieve into the butter, beating until thoroughly amalgamated.

If adding one or more of the optional extras, do so now. If you favour a super-smooth finish, pass the butter through a sieve. Scrape it on to a sheet of clingfilm or foil, and roll it into a sausage shape, closing the ends like a cracker. Store in the fridge for a few days or keep in the freezer: it can be sliced from frozen.

Also see
Passata (page 28-29)
Fried Green Tomatoes (page 409)
Tomato Ice-cream (page 151)
'Sun-dried' Tomatoes (page 395)
Classic Tomato Coulis (page 43)

tomato soups

'It's actually a cross between a soup and a salad. Cold tomato soup, made from split, roasted Sicilian tomatoes, pureed and sieved, filling no more than one third of a soup plate. It will be garnished with five different sorts of tomato, roast garlic, green and purple basil leaves and served with a mile-long breadstick. The diner is absorbed, they take in the idea of it before they eat it. It's refreshing. The acidic flavours sharpen the appetite.'

Sally Clarke, on summer menus at Clarke's, Kensington

Although I have written three books about soup, and now one about tomatoes, whenever I think of tomato soup I think of Heinz. Who doesn't? For some people it is tomato soup. What a revelation, then, when you go to the bother of making a cream of tomato soup at home. It might look the same. That familiar deep orange red, which always results from stirring cream into pureed tomato, and the same voluptuous glossy texture that is so soothing on the tongue. The taste, however, is quite different. I'm not saying it is better, because I love Heinz tomato soup, it is just different. Home-made tastes of fresh tomatoes, and it isn't sweet.

But cream of tomato isn't the only tomato soup. There is a family of Italian and Spanish soups – Pappa al Pomodoro and Gazpacho – made with bread and eaten cold or lukewarm. The former is cooked to a slop, the latter remains raw, more of a salad soup (see pages 115 and 110). By contrast, tomatoes that have been baked, their flavour concentrated and juices caramelized with sugar, make marvellous soups either on their own or with other vegetables such as red peppers, garlic and onion. Because tomatoes combine so well with so many other foods and flavourings, while providing plenty of liquid, they are a wonderful soup ingredient. They are useful in the stockpot; their skins give colour, the juice around the seeds will add a last-minute injection of flavour, and over-ripe fruit will bolster a lacklustre vegetable stock to great effect; grilling the tomatoes first and leaving on the charring skins lends a faintly smoky flavour. Tomato concassé is the perfect garnish to many soups, providing colour, freshness and a hint of acidity. Try, for example, softening 500 g concassé in butter and pouring the puree into Vichysoisse made with new potatoes. Served with a swirl of basil oil diluted with a little red wine vinegar, this is a wonderful summer soup.

Autumn, when home-grown tomatoes are heavy with flavour, is the time when tomatoes should be remembered for soups. Stewed with onions and a pinch of saffron or the grated zest from an orange, the soup will need little else. Or cooked with clams or mussels and a handful of chopped coriander, parsley or mint, tomato soups become a meal in themselves. And there is no reason not to think of tomato soups in winter: you will find several here made with canned tomatoes, which should not be regarded as second best. One of my all-time favourite tomato soups comes from a can – not Heinz, on this occasion – cooked up with red onions, red wine and orange zest (see page 77).

PURE TOMATO STOCK

If you want to enrich a meat or vegetable stock with tomatoes there are two options: either roast a few tomatoes and add them to the stock, or sweat a few tomatoes with a carrot, onion and stick of celery, and add this to the stock. In both cases, simmer everything together for 30 minutes then sieve before chilling. This stock is more drastic. Buy very cheap cooking tomatoes to make it and use it for tomato aspic, soups, risotto, sauces and stewed dishes.

- 1 kg over-ripe tomatoes, roughly chopped
- 600 ml vegetable or chicken stock

Tip the tomatoes into a food processor with the stock and blitz to a puree. Place a fine sieve or colander lined with muslin or a clean J-cloth over a bowl. Pour the tomato mixture into the sieve. Cover and leave somewhere cool to drip overnight. The stock can be frozen.

CHILLED ROAST TOMATO SOUP WITH ANGOSTURA

SERVES 4

Angostura is a secret blend of aromatic herbs, spices and flavourings developed in Venezuela in 1824 and made today in Trinidad. It is the 'pink' in pink gin and, along with a shot of vodka, is the hidden kick in this great summer soup. Definitely something that will get a meal in the garden off to a good start.

- 900 g ripe plum tomatoes, halved
- 1 garlic clove, crushed
- 3 tbsp Angostura
- 150 ml olive oil
- 1 tbsp demerara sugar
- salt and freshly ground black pepper
- vodka to taste
- sour cream (optional)
- chives (optional)

Pre-heat the oven to 450°/230°C/gas mark 8.

Toss all the ingredients, except the vodka, together in a roasting tin and season with salt and pepper. Cook, covered with foil, in the oven for 30 minutes. Transfer the tomatoes to the bowl of a food-processor, scraping up all the juices, and blitz. Pass through a sieve to catch pips and skin. Add 150 ml of water, taste and adjust the seasoning. Serve hot or cold with a dash of vodka added to the soup just before serving. If liked, decorate the soup with a swirl of sour cream and chopped chives, and a splash of Angostura.

ICED PLUM TOMATO SOUP WITH BABY MOZZARELLA AND BASIL

SERVES 8

A close relative of Gazpacho (see pages 109-112) but this time using several different kinds of tomatoes and no bread. Plum and cherry tomatoes with tomato juice go into the basic soup and a mixture of fancy little tomatoes – yellow, plum, etc. – constitutes the garnish. The soup is seasoned with balsamic vinegar and garlic and the wonderful flavour is echoed with a dribble of basil oil and marble-sized balls of mozzarella. A clever, delicious soup perfected by Mark Hix when he cooked at the Ivy in London's theatreland.

- 500 g ripe plum or other well-flavoured tomatoes, halved and seeded
- 500 g cherry tomatoes
- 300 ml tomato juice
- 3 tsp balsamic vinegar
- 1 garlic clove, peeled and blanched in boiling water for 2 minutes
- salt and freshly ground black pepper

FOR THE GARNISH

- 150 g mozzarella cheese
- 60 ml Basil Dressing (see page 225)
- a handful of small basil leaves
- 150 g mixed tomatoes, cherry, yellow, plum, etc., cut into small pieces

Process the plum tomatoes in a blender with the cherry tomatoes, tomato juice, balsamic vinegar and garlic, and pass the mixture through a fine sieve.

Taste and correct the seasoning, adding a little more vinegar if necessary. Chill the soup in the freezer for 20 to 30 minutes (or in the fridge for at least 2, preferably 4 hours).

Serve in a soup plate with small slices/balls/chunks of mozzarella, a drizzle of basil dressing, a few basil leaves, and a selection of tomato pieces.

ICED ROAST TOMATO SOUP WITH FRESH TOMATOES AND BASIL

SERVES 6

As roasting tomatoes intensifies their flavour, this is a soup that could be made at any time of the year, but the best results come from using sun-ripened tomatoes. The tomatoes are roasted together with onions and garlic, then everything is liquidized, sieved and flavoured. It is delicious at this point but it is given an extraordinary injection of intense tomato flavour with the last-minute addition of tomato concassé (see page 29) and the watery-seeming liquid around the seed cavity. Even if you use bog standard tomatoes to make the soup, do choose vine-ripened tomatoes for this last part of the recipe.

- 2 tbsp olive oil, plus a little extra (optional)
- 20 medium tomatoes (approximately 1.2 kg)
- 4 medium onions
- 2 big garlic cloves
- 400 ml iced water
- salt and freshly ground black pepper
- Tabasco
- juice of ½ lemon
- 1 tbsp tomato ketchup (optional)
- 6 vine tomatoes
- approximately 18 basil leaves
- cream (optional)

Pre-heat the oven to 400°F/200°C/gas mark 6.

Line a baking sheet with foil and smear it lightly with oil. Stand the tomatoes, core side down, in the middle of the sheet. Halve the onions through their middles, flake away all but two or three layers of skin and place them, cut side down, round the edges. Cover the garlic cloves with the flat of a knife and press hard until you hear a crack.

Place the baking sheet on a middle shelf in the oven and bake for 15 minutes, then lower the heat to 350°F/180°C/gas mark 4. Continue to cook for 30 minutes or until the skin of the tomatoes has split and the flesh is beginning to weep. The onions should feel tender to the point of a small sharp knife. Slip the garlic cloves between the tomatoes 20 minutes before the end of cooking.

Allow the vegetables to cool slightly then pinch off the tomato skins, lift off the onion skins and scrape the soft garlic flesh out of its skin. Tip everything into the bowl of a food-processor, including any juices, and liquidize. Pour the liquid through a sieve into a china or glass bowl, scraping the inside of the bowl to get every last scrap and forcing all but pips and core through the sieve.

Add half the iced water. Begin adjusting the flavour by adding and tasting as you go. Add salt, pepper, Tabasco, lemon juice, ketchup, if using, and more water if you think the flavours can take it. You want to end up with a smoky tomato and onion flavour with a hint of mellow garlic. Cover with clingfilm and place the soup in the fridge to chill.

Meanwhile core, blanch and seed the vine-ripened tomatoes and dice them quite small. Tip all the seed debris into a sieve suspended over a bowl. Press with the back of a wooden spoon to extract all the liquid. Add this and the diced tomato to the soup, stirring well. Serve the chilled soup with the basil leaves shredded or torn over the top. A splash of olive oil or a swirl of cream looks very pretty.

CHILLED TOMATO AND COUSCOUS SOUP

SERVES 4

This is a dramatically different-looking tomato soup, which would be perfect to serve as a light meal on a hot summer's day. Not only is the soup light yet satisfying, it is also very quick and easy to make using store-bought passata laced with diced fresh tomato. The soup is seasoned with basil and the flavours are fine-tuned with sugar and vinegar. Serve it in wide soup bowls with a mound of the lemon and herb couscous in the middle and a swirl of Greek yoghurt trailed round the couscous. The finishing touch is more basil and parsley scattered over the top. A wonderful soup adapted from an idea of Alastair Little and Richard Whittington in their book *Food of the Sun*.

FOR THE LEMON COUSCOUS

225 g instant couscous
juice of 2 lemons
small bunch flat-leaf parsley, leaves only
150 ml extra virgin olive oil
salt and pepper
1 small red onion, finely diced
1 red pepper, seeds and white filament discarded, diced quite small
1 yellow pepper, seeds and white filament discarded, diced quite small
10 mint leaves, shredded

FOR THE SOUP

1 litre passata (see pages 28-29)
4 large ripe plum tomatoes, cored, peeled, seeded and diced
6 drops Tabasco, or more to taste
8-12 basil leaves
1 tsp caster sugar
1 tbsp red wine or balsamic vinegar
salt and pepper
tomato ketchup

FOR THE GARNISH

300 ml Greek yoghurt
12 small basil leaves

Place the couscous in a bowl and pour over 500 ml boiling water, stirring with a fork as you go. Fork for a couple of minutes, squeeze the lemon juice over the top (through a sieve) and leave for a few more minutes until all the liquid has been absorbed.

Reserve several parsley leaves and chop the rest quite fine. Stir in the olive oil, season with salt and pepper, then stir in the onion, the peppers, the mint and the chopped parsley. Chill.

In a second bowl, mix the passata with the fresh tomato and the Tabasco. Shred the basil leaves and stir them in. Dissolve the sugar in the vinegar and stir that into the soup. Taste and adjust the seasoning with salt and pepper and tomato ketchup. Chill.

Ladle the tomato soup into flat soup bowls and place a mound of couscous in the centre of each bowl. Pour an irregular ring of yoghurt round the couscous towards the edge of the plate. Dribble over a little olive oil. Tear the garnish basil leaves and scatter them over the top with the reserved parsley.

TOMATO CONSOMMÉ

SERVES 4

This is Simon Hopkinson's recipe for tomato consommé, perfected during his days behind the stoves at Bibendum. Of all the tomato consommé recipes I have in my files, and there are many, this has the cleanest, most intense tomato flavour. It can be eaten hot or cold but is at its finest, I think, when set lightly with gelatine to become 'a trembling bowlful'. Simon suggests serving the cold or jellied version with a spoonful of crème fraîche, further sharpened by lemon juice and perfumed with fresh basil leaves. The tomatoes *must* be very ripe.

- 3 kg very ripe tomatoes, seeded and roughly chopped
- 3 cloves garlic, sliced
- salt
- a large pinch of dried red chilli flakes
- 1 large bunch of basil, 'and I mean large'
- 2 leaves gelatine (optional)

It is essential to use a stainless-steel or other non-reactive saucepan.

Put the tomatoes and the precious juices in the pan with the garlic, a little salt and the chilli, and set it over a low heat. Bring to a simmer, stir and put on a lid. The liquid that forms comes purely from the tomatoes. Cook for 40 minutes. Tear in the basil leaves and continue to simmer for a further 10 minutes. Strain through a colander into a clean bowl or other pan. Leave to drip for a good hour, but do not force the pulp (use it for another dish). At this point, if you wish to gel the consommé, soften the gelatine in cold water, squeeze it dry and warm it through in a small pan with a little of the tomato liquid to melt it, then stir it back in.

Now, either using a damp tea-towel or jelly-bag, strain the tomato liquid into another scrupulously clean bowl. It is best to support it well above the container (jelly-bags usually have strings attached so that they can be hooked up). Allow to drip until it stops completely. The liquid should settle in the bowl and be clear. However, if there is a little sediment at the bottom, simply pour off the clear liquid into another container.

TOMATO, MELON AND CUCUMBER SOUP WITH MINT

SERVES 6-8

A refreshing, quickly made soup.

- 2 medium cucumbers, peeled
- 750 g ripe tomatoes, halved
- 2 ripe Charentais, Galia, Ogen or Canteloupe melons, rind and seeds removed
- 300 g ice
- 1 medium orange
- 300 g Greek yoghurt
- salt
- 6 drops Tabasco
- a squeeze of lemon juice
- sugar
- 1 small bunch mint

Split the cucumber lengthways. Use a teaspoon to gouge out the seeds and discard them. Roughly chop it and place it in the bowl of a food processor with the tomatoes and melon. Add the ice. Blitz – you will probably have to do this in batches – and pour through a sieve into a chilled bowl, pressing down on the seeds, pips and skin to extract maximum juice.

Remove the zest (no pith) from half the orange and chop very finely, almost into dust. Add it and the juice from the orange to the puree. Stir in the yoghurt. Taste and adjust the seasoning with salt, Tabasco, lemon juice and possibly, depending on the ripeness of the fruit, a little sugar. Pick the mint leaves from the stalks and chop very finely. Stir into the soup. Serve very cold.

ROAST TOMATO SOUP WITH BASIL

SERVES 4-6

I make a lot of roast tomato soups. At its simplest it's just roast tomatoes liquidized with stock but there are all manner of variations to ring the changes with this delicious tomato nectar. Laying sprigs of rosemary or thyme over the tomatoes as they roast scents the flavour rather than overpowers it. If it's made with fresh chicken stock, the building blocks of flavour really sing out through the intense tomato flavour. A pinch of saffron and a spoonful of honey give the soup a Moorish flavour. It changes again with different garnishes. My current favourite is a crumble of feta, chopped black olives and basil. Whatever you do, this soup is wonderful hot but delicious cold. Try it with a nip of vodka or use to make a Bloody or Virgin Mary.

- 10 large vine tomatoes, approx 900 g
- 1 tbsp olive oil
- a few branches rosemary or thyme (optional)
- 750 ml chicken stock or
- 1 ½ chicken stock cubes and
- 750 ml boiling water
- about 15 flourishing basil leaves

Heat the oven to 350°F/180°C/gas mark 4. Line a shallow baking tray with foil. Halve the tomatoes round their middles and place, cut-side up, on the foil. Smear with a little oil. Lay the branches of rosemary or thyme, if using, over the tomatoes. Place the tray in the oven on a lower shelf. Cook for 60 minutes or until the tomatoes feel squashy. Remove the tray from the oven. Discard the herbs. Tip the tomatoes and their juices into the bowl of a food-processor. Blitz for several minutes until smooth. Pour through a sieve suspended over a suitable pan. Push the tomatoes through the sieve with the back of a wooden spoon, scraping underneath so nothing is wasted. Discard pips and pith. Add the chicken stock or cubes dissolved in boiling water. Simmer for 10 minutes then adjust the seasoning with salt and pepper. Serve with a swirl of best olive oil and torn or snipped basil. Good with bruschetta or garlic bread.

BLACK BEAN SOUP WITH TOMATO AND AVOCADO RELISH

SERVES 6-8

Black beans, not to be confused with black-eyed beans, are small, shiny and kidney-shaped. Their slightly sweet flavour is complemented by onions and garlic, goes well with coriander, cumin and tomatoes, and needs to be pepped up with chilli. This soup combines all those flavours and the result is an intriguingly aromatic, thick and chunky soup, freshened with a 'salad' of raw tomato and avocado seasoned with lemon juice.

4 tbsp vegetable oil
2 large onions, diced
4 garlic cloves, chopped
1 tsp ground cumin
1 tsp ground coriander
1 tsp dried oregano
1 bay leaf
250 g dried black beans, soaked in water for at least 4 hours and drained
2 x 400 g tins Italian tomatoes
1 tbsp tomato puree
1 scant tsp Tabasco
a large bunch coriander (approximately 75 g), leaves only, chopped
1.75 litres hot water or vegetable stock
salt and freshly ground black pepper
½ lemon

FOR THE GARNISH

1 firm but ripe avocado, diced
1 tbsp lemon juice
2 plum tomatoes, cored, peeled, seeded and diced
100 g soured cream
a few coriander leaves

Heat the oil in a large pan and sauté the onion and garlic for several minutes until slippery but not coloured. Stir in the cumin, ground coriander, oregano and bay leaf, then add the beans. Cook, stirring constantly, for 5 minutes.

Run a sharp knife through the tomatoes a few times while still in the tin and add them, with their liquid, the tomato puree, Tabasco and chopped coriander and the hot water or stock. Bring to the boil, turn down immediately and simmer very gently for 3 hours.

Discard the bay leaf. Puree half the soup in a food-processor or mouli-legumes. Pass the soup through a sieve, pressing down hard, into a clean pan and add the unpureed soup. Reheat the soup and adjust the seasoning as necessary, sharpening it up with a squeeze of lemon.

Make the garnish. Mix together the avocado, lemon juice and tomato. Serve the soup topped with a scoop of cream, a tablespoonful of the avocado mixture and the coriander.

CHEAT'S BLACK BEAN SOUP SERVES 2, GENEROUSLY

Canned black beans make very good soups. The flavour for this one is spicy with hints of cumin and smoky pimenton and sharpened with lime. The texture stays chunky but a quick blast with a stick blender purees some of the beans to thicken the soup. The rest is bumpy with slippery, sliced red onion, soft cherry tomatoes, masses of chopped coriander and diced avocado. Keeping the Mexican mood, turn soup into supper with pan-toasted tortilla piled with more chopped avocado, tomato and coriander, dredged generously with grated Cheddar. When you are ready to serve, pop the faux pizza under the grill; it's ready when the cheese melts. Serve cut into wedges with the soup.

- 1 large red onion
- 1 tbsp olive oil
- 400 g can black beans
- ¼ tsp ground cumin
- ¼ tsp picante pimenton
- 600 ml chicken or vegetable stock
- 12 cherry tomatoes
- 2 limes
- 1 ripe but firm avocado
- 50 g coriander

Peel and halve the onion then slice down the halves to make thin wedges. Heat the oil in a pan that can accommodate the soup and stir in the onion. Cook, stirring often, for about 10 minutes until slippery soft. Add cumin and pimenton, stirring to cook the spices then add the stock. Bring to the boil. Season with salt, pepper and juice of ½ a lime. Quarter the tomatoes. Add half to the pan. Simmer, semi-covered, for 5 minutes. Use a blender wand to blitz the soup for a couple of minutes to liquidize about half of it. Add the remaining tomatoes, diced avocado and finely chopped coriander. Re-heat, taste and adjust the seasoning with extra lime and salt. Serve very hot.

CREAM OF TOMATO SOUP

SERVES 4

The Real Thing. It might look like Heinz Cream of Tomato but try it and spot the difference.

- 50 g butter
- 2 celery sticks, finely diced
- 2 cloves of garlic, finely chopped
- 700 g very ripe tomatoes, cored, scalded, peeled and chopped
- a pinch of sugar
- salt and freshly ground black pepper
- 750 ml light chicken or vegetable stock
- 10 basil leaves
- 125 ml whipping cream

Heat the butter in a spacious heavy-bottomed pan and soften the onion and celery, allowing about 20 minutes for this, adding the garlic towards the end. Add the tomatoes with a little sugar, salt and pepper, let them melt and reduce a little, then add the stock. Cook for 15 minutes, adding the basil for the last few minutes, then liquidize.

Pass through a fine sieve into a clean pan. Stir in the cream and gently reheat, taking care not to let it boil. Taste and adjust the seasoning and, if liked, serve with buttery croutons.

THAI CREAM OF TOMATO SOUP

SERVES 4-6

On this occasion, cream means coconut milk and bean curd. An unusual take on tomato soup with Thai seasonings.

- 1 kg tomatoes, roughly chopped
- 700 ml coconut milk
- 1 tsp red curry paste
- 300 g bean curd, cubed
- 2 tbsp soy sauce
- 1 tbsp lemon juice
- 2 tbsp chopped coriander leaves
- salt and freshly ground black pepper
- pinch of sugar

Blitz the tomatoes to a puree. Pass through a sieve directly into a saucepan. Add the coconut milk, red curry paste, bean curd, soy sauce and lemon juice.

Over a gentle heat, bring slowly to the boil. Reduce the heat and cook very gently for 20 minutes. Taste and adjust the seasonings, adding a little sugar if necessary. Stir in the coriander and serve.

INDIAN CREAM OF TOMATO SOUP SERVES 4-6

I came across this soup when I was researching *A Celebration of Soup* in what I consider to be Madhur Jaffrey's finest book: *Eastern Vegetarian Cooking*. Its spicy-hot, sweet-sour flavour remains a great favourite. I leave out the butter and flour emulsion.

- 700 g ripe tomatoes, chopped
- 1 tbsp finely chopped lemon grass heart
- 1-2 curry leaves
- 5 cm piece fresh ginger, peeled and chopped
- 100 ml water
- salt and freshly ground black pepper
- 4 tbsp unsalted butler (optional)
- 2 tbsp flour (optional)
- 100 ml single cream
- 570 ml milk
- ½ tsp ground roasted cumin seeds
- ⅛ tsp cayenne pepper
- 2 tsp lime or lemon juice
- 1 tbsp chopped coriander leaves

Put the tomatoes, lemon grass, curry leaves, ginger and water in a pan. Season generously with salt and bring to the boil. Lower the heat, cover, and simmer gently for 15 minutes. Uncover, increase the heat and simmer more aggressively for 15 minutes. Puree and sieve: you should end up with about 400 ml of thick tomato juice.

Meanwhile, if you are including the butter and flour liaison, heat the butter, stir in the flour and cook on a low heat for a couple of minutes. Pour in the hot tomato juice, stirring all the time. If not, proceed directly to adding the cream, milk, cumin seeds, cayenne pepper and lime or lemon juice. Season generously with black pepper. Stir thoroughly and reheat without boiling. Serve sprinkled with the freshly chopped coriander.

HOT SOUPS

LOBSTER BISQUE

SERVES 4

Tomatoes are as vital to bisques as the shells of the seafood that qualify a soup to be called a bisque. This particularly fine version, inspired after a visit to the Carved Angel restaurant in Dartmouth, comes from *The Prawn Cocktail Years*, which I wrote with Simon Hopkinson. The flavour in the soup is the very essence of lobster: sweet and deep, rich and fragrant, and lifted by a whisper of Cognac.

- 1 x 500 g boiled lobster, plus any extra shells
- 75 g butter
- 1 carrot, peeled and diced
- 1 medium onion, peeled and chopped
- 2 garlic cloves, peeled and chopped
- 50 ml Cognac
- 400 g tin chopped tomatoes
- 150 ml dry white wine
- bouquet garni, made with parsley, thyme and a bay leaf
- 400 ml chicken stock
- 1 tbsp long grain rice
- 100 ml whipping cream
- salt and cayenne pepper

Remove the cooked lobster meat from the shell and set aside. Chop the lobster shells with a heavy knife. Heat the butter and gently fry the shell until burnished. Add the vegetables, stirring around until they brown and begin to soften. Pour in 25 ml of the Cognac and ignite. Once the flames have subsided, add the tomatoes and wine. Simmer for 10 minutes then add the bouquet garni and stock. Bring to the boil and simmer for 30 minutes.

Remove the claw shells and bouquet garni from the pan. Tip everything else into a liquidizer and process until the motor runs easily. Strain through a sieve into a clean pan, pressing down well on the solids to extract all the flavour. Reheat with the rice and cream, and simmer for 10 minutes or so until the rice is overcooked (it is only used for thickening). Liquidize once more, pass through a fine sieve and season with salt and cayenne. Chop the lobster meat and stir into the soup together with the remaining Cognac. Heat through and serve very hot.

MANHATTAN CLAM CHOWDER

SERVES 4

Tomatoes are what sets a Manhattan clam chowder apart from a creamy New England chowder. It is a hearty bowlful: brimful of potato, leeks, onion, celery, tomatoes and plenty of herbs. In America, Manhattan clam chowder will be made with giant, meaty, quahog clams. These are rarely available from British fishmongers but this wonderful soup is just as good made with whatever clams you can lay your hands on – palourdes or Venus are the most likely. The clams can be replaced by cockles, mussels, oysters and chunks of firm white fish, such as cod and smoked haddock.

- a splash of cooking oil
- 100 g rindless, streaky bacon, chopped
- 25 g butter
- 1 large onion, peeled and chopped
- 2 sticks celery, peeled and chopped
- 2 medium floury potatoes, peeled and chopped
- salt and freshly ground black pepper
- 2 leeks, washed, trimmed and thickly sliced
- 400 g tin Italian tomatoes
- 3 tbsp finely chopped flat-leaf parsley
- 1 flourishing sprig of thyme
- 1 bay leaf
- 1 litre fish stock
- 1.35 kg clams, palourdes, Venus, cherrystone or little neck clams, scrubbed and rinsed under running water
- 1 glass dry white wine, 150 ml (optional)

In a spacious pan, heat the splash of oil and slowly sauté the bacon, increasing the heat as the fat begins to melt, until cooked to a crisp. Put the bacon to one side. Add the butter and gently sweat the onion, celery and potatoes with a generous pinch of salt. When they are nicely softened, stir in the leeks, tomatoes, most of the parsley, the thyme and bay leaf. Pour on the stock and leave to simmer.

Meanwhile, put the cleaned clams in a pan (discarding any that refuse to close after a sharp rap against a hard surface) with the wine or a little stock or water. Cover and cook fiercely until all the clams open (discard any that don't). Pick the clams out of their shells and put to one side. Strain the cooking liquid carefully into the soup (through a sieve to catch grit but watch out for sand). Reheat, adjust the seasoning and stir the clams into the soup. Serve garnished with the last of the parsley and the crisp bacon pieces.

PLUM AND TOMATO SOUP

SERVES 6

Comparisons are often made between plums and tomatoes. After all, plum tomatoes look like red plums, they have similar skin and the texture of their flesh is almost identical. No wonder then, that so many recipes are interchangeable between the two. Here, in a fresh-tasting and stunning red soup that will keep your guests guessing, they are cooked together.

25 g olive oil

1 medium onion, peeled and finely chopped

450 g red plums, stoned

450 g tomatoes, cored, peeled and seeded

300 ml fresh tomato juice (see page 431)

570 ml chicken stock

1 sprig of thyme

1 tsp caster sugar

salt and freshly ground black pepper

FOR THE GARNISH

6 dsp single cream

2 red plums, scalded, peeled, stoned and diced

½ tbsp finely sliced chives

½ tbsp finely chopped flat-leaf parsley

Heat the oil and gently sauté the onion until soft but not browned. Stir in the plums, tomatoes, tomato juice, stock, thyme, sugar, a generous pinch of salt and a few grinds of pepper. Bring to the boil, turn down the heat and simmer gently for about 15 minutes.

Leave to cool slightly. Remove the thyme, then force the soup through a fine sieve. Check the seasoning and chill. Serve garnished with the cream, the raw plums and herbs.

POTATO, TOMATO AND BASIL SOUP

SERVES 4

This is a remarkably good soup from the wonderful *Greens Cookbook* by Deborah Madison. You need potatoes with plenty of flavour for this, preferably Cornish new potatoes or Jersey mids. The soup is served with an intensely flavoured basil vinaigrette. The final combination is stunning in every sense.

- 50 g butter
- 1.4 litres water
- 1 large white onion, peeled and finely chopped, or 2 bunches spring onions, trimmed and finely chopped
- 1 bay leaf
- 5 sprigs of thyme
- 700 g new potatoes, scrubbed and coarsely chopped
- salt and freshly ground black pepper
- 500 g ripe tomatoes, cored, peeled, seeded and finely chopped
- 4 tbsp olive oil
- small bunch of basil, leaves only
- ½ tbsp red wine vinegar

Melt the butter in a large pan with a little of the water, and add the onion, bay leaf and thyme. Stew over a low heat for a few minutes, then add the potatoes and a teaspoon of salt. Cover and cook for 5 minutes. Pour in the rest of the water and bring to the boil. Cook until the potatoes are falling apart.

Pass the soup through a mouli-legumes or sieve and return to the pan. In a separate saucepan, fry the tomatoes with a little seasoning in 1 tablespoon of the olive oil, until their juices have evaporated and the tomatoes have thickened slightly. Whisk them together to make a semi-smooth sauce, and add them to the sieved potato.

Puree the basil, with a splash of vinegar and salt, then add the remaining olive oil to make a dressing.

Serve the soup in individual bowls with a spoonful of the basil puree floating on top and a generous grinding of pepper. If the soup thickens between the time it is made and served, thin it with additional water or, if you prefer, a little cream.

RASAM

SERVES 6

There are many versions of rasam, a highly seasoned lentil broth which is a South Indian speciality. It is made by boiling yellow lentils in water and using the liquid as the base for a thin tomato soup flavoured with sour tamarind, chilli and soothing spices. Because it has no suspending agent, rasam has a sediment and needs a jolly good stir before it is served and before each mouthful. It is traditionally drunk like tea, but with a spoon, or served over rice, or in a bowl as a soup and is regarded as Indian consommé. This is Julie Sahni's version from her book *Classic Indian Cookery*.

- 175 g yellow lentils, washed
- 1 tsp turmeric
- 600 g ripe tomatoes, cored, peeled and chopped
- 2 tsp finely chopped garlic
- 1 tbsp tamarind paste
- 1 tbsp ground coriander
- 1 tsp ground cumin
- ¼ tsp cayenne pepper
- ¼ tsp ground black pepper
- 1 tsp black treacle or sugar
- 1 tbsp coarse salt
- 2 tbsp ghee (clarified butter) or light vegetable oil
- ¾ tsp black mustard seeds
- ⅛ tsp ground asafoetida
- 2 tbsp finely chopped coriander leaves

Cover the lentils with 1 litre of cold water. Season with the turmeric and bring to the boil. Reduce the heat, partially cover, and simmer, stirring occasionally, for about 35 minutes or until the lentils are tender.

Meanwhile, puree the tomatoes with the garlic and 100 ml cold water, and set aside. Put the tamarind pulp in a small bowl, cover with 4 tablespoons of boiling water, and leave to soak for 15 minutes. Then mash the pulp with the back of a spoon and strain, squeezing out as much juice as you can. Discard the stringy fibre.

Puree the lentils and their cooking water and whisk in 700 ml of hot water. Leave to rest for 15 minutes. The lentils will sink to the bottom (these can be used for another dish – we need only the liquid for this recipe). Strain the liquid into a clean pan, add the tomato puree, tamarind paste, coriander, cumin, cayenne and black pepper, treacle or sugar, and salt. Bring to the boil, then reduce the heat, partially cover the pan, and simmer gently for 15 minutes. In a small frying-pan, heat the ghee or oil and, when very hot, carefully add the mustard seeds (they will splutter and pop), and a few seconds later, the asafoetida (which smells vile but adds an onion flavour). Turn off the heat and pour the spiced butter into the lentil and tomato broth. Stir, cover the pan, and leave for 5 minutes. Check for salt, stir in the coriander leaves and serve.

RED ONION, RED WINE AND TOMATO SOUP

SERVES 6

Save this soup for autumn or winter when you will appreciate the whiff of summer bounty. It is hearty and thick, a red version of French onion soup, made with red onions, tinned tomatoes and red wine. Herbs, orange zest, garlic and vegetable stock combine to produce a beguiling flavour that is a perfect balance of tomato acidity and sweet, succulent onion. This rich, mellow, satisfying soup is even better heated up the next day.

- 4 tbsp olive oil
- 2 shallots, peeled and finely chopped
- 1 kg red onions, peeled, quartered and finely sliced
- 2 x 400 g tins Italian tomatoes
- 4 large garlic cloves, peeled and crushed with ½ tsp salt
- bouquet garni, made with 1 bay leaf, 6 thyme branches and 5 cm strip of orange zest
- 2 glasses red wine, approximately 300 ml
- 1 litre stock, made with garlic and herb or vegetable stock cubes
- salt and freshly ground black pepper

Using a large heavy-based pan with a good-fitting lid, heat the olive oil. Gently sauté the shallots for about 5 minutes until they are soft and beginning to colour. Add the onions and cook slowly, stirring occasionally, for 30 minutes or until they are slippery and tender.

While the onions are cooking, drain the tomatoes, reserving 300 ml of the juice. Squeeze the pips out of the tomatoes and roughly chop the flesh.

When the onions are ready, stir in the salty garlic paste, the chopped tomatoes, the bouquet garni and the tomato juice (if there are lots of pips, pour it through a sieve). Cover the pan and leave to stew over a gentle heat for 15 minutes. Add the wine and boil vigorously until the liquid is reduced by half. Add the stock and simmer, partially covered, for 25 minutes. Remove the bouquet garni, taste and correct the seasoning with salt and pepper. Serve very hot.

ROASTED RED PEPPER AND TOMATO SOUP

SERVES 4

It was tempting to call this Romesco Soup after the famous Roast Red Pepper and Tomato Sauce (see page 238) from Tarragona in Spain. Although it tastes very rich and creamy, it is surprising to discover that it is entirely fat free. It can be eaten hot or cold and looks very pretty with a few basil leaves scattered over the top. To give the soup a Moroccan flavour, add a generous pinch of saffron stamens dissolved in 1 tbsp of boiling water, to the saucepan with the sieved tomatoes and peppers. Add chopped mint and crumbled feta instead of the crème fraîche.

500 g plum tomatoes
750 g red peppers
2 medium onions, halved but unpeeled
6 garlic cloves, unpeeled, smacked with a closed fist
1 chicken stock cube dissolved in 300 ml boiling water
salt and freshly ground black pepper
½ tbsp runny honey
crème fraîche (optional)
basil leaves

Pre-heat the oven to 400°F/200°C/gas mark 6.

Cover a heavy roasting tin/baking sheet with kitchen foil. Stand the tomatoes, core end down, in the middle of the baking-sheet and place the peppers and onion halves, cut side down, around them. Roast the vegetables for 30 minutes. Remove them from the oven and turn the onions and peppers – their skins will be blistering and blackening, and juices will be starting to run from the tomatoes. Tuck the garlic between the vegetables. Roast for a further 30 minutes.

Leave the vegetables to cool for a few minutes before removing the stalks, seeds and as much of the skins as possible from the peppers. Peel away the skin from the tomatoes and onions; scrape the soft garlic flesh out of its skin. Tip the vegetables and juices into the bowl of a food-processor and pour on the stock. Blitz to liquidize. Pour the soup through a fine sieve into a saucepan. Simmer for a few moments, taste and adjust the seasoning with salt, black pepper and honey. Serve hot with a dollop of crème fraîche topped with a few snipped basil leaves. To serve cold, chill for at least 4 hours and serve with a few basil leaves scattered over the top.

SOUPE MENERBOISE

SERVES 4-6

Tomatoes are cooked in two different ways in a soup reminiscent of the more familiar Provençal summer vegetable soup, Soupe au Pistou. Both are made with young summer vegetables and served with a basil-seasoned sauce. In this version, a favourite from Elizabeth David's *Summer Cooking*, the accompanying sauce is a sort of mayonnaise made with grilled tomatoes, Parmesan and basil. It is stirred into the soup right at the end to enrich and thicken, and heighten the appetite with its aroma.

- 5 tbsp olive oil
- 2 onions, peeled and finely sliced
- 225 g courgettes, diced
- 450 g ripe tomatoes
- 2 small potatoes, peeled, diced and rinsed
- 100 g shelled broad beans, blanched and waxy skins removed
- 40 g soup pasta or broken-up spaghetti
- salt and freshly ground black pepper
- 3 garlic cloves
- small bunch basil
- 2 egg yolks
- 2 tbsp Parmesan, freshly grated
- 1 tbsp finely chopped flat-leaf parsley

Heat the olive oil, stir in the onions and 'let them melt but not fry'; this will take at least 15 minutes. Add the diced courgettes and continue cooking very gently for 10 minutes. Meanwhile, core, peel and roughly chop all but two of the tomatoes and add them to the pot. When these are softened, add the diced potatoes and a litre of water. Bring to the boil and simmer gently for 10 minutes until the potatoes are nearly cooked, then add the broad beans, the pasta, ½ teaspoon of salt and several grinds of pepper.

Meanwhile, grill the reserved tomatoes until tender. Skin them and scrape out their seeds. Pulverize the garlic cloves with a pinch of salt, adding the tomatoes and basil. Add the egg yolks, to make a sauce that resembles a thin mayonnaise.

When the pasta is cooked, stir a ladleful of the soup into the egg sauce, and then another. Pour the mixture slowly back into the soup, stirring all the time, and without letting the soup boil. Simmer for a couple of minutes. Just before serving, stir in the Parmesan and parsley.

SOUP OF BURNT TOMATO AND YOGHURT

SERVES 6

'My food is fairly in your face in terms of flavour. I like good, earthy food, tasty meals, solid combinations and robust presentation. I wouldn't regard myself as subtle, though goodness knows, I try!' said Michael Lee-Richard, chef at Michael's, Christchurch.

This is his soup: it isn't burnt – the tomatoes are roasted until caramelized then simmered with sautéed onion and garlic seasoned with hot-sour Thai tom yum paste. It is garnished with a swirl of yoghurt drizzled with more tom yum. The recipe comes from Madhur Jaffrey's *East West Food*.

- 2 kg ripe tomatoes, cored and peeled
- 6 tbsp grapeseed or light olive oil
- 2 tbsp clear honey, plus extra to taste
- 1 large onion, peeled and finely chopped
- 4 garlic cloves, peeled and finely chopped
- 2 tsp tom yum paste, or to taste, plus extra for garnishing
- 1.5 litres tomato juice or V8 juice
- salt and freshly ground black pepper
- yoghurt to garnish

Pre-heat the oven to 350°F/180°C/gas mark 4.

Cut the tomatoes in half lengthways and brush with 2 tablespoons of the oil and 1 tablespoon of the honey. Place the tomatoes, cut side up, in a large roasting-tin and roast in the oven for 1½ hours or until caramelized and slightly dehydrated.

Heat the remaining oil in a large saucepan. Add the onion, garlic and tom yum paste and cook, stirring frequently to make sure the mixture does not catch. Add the roast tomatoes with the tomato juice and the remaining honey. Bring to the boil, then reduce the heat and simmer for about 5 minutes. Taste and adjust the seasoning and honey, if necessary. Ladle into bowls and garnish with yoghurt and a little more tom yum paste.

SPICY TOMATO MUSSEL SOUP

SERVES 6

Zuppa di Cozze or *Zuppa di Cozze Piccante*, as this soup is also called, is a classic from Puglia and typical of the southern Italian style of cooking. This version, from the River Café, in West London, is particularly interesting. In summer, they make it with fresh tomatoes, hold the anchovy and chillies and add basil instead of parsley. Both are served with garlicky bruschetta. The soups are very thick; almost like a stew.

- 2.5 kg cleaned mussels
- 50 ml olive oil
- 150 ml white wine
- 4 garlic cloves, peeled and finely chopped
- 6 anchovy fillets
- 3 small dried chillies, crumbled
- 4 x 400 g tins peeled plum tomatoes, drained of most of their juices, chopped
- salt and freshly ground black pepper
- 1 bunch flat-leaf parsley, chopped

FOR THE BRUSCHETTA

- 6 slices Pugliese bread, cut at an angle
- 1 garlic clove, halved
- 6 tbsp extra-virgin olive oil, plus extra for serving

Pick over the mussels and discard any with broken shells or that do not close when tapped. Heat 25 ml of olive oil in a large saucepan, then add the mussels, the white wine and 100 ml water. Cook over a high heat until all the mussels are open, discarding any that remain closed. You may need to cook the mussels in batches: divide oil, wine and water accordingly.

Remove the mussels and boil to reduce the liquid by half. Remove half the mussels from their shells. Heat the remaining 25 ml of olive oil in a large pan and fry the garlic until lightly brown. Add the anchovies, and mash with the garlic into the hot oil until dissolved. Add the mussel liquid, the chillies and the tomatoes. Cook gently until the tomatoes have reduced to a medium-thick consistency. This should take about 30 minutes. Taste and season lightly with salt and generously with pepper, adding more chilli if necessary. Finally, put in the mussels, shelled and unshelled, and half of the parsley.

Make the bruschetta. Toast the bread. Rub the cut surface of the garlic over one side of the toast, and dribble over the olive oil.

Serve in flat, shallow soup plates with the bruschetta, the remaining parsley and a generous amount of the very best extra-virgin olive oil.

SWEET POTATO SOUP WITH TOMATOES

SERVES 4

The paucity of ingredients belies the subtlety of this delicate but satisfying Brazilian recipe. It can be made with fresh or tinned tomatoes although the results will be quite different.

450 g pink-skinned sweet potatoes, peeled and thickly sliced

50 g butter

1 medium onion, peeled and finely chopped

400 g tin Italian tomatoes or 450 g ripe tomatoes, peeled

750 ml chicken or vegetable stock

salt and freshly ground black pepper

Cook the sweet potatoes in salted water until tender. While the potatoes are cooking, heat the butter in a frying-pan and gently sauté the onion until soft and slippery. Add the tomatoes, increase the heat and boil hard for 5 minutes.

Tip the cooked, drained sweet potatoes and tomato mixture into the bowl of a food-processor. Add the stock and liquidize. Pour through a sieve, taste and adjust the seasoning with salt and pepper. Serve very hot.

TOMATO RICE SOUP WITH LEMON

SERVES 4

This is a useful store-cupboard soup. A slightly more unusual version, Tomato Rice Soup with Orange and Coriander, is made by substituting the juice and zest of an orange for the lemon, and adding coriander in place of parsley.

50 g basmati rice
zest and juice of 1 lemon
knob of butter
1 medium onion, finely chopped, or 1 bunch of spring onions, trimmed and chopped
400 g tin Italian tomatoes or chopped tomatoes
2 tbsp tomato puree
2 tbsp finely chopped parsley
salt and freshly ground black pepper
750 ml chicken stock or equivalent using stock cubes
cream to serve (optional)

Place the rice in a pan with 100 ml water. Squeeze the lemon juice over the rice. Shred half the zest very finely and chop the rest into fine dust. Add the shredded lemon zest to the rice. Bring to the boil, turn down to establish a gentle simmer, cover the pan and leave for at least 15 minutes until the rice is tender and the water absorbed.

Meanwhile, melt the butter in a pan that can hold the finished soup and gently soften the onion. If using whole tomatoes, chop them roughly in the tin, add to the pan together with the tomato puree, half the parsley and half the lemon zest dust. Boil hard for 5 minutes. Season with salt and pepper and add the stock. Bring to the boil and simmer for 5 minutes before liquidizing. Pass through a sieve to get rid of the plethora of pips then return to the pan. By now the rice will be cooked. Tip it into the soup. Check the seasoning. Give the remaining parsley and lemon dust a final chop together until it is very fine and stir into the soup. If liked, serve with a swirl of cream.

TOMATO, SAFFRON AND ROAST GARLIC SOUP

SERVES 6

'In this unusual soup the saffron gives the tomatoes a beautiful warm colour and adds an enticing fragrance; the roasted garlic deepens the flavours, and the sherry brings all of the elements together.' So writes Annie Somerville, in her book *Fields of Greens*, of this terrific soup. It has been a favourite with me since the book was published in 1993.

1 litre vegetable stock, fortified with 400 g tin chopped tomatoes

1 head of garlic, cloves separated and brushed with olive oil

900 g tomatoes, cored, seeded and chopped or 2 x 400 g tin of whole peeled plum tomatoes

1 tbsp olive oil

1 medium-sized onion, chopped

a generous pinch of dried thyme

salt and freshly ground black pepper

1 carrot, peeled and diced

1 celery rib, peeled and diced

1 red pepper, diced

5 garlic cloves, finely chopped

150 ml dry sherry

2 pinches of saffron threads, soaked in 1 tbsp boiling water

1 bay leaf

sugar (optional)

3 tbsp finely chopped flat-leaf parsley

freshly grated Parmesan

Pre-heat the oven to 350°F/180°C/gas mark 4.

Make the stock and keep it warm over a low heat. Place the garlic in a small baking dish, and roast for 30 minutes, or until the cloves are very soft. When the garlic cools, cut the tops off, squeeze the pulp out of the skins, and blitz with the tomatoes until pureed.

Heat the olive oil in a sauté pan and add the onion, thyme, and a pinch of salt and of pepper. Cook over a medium heat for 5 minutes, then add the carrot, celery, red pepper, and finely chopped garlic. Cook together until tender, then add the sherry and cook for a further minute or two, until the pan is almost dry. Add the tomato-garlic puree, half a teaspoon of salt, a pinch of pepper, the saffron, bay leaf and three-quarters of the stock. Cover and cook over a low heat for 30 minutes. Taste and adjust the seasoning, possibly with a pinch of sugar if the soup is acidic, adding more stock if it seems too thick. Garnish each serving with a sprinkle of parsley and Parmesan.

Also see:
Harira (page 360)
Gazpacho Andaluz (page 110)
Tomato Mouclade (page 347)
Oliaigua Amb Tomatics (page 113)
Pasta e Ceci (page 288)
Zuppa Cuata (page 114)
Aquacotta (page 108)
Pappa Al Pomodoro (page 115)
Gazpacho Cream (page 109)

tomatoes and bread

'Probably the most universal refreshment in summer among working men in Greece, Italy and Catalonia is a slab of bread on to which are crushed some ripe tomatoes with a garlic clove, sea salt, bathed in olive oil. It relies on the rusticity of the bread, the fragrance of the ripe tomatoes, the taste of olive oil for excellence, and the accompanying wine.'

Patience Gray, *Honey From a Weed, Fasting and Feasting in Tuscany, Catalonia, the Cyclades and Apulia*

When a ripe tomato is squashed against bread something magical happens. The magic works with all kinds of bread – it is just different magic – and it doesn't matter whether the bread is fresh or stale, toasted or turned to crumbs. You see the combination again and again in different guises in the cuisine of every country where tomatoes grow. In Italy, France, Greece, Spain and Portugal, for example, the simple pleasure of rubbing the flesh of a tomato into a piece of bread, until the bread is soaked red with tomato juices, is a daily routine of summer. With a twist of salt and a splash of olive oil, this is food for the gods. It is also a building block for other ingredients: anchovy, roasted peppers and aubergine, rocket, onions, fresh herbs, olives, ham and cheese.

The British, who have their own tradition of things on toast, make a version of tomato bruschetta or *pa amb tomaquet*, as they call it in Catalonia. We like fried bread or buttered toast covered with grilled tomatoes and we like it best of all for breakfast. Different though all these simple tomato and bread snacks might be, all are related to the Neapolitan pizza. At its best, as it is still served at Michele's, one of the original pizza parlours of Naples, the pizza is made with a thin, misshapen piece of dough. It is baked in a brick, wood-burning stove, and cooks until it puffs and bubbles, like nearby Vesuvius, sending the intensely flavoured tomato sauce swimming all over the pizza.

The Italians also make wonderful tomato sandwiches. There is something about the combination of slightly chewy, very crusty ciabatta loaded with slices of sun-ripened tomato, mozzarella and rocket that is particularly good. Many people despise tomato sandwiches because they go soggy. In Nice, they put this soggy factor to good effect in a giant sandwich called *pan bagnat*. It looks impossible to eat, loaded as it is with most of the ingredients of a salade Niçoise. The best ones have been weighted so that the tomato and olive oil combine as a sort of vinaigrette that seeps into the dough. As you bite it squelches over the thick slices of tomato, the black olives and anchovy, and whatever else has been piled in.

But don't let us forget that tomatoes on their own, in buttered French bread, can be worth shopping specially for. Think of it now: chunky slices of sun-ripened tomatoes, freshly baked crusty bread, unsalted butter and a little salt. It couldn't be much more different from the traditional British tomato sandwich, which is far more refined. We like our tomatoes neatly sliced, layered in thin slices of buttered bread (with the crusts removed) then cut into dainty little triangles.

Tomatoes work well cooked into bread, especially when the juice is separated from the flesh and used to make the dough. However, the most pronounced tomato flavour in baked bread comes from sun-dried tomatoes. In Spain and Italy, in particular, there is a peasant tradition of soaking yesterday's bread in chopped tomato. The addition of olive oil and one or two other choice ingredients, such as onion, garlic and vinegar, maybe celery and basil too, results in surprisingly luscious soups-cum-salads. And stale breadcrumbs, layered with sliced tomato and fresh herbs, and maybe a little onion or garlic, cook into elegant, surprisingly light gratins. These, of course, are deconstructed versions of Tomatoes Provençal, an appealing dish of tomatoes stuffed with garlic and parsley breadcrumbs.

This, for me, is possibly the most attractive section of the book. If you have a copy, do read Elizabeth David on tomato bread, in 'Waiting for Lunch', in *An Omelette and a Glass of Wine*.

CATALAN TOMATO BREAD

SERVES 1

'Plain *pa amb tomaquet*, made with good bread, good oil, and a nice ripe tomato,' writes Colman Andrews in his exhaustive *Catalan Cuisine* (Grub Street, 1997), 'is its own reward.' This, the favourite snack of Catalonia, clearly evokes strong feelings. Leopold Pomes has written an entire book on the subject: *The Theory and Practice of Bread with Tomato*. And author Nestor Lujan has found a written reference to *pa amb tomaquet* in Catalonia as early as 1884.

There is much to read on the subject of Catalan tomato bread in Andrews' book and I cannot resist the quote he includes to show the 'imaginative version of how the dish might first have been conceived: from Pomes, *Teoria I Practica del Pa amb Tomaquet*':

> 'An artist from the Emporda one summer day, returning to his house intoxicated by the blue sea, his skin still impregnated with salt, saw a red sun on the horizon – and, combining his great hunger with his inborn love for the products of his own countryside, wished to pay homage to the sun and give peace to his demanding stomach at the same time. He took some red tomatoes and the flat surface and slightly uneven texture of a big slice of bread – a wonderful canvas for the work he was creating – then covered the bread completely in red, without the usual dilution of water colour, and, being both an accomplished artist and a noted gourmand, polished it voluptuously with the golden brilliance of that most exquisite varnish, olive oil.'

Anchovies, sardines, herring or slices of spicy sausage are popular additions to the tomato bread but, notes Andrews, it goes with anything including ripe figs and squares of dark chocolate. His predilection is for smoked salmon and caviare. Coarse, country-style bread is what you need for Catalan tomato bread. The tomatoes are halved, their seeds removed, if you wish, and then crusty bread is rubbed with the cut side of the tomato until it is saturated with tomato juice and all you are left with is the skin. Most often the bread is toasted, bruschetta-style, on a wood-burning fire or barbecue. In Malta, where there is a tradition for something similar, called *hobz biz-zejt*, they dip the tomato in olive oil, which has been poured on to a plate, and rub the bread with the oiled tomato just sufficiently to colour it and for it to drink up excess juices from the tomato. The tomato is then sliced on to the bread. In Italy and some parts of France, the bread is always toasted and usually smeared with olive oil. Other additions include crushed garlic, sliced onions, olives, herbs, such as basil, mint or marjoram, capers and anchovies. Sometimes a little wine vinegar is added and the Majorcan version, *pamboli amb tomatiga*, the recipe for which follows, is a glorious amalgam of everything. Salt, preferably sea-salt flakes, and freshly ground black pepper are essential.

This delicious snack is something to make with very, very ripe, full-flavoured tomatoes. It needs to be eaten within 30 minutes of being made, preferably immediately, otherwise the bread turns pappy. The two recipes that follow are suggested by Colman Andrews' *Catalan Cuisine*.

- 1-2 thick slices country-style French or Italian bread or sourdough bread
- 1 small-medium fresh tomato, very ripe
- mild extra-virgin olive oil
- 2-4 anchovy fillets, soaked in water for 1 hour and patted dry, or 1-2 very thin slices cured ham (prosciutto or Serrano type)
- sea salt

Grill the bread lightly on both sides on a wood-burning stove or barbecue (if possible), otherwise in a toaster or under the grill.

Cut the tomato in half crosswise; then rub both sides of the toast (including the crust) with the cut side, squeezing gently as you do, to leave a thin red film, including some seeds and a bit of tomato flesh, on both surfaces.

Drizzle oil on both sides of the toast, then salt to taste.

Place the anchovies or ham on top of the toast and serve with a knife and fork.

MAJORCAN TOMATO BREAD

SERVES 1

'*Pamboli amb Tomatiga* is sometimes eaten as a light lunch or supper in Majorca, accompanied by an ample wedge of some Spanish-style omelette or other.' Colman Andrews, *Catalan Cuisine*.

- 1-2 thick slices country-style French or Italian bread or sourdough bread
- 4 very ripe tomatoes
- mild extra-virgin olive oil
- sea salt
- good quality red wine vinegar (optional)
- 6-8 medium-sized black olives or 10-12 Niçoise olives, stoned and coarsely chopped
- 1-2 tsp capers, rinsed and squeezed dry
- 1 tbsp samphire, fresh or pickled, finely chopped (optional)

Toast the bread on both sides as for the previous recipe.

With a very sharp knife, cut each tomato into 4 or 5 paper-thin (translucent) slices. Arrange them across the surface of the toast, one side only, and press slightly into it with a spatula or dinner knife.

Drizzle oil over the tomatoes, then salt to taste.

Carefully shake a few drops of vinegar over the tomatoes, not too much, if desired. Mix the olives, capers and, if desired, samphire together, then spread over the surface of the tomatoes and serve with a knife and fork.

CRACKED WHEAT RUSKS WITH OLIVE OIL AND TOMATOES

SERVES 2-4 (AS A SNACK)

While I was on holiday in Crete one summer, it didn't take long to single out the taverna that became our favourite. Within days our regular custom was rewarded with a pre-meal snack that wasn't on the menu. A basket of bread rusks, so dry and misshapen that they might have been taken for dog biscuits, arrived first. They were soon followed by a bowl of olive oil, a glass of water, some pieces of feta cheese and chunks of gorgeous lumpy-looking tomatoes. Fortunately, because it wasn't immediately obvious, I knew what to do. Once, years ago, I had been stranded in a Cretan mountain hamlet and saw many of these dried loaves, piled up high for the winter when the snows isolate the place. A chunk of the bread is moistened first with water and then olive oil. I was given cheese, almonds and boiled eggs to eat with it, washed down with some sort of fire-water made at a nearby illegal still. But the bread is at it finest with tomatoes. It is the combination of very dry, dense-textured wholewheat bread soaked in olive oil, topped with a mound of chopped tomato seasoned with a splash of vinegar, eaten (messily) with a slice of crumbly feta and a black olive or two that is so extraordinarily good.

On another occasion, at a different taverna, we ate something similar called *Dakos Landouristos*. On this occasion the Cretan wholemeal bread was called *zwieback* and it was served drenched with olive oil, topped, bruschetta-style, with quite dry chopped tomato mixed with garlic and onion, and oregano. With it came extra olive oil and salt. Gradually, as we began to eat, the rusks absorbed the oil, which combined with the tomato juices to soften them, leaving a few delectable crunchy patches.

Back home, I was idling in front of the biscuit section at the supermarket when it occurred to me that I could replicate this Cretan snack with the toasted Swedish rolls, sold under labels such as Krisproll. These are nowhere near as dense or hard as the Cretan bread or the similar *frisella* of Italy (which is available at some Italian grocers) but the effect is similar. *Frisella* is a round or oblong flat loaf, which is baked like ordinary bread, then thickly sliced and baked again until it is so dry that it can be kept almost indefinitely. It is the authentic ingredient in the plethora of Italian bread and tomato-based soups and salads, such as *panzanella*, and is worth seeking out.

How you prepare the tomatoes for this is a matter of choice. It is important not to discard the seeds because the juices around them will help soften the bread and contribute to the flavour. And you want plenty of tomato.

- 1 small garlic clove (optional)
- 4 pieces cracked-wheat toasted Swedish rolls
- best quality olive oil

Halve the garlic but don't bother to peel it. Rub the cut edge vigorously over the Swedish rolls. Dribble each with olive oil – you need to be generous, using at least 2 tablespoons per roll – then scoop the chopped tomatoes over the top. Dribble a few drops of balsamic vinegar over the tomatoes, crumble over some sea-

- 4 ripe plum tomatoes, cored and roughly chopped quite small
- balsamic vinegar
- sea salt and freshly ground black pepper
- a small bunch of wild rocket or watercress
- a few black olives
- slices of feta cheese

salt flakes and a few grinds of black pepper. Serve with a mound of rocket or watercress, a few black olives, slices of feta, and the olive oil for an extra splosh.

ROASTED VINE-TOMATO BRUSCHETTA WITH BLACK OLIVES

SERVES 4

If the finest bruschetta is made with sourdough bread, then the Ferrari version is made with semolina sourdough from Puglia. This dense yet tender and chewy dough with a firm crust is transformed with a smear of olive oil, a char on the grill and a rub of garlic. When it is piled with vine tomatoes, grilled until their skins pop, and a few chopped black olives, it is heaven indeed.

- 500 g cherry tomatoes, on the vine, in clusters
- 2 tbsp olive oil, mixed with 2 tsp chopped thyme leaves
- 4 thick slices sourdough bread or pain de campagne
- 1 plump juicy garlic clove, halved
- 6-8 tbsp olive oil
- 20 Provençal or other decent black olives, stoned and roughly chopped, or 3 tbsp black olive paste
- sea salt and freshly ground black pepper

Pre-heat the oven to 400°F/200°C/gas mark 6, or pre-heat the grill.

Place the tomatoes on a piece of foil resting on a baking-sheet and use a pastry brush to smear them with the thyme and olive oil. Roast near the top of the oven, or grill, for about 10 minutes or until the skins begin to split and the juices run. Meanwhile, toast the bread and rub the hot toast on one side with the cut side of the garlic. Dribble generously with olive oil (oil first, garlic second if cooking on a barbecue or griddle). Strew the toast with the chopped olives or spread with the olive paste, lay the tomatoes over the top, pressing them gently with the back of a fork into the toast. Season with a crumble of sea-salt flakes and plenty of black pepper. Grated Parmesan is good too.

TOMATO AND BLACK OLIVE BRUSCHETTA WITH MINT AND OEUF MOLLET

SERVES 1

This is a good example of how a perfectly ripe tomato and a few other choice ingredients can be quickly transformed into a small feast for one. It was lunch for me one day when I was up to my eyes in tomatoes and was so good that I had to record it.

- 1 very fresh free-range egg
- ⅓ black olive ciabatta
- 2-3 tbsp black-olive paste
- 1 large ripe tomato, cored and peeled
- 1 tbsp balsamic vinegar
- salt and freshly ground black pepper
- 1 tbsp shredded mint leaves
- a handful of wild rocket or watercress
- 2-4 tbsp best olive oil

Bring a pan of water to the boil. Carefully lower in the egg. Boil for 4 minutes. Drain it and hold it under cold running water to cool slightly, then peel it carefully. Set it aside.

Halve the ciabatta horizontally. Toast on both sides and spread thickly with black olive paste. Meanwhile, halve the tomato lengthways. Place the cut side on a chopping board and slice across the width of the tomato without disturbing the shape. Slip a knife under each half of tomato, one at a time, and lift on to a piece of toast. Fan it out very slightly. Sprinkle both halves with balsamic vinegar. Season with salt and pepper then sprinkle over the mint. Top with rocket or watercress and drizzle over the olive oil. Add the soft-boiled egg to the plate.

BRUSCHETTA WITH TOMATOES AND ROCKET

SERVES 6

The peppery tang of rocket goes well with very ripe tomatoes. Here, the tomatoes are diced and both tomato and rocket are bathed in olive oil and piled on to garlicky bruschetta.

- 6 tbsp olive oil
- 100 g wild rocket, tough stalks discarded
- 4 thick slices pain de campagne or sourdough bread
- 1-2 garlic cloves, peeled
- 300 g tomato concassé (see page 29)
- salt and freshly ground black pepper

Place half the olive oil in a bowl. Wipe the rocket through the oil, making sure each leaf glistens. Toast the bread, then smear it with the remaining oil and rub it with the garlic (if using a griddle, oil the bread first with the remaining oil). Pile the tomato concassé on the toast, season lightly with salt and lavishly with black pepper. Cover with the rocket.

TOMATO BRUSCHETTA WITH FRESH CANNELLINI

SERVES 6

Cannellini beans are creamy-white, small, slender and kidney-shaped, a bit like naked baked beans. When cooked, they have a light, fluffy texture. The Italians love them and use them in the once ubiquitous tuna and bean salad (*tonno e fagioli*), and often cook them with tomatoes and sage (*fagioli all' uccelleto*). The sweet acidity of tomatoes, either fresh or stewed, goes very well with these wonderful beans. They are widely available dried and in tins but it is worth remembering to look out for fresh beans during August and September when they are in season. Fortunately, this is also tomato season, which is the only time to make this bruschetta from the River Café in West London. It is quite something to sit on the terrace overlooking the Thames at Hammersmith and enjoy the fruits of Italy, but there is no reason why this simple excellence cannot be replicated at home.

FOR THE BEANS

- 1.3 kg fresh cannellini beans in the pod
- 3 large garlic cloves, peeled
- 1 bunch of fresh sage
- 2 large ripe tomatoes
- salt and freshly ground black pepper
- olive oil

FOR THE BRUSCHETTA

- 6 thick slices Pugliese or sourdough bread, or pain de campagne
- 1 large garlic clove, peeled
- 100 ml extra virgin olive oil, plus extra
- 3 large ripe tomatoes, halved
- 3 tsp dried wild oregano
- 3 small dried red chillies, crumbled

Pod the beans and place them in a thick-bottomed saucepan. Cover with water, and add the garlic, sage and tomatoes. Bring to the boil, then turn down the heat, and gently simmer for 30 to 60 minutes according to freshness. They must not become mushy. Drain, discard the sage, garlic and any bits of tomato skin and stalk. Season with salt, pepper and olive oil.

To make the bruschetta toast the bread on both sides, then rub it lightly with the garlic. Drizzle it with olive oil until it is saturated but not dripping (very much). Squash 1 half-tomato on to each bruschetta, then sprinkle with some of the oregano and chilli. Drizzle with olive oil, then add a ladleful of warm cannellini beans to cover half of the bruschetta. Serve immediately.

BRUSCHETTA SAPORITA

SERVES 4

Bruschetta for the jaded palate: tomatoes with salty anchovy, sour capers, aromatic oregano and basil, and a zing of raw garlic.

- 4 medium tomatoes, cored, peeled, seeded and diced
- 8 anchovy fillets, 4 of them finely chopped
- 12 capers, squeezed and finely chopped
- 2 garlic cloves, peeled and finely chopped
- 5 basil leaves, torn into pieces
- 1 pinch of dried oregano
- salt and freshly ground black pepper
- 4 tbsp olive oil
- 4 thick slices Pugliese or sourdough bread

Place the diced tomato in a bowl with the finely chopped anchovies and the capers. Add the garlic, basil and oregano. Season with salt and pepper and stir in half the olive oil.

Toast the bread (oil it first if toasting it on a griddle) and smear with oil. Spoon the mixture on top of the toast. Decorate each bruschetta with an anchovy fillet. Serve immediately.

CROUTONS WITH TOMATOES AND CHIVES

MAKES 8

A refreshing little snack to serve with drinks.

- 125 g tomato concassé (see page 29), drained
- 2 tbsp double cream or crème fraîche
- 1 tbsp finely chopped shallot
- 2 tbsp finely chopped chives
- 1 tsp lemon juice
- ½ tsp Tabasco
- salt and freshly ground black pepper

FOR THE CROUTONS

- 8 x ½ cm thick slices from a French loaf
- 25 g butter

Mix together all the tomato topping ingredients, season with salt and pepper, cover and chill in the fridge for an hour.

Just before you're ready to serve, spread the slices of bread with butter on both sides and quickly fry them or grill them on a griddle. Spread lavishly with the topping and serve immediately.

GRILLED TOMATOES ON TOASTED MUFFINS

SERVES 2 (FOR BREAKFAST OR A SNACK)

Tomatoes grilled until their flesh turns squishy, the surfaces slightly burnished and the edges charred are what you're after here. The flesh must be so soft that it slides off its skin with the push of a knife, offering no resistance. This ambrosial goo, with its intense tomato flavour, can then mingle with buttery toast to make the most wonderful mouthful. Any toast will do, so long as it's over rather than underdone. The traditional British slice (white and processed) turns quickly into a luscious tomato pulp, and a doorstep hewn from a fresh farmhouse or bloomer flops quite differently and has the advantage of a really good crust. Best of all, perhaps, for this simple treat, is an English muffin, which, as long as it's toasted properly, will keep a crisp shell with a lovely tomato-drenched gooey middle. Another delicious alternative is fried or griddled bread first spread with butter or smeared with olive oil.

This way of cooking tomatoes is good with poached, fried and scrambled eggs, with bacon and fried mushrooms. If you like garlic, rub the uncooked tomatoes with a cut clove. Another good idea is to sprinkle the tomatoes with a little sugar to give them a caramelized crust, or to arrange a few anchovy fillets over the top. Also, try spreading the toast with Dijon mustard and/or grated Cheddar cheese. Black-olive paste is a good alternative.

- 8 over-ripe tomatoes, halved through their circumference
- cooking oil or melted butter
- salt and freshly ground black pepper
- 2 English muffins, split, or 2 slices white bread
- butter

Pre-heat the overhead grill to its maximum temperature. Lay the tomatoes, cut side up, on a grill-pan. Smear them lightly with cooking oil or melted butter. Season with salt and pepper. Cook, adjusting the heat so that the tops don't burn, until completely soft and the edges slightly charred.

When they are ready, turn off the grill and toast the muffin halves until they are nicely browned, then spread them generously with butter. Top with the tomatoes, nudging them close together, and crush them lightly into the muffins with the back of a fork. Serve with a few scraps of cold butter.

AUBERGINE TOAST 'PIZZAS'

SERVES 4

Here's a delicious quick snack idea from Gary Rhodes, which shows the versatility of a tin of chopped tomatoes.

- 1 large onion, finely chopped
- 1 garlic clove, peeled and crushed

Cook the onion and garlic in 1 tablespoon of the olive oil for several minutes until soft but not coloured. Add the tomatoes and the puree or ketchup, then simmer to a thick, chunky sauce.

- 3-4 tbsp olive oil
- 400 g tin chopped tomatoes, preferably with basil
- 2 tsp tomato puree or ketchup
- salt and freshly ground black pepper
- 2 medium aubergines
- 4 thick slices crusty bread from a round loaf
- 175 g Cheddar, grated

Season.

Meanwhile, pre-heat the grill to a high heat. Cut each aubergine lengthways into 4 or 6 slices, brush with olive oil, season with salt and pepper and grill for a few minutes on each side until tender. Brush the bread with a little oil and toast until it is golden.

To serve, lay the aubergine slices on top of the toast and spoon over the tomato sauce. Sprinkle with the cheese and grill until melted.

DAINTY TOMATO SANDWICHES

Cut thin slices from a perfect wholemeal loaf. Spread with soft butter. Cover with super-thin slices of cored, peeled tomato. Not too many. Season with a twist of sea-salt flakes and a few grains of caster sugar. Cover with a second slice of bread. Remove the crusts (these are the best bit, to be eaten privately by the cook). Cut into small squares or triangles and arrange on a doily-lined tea plate. Decorate the sandwiches with sprigs of watercress and serve immediately. Ordinary white bread also makes very good tomato sandwiches. There is a peculiar charm, that will be familiar to anyone who has attended a school fête or garden party, about the white tomato sandwich that has been left until the tomato has leached past the butter into the bread.

Good additions to a dainty tomato sandwich include: a few drops of red wine vinegar; mustard and cress; super-thin slices of peeled cucumber; a thin smear of mayonnaise; chopped watercress; a thin smear of Marmite; super-thin slices of Cheddar; shredded basil.

CHUNKY TOMATO SANDWICHES

Cut slices from a French loaf – it could be a length of baguette, split but keeping a hinge, or pain de campagne. Butter them with soft unsalted butter. Cut thick slices from perfectly ripe large tomatoes. Use only the middle slices, which match, or can be cut to match, the size of the bread. Sprinkle on some salt and black pepper. If liked, tear a few basil leaves over the top. Lay another slice of buttered bread over the top (or clamp shut the baguette), and eat.

Good additions to a chunky tomato sandwich include: thick slices of unpeeled cucumber; sprigs of watercress; slices of red onion; a splash of olive oil; pitted black olives; anchovy spread; anchovy fillets; celery leaves; country ham and thinly sliced saucisson or salami.

THE ULTIMATE TOMATO SANDWICH

When I first floated the idea of writing a book about tomatoes my editor was unmoved. A tomato, she said, is a tomato. They aren't like potatoes, she went on. Is there really a book in it? Then, one day, after her usual outing with the Dummer Beagles, the beaglers were entertained for tea at the Gloucestershire farm of one Robert Wharton. It was a wonderful spread, she told me, but little had she realized that she had been about to receive tomato enlightenment. The tomato sandwich she inadvertently picked out was so extraordinarily good that she couldn't wait to tell me about it.

Intrigued, I wrote to Mr Wharton explaining that I was writing a book about tomatoes and asked if he would share his recipe with me. The surprising upshot was an invitation to lunch at Vong in Knightsbridge. Waiting for me on the bar was a pile of pretty regular-looking sandwiches: thin slices of white bread, crusts removed and a hint of red in the middle. Mr Wharton and his nephew Oliver, who was Vong's general manager, watched as I bit into a sandwich. It was the texture that struck me first. The tomatoes were neither sliced nor diced but the flavour was the very essence of tomato. Extraordinarily, the bread had no hint of sogginess and the mixture didn't squelch out of the buttered slices as I bit. This, I had to agree, was tomato-sandwich perfection.

It turns out that Mr Wharton's brother, Oliver's father, is a New York restaurateur and Oliver a trained chef, so with food in the blood, as it were, it is no surprise that Robert Wharton had decided to perfect the tomato sandwich. 'I wanted to make something that would spread nicely and wouldn't slip off the bread. A tomato sandwich that wouldn't make the bread soggy.' There was no actual recipe, he said, he did it by eye and, of course, taste. It is difficult to be precise because the quality of the tomato is paramount and the extra seasonings – red wine vinegar, tomato ketchup, sugar, Worcestershire sauce, Tabasco – are a matter of taste. Here, then, is a guideline recipe based on my experimentation. The secret ingredient? Gelatine.

250 g vine-ripened tomatoes, cored and peeled

1 tsp tomato ketchup

½ tbsp red wine vinegar

a pinch of sugar

4 drops Tabasco

3 tbsp olive oil

5 cm square piece leaf gelatine or 1 heaped tsp gelatine granules

salt and freshly ground black pepper

Worcestershire sauce (optional)

Cut the tomatoes into quarters. Place a sieve over a bowl. Scrape the seeds into it then press them with the back of a spoon against the sides of the sieve to extract as much juice as possible. You should end up with about 50 ml of tomato water. Add the ketchup, red wine vinegar, sugar and Tabasco. Whisk in the olive oil. If using the leaf gelatine, stir it into the vinaigrette and leave for 5 minutes before stirring vigorously until it dissolves completely. If using the granules, stir them into the vinaigrette. Both should noticeably thicken the vinaigrette immediately.

Chop the tomato (you should end up with about 145 g) very finely, or press it through a large-holed sieve. Stir the tomato into the gelled vinaigrette. Taste and adjust the seasoning, perhaps adding a few drops of Worcestershire sauce, more Tabasco, or more sugar. Cover and leave in the fridge for about

30 minutes. It will keep, covered, in the fridge for several days. The tomato mixture is delicious spooned over hard-boiled eggs, or stirred into hot pasta that has been moistened with a little cream and chives.

EGG AND TOMATO SANDWICHES

It doesn't matter too much what sort of bread you use for this classic British sandwich so long as it is fresh. The thickness of the slices and whether the crusts are on or off is a matter of taste. There are two ways to go: either the sandwich is made with very thin slices of crustless buttered brown bread, then filled with thin slices of cored and peeled tomato and chopped hard-boiled egg held together in the minutest amount of mayonnaise; or, and this is probably my ultimate egg and tomato sandwich, it is rough and ready, made with quite thick slices from a super-fresh bloomer with a slightly burnt crust or one of those brown loaves with a gooey, stretchy texture and a hard crust. I'd want unsalted butter, and the vine-ripened medium-sized tomatoes would be cut in chunky slices. The egg would be the freshest I could lay my hands on and it would have been boiled just long enough for the yolk to be on the cusp of setting hard, so that there was a hint of molten lava to its firmness. There would be no grey ring round the yolk and its colour would be a rich yellow ochre. I'd cut my slices lengthways so that each slice would get a share of yolk and I'd lay them over the tomato. Both tomato and egg would be seasoned with a twist of black pepper and a crumble of sea-salt flakes. For me, the perfect accompaniment would be a glass of milk from the fridge. Good additions to an egg and tomato sandwich are watercress, chives, mayonnaise, and a thin smear of black olive paste. Not all together.

CIABATTA CASARECCIA

MAKES 2 BIG SANDWICHES

A great tomato sandwich from Francesco Zanchetta and Andrea Riva of Riva, a favourite Italian restaurant in leafy Barnes, South-West London.

- 1 ciabatta loaf, split and toasted
- 1 garlic clove, peeled
- 4 plum tomatoes, cored, seeded and chopped
- 1 fresh chilli pepper, seeded and finely chopped
- 2 tbsp olive oil
- 8 basil leaves, shredded, plus a few extra whole ones
- ½ tsp dried oregano
- a handful of rocket, rinsed
- 2 buffalo mozzarella, sliced
- 1 beef tomato, cored and thinly sliced
- 1 tbsp capers
- a few black olives, very finely chopped
- black pepper
- 8 unsalted anchovy fillets
- best olive oil

Rub the cut side of the ciabatta with the garlic. Mix together the chopped tomatoes, the chilli, the olive oil, the shredded basil leaves and the oregano. Spread this like butter on one half of the ciabatta. Cover it with rocket, and then with the slices of mozzarella interspersed with the slices of beef tomato. Sprinkle with the capers and chopped black olives, season well with black pepper and top with the anchovy fillets. Drizzle with your best olive oil, and scatter over the extra basil leaves. Cover with the top of the loaf, cut it in half and serve.

CHICKEN CLUB SANDWICH

SERVES 2

Chicken Club Sandwich is without doubt one of the great sandwiches, and wouldn't work without the necessary succulence and acidity of tomato. The combination of chicken, crisp bacon, floppy lettuce and slices of tomato sliding between mayonnaise on toast can't fail to please.

- 1 whole chicken breast with bone and skin
- 1 onion, roughly chopped with skin
- 2 garlic cloves. cracked with the flat of a knife
- 3 sprigs of thyme
- 4 black peppercorns
- 6 thin rashers rind less streaky bacon or pancetta
- sea salt and freshly ground black pepper
- 4 large slices sourdough or dense-textured country-style bread
- butter
- 4 tbsp Hellmann's or other good-quality mayonnaise
- 1 Cos or romaine lettuce heart, shredded, washed and drained
- 2 ripe medium tomatoes, cored and thickly sliced

Place the chicken in a pan with the onion, garlic, thyme, peppercorns, a pinch of salt, and cover with cold water. Simmer gently for 20 minutes.

Meanwhile get everything else ready. Layout the bacon on a grill-pan or baking-sheet and grill or bake at the top of a hot oven (400°F/200°C/gas mark 6) until crisp. Set aside on absorbent kitchen paper to drain.

Remove the chicken from the pan and discard the skin. Then, using two forks, shred the meat, removing it all from the bone.

Toast the bread lightly. Spread it with butter, then generously with mayonnaise. Divide the chicken between two slices of toast and season with sea-salt flakes and pepper. Place the lettuce over the chicken. Cover with tomato slices, bacon, then the remaining toast. Cut each sandwich in half and serve with potato crisps. Eat immediately.

PATAFLA

Throughout Provence, and in Nice in particular, elaborate sandwiches, of which the Niçoise *pan bagnat* is the most famous, are made by hollowing out loaves or large rolls and stuffing them with layers of tomato and other seasonal salad foods. One of the finest is made with char-grilled vegetables. Red peppers, slices of courgette and aubergine work particularly well, and scraps of black olive, anchovy, caper and gherkin provide a burst of contrasting salty-sour. Everything is drenched with olive oil and then the sandwich is weighted and left overnight. It can be cut into wedges and eaten with salad. It is a great addition to a picnic.

Patafla is a tomato-heavy variation on this theme that I discovered in Elizabeth David's *A Book of Mediterranean Food*. She recommends using a baguette and serving it cut in thin slices as a cocktail-party canapé.

- 4 ripe tomatoes, cored, peeled and finely chopped
- 1 large onion, peeled and chopped
- 2 green peppers (I prefer red), cored, seeds and white filament removed, and chopped
- 75 g stoned green olives, chopped
- 50 g capers, squeezed, chopped
- 50 g gherkins, chopped
- 1 long French loaf
- salt and freshly ground black pepper
- a pinch of paprika
- 3 tbsp olive oil

Mix the chopped tomatoes with the chopped onion, peppers, olives, capers and gherkins, and chop them together. With a sharp knife, remove the crumb from the loaf and tear it up into little pieces. Stir the bread into the tomato mixture, season with salt and pepper and the paprika, and knead it all together with the olive oil. Now fill the two halves of the loaf with the mixture and press them together. Wrap the loaf tightly in clingfilm and place it in the fridge. Leave overnight.

To serve, cut it into slices about 0.5 cm thick, and pile them up on a plate.

CHERRY TOMATO AND BLACK OLIVE FOCCACIA

SERVES 4

At Priscilla and Antonio Carluccio's delicatessen in Covent Garden, the highlight for me, and hundreds of others, is the selection of prepared dishes. Utterly irresistible is the tomato foccacia, made every day by the shop's chef Gennaro. The flat bread has its characteristic dimples topped with a few black olives and as many tiny cherry tomatoes as can be fitted on it, with fresh basil leaves torn over the top at the end. This is Gennaro's recipe from *Italian Feast*, the book that accompanied Antonio's TV series about Northern Italy.

NB: how things have changed since I wrote this in 1999!

- 500 g strong white plain flour
- 15 g fresh yeast, or dry equivalent
- 300 ml lukewarm water
- 2 tbsp extra virgin olive oil
- 10 g sea-salt flakes

FOR THE TOPPING

- 5 tbsp extra virgin olive oil
- sea-salt flakes
- 350-500 g cherry tomatoes
- a handful of black olives
- basil leaves

Pre-heat the oven to 475°F/240°C/gas mark 9.

Sift the flour into a bowl. Dissolve the yeast in the water and pour into a well in the middle of the flour, along with the oil and salt. Mix until a dough is formed and knead for about 10 minutes, until springy to the touch. Alternatively, mix all the ingredients in a food-processor and, using the dough hook, knead the bread for 2 minutes. Put it into a bowl, cover with a damp tea-towel and leave to prove for about 1 hour, or until the dough has doubled in size.

Knead the dough again for a couple of minutes to knock out any air bubbles, and draw it together into a ball. Lightly oil a baking-sheet, approximately 30 cm x 23 cm, and dust it with flour (this will make it non-stick). Flatten the dough into an oblong or square shape with your hands until it is approximately 2.5 cm thick. Sprinkle the top of the dough with half of the olive oil, then spread it gently over the surface with your fingertips. Sprinkle with sea-salt flakes. Plant the tomatoes, stalk end down, in the dough, pressing an olive between them and deeper into the dough every now and again. Smear the tops of the tomatoes with the remaining olive oil. Sprinkle with a little more salt. Leave to rise again for about 30 minutes.

Bake for about 15 minutes until what you can see of the dough is golden and sounds hollow when flicked with your index finger. The tomatoes will be tender and beginning to weep. Remove to a wire rack to cool. Sprinkle over the basil leaves and serve in squares.

PIZZA NAPOLITANA

MAKES 6 X 25 CM PIZZAS

Napolitana is the basic tomato pizza, as demonstrated in various forms at pizza parlours all over the world. Any thick, smooth tomato sauce could be used but the usual one is flavoured with oregano and sometimes finished with basil. Pizza Margherita is a Napolitana with slices of mozzarella and a scattering of fresh basil leaves, added when the mozzarella has melted. No problem there.

Making pizza dough, however, is a sticky, lengthy business. That's the fault of the yeast, but the gummy stage is quickly over and almost nothing can go wrong. The most common mistake is to roll the pizza too thick and pile the topping too densely. This stops the dough from breathing and bursting into life and results in a flabby, slimy pizza. One solution is to part-bake the pizza, which will puff but go down again, before adding the topping. That isn't necessary for this pizza. Remember: pizzas need to be cooked quickly at a very high temperature. At Pizza Express they take 2 minutes with an above-and-below blast of 800°F. At home, pre-heat the oven to its highest setting and cook a maximum of 2 pizzas at a time on the top shelf. It is very difficult to give exact quantities and cooking times with pizza recipes but this one works for me. However, be prepared to fine-tune with extra flour and/or water. Alice Waters, for example, of Chez Panisse restaurant in Berkeley, California, whose recipe they use at the River Café in West London, adds rye flour (150 g) after the sponge stage, while Anna del Conte, author of the authoritative *The Gastronomy of Italy*, warns that in Italy pizza is seldom prepared at home or eaten there because it is so hard to make well. She recommends frying-pan pizza, and to do that, roll the dough slightly thicker (she recommends 1 cm) and cook in hot vegetable oil for a couple of minutes a side until golden.

To make Pizza Fritte, proceed as for Pizza Napolitana but cook in a hot oven just until the mozzarella has melted. Miniature pizza – *pizzelle* – cut with a biscuit cutter, are the perfect base for tomato canapés. Try spreading them with sun-dried tomato paste or pesto and topping with diced or sliced fresh tomato, or cherry tomatoes. Garnish with basil, parsley or chives. Call them *Pizzelle Fritte Pomodoro*.

FOR THE PIZZA

7 g (about half a sachet) dried yeast granules

200 ml warm water

450 g plain flour

a pinch of salt

2 tbsp milk

3 tbsp olive oil

Rinse out a small bowl with boiling water. Dissolve the yeast in a little of the warm water in the bowl. Leave for about 15 minutes (maybe longer) to bubble and 'sponge'.

Meanwhile, sift the flour and salt into a large, warmed mixing-bowl. Make a well in the middle and pour in the milk and oil, the yeasty water, plus the remaining warm water. Stir initially with a wooden spoon, then use floured or oiled hands to form the mixture into a soft dough. Mix and knead (it will be very sticky: this texture makes a crisp crust) until the dough is smooth and pliable,

FOR THE TOPPING

- 1 quantity Pizzaiola Sauce (see page 247)
- 4 mozzarella cheeses
- about 24 black olives
- basil leaves

OPTIONAL EXTRAS

- capers
- anchovies
- strips of roasted, peeled red pepper
- Parmesan or Pecorino, shavings or gratings
- prosciutto

although quite wet, and comes away from the sides of the bowl. Alternatively, put the mixture in a food-processor or mixer fitted with a dough hook, and knead for 10 to 15 minutes.

Remove the dough ball; rinse and dry the bowl, then smear it with olive oil. Return the dough ball to the bowl and dribble a little olive oil over the top. Cover with clingfilm or a damp cloth and leave to rise in a warm place for between 30 minutes and 2 hours, until double in size. Punch the dough with your fist (that's the good bit) and knead lightly to release any air bubbles. Return it to the bowl and let it rise while the oven heats up to 450°F/230°C/gas mark 8. Place a flat oven-sheet or pizza stone (terracotta tiles are a good alternative) in the oven.

When the dough is ready, divide it into six golf-ball-sized pieces and roll each into a ball on the palm of your hand. Place a dough ball on a floured work surface and roll it out with quick light motions as thinly as possible; it can be patched. Transfer to an oiled baking-sheet. Repeat with the others.

Smear a couple of tablespoons of Pizzaiola Sauce over the pizza base, leaving a small border. Slice the mozzarella and arrange several slices on top of the tomato sauce with gaps between them. Dot with olives. Repeat with the other dough balls.

Place no more than 2 prepared pizza at a time in the hot oven over the pre-heated oven-sheet/pizza stone. Check after 8 minutes and swap positions in the oven, then continue to cook until the mozzarella is molten and the crust is crisp and turning golden at the edges.

TOMATO SPOON BREAD

A quick and easy cake-cum-loaf made with polenta. Eat it hot from the oven or allow it to cool.

- 50 g butter, plus an extra knob
- 75 g finely grated Parmesan
- 15 pieces sun-dried tomatoes (see page 395)
- 600 ml milk
- 2 large eggs
- 175 g cornmeal (polenta)
- 1 tsp salt
- ¼ tsp sugar
- 2 tsp baking powder

Pre-heat the oven to 450°F/230°C/gas mark 8.

Use the knob of butter to smear a 1.5 litre soufflé dish. Dust the inside of the dish with some of the Parmesan: it will stick to the butter.

If the sun-dried tomatoes are in their dried state, rehydrate them in a little warm water for about 20 minutes or until soft. If using tomatoes stored in olive oil, drain them well. Coarsely chop the tomatoes.

Whisk half the milk with the eggs. Place the remaining milk in a medium-sized pan with the butter. Gently heat the two together, stirring as the butter melts into the milk. Increase the heat slightly and add the cornmeal in a steady stream, stirring constantly. Stir in salt and sugar. Remove from the heat, add the milk and egg mixture, beating until smooth. Sprinkle the baking powder and remaining Parmesan over the top, stir it in thoroughly. Now stir in the tomatoes. Or, if you prefer, pour half the mixture into the prepared dish, arrange the tomatoes over the top, then pour on the remaining mixture.

Bake until the bread has risen and is puffed and golden. It takes about 30 minutes, slightly less in a metal tin.

A TOMATO LOAF

MAKES 1 KG LOAF

This makes a fabulous orange-coloured loaf, with a delicate tomato flavour and a decent crust. It makes pretty sandwiches and can be livened up with a dash of Tabasco. Good additions would be chunks of prepared sun-dried or mi-cuit tomato, sliced ham, grated Gruyère, a teaspoon of herbes de Provence, and chopped green olives. This great recipe was specially devised for me by Ursula Ferrigno and Eric Treuille, authors of *Bread: The Ultimate Visual Guide to the Art of Making Bread.*

- 2 tsp dried yeast or 15 g fresh yeast
- 2 tbsp warm water
- 500 g strong white flour
- 2 tsp salt
- 300 ml good quality tomato passata

Sprinkle the yeast into the water, leave for 5 minutes to soften; stir to dissolve. Put the flour and salt in a bowl and make a well in the centre. Pour in the yeasted water and the tomato passata. Draw in enough flour to make a thick batter. Cover the bowl with a tea-towel and leave for 20 minutes to 'sponge', when it will be puffed up and slightly risen. Draw in the remaining flour to make a soft, sticky dough. Knead for 10 minutes, until smooth and shiny. Cover the bowl with a cloth and leave to rise for 1½ hours until doubled in size. Knock back and leave to rest for 10 minutes. Shape for a tin loaf and place in a lightly oiled 1 kg loaf tin. Cover with a cloth and leave to rise for 45 minutes until the dough has come to 2.5 cm above the rim of the tin.

Meanwhile, pre-heat the oven to 400°C/200°F/gas mark 6. Bake for 45 minutes, then turn the loaf out of the tin. If the bread sounds hollow when tapped underneath, it is ready. If not return it to the tin and to the oven for another 10 minutes. Cool on a wire rack.

AQUACOTTA

SERVES 4

Italy, Spain and Portugal, in particular, have a peasant tradition of doing wonderful things with bread and tomatoes. Like Pappa al Pomodoro (see page 115), which it resembles, Aquacotta is an ancient tomato and bread soup from Tuscany.

- 6 tbsp olive oil
- 2 Spanish onions, peeled and finely chopped
- 2 garlic cloves, peeled and chopped
- 1 celery heart, including leaves, strings removed and finely chopped
- 1 red pepper, cored and diced
- salt and freshly ground black pepper
- 750 g ripe tomatoes, cored, peeled and chopped
- 1 chicken stock cube dissolved in 570 ml boiling water
- 8 slices stale country-style bread
- 4 fresh eggs
- 1 tbsp roughly chopped flat-leaf parsley or coriander (optional)
- Parmesan

Heat 4 tablespoons of the oil in a medium-sized saucepan and gently sauté the onion until it begins to soften and change colour. Stir in the garlic, celery and red pepper, season well with salt and pepper, add the tomatoes and cook for 15 minutes. Pour in the stock and cook for 10 more minutes. Taste and adjust the seasoning.

Line the base of a fireproof serving-dish with the bread. Dribble over the remaining olive oil and pour on the soup. Carefully break the eggs, evenly spaced, into the soup, and simmer gently. The soup is ready when the eggs have set. Strew with parsley or coriander, if liked, and serve with freshly grated Parmesan.

GAZPACHO CREAM

SERVES 6

'This is essentially gazpacho without the water. In Cordoba and Seville it is served in individual earthenware ramekins, topped with ham and chopped egg, with a spoon and bread for dipping,' says Janet Mendel, in her book *Traditional Spanish Cooking*. This exquisite and perfectly seasoned tomato nectar is almost a meal in itself.

- 450 g stale bread, crusts removed
- 600 g ripe tomatoes, cored, peeled and chopped
- 50 g green pepper, cored, seeded, white filament removed, then chopped
- 3 garlic cloves, peeled
- 1 tsp salt
- 2 eggs
- 100 ml extra-virgin olive oil
- 4 tbsp wine vinegar
- 100 g Serrano ham, cut in strips
- 2 hard-boiled eggs, or 6 hard-boiled quail's eggs, sliced

Soak the bread in enough cold water to cover for 15 minutes. Squeeze it out. Put it in a blender or food-processor with the tomatoes, pepper and garlic. Process until smooth. Then add the salt and the uncooked eggs.

With the motor running, add the oil in a slow stream until it is incorporated. Blend in the vinegar. Serve the cream smoothed into soup plates or on a shallow serving-bowl, topped with strips of ham and sliced eggs.

GAZPACHO ANDALUZ

SERVES 6

The great thing about gazpacho is that there is absolutely no cooking involved. Instead you need a sharp knife, a sieve and a food-processor. The soup is as old as the Spanish hills whence it came and original versions would have been more like a rough and ready puree. The silky-smooth soup we've come to know as gazpacho is courtesy of the electric blender. Some people call it the salad soup and that is exactly what it is. It's a good idea to garnish the soup with shellfish. A couple of quickly fried scallops, a few oysters, perhaps, or poached prawns would be delicious, but white crabmeat works particularly well. Its succulent, sweet and curiously stranded white flesh is a superb complement to the flavour and texture of the soup, and is a dramatic contrast to its red colour.

Decent tomatoes are essential for a good gazpacho. In Spain, all tomatoes have flavour. Here, until the late summer and autumn, when our tomatoes have had a chance to ripen properly, choose tomatoes labelled 'grown for flavour'. I'd also recommend adding some good-quality tinned crushed tomato or tomato juice. One of the best is called Rustica from Italian tomato giants Cirio. Made with care, gazpacho is a meal in itself.

- 4 thick slices white bread, without crusts
- 3 garlic cloves, chopped
- 600 g very ripe plum tomatoes, cored and peeled
- 350 ml iced water
- 2 red peppers, seeds and white filament removed, then chopped
- 1 small cucumber, peeled, split and seeded, then roughly chopped
- 1 shallot or small onion, peeled and chopped
- 350 g Cirio Rustica or other good-quality crushed tomatoes, sieved
- 4 tbsp vinegar, either sherry, red or white wine

Tear the bread into pieces. Place it and the garlic in the bowl of a food-processor and blitz to make fine breadcrumbs.

Rest a sieve over a bowl. Quarter the tomatoes lengthways and scrape the pips into the sieve to catch the juice. Press down on the seeds with the back of a spoon to extract maximum juice. You will end up with about 150 ml tomato water. Top this up with chilled water to make 450 ml.

Place the tomatoes, peppers, cucumber, onion and mint in the food-processor with the breadcrumbs. Add the tomato water, the crushed tomatoes, sherry or vinegar, olive oil, mint leaves, Tabasco, and a decent seasoning of salt and pepper. Process until smooth.

Pour the soup through a sieve into a serving-bowl, pressing down to extract all the juices. Taste and adjust the seasoning with salt, pepper, Tabasco and vinegar. If you think the soup needs it – it makes it very creamy – whisk in the extra olive oil. Serve the soup very cold in chilled shallow bowls with a mound of crabmeat. If you are serving the other garnishes, arrange them in small bowls for people to help themselves.

100 ml best olive oil, plus 2-3 tbsp extra

6 mint leaves

4 shakes Tabasco

salt and freshly ground black pepper

FOR THE GARNISHES

100 g fresh white crabmeat

or

1 small red pepper, cored, seeded, white filament removed, and finely diced

3 ripe but firm tomatoes, cored, peeled, seeded and finely diced

½ small cucumber, peeled, seeded and diced

1 small red onion, peeled and finely chopped

1 peeled garlic clove, finely chopped

a few mint leaves, shredded

CHERRY TOMATO GAZPACHO

SERVES 6-8

3 large new season garlic cloves

150 g day-old white bread, preferably country-style

1 cucumber

1 red chilli

2 red peppers, preferably the pointed 'extra sweet' type

1 kg tomatoes, at least half cherry tomatoes

2 tbsp sherry or wine vinegar

about 20 small mint leaves

100 ml extra virgin olive oil plus 2 tbsp extra

3 plum or vine tomatoes

1 lemon

Tabasco

Peel the garlic. Tear the bread into pieces. Place both in the bowl of a food processor and blitz to make fine breadcrumbs. Meanwhile, peel the cucumber. Halve it horizontally and use a teaspoon to scrape out the seeds. Chop half of it roughly. Trim and split the chilli. Scrape out the seeds. Set aside ½ (half) one red pepper and chop the rest, discarding seeds and white filament. Peel and halve the onion. Coarsely chop one half and add to the breadcrumbs together with the chopped cucumber, chilli and chopped red pepper. Remove the stalks from the 1 kg tomatoes. Roughly chop regular tomatoes, leave cherry tomatoes whole. Add the tomatoes to the food-processor bowl together with the vinegar, 300 ml ice cold water, most of the mint, the 100 ml olive oil and ½ tsp salt and a generous seasoning of black pepper. Blitz for several minutes until liquidized (you may want to do this in two batches). Meanwhile prepare the garnishes. Keeping separate piles, finely dice the remaining cucumber and red pepper and finely chop the remaining red onion. Quarter the plum or vine tomatoes, discard the seeds and finely chop. Taste the gazpacho and adjust the seasoning with salt, pepper, lemon juice and Tabasco. If you think the soup needs it – it makes it very creamy – whisk in the extra olive oil. Transfer to a serving bowl and chill until required, at least 4 hours.

OLIAIGUA AMB TOMATICS

SERVES 4-6

This soup is a speciality of Menorca and a dish that, according to Pedro Ballester in his classic book on Menorcan cooking, *De Re Cibaria*, *oliaigua amb tomatics*, 'warms the stomach in the winter, cools it in the summer and refreshes the tired body all year long'. Traditionally it is made only with oil and water – *oliaigua* – garlic, parsley and salt, poured over dried bread. In this version, with tomatoes, onions, green peppers and tomatoes, it has become almost a hot gazpacho.

If you are serving oliaigua cold, use the merest amount of olive oil and omit the bread. It goes without saying that it is only worth contemplating making this soup with very, very ripe, full-flavoured tomatoes.

- 6 tbsp extra-virgin olive oil
- 2 onions, peeled and chopped
- 1 green pepper, cored, seeds and white filament removed, chopped
- 3 garlic cloves, finely chopped
- 4 beef tomatoes, cored, peeled and coarsely chopped
- 1 tbsp chopped flat-leaf parsley
- salt and freshly ground black pepper
- 4 very thin slices French or Italian bread, lightly toasted

Place the olive oil, onions, pepper and garlic in a pan. Cook, stirring frequently, over a low heat until the vegetables are tender but the onions and garlic uncoloured.

Add the tomatoes, parsley, 300 ml water and ¼ teaspoon of salt. Simmer for a further 15 minutes, then raise the heat and cook until almost ready to boil. Liquidize and pass through a sieve into a clean pan. Taste and adjust the seasoning.

Place a slice of bread in a soup bowl and spoon over the hot soup.

ZUPPA CUATA

SERVES 4

Zuppa Cuata means 'lost or hidden soup', and is a speciality of Sardinia. This version has been given the Midas touch by Simon Hopkinson, while he was 'fiddling around in a corner' at Alastair Little's cookery school, La Cacciata, in Umbria. It is one of those gorgeously soupy slops, that is almost a gratin and manages to be at once comforting and lively.

- 400 g tin chopped tomatoes
- 2 garlic cloves, peeled and chopped
- 4 tbsp good olive oil
- a pinch of dried chilli
- salt
- 150 g country bread, torn into chunks
- 12 basil leaves
- 400 ml light meat or poultry broth
- 50 g grated Pecorino

Put the tomatoes, garlic, 1 tablespoon of the oil, the chilli and a generous pinch of salt into a heavy-bottomed saucepan. Reduce to a thick sauce over a gentle heat. Expect this to take 20 minutes.

Pre-heat the oven to 400°F/200°C/gas mark 6.

Meanwhile, put the bread into a deep oven-dish, tuck in the basil leaves and cover with the broth. Allow the broth to be completely 'lost' into the bread; this should have happened by the time the tomatoes have reduced. Spread the tomatoes over the bread and scatter thickly with the Pecorino. Spoon over the remaining olive oil and put the dish in the oven for 20 minutes. Finally, heat an overhead grill to high and burnish the cheesy surface to a bubbling, crusted brown. Leave to cool to lukewarm before eating with crisp lettuce and a sharp dressing.

SOUPS AND SALADS

PAPPA AL POMODORO

SERVES 6

An ambrosial soup from Tuscany. It's a traditional peasant dish made with yesterday's bread, and tomatoes from the garden: its success relies on using sun-ripened tomatoes that are full of flavour. It can be eaten hot, warm or cold, but is at its best served warm for an alfresco meal on a hot summer day.

- 3 tbsp olive oil
- 2 plump garlic cloves, pounded to a paste with ½ tsp salt
- 750 g very ripe tomatoes, cored, peeled, seeded and chopped
- 10 basil leaves
- 200 g country bread, crusts removed, torn into small pieces
- 1 litre light chicken stock
- salt and freshly ground black pepper

TO SERVE

- extra-virgin olive oil
- basil leaves (optional)
- Parmesan (optional)

Heat the olive oil in a pan that can hold all the ingredients, and gently sauté the garlic without browning. Add the tomatoes, basil and bread, then gradually add the stock, stirring as it begins to resemble porridge. Taste and season with salt and pepper.

Serve with a swirl of your best olive oil and, if liked, a few basil leaves and/or freshly grated Parmesan.

PANZANELLA

SERVES 2

In Tuscany, where Panzanella comes from, there are many time-honoured ways of making something special out of stale bread, in fact *frisella* (see page 90) is specially pre-prepared for it. In this instance, the bread is hewn into chunky pieces, soaked in a garlicky olive-oil vinaigrette, and tossed with ripe, fruity tomato, roasted red peppers, a few salty black olives and plenty of fresh basil. The result is one of the most luscious and satisfying salads it is possible to imagine.

There are, of course, as many recipes for Panzanella as there are cooks to make it, and in Tuscany this strange-seeming salad is an open-ended feast that sometimes includes cucumber and celery. Other common additions are salt-cured anchovies and capers, and boiled eggs. Not only do the ingredients vary, and it's the sort of dish that changes from day to day depending on what's ripe and available, but the way in which they are prepared and how the bread is treated is open to interpretation. Many recipes suggest soaking the bread in water first, then crumbling it before mixing it with very finely chopped vegetables. I prefer a more rustic approach, when the bread is broken into pieces large enough to act as rafts on which to build up a sort of bruschetta – a piece of tomato, pepper and cucumber, with a sliver of red onion, a caper, an olive and a basil leaf. For me, the bread needs to stay chewy rather than soggy so that you end up with a good textural mouthful. Peeling and seeding the tomatoes is a matter of personal preference. In this version, I've done that but saved the delicious juices from the seed cavity to add to the vinaigrette. Do be sure to let the gorgeous, glistening Panzanella sit for at least 30 minutes before serving so that the flavours get a chance to develop.

½ cucumber, peeled and seeded
1 large red pepper
1 serrano or other red chilli pepper (optional)
6 ripe plum tomatoes, cored and peeled
1 tbsp red wine vinegar
8 tbsp best-quality olive oil
1 small garlic clove, worked to a paste with a little salt
½ stale ciabatta loaf
approximately 10 capers, rinsed and squeezed dry
1 small red onion, halved and finely sliced

Slice the cucumber chunkily, sprinkle it with ½ teaspoon of salt and scoop into a colander to drain for 20 minutes. Rinse then squeeze dry in a tea-towel.

If you have a gas hob, use tongs to hold the pepper, then the chilli, in the flame of the largest burner, turning as the skin blisters and blackens. Alternatively do this under the overhead grill. Then place on a plate, cover with clingfilm, leave for 15 minutes then flake away the skin. Cut down the natural lines of the pepper, open it out like a flower and cut out the seeds and filament. Then remove the four 'petals' from the stalk. Cut each one lengthways into three strips. Seed and finely chop the chilli.

Cut the tomatoes lengthways into quarters. Place a sieve over a bowl and scrape the seeds into the sieve. Press the seeds against the sieve to extract maximum juice, whisk in the vinegar and 6 tablespoons of the olive oil. Stir in the garlic paste.

Split the ciabatta in half lengthways, hold the pieces together and slice the loaf vertically. Lay out the bread in a serving bowl,

- 20 good-quality black olives, stoned
- sea salt and black pepper
- extra olive oil to serve
- a handful of basil leaves

dribble over the vinaigrette, pile on all the remaining ingredients, including the basil leaves, season with a crumble of sea-salt flakes and several grinds of black pepper, then toss and dribble over the remaining olive oil. Rest for 30 minutes, or more, and serve with the extra olive oil.

FATTOUSH

SERVES 4-6

Fattoush is a Middle Eastern salad with a wonderful mixture of fresh, slightly acidic flavours with a kickback of garlic and a nuttiness that comes from the salad's 'garnish' of toasted pitta bread. To be authentic it needs a blend of Middle Eastern herbs called za'atar, which features sumac, a tart red spice. A good alternative would be the Moroccan spice mix ras el hanout, although I'm not convinced that these extra sharp, resinous flavours are essential to the success of the dish.

Delicious on its own, it is also good with feta cheese, or as a side dish with grilled lamb, chicken or sausages.

- 1 medium cucumber, peeled, seeded and diced
- salt and freshly ground pepper
- 1 whole pitta bread
- 2 plump garlic cloves, worked to a paste with scant ½ tsp salt
- juice of 1 lemon
- 6 tbsp olive oil
- 4 large shallots or 2 medium red onions, peeled and finely chopped
- 1 celery heart (at least 4 sticks with fronds), trimmed and finely sliced
- 500 g tomatoes, cored, peeled and seeded
- 1 very large bunch flat-leaf parsley, leaves only, finely chopped
- 1 tbsp roughly chopped mint
- 3 tbsp roughly chopped coriander

Tip the cucumber into a colander, dredge with ½ teaspoon of salt and leave to drain for at least 15 minutes.

Split the pitta bread in half and toast both sides until crisp. When cool enough to handle, crumble it into small pieces.

Put the garlic paste into a salad bowl, stir in the lemon juice and whisk in the olive oil. Tip in the onions, then the celery, then the tomatoes and herbs, stirring as you make each addition. Place the cucumber in a clean tea-towel and squeeze it dry. Add it to the dish and season generously with black pepper. Toss, then strew the pitta bread over the top. Five minutes before serving, fold it into the salad.

INSALATA DI PANE, POMODORO E BASILICO

SERVES 6 AS AN APPETIZER

Bread and tomatoes from Tuscany, River Café-style.

- 1 ciabatta loaf
- 1 kg ripe plum tomatoes (they must have a strong flavour)
- 250 ml extra-virgin olive oil
- 2 tbsp best-quality red wine vinegar
- 2 peeled garlic cloves, crushed to a paste with a little salt
- salt and freshly ground black pepper
- a handful of fresh basil leaves
- juice of ½ lemon

Pre-heat the oven to 475°F/240°C/gas mark 9, or the highest it will go.

Roughly tear the loaf into eight and place it on a baking-tray. Bake until dry and toasted on the outside, but soft in the centre (no more than 5 minutes). Put it in a bowl.

Take 4 of the tomatoes and, using your hands, squeeze them over the toasted bread. Mix together a dressing using half the olive oil, the vinegar, the garlic and some salt and pepper. Pour the dressing over the toasted bread and tomato and toss.

Core and peel the remaining tomatoes. Place a sieve over a bowl. Working over it, cut the tomatoes lengthways into eighths. Scrape out the seeds into the sieve and press out the juices. Add the tomato pieces, with the basil, to the bread mixture. Dribble over the tomato juices and the lemon juice, and pour over the remaining olive oil.

BROWN TOM

SERVES 4

For brown, read bread and for tom, read tomato. This neat recipe name (not, I'm sorry to say, my invention), refers to a surprisingly elegant summer gratin made with wholemeal breadcrumbs and slices of ripe tomato. As it cooks – and the smells are indescribably good – the butter and olive oil mingle with the softened tomatoes and all these juices and flavours run into the bread, making it succulent and intensely flavoured. It is important, I think, to peel the tomatoes otherwise the strips of skin interfere with the soft textures. Serve Brown Tom hot from the oven; it goes very well with runner beans or minted peas and perhaps a few new potatoes. Another name for this dish is Scalloped Tomatoes. It could also be called Tomato Gratin.

- 150 g wholemeal bread without crust
- 2 medium onions, peeled and very finely chopped
- 1 very large garlic clove, peeled and finely chopped
- 25 g finely chopped flat-leaf parsley
- 30 g finely chopped basil
- 6 tbsp freshly grated Parmesan
- salt and freshly ground black pepper
- 4 tbsp olive oil
- 1 kg ripe, full-flavoured tomatoes, cored, peeled and thickly sliced
- 25 g butter
- extra Parmesan

Pre-heat the oven to 400°F/200°C/gas mark 6.

Chunk the bread and process it to crumbs in a food-processor. Mix together the breadcrumbs, onions, garlic, herbs and Parmesan, and season generously with salt and pepper.

Use 1 tablespoon of the olive oil to grease an approximately 25 cm x 5 cm gratin dish. Cover the bottom of the dish with a third of the bread mixture and top with half of the tomatoes laid out evenly. Season generously with salt and pepper and dribble over 1 tablespoon of the olive oil. Cover the tomatoes with another third of the bread mixture and then with the remaining tomatoes. Finish with the remaining third of bread mixture and dribble over the remaining olive oil. Finally, cover the bread with thin slices of butter.

Cook Brown Tom for 35 minutes in the middle of the oven until the top is well browned and slightly crusty.

Serve from the dish, cut like a cake using a fish slice. Dust with the extra Parmesan.

POMODORI RIPIENI CON PESTO PANGRATTATO

MAKES 20 ANTIPASTI

When I first had a copy of Alastair Little's *Italian Kitchen*, I left it open at this recipe: a whole page is filled with a photo of a dish of these tomatoes waiting to go into the oven – bright red tomato halves filled with a scoop of pesto and breadcrumbs, looking every bit like exotic bonbons.

The idea is to bake the tomatoes until squishy to the prod but still holding their form, and the pesto crusted round the edges. As Alastair says, 'The cooking times are approximate. You must make your own judgements; remember that tomatoes are good raw and delicious cooked, but an indeterminate half-way stage is not pleasant.' A good compromise to avoid overcooking the pesto is to part-cook the tomatoes before the pesto is added, but you may feel that is too much of a fiddle.

- very good olive oil
- 10 ripe plum or other ripe fleshy-variety medium tomatoes
- salt and freshly ground black pepper
- 30 g basil leaves
- 50 g pine nuts, toasted
- 100 g breadcrumbs fried in olive oil or tossed in olive oil and roasted in a low oven until crisp and golden
- 50 g freshly grated Parmesan
- 2 plump garlic cloves

Pre-heat the oven to 300°F/150°C/gas mark 2.

Oil a baking-tray or gratin-dish just big enough to hold the tomatoes in a single layer. Moisten it with a little water.

Halve the tomatoes, through their stalk if they are plum tomatoes and through their circumference, if they are round. Use a teaspoon to scoop out the seeds and discard (or save to make a tomato vinaigrette or stock; see pages 179 and 61). Season lightly and leave to drain like inverted boats, on a rack over a plate, while you make the pesto crumbs.

Combine the basil, pine nuts, breadcrumbs, Parmesan and garlic in the bowl of a food-processor. Blitz, then add enough oil for the mix to cohere lightly when pressed. Check the seasoning.

Stuff the tomatoes with this mix, but don't heap it up, and arrange them carefully in the prepared dish. Bake in the oven for 40 minutes until the tomatoes are tender but watch out that the tops don't burn (you may cover loosely with foil once brown but this will cause the crust to steam and not remain crisp). Do not allow the water in the dish to dry out completely, or the tomatoes may burn on the bottom.

TOMATES À LA PROVENÇALE

SERVES 4

This is one of the simplest recipes for stuffing tomatoes. All you have to do is cut the tomatoes in half and strew them with flavoured breadcrumbs. No peeling or seeding is necessary. Just make sure that the tomatoes are cooked through, or you will end up with the sort of tomato that comes with your average provincial hotel breakfast: hard, warm and pitiful.

Place the breadcrumbs in a food-processor with the parsley, garlic and lemon zest. Process until well blended – the crumbs will turn a lovely green colour – but don't overwork or the mixture will become pasty.

Pre-heat the oven to 350°F/180°C/gas mark 4.

Smear a shallow gratin dish with some of the olive oil and arrange the tomato halves, cut side up, in the dish without crowding, and season with salt and pepper. Carefully spoon the breadcrumbs in little piles over each tomato, trying not to let any fall off. Generously dribble more olive oil over the tomatoes and bake in the oven for 30 to 40 minutes, or until the breadcrumbs have browned and the tomatoes are cooked through. Flash under a pre-heated grill, if necessary, to burnish further. Serve in the dish at room temperature.

PLUM TOMATOES WITH ANCHOVIES AND BREADCRUMBS

SERVES 4 AS A SNACK

An idea from Nigel Slater, the *Observer*'s cookery writer, for bringing slightly lacklustre tomatoes to life.

- 12 plum tomatoes
- 200 g fresh breadcrumbs
- 8 anchovy fillets, rinsed and chopped
- a handful of basil, shredded
- 2 garlic cloves, peeled and crushed
- 6 tbsp olive oil
- freshly ground black pepper

Preheat the oven to 425°F/220°C/gas mark 7.

Slice the tomatoes in half horizontally. Scoop out the seeds into a bowl and reserve. Arrange the tomato halves, skin side down, in an oiled ovenproof dish. Mix the breadcrumbs, anchovies, basil, garlic and 2 tablespoons of the olive oil into the tomato seeds and jelly. Season with black pepper then heap the stuffing into the tomatoes. Spoon over the remaining olive oil and bake for 20 to 25 minutes until the breadcrumbs are golden and crunchy.

TOMATO AND RED PEPPER SUMMER PUDDING

SERVES 4 AS A MAIN COURSE, 6-8 AS AN APPETIZER

Some years ago, in her *Spectator* column, 'Fat Lady' Jennifer Paterson gave the following recipe for Tomato Summer Pudding.

tomatoes
tomato passata or juice
wholemeal bread (decrusted) and sliced

'Get enough tomatoes to fill the bowl you have in mind; pour boiling water over them then skin. Chop roughly, grind salt and pepper over them and sprinkle with a tiny bit of sugar. Pour the passata or juice into a flat soup plate, season with lemon and Worcester sauce, salt and pepper. Soak the bread slices in the juice briefly and line the bowl with them. Soak crushed garlic (as much as you fancy), about 20 basil leaves torn apart and a good measure of olive oil to the tomatoes and pour the lot into the bread-lined bowl. Put more soaked bread on top. Place a saucer and weights on top, leave overnight; turn out, surround with hard-boiled eggs and serve with sour cream or mayonnaise.'

Jennifer Paterson, *Spectator*, 10 August 1985

My recipe takes its cue from Jennifer but owes a debt to the Ultimate Tomato Sandwich (see page 98) and Michel Bourdin of the Connaught, who once gave me his recipe for Summer Pudding.

2 red peppers
1 kg ripe tomatoes, cored and peeled
1 tbsp tomato ketchup
1 tbsp red wine vinegar
3 shakes Tabasco
salt and freshly ground black pepper
4 tbsp olive oil
pinch of sugar
2 heaped tsp powdered gelatine

Pre-heat the oven to 400°F/200°C/gas mark 6.

When the oven is hot, lay out the peppers on a baking-tray and cook, turning as necessary, until the skin is blackened and the peppers are tender. Allow about 35 minutes for this. Transfer to a plate, cover with clingfilm and leave for at least 15 minutes before removing the skin. Discard the stalk, the seeds and the white membrane. Chop the softened flesh, pour any juices through a sieve into a large bowl and add the chopped pepper.

Meanwhile, place a sieve over a second bowl and quarter the tomatoes over it, scraping the seeds and jelly into it. Finely chop the tomato flesh. Press against the seeds and jelly with the back of a spoon to release as much juice as possible. You should have about 300 ml. Stir the ketchup, vinegar, Tabasco and a good seasoning of salt and pepper into the juice. Whisk in the olive oil.

- a handful of basil leaves, shredded
- 1 loaf slightly stale white bread, thinly sliced, crusts removed
- 250 ml fresh tomato juice (see page 431), or 350 ml Cirio Rustica (page 20), sieved
- 20 Grilled Cherry Tomatoes (see page 42)

Taste and adjust the flavour with sugar if you think it needs it. Sprinkle over the gelatine and stir to disperse. Pour this mixture into the chopped peppers and their juices. Stir the tomato flesh into the mixture with the basil. The mixture should be thick and dense with tomato and pepper.

Cut the slices of bread in half lengthways. Use them to line a 900 ml-1.2 litre pudding basin. Begin by cutting a disc to place at the bottom of the bowl. Then arrange overlapping slices (or half-slices) working your way round the bowl, thus leaving no gaps. Cut a second, larger, disc to fit the top. This way of lining the bowl means that when the pudding is turned out, you end up with a pretty ridged pattern.

Place the bread-lined bowl in a dish that is roomy enough to catch any over-spill. Spoon in the prepared tomato mixture, completely filling the bowl. Position the lid disc. Now ladle the tomato juice or Rustica carefully between the bowl and the bread, taking care not to disturb it. Pour more tomato juice over the top bread disc.

Lay a saucer on top, add weights and cover the pudding with clingfilm and chill overnight. Remove the clingfilm and the saucer, place a dinner-plate over the top of the dish and invert it quickly. Pour extra tomato juice over the top (paying special attention to any white spots). Decorate the top with Grilled Cherry Tomatoes (see page 42) and serve.

Also see:
Tomato Soup Cake (page 426)
Roast Tomato Butter (page 58)
Salade Mechouia (pages 172)

tomatoes and eggs

'One tomato, skinned and chopped small, cooked hardly more than a minute in butter, with salt and pepper, is added to the eggs already in the pan.'

Elizabeth David, on tomato omelette in *French Provincial Cooking*, 1960

It is hard to imagine an egg dish that would not be complemented by tomato. Creamy eggs and sweet-sour tomatoes are made for each other. This combination of opposites works in many different ways. You have only to think of egg and tomato sandwiches, or something as mundane as a perfectly fried egg and a squirt of tomato ketchup. How about a tomato omelette filled with fresh tomato puree that oozes between the eggy folds as your fork slices into it? My particular weakness is for poached eggs with fresh tomato sauce. And if the sauce has been spiced up, Mexican-style, with a little chilli, then I'm in heaven. I love that moment when the egg is first cut and the yolk gushes forth, making its oleaginous path through the watery tomato. I cannot eat this lovely mess politely. I like to scoop it up greedily, almost as if someone else is trying to beat me to it.

There is a similar but different alchemy with omelettes, soufflés and roulades, when the egg is cooked on the wobbly side of just set so that the tomato can almost, but not quite, melt into it. But it is the combination of scrambled eggs with tomatoes, particularly when the eggs are very fresh and carefully cooked, and the tomatoes very ripe, that is the universally popular way of serving eggs and tomato together. There is something about that combination of creamy soft scrambled eggs and tomatoes that have been cooked until melting that is irresistible. At its simplest, this is regular scrambled eggs stirred towards the end of cooking with whatever sort of tomato sauce takes your fancy. The combination gets more complex as you travel around the world. In Mexico, for example, they flavour the eggs with cumin and coriander, and make a little stew with the tomatoes, adding garlic, spring onions, roasted green peppers and tortilla strips. In North Africa, scrambled eggs come with a chilli-hot version of ratatouille, and there is something very similar on the menu in Turkey. The most famous version, however, is Basque Piperade. This is made by stewing equal quantities of red pepper and tomato with a little garlic, then, when the vegetables are so soft they have melted, the eggs are stirred into the dish with spring onions or chives. In Malta they like onion and garlic, and a little parsley or mint, with their tomatoes and scrambled egg.

There are other less familiar ways of combining egg with tomato, some of which we hardly realize have taken place. What about tomato mayonnaise, for example, or savoury tomato ice cream? Or have you ever thought to cook an egg *inside* a tomato?

TOAST RACK EGGS

SERVES 6

'. . . a pretty way of serving tomatoes and eggs as a cold hors d'oeuvre.'

Margaret Costa, *Four Seasons Cookery Book* (Thomas Nelson, 1970)

- 6 eggs
- 6 large, handsome tomatoes
- 2 flourishing bunches of large-leaf watercress
- a few black olives

FOR THE FRENCH DRESSING

- 5 tbsp olive oil
- 1 tbsp lemon juice or vinegar
- a pinch of sugar
- a little crushed garlic, to taste (optional)

Slide the eggs into boiling water, cover the pan closely, remove it from the heat and leave for 15-18 minutes. Put them into a bowl of cold water and shell them when cold. Wipe the tomatoes and, with a saw-edged knife, cut them down in thickish slices to within about 1 cm of their base so that you can open them out like a toast rack or a fan.

Slice the eggs equally thickly and slip a slice of egg between each tomato slice. Arrange on a bed of well-washed cress and garnish with black olives. Just before serving, pour over the dressing or serve with a bowl of home-made mayonnaise. Margaret Costa adds, 'Like all tomato dishes, this is much improved by adding some chopped fresh basil, tarragon or marjoram to the dressing.'

EGGS À LA WASHINGTON AND POMODORI CON UOVI

SERVES 3 OR 6

A variation on coddled eggs using a hollowed-out tomato as the receptacle. Neat.

Pomodori Con Uovi is a similar idea: it is made by seasoning the eggs with a little chopped tarragon and a nut of butter. Both types of eggs would be good served on a round base of buttered toast covered with a slice of ham.

- 6 large tomatoes
- salt and freshly ground black pepper
- 6 basil leaves
- 6 eggs
- 6 tbsp double cream
- 1 tbsp cooking oil

Pre-heat the oven to 400°F/200°C/gas mark 6.

Core the tomatoes and cut off their tops. Use a teaspoon to scoop out sufficient flesh to accommodate the egg and a spoonful of cream. Season the hollowed shell with salt and black pepper. Place a basil leaf inside each.

Crack an egg, taking care not to break the yolk, into each tomato. Anoint with a spoonful of cream, season again. Place the tomatoes on an oiled baking-sheet and bake for about 15 minutes, checking after 10, until the white is set but the yolk is till running.

SURPRISE EGGS

SERVES 4

The surprising thing about these 'eggs' is that they are actually tomatoes – plum tomatoes, which are oval-shaped and smooth-sided. It is a *nouvelle cuisine* dish, more style than content, you might say, from the Troisgros brothers for the three-Michelin-star restaurant that bears their name at Roanne, near Lyon. The recipe comes from their book, *The Nouvelle Cuisine of Jean and Pierre Troisgros*, edited and translated by Caroline Conran.

Each person gets three 'eggs', one filled with spinach, one with scrambled egg white and the other with scrambled egg yolk. The method of preparing the tomatoes, tunnelling out some of the flesh and grilling them with butter until they are cooked but firm enough to hold the filling, is something you might want to remember for other fillings. You will, of course, need twelve egg-cups.

- 12 even-shaped and sized Italian plum tomatoes, about 1 kg
- salt and freshly ground black pepper
- 80 g young spinach leaves
- 4 eggs
- 100 g butter
- 1 garlic clove, peeled

Cut the tops off the tomatoes two-thirds of the way up and remove the pips and half of the flesh with a teaspoon. Season inside lightly with salt and pepper, then stand them upright in a saucepan just large enough to hold them side by side.

Place the spinach in a colander and pour over half a kettleful of boiling water. Refresh in cold water, then drain again thoroughly, pressing it lightly to remove excess water. Chop it fairly coarsely.

Separate the eggs, putting the whites and yolks into two bowls; season both with salt and beat lightly.

Cut a third of the butter into little pieces, and put it inside the 12 tomatoes. Put them under a heated grill for about 12 minutes, until they are cooked but still firm enough to be stuffed.

While they are cooking, heat 20 g of the remaining butter to a hazelnut brown in a small saucepan. Put in the spinach and heat it through, stirring it round with a fork with a clove of garlic spiked on to the prongs. Do not allow the spinach to brown.

A few minutes before serving, cook the eggs in the following way. Take two small heavy saucepans so that the eggs won't cook too fast or, failing that, use a bain-marie, which will take longer. Melt 2 teaspoons of the remaining butter in one of the pans placed over a very low heat, pour in the egg whites and stir continuously to combine the parts that are starting to set with the unset parts. As soon as the whites are thickening slightly, remove the pan from the heat and let them finish cooking in their own heat. Keep the pan in a warm place while you repeat the process with the egg yolks in the other pan. Then stir 15 g butter, cut into small pieces, into each of the egg preparations.

To serve, put the tomatoes into the egg-cups and fill the first 4 with the scrambled egg whites, the next 4 with the scrambled egg yolks, and the last 4 with the spinach. Serve at once. With or without soldiers.

TOMATOES STUFFED WITH FETA AND COTTAGE CHEESE

SERVES 4

Another way of stuffing tomatoes – there are many throughout the book – this version is based on a Balkan dish. The stem and a tiny bit of flesh around it become the lid and the rest of the tomato is carefully excavated without breaking the outer skin. Then feta, cottage cheese and a little mint are mixed with beaten egg and poured into the seasoned tomatoes.

They are ready when the tomato is tender and the filling is puffed and golden. The recipe comes from *The Melting Pot – Balkan Food and Cookery* by Maria Kaneva-Johnson (Prospect Books, 1996).

- 8 medium tomatoes, weighing about 1 kg
- salt and freshly ground black pepper
- ½ tsp sugar
- 100 g feta cheese
- 100 g cottage cheese
- 2 eggs, lightly beaten
- ¼ tsp nutmeg
- 1 tsp dried mint

Pre-heat the oven to 400°F/200°C/gas mark 6.

With a sharp-pointed knife, cut a little circle around the stem end of each tomato, slice off a lid and reserve. With a pointed spoon, scoop out the seeds, being careful not to break the outer flesh and skin. Place the tomatoes in an oiled baking-dish, cut side up, and sprinkle lightly with salt and sugar.

Mash the feta cheese with a fork. Add the cottage cheese, eggs, nutmeg, mint, a decent seasoning of pepper and mix well. Fill the tomatoes with this. Perch the lids on top.

Bake the tomatoes for 30 minutes or until the tomato is soft and the filling puffed and golden. Take care that the tomato does not overcook and fall apart.

ENGLISH MUFFINS WITH TINNED TOMATOES AND POACHED EGGS

SERVES 2

The fruity acidity of tomatoes and the rich creaminess of egg yolk combine to perfection in this classic breakfast or excellent quick supper dish. For best results the tomatoes must be cooked through, so that the juices turn jammy and concentrate their flavours. The slightly chewy, dense texture of toasted muffins is the perfect raft. They don't go soggy like toast.

- 400 g tin Italian tomatoes
- 1 heaped tsp brown sugar
- 1 shake Tabasco
- salt and freshly ground black pepper
- 1 tbsp vinegar
- 4 eggs
- 2 English muffins
- butter

Tip the tomatoes and their juice into a small saucepan with the sugar, Tabasco and a generous seasoning of salt and pepper. Cook over a medium heat, shaking the pan a few times as the sugar dissolves, for about 6 minutes or until the juices have reduced and thickened.

Meanwhile, half fill a medium-sized pan with water and bring to the boil. Add the vinegar and reduce the heat to a steady simmer. Crack 1 egg into a cup and slip it into the pan. Repeat with the other 3, adjusting the heat so that the water simmers steadily. Cook for 2-3 minutes until the egg whites are firm but the yolk remains soft.

Split and toast the muffins, spread with butter and lay two halves side by side on each plate. Heap the tomatoes over the muffins. Remove the eggs with a slotted spoon, rest on absorbent kitchen paper to drain, then set on top of the tomatoes. Serve immediately.

HUEVOS RANCHEROS

SERVES 2

The secret of this simple and delicious Mexican version of egg on toast is making a really spicy tomato sauce and cooking it long enough so that it isn't watery. Fresh tomatoes give the cleanest flavour but canned tomatoes make a very acceptable alternative. There are countless variations on the theme of ranch eggs but the basic recipe, when a thin, crisp tortilla is topped with a generous scoop of sauce and a fried egg, garnished with grated Cheddar-style cheese and fresh coriander, seems to me the best.

- 1 medium onion, peeled and roughly chopped
- 2 garlic cloves, peeled
- 2-4 green chilli peppers, seeded and chopped
- 750 g tomatoes, cored, peeled and seeded
- 3 tbsp vegetable oil
- salt and freshly ground black pepper
- 4 corn or flour tortillas
- 4 fresh eggs
- 50 g mature Cheddar or Monterey Jack cheese, grated
- 1 tbsp chopped coriander

Place the onion, garlic and chillis in the bowl of a food-processor and blitz. Drop in the tomatoes once the onion mixture has been worked to a rough paste and process again.

Heat 1 tablespoon of the oil in a medium frying-pan, then add the tomato puree. Season with salt and pepper. Simmer briskly, stirring frequently, until the sauce is no longer watery and thickens enough to coat the back of a spoon. This takes about 12 minutes.

When the sauce is ready, place a non-stick frying-pan over a high heat. Toast the tortillas one at a time in the hot, dry pan, cooking for a few seconds on each side until they are starting to brown and crisp. Set 2 on warmed plates and keep the other 2 warm (or cook them when you've eaten the first ones).

Use the rest of the oil to fry the eggs, basting so that the top cooks properly.

Spoon a share of the tomato over each tortilla, lay an egg on top, then sprinkle over the grated cheese and the coriander.

TUNISIAN ADJA WITH EGGS

SERVES 4

Adja is a stew of onions, tomatoes, sweet red peppers and spices. It is not dissimilar to Mauritian Creole Sauce (see page 198) or Peperonata (see page 199). The idea of serving it, Spanish-style, with eggs poached in the juices makes perfect sense, and comes from Robert Carrier's *New Great Dishes of the World*. Use the freshest eggs you can lay your hands on, and be rewarded with a perfect golden yolk running into this delicious tomato stew. Serve the Adja with plenty of crusty bread and butter to mop up the juices.

- 2 Spanish onions, peeled, halved and thickly sliced
- 8 tbsp olive oil
- a large pinch of cayenne pepper
- a large pinch of paprika
- a large pinch of cumin
- 2 garlic cloves, peeled and chopped
- 400 g tin whole peeled Italian tomatoes, drained and chopped
- salt and freshly ground black pepper
- 2 red peppers
- 4 medium tomatoes, cored, peeled and thickly sliced in rounds
- 1 small bunch coriander
- 4 large fresh eggs

Pre-heat the oven to 325°F/170°C/gas mark 3.

Cook the onions in the olive oil in a roomy heavy-bottomed pan until soft and golden. Mix together the spices. Add the garlic, tinned tomatoes and half the spice mixture. Season with salt and a little black pepper. Simmer, uncovered, for 10 minutes or until the stew is quite thick.

Meanwhile, pre-heat the grill. Lay out the red peppers in the grill-pan and cook until the skin is black and blistered, turning as necessary. Transfer to a plate, cover with clingfilm and leave for at least 20 minutes before removing the skin. Quarter the peppers, remove the seeds and white filament, and slice them into chunky ribbons. Add the peppers and the sliced tomatoes to the tomato stew. Cook for 5 more minutes. Adjust the seasoning. Stir in 1 tablespoon of roughly chopped coriander leaves.

Pour the Adja into 4 individual large ramekins or earthenware dishes. Make indentations in the Adja with the back of a spoon and carefully crack an egg into each depression. Cover the dishes with foil and place in a roasting-tin. Pour boiling water into the tin to come about half-way up the dishes. Bake for 10 minutes or until the eggs are just set. Alternatively, and I prefer this method, make indentations in the Adja in the pan, break in the eggs and cook, covered, until the eggs are set. Sprinkle the eggs with the rest of the spice mix. Garnish with sprigs of coriander and serve immediately.

EGGS MASALA

SERVES 4

Tomatoes are stewed with onions and various Indian spices to make a delicious gravy-cum-sauce in which to sink hard-boiled eggs. Flavours are pointed up with a garnish of fresh coriander, and the dish is served with basmati rice, chutneys, raita and poppadums.

- 1 tsp coriander seeds
- 1 tsp cumin seeds
- ½ tsp cloves
- ½ tsp black peppercorns
- seeds from 2 cardamom pods
- 4 garlic cloves, peeled and chopped
- 2.5 cm piece fresh ginger, peeled and grated or finely chopped
- ½ tsp cayenne pepper
- 2 tbsp vegetable oil
- 2 Spanish onions, peeled and finely chopped
- 500 g ripe tomatoes, cored, peeled and roughly chopped
- salt
- lemon juice
- sugar (optional)
- tomato ketchup (optional)
- 8 fresh eggs
- 2 tbsp fresh coriander leaves

Grind the coriander, cumin, cloves, black peppercorns and cardamom to a powder (an electric coffee grinder is ideal for this), then add the garlic and ginger. Blitz to make a stiff masala paste and stir in the cayenne pepper.

Heat the oil in a wok or large saucepan over a medium-high heat and fry the onions until they turn caramel brown, stirring constantly, so that they colour evenly without burning. This will take about 20 minutes. Stir the masala paste into the onions and stir-fry for a couple of minutes. Add the tomatoes and a generous pinch of salt. Simmer vigorously for 10-15 minutes until the sauce begins to thicken. Taste and adjust the seasoning with more salt and lemon juice. If the tomatoes weren't ripe enough you may need to add a little sugar and a slug of tomato ketchup.

Place the eggs in a pan, cover them with water and bring to the boil. Cook for 10 minutes. Drain them under running water, then peel them. Halve the eggs lengthways.

Get the sauce very hot, stir in most of the coriander and place the eggs in the sauce, sunny side up. Continue simmering until the eggs are warmed through. Garnish with the last of the coriander and serve.

EGGS SCRAMBLED WITH TOMATO AND BASIL

SERVES 4

An elegant summer dish to serve for lunch in the garden.

- 4 ripe medium tomatoes, cored, peeled, seeded and coarsely chopped
- 3 garlic cloves, crushed then peeled
- 3 sprigs thyme, tied with cotton to a bay leaf
- ½ tsp sugar
- salt and freshly ground black pepper
- 3 tbsp olive oil
- 10 eggs
- 50 g butter, diced
- a handful of basil leaves

Place the tomatoes, garlic, thyme and the bay leaf in a pan with the sugar, a seasoning of salt and pepper, and the olive oil. Cook over a low flame, tossing occasionally, until the liquid in the tomatoes has evaporated and they have turned into a pulp that glistens with olive oil. Remove the garlic and herbs.

Crack the eggs into a bowl and beat them lightly with a fork. Add the butter, cut into small pieces, season with salt and pepper. Pour the eggs into the tomato and cook, stirring continuously with a wooden spoon, until the eggs begin to thicken. Remove from the heat. Snip the basil over the top. Stir and serve.

PIPERADE

SERVES 2

Piperade comes from the Basque country, that region of southern France on the Spanish border where they grow wonderful tomatoes and produce Bayonne ham. It is an imprecise dish made by stirring eggs into tomatoes and red peppers that have been cooked to melting. It often includes a little garlic, some onion and plenty of chives stirred in with the eggs. Elizabeth David thought Marcel Boulestin introduced the dish to the English public at the turn of the century. He maintained that when it is finished, it should be impossible to see which is egg and which is vegetable, 'the aspect being that of a rather frothy puree'. Or pink scrambled eggs. If you prefer the peppers and tomatoes to be distinguishable, then check out the Turkish version of this dish, Menemen, the recipe for which follows. Locally, Piperade will be served with slices of fried Bayonne ham, but rashers of thin streaky bacon are an excellent alternative. It looks very attractive served with triangles of fried bread. Dip the edges in oil and then into finely chopped parsley for a smart finish.

- 4 rashers thin streaky bacon
- 2 slices pain de campagne or sourdough bread
- 3 tbsp olive oil, plus extra for frying
- 1 red pepper, roasted or grilled, peeled, seeded and chopped
- 4 ripe tomatoes, preferably plum, cored, peeled, seeded and chopped
- 1 small garlic clove, crushed to a paste with a little salt
- 4 fresh eggs, beaten
- 1 tbsp finely snipped chives
- salt and freshly ground black pepper
- ½ tbsp chopped flat-leaf parsley

Grill the bacon to a crisp. Cut the bread into four triangles and fry in hot olive oil until golden on both sides. Heat 3 tablespoons of olive oil in a medium-size saucepan and sauté the red pepper, tomatoes and garlic until they cook into a red slop.

Pour in the eggs and chives, and cook gently, as you would for scrambled eggs. Season with salt and pepper and stir in the parsley. Serve on warm plates with two rashers of bacon criss-crossed on each and the triangles of fried bread nudged up to the eggs.

MENEMEN

SERVES 4

In this Turkish version of Basque Piperade, the tomato and peppers are sautéed in butter or olive oil until they are softened but have not disintegrated. The vegetables are cooled slightly before the beaten eggs are added. I prefer the dish this way, when there is a textural contrast between the slippery red pepper, the chunks of tomato and the soft egg. A green salad with bruschetta or crusty bread turns the dish into a light meal.

700 g mixed red and yellow peppers

500 g ripe tomatoes, cored, seeded and chopped

50 g butter or 4 tbsp olive oil

salt and freshly ground black pepper

6 eggs, beaten

Peel the peppers with a potato peeler, removing the skin in long, thin sweeps without being too meticulous about getting between the folds. Discard the seeds and the white filament and slice them into thin strips. Cook the peppers and tomatoes together in a lidded sauté pan with the butter or olive oil for about 8 minutes, until they are tender but not mushy. Add plenty of salt and pepper. Remove the pan from the heat and cool slightly. Now stir in the beaten eggs, replace on a low heat, and cook gently until set, stirring constantly as you would for scrambled eggs. Serve immediately.

PARSEE SCRAMBLED EGGS

SERVES 3-4

Scrambled eggs with tomatoes, onions, ginger, turmeric and cumin are served all over India, but in this Parsee version, onions, various spices and seasonings are cooked with tomatoes to almost melting consistency before the eggs are added. Serve them with hot naan or another Indian bread and a glass of the yoghurt drink lassi to cool the bursts of heat from the green chilli in the eggs. Savoury lassi is made by liquidizing natural yoghurt with a few coriander and mint leaves, a pinch of salt and cumin.

- 6 eggs
- salt and freshly ground black pepper
- 2 tbsp vegetable oil, ghee or butter
- 1 medium onion, halved and finely sliced
- 1cm root ginger, grated
- 1 small hot green chilli, seeded and finely chopped
- ¼ tsp ground turmeric
- ½ tsp ground cumin
- 4 medium tomatoes, cored, peeled, seeded and diced
- 1 tbsp chopped coriander leaves

Lightly whisk the eggs in a large bowl and season with salt and pepper.

Heat the oil in a medium-sized saucepan and sauté the onion until tender and golden; allow about 10 minutes for this. Add the ginger, chilli, turmeric and cumin and stir-fry for a couple of minutes, then add the tomatoes and cook gently for 3 minutes. Lower the heat, add the eggs to the pan and continue stirring gently as they begin to firm up. Just before they are ready, stir in the coriander.

MEXICAN EGGS

SERVES 6

Brunch, Mexican-style. Serve with a pitcher of Bloody Mary (page 435).

- 5 large tomatoes
- 5 serrano chillies
- 1 garlic clove
- ½ Spanish onion, halved
- salt and freshly ground black pepper
- 12 eggs, lightly beaten
- 5 tbsp butter, lard (to be authentic) or cooking oil
- 8 tortillas

Arrange the tomatoes, chillies, garlic and onion on a foil-lined grill-pan. Turn the grill to its highest setting and cook until the skins blister and blacken. Turn as necessary. Discard the tomato skin. Flake away the chilli skins and discard the seed. Scrape the garlic flesh from the peel and discard the onion skin. Purée together the tomatoes, chillies, garlic and onion. Season with salt to taste.

Season the eggs with salt and pepper and cook in hot butter, lard or cooking oil, adjusting the heat so that the eggs end up tender and creamy. Stir in the chilli puree and a splash of water if it seems too dry (unlikely) and simmer the two together for a few moments to thicken. Serve with a soft, hot tortilla for scooping.

TOMATO AND BASIL OMELETTE

SERVES 1

There is a tradition in the South of France for making thick, flat omelettes, rather in the style of a Spanish tortilla, with tomatoes. A surprisingly large quantity of tomato concassé, cut from their wonderful fleshy tomatoes, is sweated in olive oil until it dries out, almost to a paste. Cooled, it is then stirred into lightly whisked eggs and flavoured with a little garlic and fresh herbs such as thyme, basil or savory. This tomato-egg mixture is then cooked in olive oil in the French way of making omelettes, which is to stir the eggs continuously until they have set. Ideally the omelette should be golden on the bottom but still creamy within. Roger Verge recommends serving it with a few little black Niçoise olives, and eating it hot, warm or cold.

- 4 large ripe tomatoes, each about the size of a tennis ball, cored and peeled
- 4 tbsp olive oil
- 1 bay leaf
- 1 sprig of thyme
- 1 garlic clove, crushed then peeled and finely chopped
- a handful of basil leaves, coarsely chopped
- 6 fresh eggs
- salt and freshly ground black pepper

Cut each tomato in half and squeeze lightly to press out seeds and juice. Chop the flesh into coarse dice and place in a saucepan with 2 tablespoons of the olive oil and the bay leaf. Cook over a brisk heat for 15-30 minutes, depending on the texture of the tomatoes, until all the moisture has evaporated. Set aside to cool slightly.

Meanwhile, pick the leaves from the sprig of thyme and place in a bowl with the garlic and basil. Break in the eggs, season with salt and pepper and beat with a fork. Add the cooled tomato, and mix well.

Heat a frying-pan over a high heat, add the remaining oil, swirling it round the pan. Pour in the egg mixture and cook, stirring continuously with a fork in a circular motion, until the eggs have set evenly, but are still creamy. Leave the pan over the heat undisturbed for 30 seconds to brown the bottom. Remove it from the heat, place a plate over the top of the pan, and invert.

TOMATO FRITTATA

SERVES 1

The appeal of this flat omelette is the combination of the cold, melon-like tomato concassé (see page 29) and lightly cooked hot eggs. It is the brief exchange of flavours between the sweet acidity of the tomatoes and creaminess of the egg that works so well. The omelette is cooked just long enough to firm the base and set the eggs, then the pan is placed under the grill (or into a hot oven) to finish the top. The idea is to end up with an omelette that is soft, buttery and creamy, while the tomato has been hardly affected by the cooking process. It is slipped on to a warmed plate and eaten with a dusting of Parmesan and a scoop of crème fraîche, which is covered with finely sliced chives and an extra tumble of tomato concassé. This is also very good with a few rashers of very crisp bacon on the side.

3 fresh eggs
4 ripe tomatoes, cored, peeled, seeded and diced
salt and freshly ground black pepper
Tabasco
50 g finely grated Parmesan
a knob of butter
1 scoop crème fraîche
1 small bunch chives

Pre-heat the overhead grill.

Break the eggs into a bowl and whisk lightly with a fork. Add the diced tomato, reserving about 1 tablespoon. Season with salt and pepper and a few drops of Tabasco. Stir in three-quarters of the Parmesan. Heat a favourite frying-pan over a medium heat. Add the knob of butter and swirl it round. As soon as the surface is covered with tiny bubbles pour in the egg. Use a wooden spoon to push back the egg in several places round the edge of the pan so that uncooked egg can run into the spaces. As soon as most of the base has set – this takes moments rather than minutes – but the top is still runny, place the pan under the grill. Allow the surface to just set. Slip the omelette on to a warmed plate. Dust the surface with the remaining Parmesan and place the scoop of crème fraîche in the middle. Spoon over the rest of the concassé and quickly snip the chives on top. Eat immediately.

OMELETTE GRATINÉE À LA TOMATE

SERVES 4

An excellent way of serving an omelette for more than one is to make several undercooked omelettes, fill them with freshly made tomato sauce and slip them on to a buttered metal dish, side by side. Sprinkle with cheese and flash the dish under the grill until it is burnished and bubbling.

- 8 fresh eggs
- salt and freshly ground black pepper
- 2 tbsp of one of the following herbs: finely snipped chives, parsley, basil or coriander, or a mixture of one or more of them
- butter
- 300 ml Chunky Tomato Sauce (see page 236) or Smooth Tomato Sauce (see page 236) stirred with concassé (see page 29)
- 150 ml thick cream or crème fraîche
- 75 g grated Gruyère or Emmental or 2 tbsp finely grated Parmesan

Break two eggs in a mixing bowl, season with salt and pepper and whisk lightly with a fork to blend the eggs. Use some of the herbs to season the omelette mixture, but save sufficient to sprinkle over the top of the dish at the end. Butter a plate and butter a Swiss-roll tin or similar metal cooking-dish.

Heat a non-stick frying-pan over a medium heat, add a knob of butter and swirl it round. Turn up the heat, pour in the egg mixture and tilt the pan to spread it evenly. After a few seconds use a metal spoon to draw one edge of the omelette towards the centre, tilting the pan so that the uncooked egg runs into the space. When the eggs are set underneath but still slightly runny on top, tilt the pan away from you and use the spoon to fold the omelette almost in half. Slip it on to the buttered plate, flipping to form a neatish roll. Slide it into the prepared cooking dish. Make the other omelettes.

Pre-heat the overhead grill to its highest setting.

Cut slits the length of each omelette to within about 1 cm of the two ends. Open the slits slightly and fill them with the warmed tomato sauce, then spoon the cream or crème fraîche over the top. Sprinkle with the cheese and dribble over a little melted butter. Place the pan under the grill – not too close, about 7 cm away – and leave there for a few minutes until the cheese is lightly browned but not for so long that the omelettes are rubbery. Serve immediately.

HARLEQUIN OMELETTE

SERVES 4-6

Delicious though a simple tomato omelette undoubtedly is, there are many different ways, several of which are given here, of making one. *The Alice B. Toklas Cook Book* includes a complicated tri-coloured version consisting of a green omelette, made with spinach, rolled inside a saffron-flavoured omelette, and the whole lot surrounded by tomato sauce. In a similar vein, Harlequin Omelette, invented by three-Michelin-starred chef Roger Verge, comprised three separate omelettes, one filled with a puree made with very ripe tomatoes, a second with grated Gruyère cheese, and a third with fresh spinach. This tomato omelette is made and served terrine-style, in an oiled dish, and can be eaten hot or cold. It would make a spectacular hors d'oeuvre for a dinner party or a lovely summer lunch dish.

- 8 tbsp olive oil
- 400 g very ripe tomatoes, cored, peeled, seeded and chopped
- ½ tsp thyme flowers or leaves
- salt and freshly ground black pepper
- 500 g fresh spinach, rinsed and drained
- 2 garlic cloves, peeled
- 9 eggs
- 8 tbsp whipping cream
- nutmeg
- 75 g grated Gruyère

Pre-heat the oven to 250°F/120°C/gas mark ½.

Heat 2 tablespoons of the oil in a medium-sized pan. Add the chopped tomato together with the thyme and a pinch of salt, and cook until the moisture from the tomatoes has evaporated completely. Place in a bowl to cool.

Put 3 tablespoons of the olive oil in a larger saucepan and allow it to get very hot. Add the spinach, the garlic and a pinch of salt. Stir with a wooden spoon and cook until the moisture has completely evaporated. Place in a bowl to cool. Remove the garlic.

Line up three bowls and crack three eggs into each. Add the spinach, 3 tablespoons of the cream, a grating of nutmeg, salt and pepper to one bowl and whisk everything together. Add 2 tablespoons of the cream, the tomatoes, salt and pepper to the next bowl and whisk. Add the grated Gruyère, 3 tablespoons of cream, salt and pepper to the third bowl. Whisk.

Oil the inside of a pâté dish or terrine (approximately 20 cm long) lavishly, and pour in the tomato mixture. Stand the dish in a bain-marie half filled with hot water and bake for 15 minutes. Then, very gently, pour in the cheese mixture and return to the oven for a further 15 minutes. Finally, pour in the spinach mixture and cook for 20 minutes more. When the omelette is cooked, let it rest for 10-15 minutes in a warm place. Serve hot, cutting into slices or wedges according to the shape of the dish it was cooked in. A smooth tomato sauce would go well with this. Alternatively, allow the omelette to cool and serve cold, as a first course or for a picnic, with a little olive oil sprinkled on each slice.

TOMATO PANCAKES

SERVES 2

In these pancakes, diced tomato mixed with finely chopped onion is held in a soufflé-style batter. The mixture puffs as it cooks and the pancakes give a delicious eggy background to the tomatoes. Serve them for breakfast with a few rashers of crisp streaky bacon, with poached chicken or with simply cooked fish. I rather like them on their own and they are delicious dipped into Greek yoghurt sprinkled with finely chopped chives.

- 1 large egg
- 100 ml milk
- 3 tbsp self-raising flour
- 2 tbsp cooking oil
- salt and freshly ground black pepper
- 4 spring onions, trimmed and finely sliced
- 4 large plum tomatoes, cored, peeled, seeded and diced

Separate the egg. Beat the yolk with the milk, flour and ½ tablespoon of cooking oil to make a thick, smooth batter. Season with salt and pepper, then mix in the onions and tomatoes. Whisk the egg white until it is firm enough to hold its peaks. Fold into the batter. Heat the remaining cooking oil in a frying pan over a medium flame. Drop scoops of the tomato batter into the hot oil and fry for about 30 seconds a side until set and nicely puffed.

TOMATO SOUFFLÉ WITH ROAST TOMATO SAUCE

SERVES 4-6

I came across several fiddly recipes for layered soufflés while I was researching the book: tomato and spinach, tomato and macaroni, tomato and red peppers. This got me thinking that a Parmesan soufflé with a middle layer of thick, smooth tomato sauce might work rather well, the idea being that when the soufflé is cut, the tomato spurts out like the jam in a doughnut. Josceline Dimbleby had a more practical idea for individual goat's cheese soufflés, in her book *The Almost Vegetarian Cookbook*, but she put the tomato sauce at the bottom of the ramekin so you had to wait a little longer for the surprise. It just goes to show that there are many possibilities when it comes to tomato soufflés.

In the end, I took a tip from the spinach soufflés served at Langan's Brasserie in London's Mayfair. These are standard soufflés but there is a moment of drama at the table when they are served. The waiter cracks a hole in the top of the soufflé and pours in some anchovy sauce and, hey presto, the soufflés are magically reinflated. In my version the soufflé mixture is made with Roast Tomato Sauce and more of it is poured into or over the soufflé when it is served. This soufflé could also be made with Tomato and Red Pepper Sauce (see page 238).

- 1 quantity Roast Tomato Sauce (see page 245)
- 3 whole eggs plus 2 egg whites
- salt and freshly ground black pepper
- freshly grated Parmesan
- a knob of butter
- a handful of basil leaves

Pour a third of the tomato sauce into a serving jug and set it aside.

Separate the whole eggs, placing the whites in a large bowl. Add the extra egg whites and whisk to form soft peaks. Stir the egg yolks into the tomato sauce. Season with salt and pepper. Add 2 tablespoons of finely grated Parmesan. Stir some of the beaten egg whites into the cold tomato sauce with a whisk. Then add the remaining egg whites, folding them in delicately with a spatula.

Pre-heat the oven to 400°F/200°C/gas mark 6.

Lightly butter the base and sides of a 1 litre soufflé dish. Grate a little Parmesan directly into the dish then roll the dish round in your hands so that the buttered surface is stuck with Parmesan. Spoon the soufflé mixture into the dish – it will almost fill the dish. Smooth the surface with a knife. Push the mixture inwards 0.5 cm away from the edge of the dishes with your thumb, to help the soufflé rise.

Dust the surface with a thin grating of Parmesan. Bake in the middle of the oven for just under 20 minutes or until the soufflé is puffed and golden. Just before you are ready to take it out of the oven, reheat the reserved tomato sauce and snip the basil over the top.

When the soufflé is ready take it quickly to the table. If liked, crack a hole in the middle of the soufflé and pour in half of the tomato sauce. Serve immediately, passing the rest of the sauce separately with extra Parmesan for sprinkling over the top.

INDIVIDUAL FRESH TOMATO SOUFFLÉS

SERVES 4

This elegant, clean-tasting tomato soufflé is made with egg whites. The ingredients have been pared down to the essentials: fresh tomato sauce flavoured with tarragon and stiffened with gelatine. It was invented in the early seventies at the height of Michel Guérard's foray into gourmet diet food. I discovered the recipe when his book *Cuisine Minceur* was published in the UK in 1977. The recipes were, and still are, stunning, and came from the menu of his three-Michelin-starred restaurant within a health spa, at Eugénie-les-Bains, in south-west France. Unless you are dieting seriously, you might prefer to replace the gelatine with two egg yolks.

- **2 sheets gelatine or 2 level tsp of powdered gelatine**
- **1 litre Fresh Tomato Sauce (see page 243)**
- **½ tsp chopped tarragon**
- **6 egg whites**
- **butter**

Soak the gelatine for 15 minutes in cold water to soften.

Bring the tomato sauce, together with the tarragon, to the boil and reduce by two-thirds of its volume. Stir in the gelatine and allow to cool.

Pre-heat the oven to 425°F/220°C/gas mark 7.

Whisk the egg whites to a soft snow. Do not allow them to become too firm. Stir some of the beaten whites into the cold tomato sauce with a whisk. Then add the rest, folding them in delicately with a spatula.

Lightly brush the insides of four ramekins (approximately 9 cm x 4 cm deep) with butter and fill them right up to the top with the soufflé mixture. Smooth the surface with a knife. Push the mixture inwards 0.5 cm away from the edges of the dishes with your thumb, to help the soufflés rise.

Cook for 8-10 minutes and serve immediately.

ROAST TOMATO CLAFOUTIS WITH GOAT'S CHEESE

SERVES 6

It is always gratifying when you think you might have come up with an original idea to find that someone else has already thought of it. Patricia Wells includes Tomato Clafoutis in *At Home In Provence* and makes it with the luscious, firm ripe tomatoes available in the South of France. She says she has prepared it with both round and plum tomatoes with equal success.

Tomato Clafoutis is a bit like Tomato Quiche without the pastry and should you wish to make this into something more substantial, line the dish with shortcrust pastry and blind-bake it before proceeding with the recipe. My version also includes scraps of goat's cheese, which melt as the clafoutis cooks. It is at its finest eaten warm and is perfect picnic material.

4 large free-range eggs

50 g flour

salt and freshly ground black pepper

300 ml double cream or 150 ml double cream and 150 ml milk

20 roast tomato halves (see page 33) or 10 ripe, firm tomatoes, cored, peeled and halved through their middles if round, lengthways if plum

1 tbsp olive oil

a pinch of sugar

a knob of butter

150 g goat's cheese or feta, cut into postage stamp-size pieces

2 tbsp freshly grated Parmesan

crème fraîche and basil to serve (optional)

Pre-heat the oven to 350°F/180°C/gas mark 4.

Beat the eggs, then add the sieved flour, salt and cream and continue to beat until thick and smooth. This is quickly done in a mixer but if done by hand with a whisk, any lumps could be eliminated by pouring/pushing through a sieve and scraping under it to get the thick residue. Leave to rest while you prepare the tomatoes.

If using fresh tomatoes, pre-heat the grill to its highest setting. Lay the tomatoes, cut side up, on a grill-pan. Smear the cut surfaces with olive oil, season with salt, pepper and sugar. Grill until the sides feel soft and the tops are beginning to burnish; you want the tomatoes tender but not mushy.

Butter an approximately 20 cm x 25 cm ceramic or earthenware gratin dish liberally so that the clafoutis can puff up with ease. Arrange the tomatoes, cut side up, in the dish. Place pieces of goat's cheese or feta in the gaps. Pour over the batter. Cook near the top of the oven for about 35 minutes until the pudding has billowed and the top is appetizingly browned in patches.

Tempting though it is to eat the Clafoutis immediately, the flavours will be more pronounced if it is left to settle back into itself and cool to lukewarm. Before serving, dust the surface with Parmesan and, if liked, serve with a dollop of crème fraîche laced with shredded basil.

FRESH TOMATO CLAFOUTIS

SERVES 8 AS A STARTER

This is Patricia Wells's recipe from *At Home In Provence.*

- 1 kg firm ripe tomatoes, cored, peeled and quartered
- salt
- 2 large eggs plus 2 extra-large egg yolks
- 5 tbsp crème fraîche or double cream
- 50 g freshly grated Parmesan
- 2 tsp fresh thyme leaves, carefully stemmed

Pre-heat the oven to 375°F/190°C/gas mark 5.

Place the tomato quarters side by side, on a double thickness of paper towelling. Sprinkle generously with salt. Cover with another double thickness of paper towelling. Set aside for at least 10 minutes, and up to 1 hour, to purge the tomatoes of their liquid.

In a small bowl, combine the eggs, extra egg yolks, the crème fraîche, half of the cheese, and half of the thyme leaves. Season lightly with salt and whisk to blend.

Lay the tomatoes on the bottom of a 27-cm diameter baking-dish. Pour the batter over the tomatoes. Sprinkle with the remaining cheese and thyme. Place in the centre of the oven and bake until the batter is set and the tart is golden and bubbling, about 30 minutes. Serve warm or at room temperature, cut into wedges.

TOMATO AND ROASTED RED PEPPER CAKE

SERVES 4-6

This is a flan without pastry made in a removable-base cake tin and served as an hors d'oeuvre. It is cooled in the tin, then lifted on to a cake stand to be decorated as you will. Branches of tiny grilled vine tomatoes laid over the top look attractive. Another idea is to cover the whole thing with roasted tomato halves, or with slices of peeled tomato laid out, French apple tart-style, in overlapping concentric circles. Finish with a vinaigrette made with the juice from the concassé.

- 3 tbsp olive oil
- 500 g tomato concassé (see page 29)
- 1 garlic clove, peeled and finely chopped
- ½ tsp thyme leaves
- salt and freshly ground pepper
- 2 tsp balsamic vinegar
- ½ tsp sugar
- 2 red peppers, roasted, peeled, seeded, white filament removed, and chopped
- a squeeze of lemon juice
- 2 eggs
- 3 egg yolks
- a handful of basil leaves
- 40 g fresh breadcrumbs
- 40 g grated Parmesan

Pre-heat the oven to 350°F/180°C/gas mark 4.

Heat the oil in a heavy frying-pan. Add the tomato concassé, garlic, thyme and a seasoning of salt and pepper. Cook over a medium-low heat, stirring frequently, until all the liquid in the tomatoes has evaporated. Add the balsamic vinegar and sugar and cook, stirring constantly, for a couple more minutes.

Puree the tomatoes and red pepper together. Leave to cool. Taste and adjust the seasoning with salt, pepper, sugar and lemon juice.

Whisk the eggs, season with salt and pepper and snip the basil over them. When the tomato mixture is cool, stir it into the eggs with the Parmesan and breadcrumbs.

Line a removable-base cake tin of approximately 20 cm in diameter with greaseproof paper. Spoon the mixture into the tin. Bake for about 30 minutes until the low-rise 'cake' is lightly set and quite firm. Remove from the oven, allow to cool slightly before removing the collar. Peel off the paper and serve warm or cold in slices or wedges with a watercress or rocket salad.

ROAST TOMATO MAYONNAISE AND TOMATO AÏOLI

SERVES 4-6

Using roast tomatoes to flavour mayonnaise gives it a deep tomato flavour and dark colour that is far more pronounced than using fresh tomatoes. A spoonful of sun-dried tomato puree will give similar results. To turn the mayonnaise into Tomato Aïoli, follow this recipe but begin by pounding two large, new-season garlic cloves to a paste with a little salt. Blend in the egg yolks and add 1 heaped tablespoon of sun-dried tomato puree.

- 2 egg yolks
- 1 tsp smooth Dijon mustard
- salt and freshly ground white pepper
- 8 roast tomato halves (see page 33)
- 200 ml vegetable oil
- 1 tbsp balsamic vinegar
- 75 ml light olive oil (pure, not virgin)

Whisk the egg yolks with the mustard. Season with salt and white pepper.

Place a sieve over a bowl and press the tomato halves through, scraping all the paste off the bottom of the sieve. If it seems very wet – unlikely – drive off the liquid by transferring to a small saucepan and briefly cooking over a medium heat. Stir the dry paste into the egg yolks and add, whisking all the time, a few drops of the vegetable oil. Continue until the mixture is very thick and sticky. Now add a little of the vinegar to loosen it and carry on adding the oil, a little faster now, in a very thin stream. Once the mixture starts to thicken again, add a little more vinegar then return to the oil, and so on, finishing the mayonnaise with the olive oil. Check the seasoning and add any extra drops of vinegar if necessary.

TOMATO REMOULADE

SERVES 6

A spicy thick sauce-cum-dip to serve with fish cakes or goujons of cod.

300 ml mayonnaise
2 tbsp smooth Dijon mustard
1 tbsp finely grated fresh horseradish
1 tbsp lemon juice
75 g finely chopped celery heart
50 g coarsely chopped capers
6 drops Tabasco
1 garlic clove, worked to a paste with a pinch of salt
250 g tomato concassé (see page 29)
2 tbsp snipped chives
salt and freshly ground black pepper

Mix together all the ingredients, adjust the seasoning with salt and black pepper and chill thoroughly before serving.

TOMATO ICE CREAM

SERVES 4-6

If you were to find yourself with some left-over Tomato Mayonnaise, or ordinary mayonnaise, you might care to have a go at turning it into ice cream. This is simply done by folding partially whipped cream and cooked tomato concassé (see page 29) into the mayonnaise, and freezing the mixture. It could be frozen in a ring mould in the style of Tomato Aspic (see page 54) or in a block. Either way, it should be allowed to soften in the fridge for about 30 minutes before it is served, in scoops from the block, as an unusual hors d'oeuvre, decorated with slices of avocado and prawns, and extra fresh tomato sauce to pour over the top. Arabella Boxer, who offered something similar in her *Garden Cookbook*, suggests serving this after a hot main course, especially a curry.

- a pinch of sugar
- 1 garlic clove, crushed to a paste with a pinch of salt
- 300 g tomato concassé (see page 29)
- 150 ml sour cream
- 150 ml Tomato Mayonnaise (see page 149), or ordinary mayonnaise
- salt and freshly ground black pepper
- a squeeze of lemon juice

Sprinkle the sugar and garlic over the tomato concassé. Press it through a sieve or blitz in a food-processor to make a smooth puree. Mix the sour cream into the mayonnaise. Stir in the tomato puree. Season to taste with salt and pepper and a little lemon juice.

When well mixed, pour into a clean plastic container, and freeze for two hours or until set. Use a large spoon to scoop from the centre of the ice cream.

CRAB MAYONNAISE STUFFED TOMATOES

SERVES 4

The acidity of tomato goes extremely well with the creamy flavour of crab. In this simple appetizer, ripe tomatoes are hollowed and filled with white crabmeat mixed into mayonnaise seasoned with fresh herbs and a hint of lime and chilli. If you want to be fancy, and it does look very attractive, then peel the tomatoes but it isn't really necessary.

- 4 large ripe tomatoes
- 150 g mayonnaise
- 2 limes
- 4 drops Tabasco (or more to taste)
- salt and freshly ground black pepper
- 200 g white crabmeat
- 3 tbsp finely chopped coriander or chives

Remove the stalks from the tomatoes. Turn up the other way and slice the top quarter off each tomato. Set aside the smooth lid. Use a teaspoon to scoop the flesh and seeds out of the tomatoes leaving a 0.5 cm wall of flesh. Discard or put this aside for another dish.

Spoon the mayonnaise into a bowl and add 1 tablespoon of lime juice, the Tabasco and a little salt and pepper. Stir well, then shred the crabmeat with a fork into the bowl. Add most of the coriander or chives, stir well.

Taste and adjust the seasoning. Heap the crab mayonnaise into the hollowed-out tomatoes, sprinkle with the remaining herbs and replace the tomato 'hats' at a jaunty angle. Chill before serving with the other lime, cut into wedges.

Also see:
Tomato and Black Olive Bruschetta with Mint and Oeuf Mollet (page 92)
Andalusian Salad (page 181)
Salade Niçoise (page 172)
Creamed Tomato Quiche (page 224)

salads, vinaigrettes and dressings

'Salad tomatoes in Greece and Catalonia seem to be of a different race, larger, firmer, tasting like fruit. They are always used green, with only the faintest tinge of pink, in salads. Crisp in texture, they are perfumed and sweet.

At Vendrell lunch began every day (this is universal Catalan practice) with these fruits cut in half across, scored with the point of a knife on the exposed surfaces, some slices of peeled garlic inserted, then sprinkled with salt and orenga, wild marjoram. Some very fine slices of raw sweet onion were laid on top of each half, and sometimes one or two desalted anchovy fillets. Always prepared at the last moment for the sake of freshness. Everyone helped themselves to olive oil from the setrill, a little glass bottle with a fine spout.'

Patience Gray,
Honey From A Weed, Fasting and Feasting In Tuscany, Catalonia, the Cyclades and Apulia

A simple tomato salad, the tomatoes cut any way you like but sun-ripened, luscious ones, their juicy flesh dense and meaty yet soft and succulent, is one of life's greatest pleasures. The salad changes not only by the way in which the tomato is cut, be it in the traditional slices, wedges or tiny dice, but by the size of the tomato. Combining different-sized tomatoes in one salad, particularly if the tomatoes are of different colours, offers great scope for ringing the changes. Once they are peeled – rarely necessary but sometimes welcome – the salad is different again.

When the tomatoes are a good variety, and have been ripened in the full strength of the sun, the flesh has such an intense tomato flavour, the sweet and sour in perfect harmony, that they need no more than a twist of salt to accentuate their perfection. But why stop there? There is so much more to discover with tomato salad – a little garlic and onion, or herbs, such as basil, chives, parsley, coriander, mint, savory and marjoram. It is difficult to think of ingredients that aren't good in a tomato salad: red peppers, green beans, chicory, lettuce and cucumber, scraps of lemon or orange zest, the juice of citrus fruits, salty and sour seasonings, such as black olives, capers, and anchovy, all work well in very different ways. So do soft, creamy cheeses like mozzarella, and goat's cheese, and more vibrantly salty cheeses such as feta and Parmesan.

Boiled eggs are a well-known addition to a tomato salad, but fruits such as orange, melon and peaches, which might seem odd couplings, can be very good with a simple lemon juice and olive oil dressing. Almost any dressing, be it a modest swirl of balsamic vinegar and a splosh of olive oil, a delicate cream dressing, or a full-bodied vinaigrette, works well in a tomato salad.

Tomato salad can begin a meal, punctuate a meal, be a meal or finish a meal. It can be all things to all people on all occasions. I cannot imagine ever tiring of tomato salad, although it is not something I would wish to eat on a chilly day. The following selection of tomato salads, vinaigrettes and dressings, is made with whole tomatoes, sliced tomatoes, chopped tomatoes, pureed tomatoes, and roasted and grilled tomatoes. The selection couldn't possibly be considered comprehensive, but is chosen to show off the tomato's versatility as a salad vegetable.

CHUNKY TOMATO SALAD WITH RED ONION AND BLACK OLIVES

SERVES 4

This is one of those great tomato salads that goes well with almost anything. I particularly like it with a slab of feta or mozzarella cheese, and it is very good with an omelette, chicken kebab or cold cuts of meat.

- 1 scant tbsp balsamic vinegar
- sea salt and freshly ground black pepper
- a pinch of sugar
- 3 tbsp olive oil
- 1 red onion, approximately 125 g
- 3 large ripe tomatoes, a craggy type such as Marmande (approximately 300 g each)
- 12 pitted black olives, roughly chopped
- 2 tbsp roughly chopped parsley

Mix the vinegar, salt, sugar and pepper in a mixing bowl before whisking in the oil. Peel, halve and slice the onion wafer-thin.

Use a small sharp knife to cut out the tomato cores in a cone shape. Quarter the tomatoes and cut into chunky wedges. Tip them into a shallow salad bowl, add the olives and parsley, season with a crumble of sea-salt flake and black pepper. Give the dressing one more whisk, then dribble it over the tomatoes.

CLASSIC TOMATO SALAD WITH A CHOICE OF THREE DRESSINGS

SERVES 1

Plain and simple. Elegant and delicious.

2 large, ripe tomatoes, cored, peeled and thinly sliced in rounds

FOR THE ITALIAN DRESSING

3 tbsp best olive oil

1 tbsp balsamic vinegar

basil leaves

salt and pepper

FOR THE CREAM DRESSING

1 tbsp red wine vinegar

salt and pepper

150 ml double cream

a few shakes of Tabasco (optional)

1 tbsp freshly snipped chives or a few finely sliced spring onions

FOR THE TAHINI DRESSING

3 tbsp tahini (sesame-seed paste)

4 tbsp warm water

juice of 1 lemon

2 garlic cloves, peeled and ground to a paste with salt

½ tsp cumin seeds, crushed to powder

freshly ground black pepper

Lay out the tomato slices in a single layer on a large plate.

For the Italian dressing, dribble the olive oil into the balsamic vinegar while whisking continuously. Spoon the dressing over the tomatoes. Season with salt and pepper and snip the basil over the top.

For the cream dressing, whisk together the vinegar and seasoning, then pour in the cream, continuing to whisk until frothy and slightly thickened (the vinegar will help this to happen naturally). Add the Tabasco and carefully spoon over the tomatoes. Sprinkle with the chives or spring onions and allow to sit for 20 minutes or so before serving.

For the tahini dressing, spoon the tahini into a bowl. It is thick, stiff and difficult to deal with. Gradually incorporate the warm water, then the lemon juice. Stir in the garlic and the cumin, adding more juice to taste and more water to arrive at a pouring consistency. Season with black pepper. Spoon over the tomatoes.

COOKED TOMATO SALAD WITH SPRING ONIONS

SERVES 4

One of the gastronomic highlights of my first trip to Sydney in 1995 was a visit to Paul Merrony's restaurant, Merrony's, by Circular Quay. It was a lucky coincidence that Simon Hopkinson was also in town and it's thanks to him that I went. Simon had often talked about Paul – he did a stint with him at Bibendum – and had told me about his wonderful cooked tomato salad.

I wasn't disappointed. In fact, Paul's salad is now one of my favourite summer treats. One little adjustment Simon suggested, with which I agree, is to use the flavoured oil from cooking the tomatoes – rather than fresh oil – in the vinaigrette. So, it is with thanks to Paul, and Simon, that I can reproduce this great recipe.

10 ripe medium tomatoes, peeled
salt and freshly ground black pepper
a little sugar
150 ml good olive oil
2 garlic cloves, peeled and finely sliced in rounds
1 small bunch thyme
10 bulbous spring onions
20 g butter
1 tbsp finely shredded flat-leaf parsley

FOR THE DRESSING

salt and pepper
50 ml red wine vinegar
1 tsp Dijon mustard
the oil from cooking the tomatoes

Pre-heat the oven to 275°F/140°C/gas mark 1.

Cut the tomatoes in half through the circumference. Gently squeeze out most of the seeds and place the shells in a shallow dish, cut side uppermost. Season with salt, pepper and a little sugar, and spoon over the olive oil. Sprinkle over the garlic and distribute the thyme twigs over the surface. Place in the oven and leave the tomatoes to stew gently for about 30 minutes or until they feel soft to the prod of a finger.

Remove the dish from the oven and leave to cool slightly. Discard the garlic and thyme, then, using a slotted spoon, transfer the tomatoes to a serving-dish or plates, arranging them cut side down. Strain the cooking oil through a fine sieve into a jug and allow to cool and settle.

While the tomatoes are cooling, peel and trim the spring onions to leave about a centimetre of green stalk above the bulb. Place them in a saucepan with the butter, a little seasoning and water just to cover. Simmer for several minutes until tender to the point of a small sharp knife. Lift out with a slotted spoon and cool on a plate. Carefully cut in half lengthways and gild the cut sides in a lightly oiled frying-pan. Arrange each onion half (browned side uppermost) on top of a tomato half.

To make the dressing, dissolve a generous pinch of salt in the vinegar, season with pepper then stir in the mustard before whisking in sufficient oil and tomato cooking juices to achieve a creamy dressing. Spoon as much or as little of the dressing as you wish over the tomatoes and onions. Scatter over the parsley, and finish with a little freshly ground black pepper. Serve with good bread to mop up those delicious juices.

EGG AND TOMATO SALAD AND SALAD CLEMENTINE

SERVES 6

Most people love egg and tomato salads and everyone has their favourite ways of presenting them. It could be a simple pile-up, for example, of round slices of egg and tomato. There again, you may prefer the eggs sliced lengthways, so that every slice gets some yolk, with the tomato chopped and served as a garnish. Or how about chopped egg and chopped tomato, or sliced tomato and chopped egg? And what about other ingredients? A little onion, perhaps, or chives, and parsley too? Will the dressing be creamy, or a straightforward vinaigrette? Perhaps it will be salad cream, from a bottle, or pukka mayonnaise. Perhaps the egg will be the mayonnaise. You can't go wrong with egg and tomato salads.

Salad Clementine is the most elaborate egg salad I've ever come across and it originates from the Cordon Bleu course. It looks stunning. The eggs are sliced and arranged on a dish and scattered with capers and sliced gherkins. The whole lot is hidden by upturned, hollowed out and briefly fried tomato halves, decorated with a lattice of anchovy strips and dressed with a tasty vinaigrette seasoned with mustard, tomato ketchup and herbs. It is served chilled with slices of brown bread and butter.

6 medium tomatoes, cored and peeled
salt and freshly ground black pepper
2 tbsp cooking oil
6 hard-boiled eggs
1 tbsp capers, lightly squeezed
1 tbsp sliced or chopped gherkins
6 anchovy fillets
brown bread and butter to serve

FOR THE SALAD DRESSING
salt and freshly ground black pepper
2 tbsp wine vinegar
1 tsp dry mustard (English mustard)
6 tbsp salad oil
3 dsp tomato ketchup
1 tbsp mixed chopped herbs such as parsley, chives and mint

Cut the tomatoes in half through the stalk (or where the stalk would have been) and scrape out the seeds. Season the flesh lightly. Heat the oil in a pan and sauté the tomatoes very quickly on both sides. Lift them out carefully and leave to cool.

Peel and slice the eggs and arrange them on a platter. Scatter the capers and gherkins over the top. Season with salt and pepper. Set the tomatoes, cut side downwards, on top.

Split the anchovy fillets in half or cut thinner strips if possible. Arrange them in a lattice over the tomatoes. Make the dressing by stirring salt and pepper into the vinegar, then combining all the ingredients. Carefully spoon the dressing over the tomatoes. Chill for 1 hour before serving with the brown bread and butter.

EZME

SERVES 6-8

Ezme is the Turkish version of salsa (see pages 184-192) with tomatoes and various other ingredients all neatly chopped and mixed together, but it is dressed with a vinaigrette and thus ends up as more of a salad. It is a wonderful dish to make for a buffet or a barbecue. Dried mint, incidentally, is characteristic of Turkish food. You may prefer to substitute fresh. I do.

- 450 g ripe tomatoes, cored, peeled, seeded and chopped
- ¼ cucumber, peeled, seeded and chopped
- salt and freshly ground black pepper
- 1 green or red pepper, seeded and white filament discarded, chopped
- 4 spring onions or 1 red onion, finely chopped
- 1 garlic clove, chopped
- ½ tbsp dried mint or 2 tbsp finely chopped fresh mint
- 1 tbsp tomato puree
- 4 shakes Tabasco
- ¼ tsp caster sugar
- 1 tbsp wine vinegar
- 3 tbsp olive oil

Place the chopped tomato and cucumber in a colander. Sprinkle lightly with salt (about ½ teaspoon) and leave to drain for 30 minutes. Mix with the other vegetables and garlic, and chop everything together very, very finely, until you have a coarse, lumpy puree. Stir in the mint. Make a vinaigrette by mixing together the tomato puree, Tabasco, sugar and vinegar. Whisk in the olive oil, then stir it into the pureed vegetables. Taste and adjust the seasoning. This salad is best made by hand but if you attempt it in a food-processor, use the pulse button, working in short bursts to avoid making a slushy mush.

FOUR TOMATO SALAD

SERVES 6

This is a smart hors d'oeuvre salad, perfected by Joan Campbell who wrote wonderful recipes for *Australian Vogue Entertaining*. A thick slice of beef tomato becomes a sort of plate and is decorated with halved cherry tomatoes (Tom Thumb, as they call them in Sydney) and halved yellow pear (teardrop) tomatoes. The salad is dressed with basil vinaigrette.

- 2 ripe beef tomatoes, cored and peeled
- 4 sun-dried tomatoes preserved in olive oil, sliced into strips
- 1 tsp caster sugar
- 24 cherry tomatoes, halved through the circumference
- 24 yellow mini pear or plum tomatoes, halved lengthways
- sea salt and freshly ground black pepper

FOR THE BASIL SAUCE

- 200 ml garlic-flavoured vinaigrette
- bunch of basil, leaves only

Cut three thick slices from the middle of the two beef tomatoes. Place a slice on each plate and sprinkle with some of the sun-dried tomato strips. Sprinkle with a little of the sugar and dribble over lightly about a tablespoon of vinaigrette.

Arrange the cherry and mini pear or plum tomatoes on top and season with sea-salt flakes, black pepper and sugar. Blend the remaining vinaigrette with the basil leaves and spoon over the top.

GOLDEN TOMATO SALAD WITH MARJORAM

SERVES 4

Yellow or orange tomatoes are what you need for this salad with novelty appeal. It looks dramatically different but the flavour of the tomatoes with names that include the word 'gold' is as variable as it is in red tomatoes. It is a pity to peel gold tomatoes because their skin is a far deeper colour than the flesh.

- 400 g regular-size golden tomatoes
- 200 g cherry or small plum golden tomatoes
- 2 tbsp marjoram or oregano leaves
- 1 tbsp red wine vinegar
- 5 tbsp olive oil
- sea salt and black pepper

Core and thickly slice the regular-size tomatoes. Halve the cherry tomatoes, slicing lengthways if using a plum-shaped variety. Arrange the two sets of tomatoes in a shallow bowl. Blitz together most of the marjoram or oregano leaves with the vinegar and olive oil in a food-processor to make a green vinaigrette. Spoon it over the tomatoes, season with a crumble of sea-salt flakes and freshly milled black pepper. Sprinkle the reserved leaves over the top.

GREEK SALAD

SERVES 2-4

Made with knobbly, sun-ripened tomatoes, sweet, crunchy onion and cucumber, with slightly sour feta cheese and black olives, Greek salad is a meal in itself and one I could eat every day. For a simplified version, known as *Horiatiki*, include only tomatoes, feta cheese, red onion, black olives and flat-leaf parsley. This salad is known as *Coban* in Turkey.

- ½ large cucumber, peeled, halved lengthways, seeded and thickly sliced
- 450 g ripe tomatoes, cored and cut into thick wedges
- 1 large red onion, cut into wafer-thin slices, or a few spring onions, sliced
- a few pale green pickled peppers
- salt and freshly ground black pepper
- 1 tbsp chopped mint
- 1 tbsp flat-leaf parsley
- 6 tbsp fruity olive oil
- 2 tbsp lemon juice
- 225 g Greek feta cheese
- 10 good-quality black olives, preferably Kalamata
- 1 tsp dried oregano

Make layers with the cucumber, tomato and onion, seasoning as you go with salt and pepper, mint and parsley adding the occasional pickled pepper and olives.

Whisk together most of the olive oil and lemon juice, pour over the salad. Add slabs of feta, a sprinkling of dried oregano and the last splash of olive oil.

GREEN BEANS WITH TOMATO AND BASIL

SERVES 2

A simple little salad made with peeled, diced tomato, quickly cooked fine green beans and an intensely tomato-flavoured creamy dressing. Delicious on its own, with cold cuts, a kebab or a plainly cooked piece of fish.

- 100 g extra-fine green beans
- 3 firm, ripe, medium-sized good-flavoured tomatoes
- 1 tbsp mayonnaise (Hellmann's is fine for this)
- 1 tbsp vinaigrette
- 1 small shallot, finely diced
- 1 tsp red wine vinegar (optional)
- sea salt and freshly ground black pepper
- 10 basil leaves, shredded

Bring a large pan of salted water to the boil. Drop in the beans, bring the water back to the boil and cook for 1 minute. Drain, then plunge the beans into ice-cold water. Drain again.

Peel, core and seed the tomatoes in the usual way but do so over a sieve suspended over a bowl to catch the juices. Dice the tomato flesh.

Place the mayonnaise in a bowl, stir in the vinaigrette and diced shallot. Add the tomato juices and hold the sieve over the bowl, gently crushing the tomato debris against the sieve so the juices drip into the vinaigrette. Stir to make a creamy dressing. Taste and add a little wine vinegar as necessary. Add the drained beans and diced tomato, season with sea-salt flakes and black pepper then toss. Add the shredded basil leaves, toss again and serve.

GRILLED RED ONION AND TOMATO SALAD

SERVES 4

The frizzled red onions, with balsamic vinegar and ripe, fruity tomatoes, make an excellent salad that is particularly good with barbecued meat and sausages.

- 4 medium red onions, quartered and each quarter cut lengthways into 4
- 3 tbsp olive oil
- 1 tbsp balsamic vinegar
- 8 medium vine tomatoes quartered
- salt and freshly ground black pepper
- 2 tbsp freshly snipped chives

Place the onion slices in a bowl with 1 tablespoon of the olive oil. Use your hands to toss the onions to get all of them lightly coated with the oil. Heat a ridged griddle or heavy-bottomed frying-pan, and when it is very hot, cook a single layer of onions over a medium-fierce heat for 5-10 minutes, tossing and turning the onions until the edges begin to wilt and some to frizzle. Remove to a salad bowl. Continue with the rest of the onions. Pour the rest of the olive oil into the bowl with the balsamic vinegar, toss and leave for at least 10 minutes (an hour, or overnight would be better) before adding the tomatoes, a generous seasoning of salt and black pepper and the chives. Toss again and serve.

GRILLED TOMATOES WITH A MUSTARD DRESSING

SERVES 4-6

A simple and effective way of turning grilled tomatoes into a Salade Tiède de Tomates. It makes a delicious light summer starter.

- 6 ripe plum tomatoes, halved through the core
- 4 tbsp olive oil, plus a little extra for grilling
- salt and freshly ground black pepper
- 1 tsp caster sugar
- scant tsp Dijon mustard
- juice of ½ lemon
- 1 tbsp finely chopped flat-leaf parsley

Arrange the tomato halves, cut side up, on a grill-pan lined with lightly oiled kitchen foil. Brush the cut surfaces with olive oil and season with salt and pepper. Place under the grill to cook.

Make a dressing by dissolving the sugar and mustard in the lemon juice, then whisk in the olive oil.

Baste the tomatoes with the dressing while they are grilling. When they are quite tender, transfer them to a serving-dish and tip over the top any juices that have collected along with any remaining dressing. Sprinkle with the parsley and serve immediately, or allow to cool slightly and then add the parsley.

INSALATA DI POMODORO CON INSAVURIDA

SERVES 4

An Italian way of preparing a tomato salad, when the dressing and any herbs and other seasonings, such as garlic and onion, are chopped so finely that they are almost emulsified. This particular Insavurida comes from Franco Taruschio of the Walnut Tree at Abergavenny. Franco recommends using Italian salad tomatoes, which would be ridged and swollen, very fleshy and very ripe. Choose the nearest equivalent, but be sure the tomatoes have plenty of flavour.

- 1 tbsp very finely chopped parsley
- ½ tbsp very finely chopped basil
- 1 tbsp very finely chopped onion
- ½ garlic clove, very finely chopped
- 3 tbsp extra virgin olive oil
- 1 tbsp balsamic vinegar
- salt and freshly ground black pepper
- 4 medium-large Italian salad tomatoes (Marmande style), thinly sliced

Mix together the herbs, onion and garlic, and add the olive oil and balsamic vinegar. Season with salt and pepper and mix well together. Lay the tomato slices on a serving-dish and dress with the Insavurida.

INSALATA TRICOLORE

SERVES 4-6

A classic dish: slices of tomato, mozzarella and avocado dressed with olive oil and lemon juice and garnished with basil. There are countless ways of presenting this simple yet delicious salad: on a large platter, for example, in overlapping slices starting first with slices of tomato, then mozzarella, and ending with the avocado, or it looks stunning laid out on an oblong plate, making layers of red, white and green.

For a more formal approach, make individual salads by choosing a large tomato, slicing it through its middle and reassembling the tomato with the cheese and avocado, with whole basil leaves tucked between the slices. Whichever presentation you go for, the salad is finished with a splash of olive oil and, if liked, a few basil leaves. It is only worth making Insalata Tricolore with ripe, full-flavoured tomatoes, the finest buffalo mozzarella available and avocado that is fully ripe but not squishy. Another delicious twist is to make a lemon or lime juice dressing with balsamic vinegar, a hint of sugar, and olive oil, and pour a little of it over the layers: 2 tbsp lemon or lime juice, 1 tsp balsamic vinegar, ½ tsp sugar, 4 tbsp olive oil.

- 6 medium-large tomatoes, peeled and thickly sliced through the circumference
- sea salt and freshly ground black pepper
- approximately 6 tbsp good-quality olive oil
- 3 buffalo mozzarella cheese
- 3 firm but ripe avocados
- juice from 1 lemon
- basil leaves

Lay out the tomatoes in overlapping slices on a large white plate. Season lightly with sea-salt flakes and black pepper and dribble over about 1 tablespoon of the olive oil. Slice the mozzarella thickly and arrange over the tomatoes, leaving a border of tomato. Repeat the seasoning and oiling.

Peel the avocado, halve, remove the stone and slice thickly. Pile in the centre of the mozzarella. Squeeze the lemon juice over the avocado and pour over the last of the olive oil. Season with salt and a few grinds of pepper. Decorate with the basil leaves. It is important to allow it to rest before it is served so that the juices have a chance to mingle and develop, but not for too long because the avocado will discolour.

LIME-ROASTED VINE TOMATOES AND WILD ROCKET SALAD

SERVES 4

Simple to make, stunning to look at and great to eat.

- juice of 2 limes
- 1 tbsp balsamic vinegar
- sea salt and freshly ground black pepper
- 3 tbsp olive oil
- 500 g small vine-ripened tomatoes, stalks removed
- a handful of wild rocket

Squeeze the lime juice into a bowl, add the balsamic vinegar, season with a pinch of salt then pour in the olive oil, whisking as you go. Add the tomatoes and toss around to coat with the dressing. Tip everything into a frying-pan, and heat the grill. Season the tomatoes with black pepper, place the pan under the grill and cook for a few minutes, shaking the pan a couple of times, until the tomato skins split and the flesh softens. Leave to cool in the juices.

Carefully drain the juices into a mixing bowl, add the rocket and toss. Tip the rocket and the juices on to a serving platter, arrange the tomatoes alongside and season with a crumble of sea-salt flakes and a grinding of black pepper.

MELON, CUCUMBER AND TOMATO SALAD WITH MINT

SERVES 4-6

A surprisingly successful combination dreamed up by Anton Mosimann in the early nineties for his Channel 4 TV series and book called *Naturally*.

- 1 cucumber, peeled and seeded
- sea salt and freshly ground black pepper
- 1 Cantaloupe melon
- 1 Charentais or Ogen melon
- ¼ small watermelon
- 100 g red cherry tomatoes
- 100 g yellow cherry-sized pear tomatoes
- 2 tbsp finely sliced mint

FOR THE DRESSING

- 1½ tbsp clear honey
- 1 tbsp balsamic vinegar
- 1½ tbsp orange juice
- 3 tbsp olive oil

Slice the cucumber into crescents approximately 0.5 cm thick. Place it in a colander and sprinkle with a little salt. Leave for 20 minutes to drain. Wrap in a tea-towel and squeeze dry.

Halve the melons and remove the seeds. If you have one, use a melon baller to make balls. If not, and I don't know anyone who does, cut the melon into cherry-size dice. Make sure you get rid of the watermelon seeds.

Combine the cucumber, melon, tomatoes and mint in a bowl. Mix together the salad dressing ingredients and pour over the salad. Season with black pepper and a little salt. Toss and serve.

MIXED TOMATO AND BASIL SALAD SERVES 4

This is a stylish idea pinched from Mark Hix and the Ivy, featuring two distinct dressings for one salad.

- 500 g mixed seasonal tomatoes, plum, beef, cherry or golden
- ¼ tsp caster sugar
- sea salt and freshly ground black pepper
- 1 tbsp balsamic vinegar
- 4 tbsp olive oil
- 50 ml Cherry Tomato Basil Dressing (see page 179)
- a handful of basil leaves, red if possible

Cut the tomatoes into different shapes – halves, wedges, either whole or halved if they are very small. Arrange them on a plate or in a bowl. Dissolve the caster sugar and a generous pinch of salt in the balsamic vinegar and whisk in the olive oil to make a creamy, dark vinaigrette. Spoon this vinaigrette and then the basil dressing over the tomatoes so that they remain separate. Season with black pepper and a crumble of sea-salt flakes. Scatter torn basil leaves over the top.

PEACH AND TOMATO SALAD

SERVES 6

'A traditional Tuscan thing,' wrote Rowley Leigh (when chef of Kensington Place in West London, before running Café Anglais at Whiteleys in Paddington), of this salad, in an article about peaches published in *The Guardian*. It makes an unusual start to a summer meal, and should only be made if you have very ripe tomatoes and perfect white peaches. It also works, Rowley says, with nectarines, and walnut oil instead of olive oil.

- 6 large tomatoes, cored and peeled
- salt and freshly ground black pepper
- 6 white peaches, scalded and peeled
- 1 lemon
- olive oil
- 6 shelled walnuts, chopped
- 6 basil leaves, torn

Slice the tomatoes thinly and salt them; then cut the peaches into thin segments. Arrange both fruits in an overlapping circle, alternating the two. Squeeze the juice of a lemon over the salad and drizzle lightly with oil (very lightly if you are using walnut oil). Scatter the walnuts and basil over the salad. Grind over some black pepper, and serve cold.

PORTUGUESE TOMATO SALAD

SERVES 4-6

Lightly grilling the peppers and tomatoes gives this salad an interesting smoky flavour. Excellent, as you might expect, with grilled sardines.

- 1 small cucumber, peeled and thinly sliced
- salt and freshly ground black pepper
- 3 green or red peppers
- 4 large ripe tomatoes
- 1 garlic clove, peeled and finely chopped
- 3 tbsp olive oil
- 1 tbsp white wine vinegar

Spread out the cucumber and sprinkle with ½ teaspoon of salt. Collect it all up and leave to drain for 30 minutes in a colander, then squeeze out all the water in a tea-towel.

Pre-heat the grill and cook the peppers, turning as the skin blackens. Transfer to a plate, cover with clingfilm and leave for 20 minutes before removing the skin. Core and seed them, slice into strips about 1.5 cm wide and arrange them in a large shallow bowl.

Spear a tomato with a fork and turn until the skin bursts and blackens. Remove from the heat and peel away the black skin. Repeat with the others. Cut out the cores and slice into slim wedges.

2 tbsp coarsely chopped fresh coriander

Arrange the tomato pieces, then the cucumber over the peppers. Sprinkle over the garlic and a decent seasoning of black pepper. Drizzle over the olive oil, then the vinegar. Toss lightly. Scatter over the coriander, cover and leave to marinate at room temperature for 1 hour. Toss lightly again and serve.

ROAST TOMATO SALAD WITH MINT, BLACK OLIVES AND FETA

SERVES 2

Serve with crusty bread for a summer lunch. You could vary the choice of herbs. In this one, mint predominates with a background hint of coriander.

- 15 good-quality black olives, preferably Provençal-style with herbs
- 8 roast tomato halves (see page 33)
- 1 tbsp capers, drained
- a handful of mint leaves, roughly chopped
- a few coriander leaves, finely shredded
- 3 tbsp olive oil
- 1 tbsp balsamic vinegar
- 100 g feta cheese
- sea salt and freshly ground black pepper

Cut the flesh off the olive stones in big pieces. Lay the tomato halves on a platter, scatter with capers, the olives and the herbs. Whisk the olive oil into the balsamic vinegar and dribble it over the salad. Break the cheese into pieces and scatter over the top. Season with a crumble of sea-salt flakes and black pepper.

SALADE MECHOUIA

SERVES 4

When I was in my early twenties I worked for several weeks on an international arts festival at a little-known town called Tabarka on the coast of northern Tunisia. My job was interviewing the artists – as diverse as Joan Baez, the Kipper Kids and some Parisian African drummers – and writing a daily paper about them and the other goings-on in this heavenly place. Part of the job was sussing out all the restaurants – of which there were many – and I became an aficionado of Tunisian food. The salads were stupendous but Mechouia, sometimes served on a slab of bread soaked in olive oil and tomato juice, was the mutt's nuts, as someone once put it. It is clearly related to Salade Niçoise although, if you're lucky, the red peppers and tomatoes will have been grilled (mechoui means 'grilled' and often refers to lamb cooked with peppers and tomatoes). This salad is often served with chunks of tinned tuna and scraps of preserved lemons, which can often be found at Cypriot green-grocers, in some delicatessens and large supermarkets.

To make this recipe into Salade Niçoise, don't bother to grill the tomato, omit the red pepper, and add a handful of blanched green beans, a couple of round lettuce hearts, a few small boiled new potatoes, and some sliced spring onions. Artichoke hearts, shelled broad beans and a few basil leaves are optional extras. Canned tuna also turns up often in Salade Niçoise, but pink Spanish anchovies preserved in olive oil would be a good alternative. The dressing in this case should be made with red wine vinegar, olive oil and garlic.

FOR THE SALAD

3 red peppers

6 firm but ripe medium tomatoes, cored and peeled

4 tbsp olive oil, plus a little extra for grilling

sea salt and freshly ground black pepper

sugar

3 fresh eggs, hard-boiled, peeled and quartered

FOR THE TOMATO BREAD (OPTIONAL)

6 over-ripe tomatoes

1 tbsp red wine vinegar

a pinch of sugar

Pre-heat the grill. Lay the peppers on the grill-pan, turning them as their skins blacken. Transfer to a plate, cover with clingfilm and leave for 20 minutes before removing the skin. Slice them into chunky ribbons, discarding seeds and white filament. Halve the tomatoes through their cores, lay them on the grill-pan and paint the cut surfaces with a smear of olive oil. Season with salt and pepper and a little sugar. Cook under the grill at a slightly reduced heat until the cut surface is blistered and scorched and they are tender all the way through. Leave to cool.

Meanwhile, make the tomato bread. Place the over-ripe tomatoes in the bowl of a food-processor. Blitz to a puree with the vinegar and sugar. Pass through a sieve (or not) and whisk in 1 tablespoon of the olive oil. Season with salt and pepper. Toast the bread, rub it with garlic and smear one side with olive oil. Place the bread in shallow soup bowls or on large plates and drench it with the pureed

- salt and freshly ground black pepper
- 8 black olives, pitted and halved
- 1 tbsp capers, rinsed and squeezed
- 4 anchovy fillets, rinsed and split lengthways
- 1 tbsp coarsely chopped flat-leaf parsley
- ½ preserved lemon, chopped (optional)
- juice of 1 small lemon
- 4 slices pain de campagne or sourdough bread
- 1 garlic clove, cut in half but don't bother to peel

tomato. Now arrange all of the salad ingredients on top. Whisk the lemon juice with the remaining olive oil and spoon over the top. Season with sea-salt flakes and freshly ground black pepper.

SUGOCASA SALAD WITH BASIL

SERVES 4

Sugocasa is an Italian name for premium chopped tomatoes and in this salad-cum-salsa, ripe tomatoes are peeled and diced but the juice around their seed cavities is used in the vinaigrette. The finishing touch to this stunning salad is a couple of teaspoons of gelatine granules. They don't set the salad, but give the dressing a jammier texture.

- 500 g ripe plum tomatoes, cored and peeled
- 1 tbsp red wine vinegar
- ¼ tsp caster sugar
- sea salt and freshly ground black pepper
- 1 shake Tabasco
- 4 tbsp olive oil
- 2 tsp gelatine granules
- 10 basil leaves, shredded

Quarter each tomato lengthways. Place a sieve over a bowl and use a teaspoon to scoop the seeds and their juices into the sieve. Press the seeds against the sides of the sieve to extract all the juice. Slice each tomato quarter into 2-3 strips then chop into chunky dice.

Place the red wine vinegar in a bowl, stir in the sugar and a generous pinch of salt until both dissolve. Add Tabasco and 2 tablespoons of the reserved tomato juices. Whisk in the olive oil and gelatine granules. Stir in the tomatoes. Strew the basil over the top, season with sea-salt flakes and freshly grated black pepper, stir again and serve.

HOT AND COLD SALAD

SERVES 4

Salads made with different-sized and different-coloured tomatoes look smart and interesting. Even more interesting, however, and this is a weakness of mine, is the combination of cooked and raw tomatoes. In this salad, both ideas come together and the juices from squashy roast tomatoes ooze into the salad and make their contribution to the simple dressing of olive oil and balsamic vinegar. Oregano, the pizza herb, is scattered over the hot tomatoes to give the salad a wonderful aromatic pungency.

- 450 g vine-ripened small tomatoes, cored, peeled and halved
- 6 tbsp best-quality olive oil
- ½ garlic clove
- salt and freshly ground black pepper
- 1 tbsp sugar
- 2 tbsp lightly chopped oregano or marjoram leaves
- 350 g ripe plum tomatoes, cored and sliced into rounds
- 250 g cherry plum tomatoes, red or golden, halved lengthways
- 2 tbsp balsamic vinegar

Pre-heat the oven to 400°F/200°C/gas mark 6.

Lay the small tomatoes, cut side up, closely together on a sheet of foil, spread lightly with a little of the olive oil, laid over a baking sheet. Rub the cut end of the garlic over the tomato surfaces then season with salt, pepper and a little sugar. Bake for 20 minutes or until they are soft, squashy and the tops lightly burnished. Remove from the oven and sprinkle with the chopped herbs. Leave to cool slightly.

Arrange the plum tomato slices in a shallow serving bowl or plate. Season with salt and pepper. Arrange the roast tomatoes and cherry plum tomatoes over the top, season with salt and pepper and dribble the balsamic vinegar and the rest of the olive oil over the top.

TOMATO AND CORIANDER SALAD
(CHILEAN SALAD/MIDDLE EASTERN SALAD /MOROCCAN SALAD)

SERVES 6

Equal quantities of finely sliced onion and tomato, dressed with olive oil and topped with masses of fresh coriander are a combination that turns up in various guises in many countries. Often a pinch of paprika is added and the onion may be omitted. Sometimes lemon is mixed with the olive oil, and sometimes there are equal quantities of coriander and flat-leaf parsley.

- 750 g onions, peeled and finely sliced
- 750 g tomatoes, cored, peeled and thinly sliced
- salt and freshly ground black pepper
- 4 tbsp olive oil
- juice of ½ lemon
- big bunch of coriander, leaves only, chopped

Rinse the onions thoroughly in cold water. Drain and shake dry. Place in a bowl, add the tomatoes and season with salt and pepper. Drizzle over the olive oil, squeeze over the lemon juice and mix well. Sprinkle with chopped coriander and serve.

TOMATO AND ORANGE SALAD

SERVES 2

Once considered a very daring combination. Not as daft as it might seem.

- 2 perfect oranges, peeled
- 20 small vine-ripened or golden tomatoes, cored and peeled
- 2 tbsp vinaigrette
- 4 tbsp single cream
- salt and freshly ground black pepper
- brown bread and butter to serve

Working round each orange from top to bottom, carefully slice away the inner membrane and peel. Remove each segment by slicing on either side towards the centre of the orange. Quarter each tomato. Mix the vinaigrette thoroughly with the cream. Arrange the orange segments and tomatoes on a plate and spoon over the vinaigrette. Season lightly with salt and pepper. Serve with the thin slices of brown bread and butter.

TOMATES PROVENÇALE EN SALADE

SERVES 4

Tomatoes, parsley and garlic with a little olive oil: a lovely way to combine them, from Elizabeth David's *French Country Cooking*:

> 'Take the stalks off a large bunch of parsley; pound it with a little salt, in a mortar, with two cloves of garlic and a little olive oil.
>
> 'Cut the tops off good raw tomatoes; with a teaspoon soften the pulp inside, sprinkle with salt, and turn them upside down so that the water drains out. Fill the tomatoes up with the parsley and garlic mixture. Serve them after an hour or two, when the flavour of the garlic and parsley has permeated the salad.'

TOMATO, BLACK OLIVE AND BASIL SALAD

SERVES 4-6

When made with ripe, tasty, firm tomatoes, decent meaty black olives and aromatic, strong basil, this is a salad in perfect harmony. It should be rough and ready, quickly made and enjoyed for what it is: the tomatoes are left unpeeled and cut in chunks, and the olives still have their stones intact.

- 6 ripe plum tomatoes
- salt and freshly ground black pepper
- 1 tbsp balsamic vinegar
- 5 tbsp olive oil
- about 24 black olives
- a handful of basil leaves

Quarter the tomatoes lengthways and cut across the quarters to make eighths. Dissolve a pinch of salt in the vinegar in a shallow serving-bowl, whisk in the olive oil. Add the tomatoes and the olives, season with black pepper and toss thoroughly. Tear the basil leaves over the top.

TOMATO SALAD WITH PESTO

SERVES 6

A simple idea: tomato salad dressed with pesto. A hot version of this could be made by placing tomato halves on a foil-lined baking-sheet and smearing them liberally with thick pesto. Cover the pesto with grated Parmesan and cook in a hot oven for about 20 minutes until the tomatoes are tender and the Parmesan has made a thin crust over the pesto. Another idea is to choose small, ripe plum tomatoes. They must be peeled and halved horizontally, and the seeds and liquid removed. Then, thick pesto is spooned into the empty seed pockets, and the tomatoes are nudged close to each other on a serving platter and chilled in the fridge for several hours. They are ready when the olive oil in the pesto has solidified. The pleasure is to eat a tomato half whole and to experience the burst of flavour as the olive oil melts on your tongue.

- 900 g tomatoes, cored and sliced thinly
- 4 tbsp pesto (see page 281)
- 4-5 tbsp best olive oil
- 1 tbsp grated Parmesan (optional)

Arrange the tomato slices on a platter. Place the pesto in a bowl and gradually add the olive oil, stirring vigorously and continuously to make a dressing with the consistency of ketchup or salad cream. Dribble the dressing over the tomatoes ensuring that all of them are covered. If liked, sprinkle Parmesan over the top.

TOMATOES WITH HONEY AND BLACK PEPPER

Lee Bailey is an American cookery writer who has written a lovely little book called *Tomatoes* with photos by Tom Eckerle. He hit on this neat way of serving tomatoes. It hardly needs a recipe: a beautiful ripe tomato is peeled and cored and cut into thick slices. Each slice is spread with runny honey, seasoned lightly with salt and generously with freshly ground black pepper. The tomato is then reassembled upside down so that the core end is hidden. Brush the tomato lightly with honey and sprinkle it with salt and pepper. Refrigerate for about 20 minutes and serve chilled. Decorate, if you wish, with a sprig or two of chervil.

WHOLE TOMATOES IN HORSERADISH DRESSING

SERVES 6

Excellent with cold roast beef.

- 750 g small ripe tomatoes, peeled
- 150 ml mayonnaise
- 150 ml sour cream
- 4 tbsp grated horseradish, fresh if possible
- lemon juice, to taste
- Tabasco, to taste
- salt and freshly ground black pepper

Place the tomatoes in the fridge to chill.

Make the dressing by spooning the mayonnaise into a bowl and adding the sour cream, then beating it until fluffy and smooth. Stir in the horseradish, add the lemon juice and a few drops of Tabasco to taste.

Pile the tomatoes in a pyramid on a flat dish, season with salt and pepper, then spoon the sauce over the top. Chill in the fridge until you are ready to serve.

FRESH TOMATO VINAIGRETTE

Tomatoes are acidic and as such their juices can be used to make vinaigrette. This is particularly useful in tomato salads made with pieces, as opposed to whole slices, of tomato. For example, should you wish to ring the changes with a tomato salad, cut the tomatoes into strips or dice, and whisk the liquid from the seed cavity with oil or cream to dress the tomatoes. The ratio, depending on the flavour of the tomatoes, is approximately one of tomato 'water' to two of oil, and you may need a little red wine vinegar to sharpen up the flavours. This recipe is an excellent way to use a couple of over-ripe tomatoes.

- 2 ripe tomatoes
- 1 tsp smooth Dijon mustard
- ½ tbsp red wine vinegar
- salt and freshly ground black pepper
- ¼ tsp sugar
- 3 tbsp olive oil

Place the tomatoes in a food-processor and blitz at high speed to liquidize. Rest a sieve over a bowl and scrape the tomato puree into it. Push the pulp through, until only the pips and skin are left. In a second bowl, dissolve the mustard into the vinegar with a pinch of salt and the sugar. Season with black pepper then whisk in the olive oil in a gradual trickle. Then whisk the vinaigrette into the tomato.

CHERRY TOMATO BASIL DRESSING

The perfect use for cherry tomatoes that have gone a bit too soft to eat raw.

- 15 cherry tomatoes, a mixture of orange and red is fine
- a pinch of sugar
- 15 basil leaves
- 4 drops Tabasco
- ½ tsp red wine vinegar
- salt and freshly ground black pepper
- 4 tbsp olive oil

Place all the ingredients, except the olive oil, in the bowl of a food-processor. Blitz, then pour through a sieve (or don't bother, as you wish), and whisk in the olive oil. Taste and adjust the seasoning.

ROAST TOMATO VINAIGRETTE

A gorgeous dressing: good with leeks, green beans and cauliflower.

- 6 pieces roast tomato (see page 33)
- ½ tbsp balsamic vinegar
- salt and freshly ground black pepper
- a little sugar
- 4 tbsp olive oil

Scrape the tomatoes through a sieve. Season the pulp with vinegar, salt and pepper and sugar to taste, then whisk in the olive oil.

HOT TOMATO VINAIGRETTE

SERVES 6

An idea sighted on several fashionable menus. Instead of blitzing fresh tomatoes and mixing them with all the usual ingredients for vinaigrette, the tomatoes are cooked in olive oil then seasoned with wine vinegar and whisked with more olive oil. Try it with cauliflower, fresh and dried beans, with poached fish and chicken. Vary the flavours with different herbs.

- 100 ml olive oil
- 750 g very ripe tomatoes, roughly chopped
- 4 mi-cuit tomatoes (see page 21) or 1 tbsp sun-dried tomato puree
- 12 tarragon leaves
- 2 sprigs of flat-leaf parsley
- 1 tsp runny honey
- ½ tsp salt
- freshly ground black pepper
- 1 tbsp red wine vinegar
- a squeeze of lemon juice

Heat 3 tablespoons of the olive oil in a pan. Add both sorts of tomatoes and cook over a high heat for 4 minutes. Add the tarragon, parsley, honey, salt and plenty of pepper. Return to the boil, then reduce the heat and add the vinegar. Return to the boil again and simmer for 15 minutes. Pass through a sieve into a clean pan. Return to a simmer and add the olive oil in a trickle, giving it a good whisk as you pour. Taste and adjust the seasoning with salt, pepper and lemon juice.

ANDALUSIAN SALAD

SERVES 8

This recipe comes from Janet Mendel's *Traditional Spanish Cooking*. The highly seasoned tomato dressing goes well with cooked vegetables such as potatoes, green beans, cauliflower and artichokes, but here is matched with the Spanish equivalent of Salade Niçoise.

FOR THE SALAD DRESSING

- 450 g ripe tomatoes, cored, peeled and seeded
- 2 garlic cloves, peeled
- 1-2 tsp paprika
- 1 tsp ground cumin
- salt
- 100 ml olive oil
- 100 ml wine vinegar

FOR THE SALAD

- 2 heads endive or lettuce
- 2 hard-boiled eggs, sliced
- 2 spring onions, sliced
- 100 g Serrano ham, cut into strips
- 50 g green or black olives

In a blender or food-processor, puree the tomatoes, garlic, paprika, cumin and one teaspoon of salt. With the motor running, add the oil and vinegar.

Tear the endive or lettuce into pieces and toss with some of the dressing. Arrange on a platter and top with the eggs, onions, strips of ham and olives. Spoon the remaining dressing over the top.

TOMATO AND BLOOD ORANGE DRESSING

SERVES 4

I saw the Scottish TV chef Nick Nairn make this neat little sauce on his BBC television series called *Island Harvest*. Quick and simple, it is an unusual accompaniment to simply cooked fish. He teamed it with steamed cod served on wilted spinach but it goes with green bean and other salads.

- 225 g cherry tomatoes
- juice from 1 small blood orange
- 2 tbsp olive oil

Blitz the tomatoes with the orange juice until liquidized. Pass through a fine sieve to catch pips and skin, then whisk in the olive oil. Warm to blood temperature before serving.

LEMON AND TOMATO DRESSING

SERVES 4

Tomato and citrus juices go well together, and here segments of lemon and diced tomatoes are warmed through in olive oil until the juices begin to run and are then mixed with more olive oil and shredded fresh coriander. It is one of those mixtures that falls between all camps and is neither a salad nor a salsa and isn't a dressing in the usual sense of the word. It goes very well with simply boiled new potatoes or lightly cooked young zucchini and I like it with lamb kebabs. It was devised by Gary Rhodes to go with quickly fried spicy tuna. The entire recipe is in his book *Fabulous Food* from his BBC TV series.

8 plum tomatoes, cored, peeled and seeded

2 lemons, peeled and segmented

4 tbsp olive oil

salt and freshly ground black pepper

1 tbsp coriander leaves, shredded

Cut the tomato flesh into 1cm dice. Thinly slice the lemon segments. Warm 2 tablespoons of the olive oil and add the tomatoes and lemon. Season with salt and pepper and warm through, allowing the tomatoes to just soften. Add the remaining olive oil with the shredded coriander.

TOMATO AND BASIL VINAIGRETTE

SERVES 4

An elegant derivation of Sauce Vierge (see page 333), which works well with lettuce and other green salad, green beans, courgettes, new potatoes and poached fish or poultry. A spicy version, Spicy Tomato Vinaigrette, is made by substituting ½ teaspoon of red chilli flakes or finely chopped fresh chilli for the garlic. This is particularly good with Tuna and Guacamole (see page 192) or Lentils in Wine and Tomato (see page 324).

- 4 very ripe plum tomatoes, cored and peeled
- ½ tbsp red wine vinegar
- 2 new-season garlic cloves, peeled and sliced wafer-thin
- salt and freshly ground black pepper
- 150 ml best-quality olive oil
- a handful of basil leaves

Place a sieve over a bowl. Halve the tomatoes and, working over the bowl, scrape the seeds into the sieve and press out the juice. Dice the flesh. Measure off 2 tablespoons of the clear tomato juice and pour it into a large bowl. Add the vinegar and garlic. Season generously with salt and pepper.

Stir the chopped tomatoes into the bowl and leave to macerate for 30 minutes. Stir in the olive oil, tear the basil over the dressing, stir again and serve.

Also see:
Roast Tomato Mayonnaise and Tomato Aïoli (page 149)
Clear Tomato Extract (page 433)
Sauce Vierge (page 333)

salsas

'They are eaten the same ways as eggplants, with pepper, salt, and oil, but give little and bad nourishment.'

Castore Durante, on the tomato in *Herbario Nuovo*, 1585

It is confusing that salsa is the Italian word for a sauce but also the name of a Latin American side dish of tomatoes that is neither sauce nor salad. It is best described as a fresh relish or chutney, and a fiery, sour one at that, because it is heavily laced with chilli and mixed with fresh lime juice. It should have a good balance of sweet-sour-hot-salt, and be all at once crunchy and soft.

Salsas began life in this book as an adjunct to salads. But as the number of crunchy little salsas, raw sauces, fresh chutneys, and relishes that are often lumped together under the name salsa began to grow, it was obvious that they needed their own section.

The perfect tomatoes for the recipes in this section are ripe and firm rather than ripe and squashy. Plum tomatoes, or another variety with a dense flesh that is juicy without being watery, would be ideal. Do not be tempted to make a salsa or fresh chutney with one of those hard, tasteless billiard-ball tomatoes, grown out of season in the UK. You must have *real* tomatoes for salsa.

TOMATO SALSA/SALSA CRUDA/ SALSA FRESCA

SERVES 4

Salsa Cruda is the real name of what has become known as tomato salsa but it is also called Salsa Fresca. In Mexican cooking, salsa is the staple garnish that accompanies just about everything. It is a simple combination of freshly chopped tomato, onion, chilli and coriander, all mixed together with a little lime juice. The proportion of tomato to the other ingredients is a matter of taste. This combination, to which I sometimes add garlic and mint for extra zing, is my favourite.

½ tsp sugar
salt and freshly ground black pepper
juice of 2 limes
6 plum tomatoes, cored, peeled and diced
2 small red onions, finely diced
2-3 new-season garlic cloves, finely chopped (optional)
3 tbsp chopped fresh coriander
1 tbsp chopped mint (optional)
2-3 green chillies, seeded and finely chopped

Dissolve the sugar and a generous pinch of salt in the lime juice. Toss with all the other ingredients. Season with black pepper, toss again and serve immediately.

TOMATO SALSA WITH AVOCADO AND WATERCRESS

SERVES 4

Quick and easy.

3 medium-sized squashy tomatoes (approximately 300 g)
salt and freshly ground black pepper
¼ tsp sugar
4 drips Tabasco or similar chilli sauce

Place the tomatoes in the bowl of a food-processor. Blitz briefly until they are coarsely chopped into a chunky, thick sauce. Do not over-process into a puree. Season with salt, pepper, sugar and Tabasco then turn into a bowl and stir.

Halve the avocado lengthways and twist apart. If using a large avocado, cover the half with the stone with clingfilm and store in the fridge. If using a small avocado, discard the

1 small, or ½ large, ripe avocado (tender to the squeeze)
a squeeze of lemon or lime juice
1 small red onion or shallot or 2 spring onions, finely chopped
a handful of watercress (approximately 50 g)

stone. Dice the avocado in the shell, then run the knife round the edge to loosen the flesh. Squeeze a little lemon or lime juice over the avocado to bathe it all over (it seasons as well as stopping it discolouring), then scrape it into the tomato together with the onion. Place the watercress in the food-processor. Blitz briefly until coarsely chopped and the stalks indistinguishable. Scrape the watercress into the tomato. Stir thoroughly, taste and adjust the seasoning.

BLOODY MARY SALSA

SERVES 4

A salsa with a different sort of kick: a deconstructed Bloody Mary. Serve with prawns fried with chopped garlic and fresh coriander.

2 beef tomatoes, cored, peeled, seeded and diced
2 shallots or 1 red onion, finely diced
25 ml (or more) vodka
1 dsp Worcestershire sauce
6 drops Tabasco or more to taste
a pinch of celery salt
½ tsp sugar
½ tbsp lemon juice
50 ml olive oil
50 g tomato concassé (see page 29), crushed
salt and freshly ground black pepper

Mix all the ingredients thoroughly and check the seasoning.

CHERRY PLUM TOMATO SALAD RELISH

SERVES 4-6

A salad-cum-relish-cum-salsa made with intensely flavoured little plum tomatoes. They are tossed in vinaigrette sweetened with tomato ketchup, with a good contrasting burst of acidity from the capers and the oily, metallic tang of coriander.

- 1 tbsp red wine vinegar
- salt and freshly ground black pepper
- 2 tbsp tomato ketchup
- 2 tbsp vegetable oil
- 1 heaped tbsp capers, squeezed and chopped
- 325 g baby plum tomatoes, halved
- 2 tbsp roughly chopped coriander leaves

Dissolve a decent pinch of salt in the vinegar. Season with pepper then stir in the ketchup. Whisk in the oil and add all the other ingredients. Toss.

FRESH TOMATO CHUTNEY

SERVES 6

Not really a chutney, more salsa-meets-sauce flavoured with fresh ginger and capers, enriched with olive oil.

- 50 ml olive oil
- 450 g tomato concassé (see page 29)
- 3 tbsp capers, rinsed and drained
- 2 tbsp finely chopped fresh ginger
- 2 garlic cloves, finely chopped

Heat a non-stick pan over a medium heat. Add the olive oil and the concassé and stir continuously until all the liquid evaporates – about 6 minutes, turning up the heat for the last minute.

Add the capers, ginger and garlic and cook for 1 more minute. Pour into a bowl and place in the freezer or over ice to chill quickly to room temperature. Bring to room temperature before serving.

SALSA ROSSA (RAW)

SERVES 6

Tomatoes, red pepper, red onions and a mass of fresh herbs are held in a lemon vinaigrette to make the red equivalent of Salsa Verde. Both are regarded as a relish-cum-fresh-sauce to perk up the flavours of bland foods, such as poached meat or fish, but both have a life beyond. I like it piled into toasted pitta bread with crusty lamb kebab and a dollop of Greek yoghurt; it's a great bruschetta topping and perfect for a barbecue or a cold spread.

- 3 red peppers
- 1 small red onion
- 400 g tiny plum tomatoes
- 200 ml olive oil
- 2 tbsp fresh lemon juice
- 30 g basil leaves, shredded
- 15 g mint leaves, finely shredded
- 15 g chives, finely sliced
- 15 g flat-leaf parsley, finely chopped
- salt and freshly ground black pepper

Pre-heat the grill to its highest. Cook the peppers, turning as their skins blister and blacken. Transfer to a plate, cover with clingfilm and leave for 20 minutes before removing the skin. Halve the peppers, discard the seeds and white filament, then chop them into small dice. Meanwhile, peel and finely chop the red onion and place in a large bowl. Quarter the tomatoes lengthways and chop them into dice. Beat the olive oil into the lemon juice, adding it gradually so that you end up with a thick, creamy dressing. Fold in all the other ingredients, season with salt and pepper and leave for 30 minutes before serving so that all the flavours can develop.

CREOSA SAUCE

SERVES 8-10

This recipe was first published in 1979 in *Cuisine of the Sun*, a book which has more recently been published as *Cuisine Provençale*. At the end a note from Roger Verge explains: 'I found this sauce in South America where it appears on every table, though in a much simpler version. This usually consists of diced tomato, onion and pepper in wine vinegar and is often very hot . . . This is an excellent sauce which is served – almost like a salad – with grilled or roasted beef and with all kinds of barbecued foods, including fish.' Creosa Sauce is most definitely based on salsa, thus making Vergé the first chef to realize the potential of the fresh little salad sauces with which we are now so familiar.

- 1 onion, approx 150 g, cut into tiny dice
- 3 tomatoes, approximately 400 g in total, cored, peeled, seeded and finely diced
- 1 small cucumber, approximately 200 g, peeled, seeded and finely diced
- 1 red pepper, approximately 150 g, seeds and white filament discarded, finely diced
- 100 g pickled gherkins, finely diced
- 100 g pickled capers, chopped
- 1 tsp chopped tarragon
- 50 g chopped flat-leaf parsley
- 200 ml olive oil
- 3 tbsp wine vinegar
- 4 tbsp Dijon mustard
- salt and freshly ground black pepper

Mix together all the ingredients in a bowl and season generously. Cover the bowl and keep in a cold place (not, Vergé says, in the fridge, but I don't know why) for 24 hours before serving.

INDIAN TOMATO RELISH WITH LEMON

SERVES 4

If you prefer, swap the onion, in this classic Indian relish, with cucumber. Serve with any Indian dish.

- 1 medium tomato, cored and chopped into 0.5 cm cubes
- 1 medium, sweet onion, finely chopped
- 1 tsp roasted cumin seeds, ground to powder
- 1½ tbsp lemon or lime juice
- a generous pinch of cayenne pepper

Mix all the ingredients except the cayenne pepper in a serving bowl. Cover and chill for 30 minutes. Toss, then sprinkle with the cayenne.

POMODORO E CIPOLLA CHUTNEY

SERVES 4

This chutney must be eaten within three or four days of making it. The recipe is a little gem from Franco Taruschio when he was cooking at the Walnut Tree and appears in his book *Bruschetta, Crostoni and Crostini* (Pavilion, 1995).

- 100 g semi-ripe tomatoes, cored, peeled, halved and seeded
- 100 g small red onions, peeled
- 2 tbsp red wine vinegar
- 50 g sugar

Slice the tomatoes into 8 sections. Cut each onion into 8 sections, Place the onions in a bowl and cover with boiling water. Leave for 5 minutes, then drain and shake dry.

Meanwhile, pour 1 tablespoon of the vinegar into a small pan over a medium-low heat and add the sugar, shaking the pan as the sugar dissolves. Toss the tomato and onion in the caramel, reduce the caramel by half, then add the remaining vinegar and reduce to a syrup.

SALSAS

GUACAMOLE

SERVES 4

The sweet acidity of tomato goes well with the rich oiliness of avocado. The combination, pointed up by chilli, lime juice and onion, is at its most beguiling in guacamole, the Mexican sauce-cum-relish-cum-dip. There are as many recipes as there are cooks for guacamole. My favourite includes fresh coriander and a hint of onion. The final texture is a matter of taste. Some people like to puree the avocado and fold all the other ingredients into it. Others prefer a chunkier mixture with lumps of avocado as well as puree. I like it somewhere in between but it all depends on the state of the avocados. It is best made and eaten straight away but will keep for a few hours without spoiling when covered with clingfilm and stored in the fridge. If the top does go brown, stir it in because it will do no harm.

Eat guacamole scooped up with tortilla chips, but remember it, too, as part of a mezze selection with hummus, tzatziki and Grilled Tomato Salad (page 164). It goes particularly well with char-grilled tuna steaks, ceviche of salmon and poached and barbecued chicken, and is a great dip for chunky chips and par-boiled, deep-fried small new potatoes.

- 2 large or 4 small tender avocados
- 3 medium plum tomatoes, cored, peeled, seeded and diced
- 1 small red onion, very finely chopped
- 1 chilli pepper, seeded and finely diced
- 1 tbsp chopped coriander
- juice of 2-3 limes or 1 large lemon
- salt and freshly ground black pepper

Cut the avocados in half lengthways, winkle out the stone and use a fork to mash the flesh into its shell. Scoop out with a spoon and transfer to a bowl, mashing further if you think it's necessary. Mix in all the other ingredients, seasoning well with salt and pepper.

Also see:
Sugocasa Salad with Basil (page 173)
Dealing With a Glut (pages 392-406)
Tomato Compote (page 207)

tomatoes with other vegetables

'Out in the big open spaces, in a glory of golden light, were piled tons of grapes, peaches, melons, pumpkins, gourds, glowing heaps of scarlet and orange tomatoes, shiny paprikas (peppers), yellow, green and red, black purple patajans (aubergines), long green bamias, cabbage, lettuces, beans, in Arabian Nights profusion.'

M. Edith Durham, *High Albania*, 1909

Tomatoes and aubergines, tomatoes and onions, tomatoes and red peppers, tomatoes and chillies, tomatoes and courgettes, tomatoes and beans, tomatoes and potatoes . . . The list goes on and on, endlessly, because there is hardly a vegetable that *doesn't* go with tomatoes. And there are so many different ways that all these vegetables marry up with tomatoes. Many, particularly courgettes, aubergine, okra, fennel and potatoes, combine with tomato to make marvellous gratins. These can be made by alternating layers of vegetable and tomato or interleaving slices, arranging them in much the same way as you would the apple in a French apple tart. Sometimes, the tomato element is in the form of a sauce. A few breadcrumbs sprinkled over the top to soak up the juices and a crusty topping unify the dish.

The compote of tomato, with, say, red peppers, onions, or both, is found in all the tomato-growing countries. Sometimes eggs are added, or ham, and other Mediterranean vegetables too, to make well-known dishes such as Basque Piperade, Provençale Ratatouille and Ciambotta. Tomatoes with chillies and onion make a ubiquitous trinity that can be fine-tuned to create a wide range of subtly different flavours, a balance of taste rooted in sour, sweet and hot. When cooked with, or added to, bland vegetable dishes, the trinity enhances rather than overwhelms.

Apart from these popular combinations, there are less obvious recipes. The sweetness of beetroot, for example, is well matched by the acidity of tomato and their combined flavours are offset to great effect with a hint of cumin and turmeric. Okra, often disliked because of the slimy juices it weeps when cut, is also marvellous stewed with tomato: one of the most stunning dishes, Bamia Marsousa, from Egypt, presents okra layered with tomato in a circular 'pie'. Another spectacular and unexpected combination occurs in Michel Guérard's spinach and tomato 'tart': a thick coulis is spooned into a case of spinach and briefly baked until it sets and stiffens.

BISTE AND BOHÉMIENNE

SERVES 4

Biste and Bohémienne, or Boumiano, as the dish is also known in the Vaucluse dialect, are old Provençal names for an aubergine and tomato stew-cum-puree in the ratatouille tradition. Biste is the purest version, made with equal quantities of aubergine and tomato, flavoured with garlic and marjoram. Bohémienne, which is closer to ratatouille, is made with onion too, and the vegetables are cooked into a coarse puree before they are mixed with anchovy fillets fried in olive oil. Both stews can be served hot, tepid or cold, and may have breadcrumbs scattered over the top to make a gratin. Most often, however, they are served as a starter or appetizer on bruschetta or a garlic croûte, or served as a vegetable garnish.

In Italy, a similar stew of aubergine and tomatoes, also cooked in olive oil and flavoured with garlic, is called Pomodori e Melanzane. To make it, cut 4 aubergines into cubes, disgorge them with salt for 30 minutes, then fry the dried cubes in 2 tablespoons of oil until brown all over. Add the aubergine to 800 g of canned tomatoes that have been stewed in garlicky olive oil for about 40 minutes. Finally, stir in a handful of chopped basil leaves, season and serve cold.

To make Tomato and Aubergine Confit, begin by softening a large finely sliced onion, then add 3 crushed and peeled garlic cloves and 1 kg of cubed or sliced unpeeled aubergine, which has been disgorged for about 30 minutes. Season and cook until the aubergine is beginning to soften, then add 1 kg of peeled, seeded and chopped tomatoes and bouquet garni. Turn up the heat and simmer for about 1 hour until the stew is thick.

BISTE

- 1 kg aubergines
- salt and freshly ground black pepper
- 6 tbsp olive oil
- 2 tbsp vegetable oil
- 4 garlic cloves, chopped
- 1 kg plum tomatoes, cored, peeled, seeded and chopped
- ½ tbsp marjoram or oregano leaves

Cut the aubergine lengthways in slices about 1 cm thick. Sprinkle the slices with a little salt on both sides and lay them in a colander to drain for at least 30 minutes.

Rinse the aubergines and pat dry. Mix together 2 tablespoons of olive oil and the 2 tablespoons of vegetable oil. Lightly smear the aubergine slices on both sides. They can be cooked either on a ridged, cast-iron griddle or in a pre-heated oven at 375°F/190°C/gas mark 5. If using a griddle, get it very hot, then lay out the oiled slices, pressing them down so they cook evenly. Cook for 2-3 minutes until the flesh begins to soften, then turn and cook the other side. If using the oven, lay out the slices on a baking sheet and cook for 10 minutes in total, turning the slices so that they cook evenly.

Meanwhile, heat the remaining olive oil in a large pan. Stir in the garlic, and before it has a chance to brown add the tomatoes and marjoram. Season with salt and pepper, and simmer uncovered while the aubergine cooks. When all the slices are soft, chop them and stir them into the tomatoes. Stew for 30 minutes, taste and adjust the seasoning before serving hot, tepid or cold.

BOHÉMIENNE

- 6 tbsp olive oil
- 1 large onion, peeled, halved and finely sliced
- 3 garlic cloves, peeled and crushed
- 1 kg aubergine, trimmed and peeled
- 1 kg tomatoes, cored, scalded, seeded and coarsely chopped
- salt and freshly ground black pepper
- 6 anchovy fillets from a tin

Warm 4 tablespoons of olive oil in a large pan and add the onion. Cook over a low heat, stirring regularly, until softened but uncoloured. Cut the peeled aubergine into 1 cm thick slices.

Add the garlic and aubergine to the onion and cook until softened, stirring frequently. Add the tomatoes, turn up the heat, then stir as they begin to break up and the mixture boils. Reduce the heat to establish a steady simmer and cook, uncovered, for about 1 hour. Stir regularly, breaking up the mixture as it softens, to create a thick, uneven puree. Towards the end, when almost all the liquid in the tomatoes has evaporated, stir constantly to avoid sticking.

Heat the remaining 2 tablespoons of oil in a small pan and lay out the anchovy fillets. Cook over a very low heat until they disintegrate then stir the anchovies and their oil into the tomato and aubergine puree. Taste and season with salt, if needed, and plenty of pepper. Transfer to a bowl and leave, uncovered, to cool completely before covering and refrigerating.

CIAMBOTTA WITH ROASTED VINE TOMATOES AND BASIL

SERVES 4

Ciambotta is a variation on ratatouille when red pepper, onion, new potatoes, courgettes and tomatoes are all cut differently, cooked separately then mixed together. It's a very satisfying dish to make because as each vegetable is cooked, it is piled into a bowl and a sort of osmosis of flavours occurs. Right at the end, everything is tossed together and covered with a carpet of shredded basil or mint leaves, which wilt slightly in the remains of the heat.

It is at its best eaten lukewarm when the flavours intensify and the juices run to make a wonderful 'vinaigrette'. It's a great partner to a slab of crumbly feta cheese and a few black olives, and a good companion to barbecued fish or meat, or roast chicken. Another way of serving it is to cover individual portions with slices of a creamy soft cheese such as taleggio or mozzarella and whack it into a very hot oven or under the grill for a few minutes until the cheese melts, blisters and runs into the vegetables. This also works well with grated Cheddar.

- 250 g vine-ripened small tomatoes, stalks removed
- 6 tbsp olive oil
- 1 flourishing sprig of rosemary or 2 sprigs of thyme
- sea salt and freshly ground black pepper
- 3 red peppers (approximately 400 g)
- 2 medium red onions (approximately 400 g), peeled, halved and sliced in wedges
- 2 garlic cloves, preferably new season, peeled and thinly sliced in rounds
- 1 large aubergine (approximately 350 g), trimmed, quartered lengthways and thickly sliced
- 3 medium courgettes (approximately 300 g), trimmed and diagonally sliced, 2 cm thick
- 300 g new potatoes, peeled and boiled
- lemon olive oil for serving, if possible
- 1 heaped tbsp shredded basil or young mint leaves

Pre-heat the oven to 425°F/220°C/gas mark 7.

Place the tomatoes in a bowl and toss with ½ tablespoon of olive oil. Tip them on to a foil-lined baking sheet, season with salt and pepper and lay the rosemary on top. Arrange the peppers on a second foil-lined sheet.

By now the oven will be ready. Place the peppers on the top shelf. After 10 minutes, when the skin will be blackening, turn them, and after 5 more minutes, turn again. Put the tomatoes in the oven on a lower shelf. Cook for 10 minutes. Take out the peppers. Transfer to a plate, cover with clingfilm and leave for 20 minuts before removing the skin. Peel away the pepper skin and, following the natural lines of the pepper, cut them into chunks, discarding core and pips. Slice into strips and place in a serving bowl.

Fry the onions in 1 tablespoon of oil over a medium-high flame. After 15 minutes, when the onions will have wilted and browned in places, add the garlic and season with salt. Cook for a couple more minutes and add to the bowl. Toss the aubergines in 2 tablespoons of olive oil and fry until brown on the surface and tender within. Allow 5 minutes for this. Tip into the bowl. Use 1 tablespoon of oil to fry the courgettes until the surfaces are brown and crusted but the inside remains al dente. Use the last of the oil to briefly fry the potatoes until the edges are crusty. Mix everything together, seasoning with salt and plenty of pepper. Tip the tomatoes over the top, douse with 1 tablespoon of lemon olive oil, if using, gently mix in then sprinkle over the basil or mint.

CREOLE SAUCE

SERVES 4-6

Creole Sauce is a highly seasoned tomato and onion stew, which goes with everything. It is regarded as the backbone of Mauritian cooking and varies from cook to cook but is always chilli-hot. What makes it special is that the onions are cooked until they are sweet and succulent and the tomatoes, ginger, garlic and chillies, which are added later, only get a brief stewing. Like ratatouille, which it resembles, Creole Sauce is good hot or cold and the flavours improve if it is made twenty-four hours in advance. Serve it with pasta, rice, kebabs, grilled meat and fish from the barbecue.

4 tbsp olive oil

3 Spanish onions, halved and sliced

1 bunch spring onions, sliced

2 red peppers, seeded, white filament removed, and sliced into strips

1 red chilli pepper, trimmed and finely chopped

3 plump garlic cloves, crushed to a paste with 1/4 tsp salt

2 tbsp grated fresh ginger

2 sprigs of thyme

1 heaped tbsp chopped flat-leaf parsley leaves

2 heaped tbsp chopped coriander leaves

salt and freshly ground black pepper

750 g ripe tomatoes, cored, peeled and cut into 6

Gently heat the oil in a spacious pan. Stir in the onions and cook until soft and juicy but uncoloured. Allow about 30 minutes for this.

Add the spring onions, peppers and chilli to the pan. Raise the heat slightly and cook briskly for 3 minutes. Stir in the garlic, ginger, thyme, parsley and half the coriander. Season with salt and pepper, add the tomatoes and cook for a further 5 minutes. Allow to cool (or not), garnish with the reserved coriander and serve.

PEPERONATA

SERVES 4

A soft, gooey stew of red pepper, onion and tomato, seasoned with garlic and a little wine vinegar. In this version, I've used balsamic vinegar to give a richer, rounder flavour. To get the almost jam-like texture you're after, with the strips of pepper the only discernible shape, the onion must cook until it is sloppy before you add the peppers. They in turn must partially cook before the tomatoes are added. Peperonata is at its best eaten lukewarm with a splash of your finest olive oil. A good convenience version is made by draining and slicing a tin of whole pimientos and adding them with a tin of chopped Italian tomatoes to a sliced red onion and a garlic clove softened in olive oil. The flavours are fine-tuned with a splash of wine vinegar and a spoonful of honey.

- 1 large Spanish onion, chopped
- 5 tbsp olive oil
- salt and freshly ground black pepper
- 4 red peppers or 2 red and 2 yellow
- 2 cloves garlic, sliced in wafer-thin rounds
- 900 g large plum tomatoes, cored, peeled, seeded and chopped
- 1 tbsp balsamic vinegar

Choose a spacious heavy-bottomed pan and cook the onion in the olive oil with a little salt over a gentle heat, cooking until very soft.

Meanwhile, use a potato peeler to remove the skin from the peppers. Don't be too meticulous about this. Discard seeds and white membrane, then slice the peppers into strips. Add them and the garlic to the onions. Season lightly with salt and pepper, reduce the heat slightly, cover the pan and cook for several minutes, giving the occasional stir. Add the tomatoes and balsamic vinegar and leave to cook uncovered for 45 minutes or until the tomatoes and onions have cooked into a thick, creamy, jammy sauce and the strips of pepper are very soft. Check the seasoning. Allow to cool before serving.

SHOUCOUKA

SERVES 4

This is a North African appetizer, eaten cold scooped up with toasted pitta bread. The idea is to cook tomatoes with garlic and chilli until very thick so that when cold the mixture will set (thanks to the pectin in the tomato pips) like jam. Then, squares of slippery, soft-cooked red and yellow peppers are mixed in. You sometimes see it on the menu in Tunisia as Marmouma. It is often seasoned with caraway and served with lemon wedges to squeeze over the top.

- 3 red peppers or 2 red and 1 yellow
- 2 plump garlic cloves, finely chopped
- 3 tbsp olive oil
- 500 g very ripe plum tomatoes, cored, peeled and chopped
- 1 tsp sugar
- ½ tsp paprika
- a pinch of ground chilli, or more to taste
- salt

Pre-heat the overhead grill. Lay out the peppers and cook, turning as necessary, until blackened all over. Transfer to a plate, cover with clingfilm and leave for 20 minutes before removing the skin. Discard the seeds and white filament, then cut into dice, saving the juice from inside the peppers.

Meanwhile, gently cook the garlic in the olive oil until aromatic. Add the tomatoes, sugar, paprika and chilli. Season with salt and cook gently, uncovered, for about 45 minutes until thick and jam-like. Taste and adjust the seasoning, adding more chilli if liked. Add the diced red pepper and juices. Serve cold.

SOFRITO

MAKES APPROXIMATELY 570 ML

Sometimes called *Sofregit*, *Soffritto* in Italy and *Refogado* in Portugal, this is a slowly cooked stew of mild, sweet Spanish onions with tomatoes and garlic, perhaps with chillies and other aromatics. It is a hallmark of Catalan cooking and is made up in batches to be kept in the fridge as a dressing for cooked dried beans, with rice or pasta, and as a starting-point for soups and stews. It is also the perfect dressing for blanched green beans or chunks of courgette. Sofrito recipes vary from cook to cook but the idea is to end up with a rich, thick puree. When okra are added the dish becomes Bamia.

A Mexican version is made by roasting the tomatoes, removing their skins and seeds, and cooking them quickly in a little oil over a very high heat with half as much pureed raw onion. This makes a concentrated tomato-onion jam that is a surprisingly exquisite seasoning for refried beans – simply heat the two together and serve.

- 100 ml olive oil
- 900 g Spanish onions, peeled and finely chopped
- 2 plump garlic cloves, peeled and chopped
- 750 g ripe tomatoes, cored, peeled, seeded and chopped
- salt and freshly ground black pepper

Heat the olive oil in a large, heavy-bottomed pan. Add the onions and cook, stirring every now and again, on the lowest heat.

When the onions have softened and turned a reddish brown – after about 1 hour – turn up the heat and add the garlic. Cook for 1 minute, then add the tomatoes and a generous seasoning of salt and pepper. Simmer at a steady pace until all the water in the tomato evaporates and you are left with a rich, thick puree.

SUMMER TOMATO STEW WITH GREMOLATA

SERVES 4

Just-dug new potatoes, skinny green beans, juicy onions and leaf spinach, held in a lightly cooked partial stew of ripe tomatoes, are perked up by a last-minute seasoning of gremolata, an aromatic mixture of finely chopped parsley, lemon zest and garlic. Serve it in a bowl to spoon like soup or as an accompaniment with simply cooked fish. It is good hot, warm or cold.

- 40 g butter
- 2 bunches spring/salad onions, finely sliced, including tender green parts
- 450 g small new potatoes, scraped
- 5 cm strip lemon zest
- 150 ml vegetable stock
- salt and freshly ground black pepper
- 200 g fine green beans, cut in half
- 750 g ripe plum tomatoes, cored, peeled, quartered lengthways then halved
- ½ tbsp sugar
- 200 g young spinach leaves

FOR THE GREMOLATA

- zest (no pith) from 1 large unwaxed lemon, chopped
- 2 plump garlic cloves, peeled and chopped
- 20 g flat-leaf parsley leaves, chopped

Melt the butter in a spacious heavy-bottomed pan and stir in the onion. Cook gently for several minutes until it is beginning to soften. Add the potatoes, the lemon zest, the stock and a generous seasoning of salt and pepper. Bring to the boil, establish a steady simmer and cover the pan. Cook for about 10 minutes until the potatoes are tender.

Meanwhile, drop the beans into a large pan of vigorously boiling salted water. Cook for 1 minute, drain and hold the colander under cold water for a few seconds to arrest cooking. When the potatoes are ready, remove the lid and add the tomatoes and sugar. Cook uncovered for several minutes until the tomatoes turn juicy and soften. Stir the spinach into the tomatoes and when, after a couple of minutes, it begins to flop, stir in the beans. Taste and adjust the seasoning with salt and pepper.

Make the gremolata by chopping together the chopped lemon zest, garlic and parsley. Stir half of it into the stew. Transfer the stew to a serving bowl. Scatter the remaining gremolata over the top and serve.

LEEK NIÇOISE

SERVES 4

This dish looks spectacular when made with whole, slim leeks. It is a classic combination: leeks in a chunky, garlicky tomato sauce garnished with flat-leaf parsley, which pops up throughout the Mediterranean. Everything is cooked in one dish so that the leeks actually braise in the tomato juices and are thus imbued with their flavour. Leek Niçoise is best eaten lukewarm. It is also very good made with coriander or mint instead of the parsley.

- 4 tbsp olive oil
- 1 medium onion, peeled and finely chopped
- 8 slim young leeks, trimmed and washed
- salt and freshly ground black pepper
- 2 garlic cloves, finely chopped
- 500 g tomatoes, cored, peeled, seeded and chopped
- 2 tbsp chopped flat-leaf parsley
- lemon juice

Warm the oil in a heavy pan large enough to hold the leeks in one layer. Add the onion to the pan and cook gently until it softens and begins to colour. Lay the leeks among the onions, add a little salt and cook gently, turning so that the leeks cook evenly, for about 10 minutes. Add the garlic and tomatoes, a little more salt and some pepper, then cover the dish and simmer gently for about 10 minutes until the leeks are tender to the point of a sharp knife.

Carefully lift the leeks to a serving platter. Return the pan to the heat and boil hard to reduce the sauce slightly. Stir in most of the parsley and adjust the flavours with lemon juice. Check the seasoning. Pour the sauce over the leeks, leave until lukewarm, sprinkle with the remaining parsley and serve.

POTATOES WITH ROAST TOMATO SAUCE, FETA AND MINT

SERVES 2-4

In Morocco, they are keen on adding fruit to their stews, or tagines. Tomatoes – which, after all, are a fruit – are often cooked with honey, sometimes with sultanas too, and scented with saffron. This combination might provide the sauce for fish or vegetables but when it is sieved and simmered until very thick, it makes the most heavenly relish. I was served a dollop of it on top of a classy beef tagine at La Gazelle D'Or, the Manoir aux Quat' Saisons of Taroudant. They make it, if I understood the waiter correctly, by roasting their wonderfully flavoured green-shouldered tomatoes with a smear of honey, and that is where I got the idea for this sauce, which turns simply boiled potatoes into an elegant supper.

It goes very well with scrambled egg, stirred with a mound of silky caramelized onion.

- 500 g small waxy potatoes such as scraped Jersey Royals, Charlotte, Pink Fir Apple, Anya, Cornichon or La Ratte
- salt and black pepper
- 4 plump garlic cloves
- 6 large tomatoes, halved
- 1 tsp olive oil
- ½ tbsp runny honey
- a small pinch of saffron stamens
- a squeeze of lemon juice
- Tabasco to taste
- 100 g feta cheese, diced small
- a handful of mint leaves, shredded

Pre-heat the oven to 325°F/170°C/gas mark 3.

Cook the potatoes in plenty of boiling salted water until tender. Drain. Return to the pan with cold water to cover and leave for about a minute. Drain again and whip off their skins.

Meanwhile, smack the garlic cloves with your fist or the flat of a knife until you hear the cloves crack. Smear the cut surface of the tomatoes with a little olive oil. Place them on a baking tray lined with cooking foil and season with salt and pepper. Dribble a little honey over the top of each. Pop the garlic between the tomatoes in the middle of the tray and cook for 20 minutes. Place the tray near the bottom of the oven and cook for a further 30 minutes. Remove the tray from the oven and leave the tomatoes to cool slightly.

Place the saffron in an egg-cup and cover with a splash of boiling water. Using a spoon, scrape the flesh off the tomato skins. Squeeze the garlic flesh out of its skin. Tip the tomato flesh and garlic into a blender and briefly blitz. Place a sieve over a medium saucepan and force the puree through with the back of a spoon. Add the saffron liquid and a squeeze of lemon juice. Taste and adjust the flavours with salt, pepper, and a drop or two of Tabasco.

Add the potatoes and warm them through. Just before serving stir in the feta and mint.

PATATAS BRAVAS

SERVES 4 AS A SIDE DISH, 8 AS A TAPA

'*Bravas*' means fierce, which these potatoes are, with the chilli-hot tomato sauce. They are deep-fried first – either cut into cubes or chunkier pieces – and the gorgeous sauce is spooned over the top. You might describe it as the Spanish version of chips and tomato ketchup. Anyway, Patatas Bravas, named after *toro bravo*, the fighting bull, is to be found on every tapas menu. Great though it is as a nibble (often served cold – and particularly good with the sauce cold, the potatoes hot), it makes an excellent accompaniment to simply cooked fish or meat. A scoop of sour cream or Greek yoghurt, with a few chives to pretty it up, will soothe the palate. This recipe comes from *Traditional Spanish Cooking* by Janet Mendel.

175 ml Salsa di Pomodoro (see page 236)

2 tbsp olive oil

1 clove garlic, crushed

1 tbsp wine or sherry vinegar

1 tsp paprika olive

½ tsp ground cumin

¼ tsp ground oregano

cayenne or dried chilli flakes, to taste

salt

500 g potatoes, peeled

olive oil for frying

Combine the tomato sauce, olive oil, garlic, vinegar, paprika, cumin, oregano and enough cayenne or chilli flakes to make the sauce 'fierce'. Add salt if necessary.

Cut the potatoes into cubes, chunks or chips of your desired thickness. Rinse, drain and pat them dry. Deep-fry them in hot oil until brown and tender, then drain on absorbent kitchen paper and sprinkle with salt. Serve with the sauce spooned over the top.

STEWED BEETROOT WITH LEMON TOMATOES

SERVES 6

Serve hot, lukewarm or cold, when it is very god stirred with 50 g chopped coriander.

- 5 or 6 medium beetroot, approximately 750 g
- salt and freshly ground black pepper
- zest and juice of 1 small lemon
- 2 tbsp vegetable oil
- ½ tsp cumin seeds
- ½ tsp dried red chilli flakes
- 1 red onion, peeled and finely sliced
- 750 g tomatoes, cored, peeled and chopped

Rinse the beetroot to remove any mud, without scratching the skin. Place in a suitable saucepan, add 1 teaspoon of salt and cover with water. Bring to the boil, partially cover the pan and cook at a brisk simmer for 30 minutes. Drain, and when cool enough to handle, trim the beetroot and peel. (To avoid staining hands, wear rubber gloves.) Cut into dice the size of a sugar lump.

Meanwhile, remove the zest from half the lemon and shred it finely. Heat the oil in a medium-sized saucepan over a medium flame. Stir the cumin seeds and chilli flakes into the hot oil then add the onion. Cook, stirring frequently, until the onion is tender, then add the lemon zest, tomatoes and lemon juice. Season with salt and pepper and cook uncovered for 15 minutes. When the beetroot is ready, add it to the pan and cook, partially covered, for about 20 minutes until the flavours have merged and the stew is thick. Taste and adjust the seasoning.

GREEN BEANS WITH CHERRY TOMATO COMPOTE

SERVES 6

Greek Stewed Beans are made by stewing onion and garlic in olive oil until both are very tender, then placing topped and tailed beans on top and covering the beans with tomatoes mixed with masses of parsley. Sometimes oregano or cumin are added. If whole baby onions are added, the dish becomes French Beans Provençale. My own favourite way of combining beans with tomatoes is to choose the youngest, smallest beans, cook them very quickly in plenty of salted boiling water and dress them with tomatoes. If the tomatoes are particularly ripe and luscious, they are peeled, diced and left raw. At other times I make a little tomato stew with onions and garlic. This version, when tasty little tomatoes are briefly fried until their juices run into soft shallot and garlic, then mixed with herbs, is a merging of both.

- 3 shallots, peeled and finely chopped
- 1 garlic clove, peeled and finely chopped
- 2 tbsp olive oil
- 450 g cherry tomatoes
- 1 tsp finely snipped chives
- ½ tsp finely chopped tarragon
- salt and freshly ground black pepper
- 450 g very fine French beans, topped but not tailed

Soften the shallots and garlic in the olive oil in a small pan without browning. Add the tomatoes, increase the heat and sauté for 3-4 minutes until the skins begin to split. Stir in the herbs, and season to taste.

Meanwhile, bring a large pan of salted water to the boil. When it is boiling vigorously, drop in the beans. Bring back to the boil, boil hard for 1 minute. Drain, arrange on a warm serving plate and spoon the tomato compote over the top.

RATATOUILLE

SERVES 6

I learned from Michel Guérard's book *Cuisine Minceur* how to make ratatouille in the oven. Each vegetable is initially fried separately and briefly in a little olive oil, then everything is mixed together, poured into a suitable oven dish, covered and baked. I have also adopted his way of slicing the vegetables thinly and taking the trouble to peel the tomatoes. The result is perfection every time, vegetables that keep their shape and identity yet merge together almost like a vegetable terrine. There is none of the watery slop that so often spoils this dish, and when left overnight for the flavours to develop, it is extraordinarily good. In fact, I think I prefer ratatouille cold; try it thus, with eggs poached in red wine or with hot roast chicken.

- 6 tbsp olive oil
- 1 large onion, peeled , quartered and thinly sliced
- 4 garlic cloves, very finely chopped
- 1 large red pepper, quartered lengthways, seeded and finely sliced
- 1 medium aubergine, trimmed, quartered lengthways and finely sliced
- 3 medium courgettes, trimmed and finely sliced
- 8 ripe tomatoes, cored, peeled, seeded and cut into 8 pieces
- salt and freshly ground black pepper
- 1 bay leaf
- 3 sprigs of fresh thyme
- 12 basil leaves, torn
- 1 level tsp crushed coriander seeds

Pre-heat the oven to 400°F/200°C/gas mark 6.

Heat half the olive oil in a large frying-pan and brown the onion; adding the garlic after a couple of minutes. Add the red pepper and allow it to wilt slightly. Remove from the pan to a roomy mixing-bowl.

Meanwhile, place the aubergine in a bowl and sprinkle over half the remaining olive oil. Use your hands to smear the slices thoroughly. Add to the pan, fry quickly and briefly until coloured then transfer to the bowl along with the other vegetables. Using the last of the olive oil, repeat the smearing business with the courgettes and cook in the same way as the aubergines, then add them to the other vegetables. Finally, give the tomatoes a quick fry so that they collapse slightly, and put them into the mixing-bowl.

Season generously with salt and pepper and, using your hands, mix everything carefully together.

Put the mixture into a shallow earthenware baking-dish. Lay the bay leaf and thyme over the top and cover with a lid or foil. Bake for 40 to 45 minutes. Remove from the oven, poke in the basil and coriander seeds, cover once more, and allow to stand for 15 minutes before serving.

FRESH TOMATO TARTS WITH THYME

SERVES 6

More gourmet health food from Michel Guérard's *Cuisine Minceur*. Serve as an appetizer or to accompany roast lamb.

500 g tomato coulis (see page 242), made with 1.5 kg tomatoes

300 g organic (large leaf) spinach, stalks removed

5 small sprigs of thyme

Pre-heat the oven to 425°F/220°C/gas mark 7.

Bring a large pan of water to the boil. Briefly blanch the spinach in the boiling water. Spread the leaves carefully on a cloth to drain. Use them to line 6 ramekins, or small flan tins, leaving enough falling over the edges to cover the top.

Fill each dish or tart tin with tomato coulis, reserving 5 teaspoons for decoration. Fold the spinach 'jacket' over the top so that the tomato is no longer visible.

Bake for 15 minutes. Serve the tarts in their dishes, with a teaspoon of cooked tomato poured over each to give a pretty effect of contrasting red and green. Decorate each dish with a sprig of thyme.

AUBERGINE 'LASAGNE' WITH MINT

SERVES 2-3

Long, thin slices of aubergine become 'lasagne' when layered with a chunky tomato sauce and thick béchamel, the whole interleaved with a generous seasoning of fresh parsley and mint. The top is dredged with grated Parmesan and the dish briefly cooked in the oven for just long enough to heat everything through but not merge into a gooey mess. The idea is to keep the flavours of the layers distinct yet allow them to soften against each other.

This is not a dish that is intended to look neat and precise with all the ingredients fitting right up to the edges of the container. In fact, it is all the better for being haphazardly arranged so that the thick béchamel sauce drips down the sides of the stack like icing on a bun.

FOR THE TOMATO SAUCE

500 g medium-sized tomatoes, cored, peeled and roughly chopped

2 medium onions, grated

2 plump garlic cloves, chopped

1 tbsp tomato ketchup

salt and pepper

FOR THE BÉCHAMEL SAUCE

1 garlic clove

425 ml milk

6 black peppercorns

4 cloves

1 small onion, chopped

1 bay leaf

4 branches fresh thyme

40 g butter

2 heaped tbsp flour

4 tbsp thick cream

TO ASSEMBLE

3 tbsp chopped flat-leaf parsley

First, place all the tomato sauce ingredients in a pan, season with salt and pepper and cook at a vigorous simmer until thick and jam-like. This takes at least 15 minutes.

Make the béchamel sauce. Crack the garlic with your fist and place in a pan with the milk, peppercorns, cloves, onion, bay leaf, thyme, and a pinch of salt. Bring slowly to the boil, simmer for 5 minutes, then cover and turn off the heat. Leave for at least 10 minutes. Melt the butter in a pan, stir in the flour and when it is amalgamated, pour the milk through a sieve into the pan, whisking as it comes to the boil. Leave to simmer gently for 5 minutes, stir in the cream and cook for a further 5 minutes.

Meanwhile, sprinkle both sides of the aubergines with salt and leave in a colander for 30 minutes to disgorge. Rinse and pat dry. Lay out the slices and sprinkle with the olive oil; then, working quickly, smear it all over the slices. Heat a cast-iron grill-pan or heavy frying-pan over a medium heat and lay the slices in it, turning them after about 3 minutes to repeat on the other side. They should be tender but not overcooked. Drain on absorbent kitchen paper.

Smear a shallow ovenproof dish with a little olive oil and spread 2 tablespoons of the béchamel across the base. Repeat with the tomato and cover with slices of aubergine. Season generously with salt, pepper and a third of the herbs. Repeat this process twice, being more generous with the tomato and béchamel, but make sure that you reserve

1 tbsp chopped fresh mint
2 tbsp freshly grated Parmesan

FOR THE AUBERGINE 'LASAGNE'
2 plump aubergines, sliced lengthways 0.5 cm thick
4 tbsp olive oil

enough béchamel to cover the top. Sprinkle over the grated Parmesan and cook in a hot oven (400°F/200°C/gas mark 6) for 15-20 minutes until the top is blistered and bubbling but the layers are still defined.

MELANZANE ALLA PARMIGIANA

SERVES 4 AS A MAIN DISH, 6-8 AS A STARTER

Although made all over Italy, this classic dish of pre-cooked slices of aubergine, which sandwich tomato sauce, basil and oregano leaves with Parmesan, is thought to have originated in Sicily. Traditionally the aubergine is fried but the dish is less oily if they are cooked on a griddle or in the oven.

2 large aubergines
salt and freshly ground black pepper
approximately 4 tbsp olive oil
600 ml Tomato Sauce (see page 243)
handful of basil leaves
1 tsp dried oregano
75 g freshly grated Parmesan

Cut the aubergines lengthways into 0.5cm thick slices, sprinkle both sides with salt and leave in a colander for 30 minutes to disgorge. Rinse and pat dry. Lay out the slices and sprinkle over the olive oil; then, working quickly, smear it all over the slices. Don't be mingy about this but, equally, don't drench them. Heat a cast-iron grill-pan or heavy frying-pan over a medium heat and lay the slices in it, turning them after about 3 minutes to repeat on the other side; you want them tender but not overcooked. Drain them on absorbent kitchen paper.

Pre-heat the oven to 400°F/200°C/gas mark 6.

Choose a baking dish that can accommodate the aubergine slices in 3-4 layers. Spread a thin layer of tomato sauce on the base. Cover it with aubergine slices. Spread with a more generous layer of tomato sauce, season with salt, pepper, a third of the basil leaves, then sprinkle over a little oregano, and about a quarter of the Parmesan. Make two more layers, using the last of the tomato, basil and oregano, and finish with the rest of the Parmesan. Bake for 20 minutes, until browned and bubbling round the edges. Serve hot, tepid or cold.

PIZZELLE DI MELANZANE

SERVES 4

Big round aubergines are best for this dish. That is because fried slices of aubergine will be used as 'plates' for diced tomato and mozzarella. The constituent parts could be prepared in advance, the whole completed quickly to order. Serve as a snack or appetizer, as they used to do at the Walnut Tree at Abergavenny when Franco Taruschio reigned and where this recipe originated.

- **450 g plum or other fleshy tomatoes, cored, peeled, seeded and cut into small dice**
- **a generous pinch of dried oregano**
- **1 tbsp salted capers, thoroughly rinsed, or vinegar-preserved capers, squeezed dry and roughly chopped**
- **olive oil**
- **salt and freshly ground black pepper**
- **12 x 1.5 cm thick slices cut from plump round aubergines**
- **200 g mozzarella, diced**
- **12 black olives, stoned and halved**

Place the diced tomato in a bowl, sprinkle over the oregano, add the capers, 2 tablespoons of olive oil and a generous seasoning of salt and pepper. Toss together and leave to marinate while the aubergine 'pizzas' are prepared.

Season the aubergine slices lightly with salt. Heat a frying-pan over a medium heat, then add sufficient olive oil to cover the base. Fry the aubergine slices in a single uncrowded layer, adjusting the heat so that they cook until golden on both sides. Repeat until all the slices are cooked. Press them between two sheets of absorbent kitchen paper to drain them of excess oil.

Heat the grill. Lay out the aubergine slices on a sheet of kitchen foil laid on a baking tray. Divide the tomato between them, add the mozzarella and olives. Grill until the mozzarella has just melted. Serve at once.

GRATIN OF TOMATO, COURGETTES, RED ONIONS AND BLACK OLIVES

SERVES 2 AS A MAIN DISH, 4 AS A STARTER OR ACCOMPANIMENT

This is an immensely versatile dish: it is easy to make and attractive to look at, and the smell as it cooks, while the aromatic herbs mingle with onions, tomatoes and courgettes, will make your mouth water. It will serve you well as a fast and satisfying summer supper, as a starter, or as an accompaniment to lamb, chicken or white fish such as cod or haddock.

It's one of the many tomato-based gratins that can be served piping hot from the oven or left on the side until you are ready to eat because it's as good warm as it is cold. It's ideal for a barbecue, when it's essential to have the supporting cast ready in advance.

It is, however, a summer dish, which gives of its best when made with meaty plum tomatoes that keep their shape. A layer of fresh breadcrumbs mixed with grated Parmesan and finely chopped flat-leaf parsley protects the top layer of vegetables and gives a welcome change of texture and flavour.

- 18 black olives
- 1 large bay leaf
- 1 heaped tbsp chopped thyme leaves
- 2 tbsp fresh fine breadcrumbs
- 2 tbsp freshly grated Parmesan
- 1 tbsp finely chopped flat-leaf parsley
- olive oil
- 225 g red onions, halved and cut into thick half-moons
- 2 plump garlic cloves, finely sliced in rounds
- 500 g courgettes, trimmed and thickly sliced
- salt and freshly ground black pepper
- 500 g plum tomatoes, cored, peeled and cut into thick slices

Pre-heat the oven to 425°F/220°C/gas mark 7.

Slash the olives and pick out their stones, leaving them hinged. Finely chop the bay leaf and mix it with the thyme. Place the breadcrumbs in a bowl and mix thoroughly with the grated Parmesan and parsley.

Heat a frying pan, add 1 tablespoon of olive oil and stir-fry the onions over a medium heat for several minutes until they are floppy. Add half the garlic and half the thyme mixture and cook on for a couple of minutes. Remove to a plate. Add a little more oil and quickly fry the courgettes, tossing them after about 30 seconds as they brown slightly, then adding the rest of the garlic and thyme. Remove to a second plate.

Now assemble the dish. Smear an ovenproof dish with olive oil, then tip in half the onions and half the olives. Season well with salt and pepper and cover with half the courgettes. Season again and cover with half the tomatoes. Repeat, aiming to cover the surface almost entirely with tomatoes. Dribble over 1 tablespoon of olive oil and sprinkle the surface with the breadcrumb mixture. Criss-cross the surface with a dribble of oil and bake for 40 minutes.

GRATIN OF COURGETTES AND TOMATOES

SERVES 2-3

Tegliete Gratinate is the Italian name of this lovely summer gratin made with tomatoes and courgettes. It never fails to please, however the vegetables are sliced and whatever the seasoning. In this version, designed by Franco Taruschio when at the Walnut Tree at Abergavenny, small courgettes are cut into very long, thin slices and layered with slightly thicker slices of tomato. It is one of those combinations that is at its best served tepid. Franco arranges the layers in flower shapes and serves *Tegliete Gratinate* in individual dishes as a first course. Here it is made to share and is particularly good with lamb or chicken. For larger quantities, simply scale up the ingredients.

5 tbsp olive oil

350 g courgettes, trimmed and thinly sliced lengthways

salt and freshly ground black pepper

350 g tomatoes, cored, peeled and sliced

75 g wholemeal bread without crusts

½ tbsp finely chopped thyme leaves

½ tbsp finely chopped marjoram leaves

Pre-heat the oven to 425°F/220°C/gas mark 7.

Use about 1 tablespoon of the oil to smear the base of a gratin dish and cover it with half of the courgette slices. Season with salt and pepper, then use half the tomatoes to cover the courgette. Repeat. Blitz the bread to crumbs and add the thyme and marjoram for the final few seconds. Strew the surface with the herbed breadcrumbs and criss-cross all over with the olive oil. Bake for 15 minutes or until the topping is crusty and the juices are bubbling round the edges.

GRATIN OF FENNEL IN TOMATO SAUCE

SERVES 6

Also good with grated Parmesan mixed with the breadcrumbs used for the crusty topping.

- 1 kg small fennel bulbs, trimmed and halved
- 500 ml Tomato Sauce (see page 243)
- salt and freshly ground black pepper
- 75 g breadcrumbs
- 2 tbsp olive oil

Bring a large pan of salted water to the boil. Drop in the fennel and cook for 10 minutes. Drain.

Pre-heat the oven to 350°F/180°C/gas mark 4.

Arrange the fennel in a gratin dish smeared with a little of the tomato sauce. Cover generously with tomato sauce, season with salt and black pepper and strew with the breadcrumbs. Dribble a thread of olive oil back and forth across the surface, and bake for 35-40 minutes, until the gratin has formed a crust and the tomato sauce is bubbling round the edges.

BAKED TOMATOES WITH MUSHROOMS AND GARLIC HERBS

SERVES 6

There are countless different recipes for stuffing a tomato. Generally speaking, the simplest ones are the best. Round tomatoes, the bigger the better, are best for stuffing. They are either halved equally or about a third of the tomato is removed and might be replaced as a hat. There are two ways in which to prepare the tomatoes. Either scrape out the seeds and push the stuffing into the little cavities or excavate the entire tomato half leaving a thick fleshy shell. The removed pulp may be added to the filling. If the inside of the tomato is sprinkled with salt and left upside down to drain for half an hour or so, the flesh will be dryer, and thus won't weep so much, than if you didn't bother. Don't peel the tomatoes before stuffing them: although the skin may split during cooking and end up round the tomatoes' 'ankles', it will have played a protective role. The idea is to end up with a tomato that is soft and squashy but neither split nor burst. Properly cooked stuffed tomatoes look stunning, specially when several are arranged together – they smell divinely appetizing too, and taste heavenly: the tomato flesh makes a juicy, soft sauce for the stuffing.

Peeled raw tomatoes, cut in half through the middle, make a smart garnish: the inside is scraped out, then stuffed – with, for example, guacamole, scrambled egg or prawn mayonnaise – and its 'hat' replaced. A perfect basil or mint leaf, whichever seems appropriate, looks jaunty tucked between the two halves.

In this simple recipe, finely sliced mushrooms are fried in olive oil with garlic then mixed with parsley and chives. The aromatic yet insubstantial mixture is spooned into hollow tomatoes and the whole surface covered with plenty of grated Parmesan, then baked until the tomato is soft and the cheese has hardened into a thin crust. They can be eaten hot from the oven or left to cool and arranged with other antipasta.

- 6 closed-cap mushrooms, finely sliced
- 1 tbsp olive oil
- 1 garlic clove, peeled and finely chopped
- salt and freshly ground black pepper
- ½ tbsp finely chopped flat-leaf parsley
- ½ tbsp finely snipped chives
- 6 ripe medium tomatoes, halved and seeded
- 3 tbsp freshly grated Parmesan

Pre-heat the oven to 350°F/180°C/gas mark 4.

Gently fry the mushrooms in the olive oil with the garlic until tender. Season with salt and pepper, then mix in the parsley and chives. Fill the tomatoes with the stuffing and cover thickly with Parmesan. Arrange the tomatoes on a lightly oiled baking-tray and bake in the middle of the oven for 20 minutes or until the tomatoes feel very squashy and the top is crusted.

BAKED BEANS

SERVES 6

No book on tomatoes would be complete without Baked Beans. This recipe is the best I have come across, from Richard Whittington's book, *Cutting Edge* (Conran Octopus, 1996). '. . . it sits somewhere between Boston and San Diego, *pace* Mr Heinz. These beans are great with a grilled pork chop, with sausages or bacon and eggs.'

- 450 g dried haricot beans
- 900 g tinned plum tomatoes
- 175 g piece pancetta
- 350 g onions, finely chopped
- 2 garlic cloves, chopped
- 4 tbsp Heinz tomato ketchup
- 25 g demerara sugar
- 1 tbsp dried oregano
- 2 bay leaves
- 1 tbsp English mustard powder or paste
- 1 red chilli
- 1 tbsp black treacle or molasses
- 1 tsp salt
- 2 tsp freshly ground black pepper
- 1 glass (150 ml) dry white wine

Soak the beans overnight in cold water, then bring to the boil. Boil for 3 minutes and discard the water.

Pre-heat the oven to 275°F/140°C/gas mark 1.

Place the beans in an ovenproof casserole. Tip the tomatoes and their juice into the bowl of a food-processor. Blitz, then add to the beans with the pancetta, onions, garlic, tomato ketchup, sugar, oregano, bay leaves, mustard, chilli, treacle, salt and pepper. Stir to mix. Pour over the wine and cover with water.

Bring to the boil, cover and cook in the oven for 8 hours. Check from time to time, adding more water if it starts to dry out. Remove the bay leaves, chilli and pancetta before serving.

PIEDMONTESE PEPPERS

SERVES 6

Tomatoes tucked inside pepper halves that have been strewn with scraps of garlic are roasted with olive oil and garnished with slivers of anchovy. This excellent combination originates from Elizabeth David's *Italian Food*, published in 1954. Make it when red, possibly yellow but never green, peppers and tomatoes are at their most plentiful. Plenty of crusty bread is essential for mopping-up purposes.

6 even-sized red peppers
salt and freshly ground black pepper
6 or more plump garlic cloves, sliced into wafer-thin rounds
12 ripe tomatoes, preferably plum, cored, peeled and halved lengthways
16 tbsp olive oil
12 anchovy fillets

Pre-heat the oven to 425°F/220°C/gas mark 7.

Slice the peppers in half through the stalk, keeping the stalk intact. Use a small sharp knife to remove the seeds, the white membrane and any unformed baby peppers. Rinse inside and out. Drain. Choose a heavyweight roasting-tin and lay out the pepper halves, cut side up. Season with salt and pepper and spread with a few garlic slices. Tuck two tomato halves inside each pepper half, cut side down, to fill the cavity, and season again. Pour ½ tablespoon olive oil over each pepper.

Place the tray near the top of the oven and cook for 20 minutes, then lower the heat to 350°F/180°C/gas mark 4, and cook for a further 20 minutes. Remove from the oven. While the peppers are cooking, cut each anchovy fillet into two strips and as soon as the peppers come out of the oven use them to make a cross over the centre of each pepper.

Leave the peppers to cool in the dish. Use a fish slice to scoop them on to a serving-dish – a white one is best for this – and spoon over the juices. If you need to keep the peppers hanging around, cover them generously with clingfilm and store in the fridge. They keep perfectly for about 4 days.

BAMIA MARSOUSA

SERVES 6

A stupendous-looking recipe by Claudia Roden, from her book *Mediterranean Cookery*. Okra is arranged like the spokes of a wheel to sandwich a lemon and garlic tomato sauce. It looks like a cake with the tomato showing through the green and is served in wedges.

- **1 kg okra**
- **500 g tomatoes, cored, peeled and sliced**
- **2-3 garlic cloves, crushed**
- **salt and freshly ground black pepper**
- **juice of 1 lemon**
- **75 ml olive oil**
- **1 tbsp sugar (optional)**

Pre-heat the oven to 325°F/170°C/gas mark 3.

Wash the okra and trim off the stem ends. Pack it in one or two layers in a round, shallow mould or baking-dish with the pointed end converging like rays towards the centre. If you pack them tightly they should stay in place. Put a layer of tomatoes in between or on top of the okra, sprinkling a little garlic here and there. Season each layer with salt and pepper. Beat together the rest of the ingredients with about 150 ml of water and pour over the top, adding a little more water, if necessary, to cover the vegetables.

Bake for 45 minutes or until the okra are tender. Cool, then carefully turn out on to a large flat plate, letting any excess juices run out and being careful not to upset the okra pattern. Serve hot or cold.

Also see:
Tomatoes Alone (pages 31-58)

tomato tarts

'Anchovy Heaven: Tomatoes are the heart of this savoury tart. In a shallow pan, sauté 1 crushed garlic clove and 1 diced onion in olive oil until soft. Add 6 diced tomatoes and 2 tablespoons of tomato paste, reduce the heat and cook until soft, about 10 minutes. Remove from the heat, add 2 eggs, salt and pepper. Mix well to incorporate and pour into a blind-baked tart shell. Take anchovy fillets and cut in half lengthways, remove the stones from olives and cut into half. Over the tomato, lay the anchovies in a lattice, in each square put an olive half. Bake at 180°C for 40 minutes, or until the tomato is set and lightly brown.'

10 March, *The Seasonal Produce Diary*, 1996, published by Purple Egg, Allan Campion and Michele Curtis

Take a piece of puff pastry and cover it with slices of tomato. You can lay them directly on the pastry or over a smear of something like pesto, black olive paste, or cream of red peppers. Pop the pastry into the oven. Come back half an hour later, and you will have something utterly delicious. That combination of crisp flaky pastry and sweet, succulent tomatoes is irresistible, a feast for the eye as well as the tastebuds.

There are countless variations on this theme. It works just as well, for example, made with whole cherry tomatoes, or with tomato halves, or with roasted red peppers mixed with the tomatoes. It is very good made with a combination of sun-dried tomatoes and fresh tomatoes. Or, for a change, make a tomato tart with different-sized tomatoes, or with yellow or green ones.

Different types of pastry also make a huge difference to a tomato tart: crumbly short pastry, perhaps made with olive oil instead of butter, or flavoured with herbs or cream cheese, crisp, chewy pizza dough, egg pastry, egg and lemon pastry, pastry made with tomato juice, home-made pastry, bought pastry. They all taste good with tomato, however it is prepared. It could be tomato as a thick puree, or finely diced and laced with fresh herbs. It might be thin slices or chunky slices. The slices might be jumbled anyhow or laid out very neatly in overlapping circles. Or the tomatoes could be cut into quarters with seed and skin intact. Big tomatoes, small tomatoes, cherry tomatoes. Why not introduce flavourings to the pastry, such as roast garlic to shortcrust pastry or grated Parmesan between the sheets of filo pastry, to ring the changes in a tomato tart?

There are, of course, other ways of combining pastry and tomatoes to make delicious dishes that aren't straightforward tarts. Take Tomato Cobbler, for example, where the topping is a circle of golden scones, and Spanakopitta with Herbed Tomatoes, an adaptation of the Greek spinach pie in which the tomatoes are held under several layers of crisp filo pastry in a feta cheese custard.

I never tire of the recipes in this section. Fortunately, it is hard to go wrong when tomatoes and pastry are combined.

TOMATO TARTS

SERVES 2

This tart involves only three ingredients – puff pastry, tomatoes and Parmesan cheese – and you end up with a dish that looks and tastes like something you might be offered in a fashionable restaurant. It can be put together with any ready-made puff pastry, either the ready-rolled sheets or a slab. Whichever you choose, it must be rolled very thin. Any medium-sized tomatoes will do for this tart but the better quality you choose – vine-ripened, grown for flavour, etc. – the better the result. The tomatoes are peeled and cored, cut in half and sliced then laid over the pastry, nudged up quite close, in the style of a French apple tart. Parmesan is finely grated over the top before the tart is cooked for about 15 minutes in a hot oven; the idea is to end up with crisp tender pastry and soft, juicy tomatoes.

The tarts look great and need a second grating of Parmesan to set off the flavours. Alternatively, serve them topped with a salad of rocket and finely chopped shallot, dressed with a little balsamic vinegar and olive oil.

150 g puff pastry, preferably all-butter

flour for dusting

1-2 tbsp olive oil

6 medium-sized tomatoes, approximately 350 g, cored and peeled

2 heaped tbsp freshly grated Parmesan

salt and freshly ground black pepper

Pre-heat the oven to 400°F/200°C/gas mark 6.

Dust a work surface with flour and roll out the pastry approximately 30 cm x 18 cm. Cut it into 2 equal pieces. Use a little olive oil to grease a flat baking-sheet. Transfer the sheets of pastry to the baking-sheet. Prick them all over with a fork, leaving a 1 cm border. Paint the border with olive oil.

Halve plum tomatoes lengthways, round tomatoes across their middles, and cut them into medium-thin slices. Arrange the slices so that they are nudged up close and come up to the edge of the border. Dribble the remaining olive oil over them and sprinkle them with half the Parmesan. Place the baking-sheet on a shelf near the top of the oven and cook for 15-20 minutes until the border is puffed and golden, the tomatoes are soft and juicy and the pastry underneath is cooked. Remove from the oven, season with salt and pepper and sprinkle over the remaining Parmesan.

CHEESE AND TOMATO TART WITH MUSTARD

SERVES 4

Cheese and tomato, like egg and tomato, is a classic combination. Here the cheese melts into slices of peeled tomato, which flop against pastry flavoured with sage and Dijon mustard. It is as good hot from the oven as it is cold but is at its finest eaten lukewarm. Excellent for a picnic. The idea is an old one from the *nouvelle cuisine* days of the famous Troisgros brothers of Roanne. A similar tart, this time flavoured with tarragon mustard, and again utilizing seeds and tomato juice to make a vinaigrette with olive oil, is excellent made with puff pastry. For Cantal Cheese Tart you will need 150 g ready-made puff pastry, 3 tomatoes weighing 300 g each, 2 tablespoons of olive oil, 175 g Cantal or Cheddar cheese, and 1 tablespoon of tarragon mustard. Roll the pastry to fit a 26 cm flan ring. Prepare the tomatoes as below. Spread the mustard on the base of the tart, cover with thin slices of cheese and arrange the thick slices of tomato on top. Sprinkle the tomato marinade over all. Bake for 20 minutes; it is best eaten warm.

- 100 g butter
- 8 fresh sage leaves
- 1 egg yolk
- 2 tbsp smooth Dijon mustard
- 150 g flour
- salt and freshly ground black pepper
- 10 ripe medium tomatoes, cored, peeled and sliced into 4
- 2 tbsp olive oil
- 100 g Wensleydale cheese

Pre-heat the oven to 400°F/200°C/gas mark 6.

Cut a small knob of butter and heat it until it froths in a small frying-pan. Add the sage leaves and cook briefly on both sides. Set aside on absorbent paper to drain and crisp.

Dice the remaining butter into the bowl of a food processor, add the egg yolk and one tablespoon of the mustard, and crumble in the sage. Process briefly before adding the flour with a generous pinch of salt, then continue until the mixture forms a clump. Remove, cover and set aside to rest while you fix the tomatoes.

Lay the tomato slices on a plate, season with salt and pepper and drizzle with olive oil. Turn after 5 minutes and repeat.

Roll the pastry to line a 20 cm non-stick or buttered-and-floured flan ring with detachable base. Cover loosely with foil and spread rice or baking beans over the base. Bake the pastry case for 10 minutes. Remove the foil and bake for a further 5 minutes. Reduce the oven temperature to 350°F/180°C/gas mark 4.

Smear the base of the tart with the remaining mustard, cover with thin slices of cheese and arrange the tomatoes on top. Strain the olive-oil juices over the tomatoes. Bake for 25 minutes, then allow the tart to settle for 15 minutes before removing the ring and serving. This is also excellent cold.

CREAMED TOMATO QUICHE

SERVES 8

It was while eating a slice of lemon tart that it occurred to me to try a version with tomatoes. I envisaged it as something to make at the height of the tomato season using sun-ripened fruit with full-on intensity of flavour. It looks stunning: a pale orange cream cooked until it is just set so that it has the luscious wobble of the perfect quiche. The texture is smooth and comes from making a well-flavoured, thick tomato sauce, allowing it to cool, then mixing it with beaten egg and cream. The exact seasoning – herbs, garlic, celery, etc. – can be fine-tuned according to what you have to hand. You may care to make a sauce with roast tomatoes or sun-dried tomatoes or a mixture of the two – or to be dead lazy and sieve a bottle of Cirio's Rustica (see page 20).

The tart is at its finest, I think, eaten lukewarm. However, here's a couple of ideas for smartening up its appearance to serve cold. Make some tomato jelly with liquidized tomato concassé, or roast tomatoes, and a little gelatine, and smear it over the surface so that it sets to a glossy sheen. Alternatively, decorate the top with wafer-thin slices of peeled tomato and glaze the entire surface with olive oil and balsamic vinegar.

Any salad will go well with the tart but wild rocket and black olives is particularly good.

FOR THE PASTRY

- 225 g flour, plus a little extra
- 100 g cold butter
- a pinch of salt
- 1 egg yolk lightly beaten with 2 tbsp cold water

FOR THE FILLING

- 2 large eggs
- 1 egg yolk
- 100 ml double cream
- salt and freshly ground black pepper
- 570 ml Cooked Tomato Coulis (see page 242)

Pre-heat the oven to 350°F/180°C/gas mark 4.

To make the pastry, blend the flour, butter and salt in a food processor until it resembles coarse breadcrumbs and tip it into a roomy bowl. Gently mix in the egg yolk and water with cool hands or a knife, until the pastry is well amalgamated. Put it into a plastic bag and chill in the fridge for at least 30 minutes before rolling.

Roll out the pastry thinly and use it to line a greased 23 cm loose-bottomed flan tin. Cover the pastry loosely with foil and spread rice or baking beans over the base. Bake for about 15 minutes, remove it from the oven, discard the foil and beans, then brush the inside with a little beaten egg or spare egg white, which will form a seal and prevent any leaks, and put it back in the oven for a further 5-10 minutes until biscuit coloured. Then take it out and allow it to cool.

Turn down the oven to 325°F/170°C/gas mark 3.

Now make the filling. Whisk the eggs with the egg yolk, stir in the cream and season with salt and pepper. Add the cooled tomato coulis and taste for seasoning. Place the flan tin with the cooled pastry case on a flat baking-sheet. Carefully ladle in the tomato custard, letting it come right up to the rim of the pastry. Transfer to the oven and bake for 20 minutes, or until the custard is just set but the centre is still wobbly. Allow to cool for at least 45 minutes, when it will set firmly, before decorating or slicing into wedges.

PLUM TOMATO AND BASIL GALETTE

SERVES 8

This is one of my favourite starters and appears on the wonderful menu at the Ivy, London's enduringly fashionable thespian restaurant. It is one of those inspired simple ideas and this one involves pre-cooking a circle of thin puff pastry, spreading it with sun-dried tomato paste and topping that with overlapping slices of tomato. The tarts are then given a quick blast in a hot oven and dribbled with freshly made basil oil. The galette was the inspiration for my Roasted Pesto and Tomato Tarts which follow, and the idea for pre-cooking sheets of puff pastry that aren't allowed to puff is one that came originally, I think, from Marco Pierre White.

This is the restaurant's recipe, published in their book, *The Ivy, The Restaurant and Its Recipes*, by A. A. Gill with recipes by Mark Hix (who now has his own string of restaurants).

- 8 x 16 cm rounds puff pastry, rolled 3-4 mm thick
- 240 g sun-dried tomatoes in oil
- 2 tsp tomato puree
- 8 large, or 12 medium, ripe plum or well-flavoured tomatoes, cored, peeled and sliced
- sea salt and freshly ground black pepper

FOR THE BASIL DRESSING

- 120 g basil
- 150 ml extra virgin olive oil

Pre-heat the oven to 325°F/170°C/gas mark 3.

Prick the pastry bases with a fork, lay them on a flat oiled baking-sheet and bake for 5 minutes, turning them after 2 minutes to ensure that the pastry doesn't rise. Turn up the oven to 400°F/200°C/gas mark 6.

Drain most of the oil from the sun-dried tomatoes, then process them with the tomato puree to make a fine paste. Transfer to a bowl. Rinse out the blender and wipe it dry. Make the basil dressing: process the basil with the olive oil, adding a little more oil if the dressing seems too thick.

To assemble the galettes, spread a thin layer of the sun-dried tomato puree on the pastry bases. Lay the sliced tomatoes in a circle on top, overlapping slightly. Season with black pepper and bake for 10 minutes.

Serve on a warm plate. Drizzle the basil dressing generously over the tomatoes and sprinkle with a twist of sea-salt flakes.

ROASTED TOMATO AND PESTO TARTS

SERVES 4

This is a tomato tart recipe that bypasses the sometimes unwelcome inevitability of soggy pastry and insipid tomatoes. Here, these elements are cooked separately. While the puff pastry cooks the tomato halves are roasted until their flesh is soft and flavour concentrated. Here I've made two tarts but the same ingredients could be used to make one big or several small ones. Try it with rocket or watercress salad.

- **14 ripe medium tomatoes, cored, peeled and halved through their middles**
- **3 tbsp olive oil**
- **salt and freshly ground black pepper**
- **250 g ready-rolled puff pastry**
- **4 tbsp pesto (see page 281)**

Pre-heat the oven to 400°F/200°C/gas mark 6.

Lay out the tomato halves, cut side up, on a lightly oiled sheet of foil on a baking-sheet. Paint the cut surfaces with a little oil, season with salt and pepper. Place on the bottom shelf in the oven (before it's come up to temperature).

Meanwhile cut four 15 cm circles from the pastry using a small plate to guide you. Paint one side liberally with olive oil and flip it over on to a foil-lined baking-sheet. Prick the unoiled surface all over with the tines of a fork, then oil this surface as before. When the oven is ready, put the baking-sheet on the top shelf and cook for 10-15 minutes until the surface is brown and semi-risen. Use an egg slice to flip the pastry discs so that the still-flabby underside is uppermost. Press down to flatten and return to the oven for a further 5 minutes or until flaky and golden. If necessary flatten the now thoroughly cooked pastry again. The tomatoes should be nicely squashy now, but if they are not continue cooking them until they are.

Spread each pastry circle thickly with pesto right up to the edge. Cover the pesto with tomato halves, nudging them up closely. Once assembled the tarts will remain sag-free for around 4 hours. Serve hot or cold.

SLOW-ROASTED TOMATO TARTS WITH RED PEPPER PUREE

SERVES 4

In the spring of 1999, I took part in a series of TV programmes highlighting the Heritage Seed Programme at Ryton Organic Gardens near Coventry, which helps save some of the hundreds of vegetables not protected by the National List. As I prepared recipes for the programme, I didn't have access to the magnificent pile of tomatoes from Ryton that featured in the programme: huge, craggy pale-yellow ridged White Hugh, sexy little Porter, with its distinctive 'crown' stalk, and big, beefy, ridged Abraham Lincoln. Instead, I had to make do with tasteless out-of-season supermarket tomatoes, and that is how I discovered that if you roast bland tomatoes in a low oven for at least an hour their flavours concentrate and sweeten. They stay moist and juicy and are exquisite on buttered toast or with peppery rocket salad, or with a couple of slices of salty feta cheese and a few black olives. In this recipe, these intensely flavoured tomatoes are laid out on a square of puff pastry spread with red pepper puree. In the original I tucked wafer-thin slices of garlic in the seed cavities. Amazingly they hardly softened but their flavour was gentle.

- 18 medium tomatoes, peeled
- 6 garlic cloves, sliced into wafer-thin rounds (optional)
- olive oil
- 225 g ready-rolled puff pastry
- 4 tbsp red pepper puree or Red Pesto (see page 296) or sun-dried tomato puree
- salt and freshly ground black pepper

Pre-heat the oven to 300°F/150°C/gas mark 2.

Slice the tomatoes in half across their circumference. Insert three slivers of garlic, if using, between the seeds of each tomato half and brush the tops with olive oil. Lay out the tomatoes on lightly oiled foil on a flat baking-sheet and bake for 1 hour until they feel soft to the touch. Remove from the oven and turn the temperature up to 450°F/230°C/gas mark 8.

Use a sharp knife to cut the pastry into 4 equal pieces. On a lightly floured surface, roll out each piece of pastry until it measures 15 cm square. Transfer the squares to an oiled baking-sheet. Prick the pastry with a fork, going right through so that it doesn't rise in the middle and push off the tomatoes. Leaving a 1 cm border, spread each square with some of the red pepper puree or red pesto.

Place 9 tomato halves on each square and brush the border with olive oil. Grind over a little black pepper and season with salt. Bake the tarts in a hot oven for 15 minutes until the sides are puffed and golden and the underneath is nicely crisp.

SPANAKOPITTA WITH HERBED TOMATOES

SERVES 6

Spanakopitta is a sort of savoury baklava. It is made by lining an ovenproof dish with layers of flaky filo pastry and filling it with spinach and spring onions suspended in an egg and feta cheese custard. In this version, however, spinach takes a minor role and spring onions are replaced with butter-softened leeks. As you might expect, the main ingredient is tomato. And you need plenty of really well-flavoured ones. The combination of sweet, herby tomatoes against a soufflé flecked with buttery leeks pitted with nuggets of feta cheese and black olives, all encased in sheets of crisp pastry, is exquisite. It is a lovely dish to eat in the garden on a hot summer day and, although at its best eaten lukewarm, it is irresistible hot from the oven. It reheats remarkably well.

- 50 g butter
- 1 medium onion, finely diced
- salt and freshly ground black pepper
- 4 leeks, trimmed
- 1 tbsp finely chopped mint
- 225 g young spinach
- 750 g ripe plum or other firm-textured tomato, cored, peeled, seeded and sliced
- 2 tbsp finely chopped flat-leaf parsley
- 2 tbsp finely shredded basil leaves
- 10 pitted black olives, chopped
- 4 large eggs
- 250 g feta cheese
- 2 tbsp freshly grated Parmesan cheese
- 450 g filo pastry
- approximately 10 tbsp olive oil

Pre-heat the oven to 375°F/190°C/gas mark 5.

Melt the butter in a heavy-bottomed pan over a medium-low heat and stir in the onion. Season with salt and pepper and leave to soften while you slice the leeks in 1 cm thick rounds. Add it to the onion, reduce the heat, cover the pan and cook until the leek is soft but not coloured. Turn off the heat and stir in the mint.

Bring a second pan of water to the boil. Add a teaspoon of salt and the spinach. Return the water to the boil, cook for 30 seconds then scoop out the spinach to drain in a colander, pressing it against the sides to remove all the liquid. Slice it into ribbons and stir it into the leeks. Add the tomato slices and stir in the remaining herbs and the olives. Season again with salt and pepper.

Break the eggs into a mixing bowl. Whisk lightly then crumble in the cheese before stirring in the leek, spinach and tomato mixture.

Using a pastry brush, lightly paint a rectangular tin, approximately 25 cm x 30 cm, with oil and build up a case for the filling with two-thirds of the sheets of filo, using olive oil to paint each sheet as you go. Leave plenty of overhang. Pour in the filling, smooth it carefully, and fold over any overlapping sheets of pastry. Use the remaining filo, sheet by sheet and painting each with oil, to cover the filling, tucking in the edges to make it leak proof. Brush the top generously with oil, then use a sharp knife to cut the pie into portion-sized squares or diamonds, but don't cut right through to the filling. Bake for 40 minutes, until the pie is puffed and golden.

TARTE AUX TOMATES ET AU PROSCIUTTO

SERVES 4

Wonderful little tomato *feuillettes* are served at Michel Rostang's Bistro d'à Coté, next door to his eponymously named Michelin-starred restaurant in Paris. It isn't until you deconstruct their gorgeous savoury flavour that you realize the thin sheet of puff pastry has been spread with a paste made of prosciutto. The final embellishment is a dribble of aromatic home-made basil oil. In my adaptation, the tarts are the size of a small pizza and are served as such.

- **225 g ready-rolled puff pastry**
- **125 ml olive oil**
- **3 garlic cloves, peeled**
- **225 g prosciutto**
- **½ tsp freshly ground black pepper**
- **10-12 ripe, firm plum tomatoes, cored, peeled and cut into 0.5 cm thick slices**
- **1 tsp chopped thyme leaves**
- **4 tbsp finely chopped basil leaves**

Pre-heat the oven to 375°F/190°C/gas mark 5.

Flour a work surface, divide the pastry into 4 pieces and roll each very thinly. Using a plate to guide you, cut each piece into an approximately 15 cm circle. Oil a baking-sheet and sprinkle with water (this helps the pastry to rise) and lay out the dough circles with space between them. Fork all over the pastry to stop it rising.

Place the garlic, 50 ml of the olive oil and the torn sheets of prosciutto in the bowl of a food-processor with the pepper. Blitz briefly to make a rough puree. Place a dollop in the centre of each dough circle and carefully spread it as best you can to leave a 1 cm border uncovered.

Arrange the tomato slices over the puree in overlapping concentric circles. If appropriate, use 1 slice to fill the central gap. Dribble a little olive oil over the tomatoes then sprinkle with thyme. Turn up the unadorned edges of each tart to make a little border. Bake in the centre of the oven for 15-18 minutes until the pastry is golden, lightly risen and properly cooked.

While the tarts are cooking, blitz the basil leaves with the remaining olive oil (approximately 50 ml) to make the basil oil. Serve the tarts with a dribble of the oil.

TOMATO COBBLER

SERVES 4

A cobbler is a lazy sort of tart – scone-cum-biscuit dough is rolled out thickly, cut into rounds then usually arranged over soft fruit. However, as I tucked into a plum cobbler one day, why not, I thought, make a savoury version with tomatoes?

To avoid the dish becoming excessively juicy, it is important to use a firm-textured plum tomato. Even so, the tomatoes are salted and drained first and a handful of basil breadcrumbs mixed in with them. The scones are flavoured with Parmesan and, as they cook, they flop slightly and merge into each other under a crumbly, buttery, lightly crusted topping. Juices from the tomatoes will bubble up and over any gaps in the scones, so the dish looks particularly appetizing. It also smells divine. Also see Green Tomato Tarte Tatin, page 412.

- 1 kg ripe plum tomatoes
- salt and freshly ground black pepper
- 175 g self-raising flour, plus a little extra
- 2 heaped tsp baking powder
- 4 tbsp freshly grated Parmesan
- 50 g unsalted butter at room temperature
- 100 ml milk
- 1 large egg
- 1 tbsp thick cream or Greek yoghurt
- 4 tbsp fresh white breadcrumbs
- 1 small garlic clove, worked to a paste with a pinch of salt
- a large bunch of basil, leaves only, finely shredded
- butter

Pre-heat the oven to 450°F/230°C/gas mark 8.

Slice the tomatoes in half horizontally and make a small triangular cut to remove the core. Poke your index finger into each tomato cavity to loosen the seeds slightly then shake them out. Place the halves on a baking-sheet and sprinkle the cut surfaces generously with salt. Cook in the hot oven for 10 minutes, by which time the tomatoes will have filled with water and the skins loosened. Have ready a cake rack positioned over the sink. Using a spatula, knife or fish-slice, carefully upturn each tomato half and leave them to drain and cool on the rack.

Meanwhile, sieve the flour and a pinch of salt into a mixing bowl, stir in the baking powder and 2 tablespoons of the grated Parmesan. Add small pieces of butter (mine was floppy-soft) and rub it into the flour. Make an indentation in the middle and, using a knife or fork, stir in the milk quickly to make a sloppy, damp dough that clumps together into a sort of ball. Sprinkle a handful of flour on to a work surface, and roll the dough in it to firm it up so that it is soft and floppy.

Whisk the egg and cream together in a mixing bowl, then stir in the breadcrumbs. Add 1 tablespoon of the remaining Parmesan and the garlic paste. Season lightly with salt and generously with pepper. Stir in the basil. Pull the skins off the tomatoes and fold the tomatoes into the egg and breadcrumb mixture.

Butter a deep, approximately 20.5 cm diameter dish (I used a ceramic soufflé dish) with a minimum 1.5 litre capacity and spoon in the tomato mixture.

Pat the dough flat with your hands and form it into a disc

approx 15 cm. Use a biscuit cutter or an upturned wine-glass and cut out 4 circles. Place them over the tomatoes and form a small disc with leftovers to sit in the middle. Sprinkle with the remaining Parmesan and top with scraps of butter. Bake for 20 minutes until the pastry is golden and firm on top.

TOMATO AND ROCKET PESTO TARTLETS

MAKES APPROXIMATELY 20

This is a neat summer canapé idea. One slice of a ripe, full-flavoured tomato rests on a thick smear of pesto spread on a disc of pre-cooked, flattened puff pastry. Delicious finger food.

flour for dusting

375 g ready-rolled puff pastry

3-4 tbsp vegetable oil

8-10 medium vine-ripened tomatoes, peeled and thickly sliced through the circumference

FOR THE PESTO

3 tbsp pine nuts

½ tbsp cooking oil

60 g rocket or watercress leaves

2 garlic cloves, peeled and roughly chopped

7 tbsp best olive oil

3 tbsp freshly grated Parmesan

salt and freshly ground black pepper

small basil leaves to garnish

Pre-heat the oven to 400°F/200°C/gas mark 6.

Dust a work surface with flour and lightly roll the pastry, approximately 0.5 cm thick, so you can cut out at least 20 biscuit-size circles, to fit the tomato slices. Dip a pastry brush in the oil and paint it lightly on each circle. Place them, oiled side down, on lightly oiled foil laid on a flat baking-sheet. Prick the un-oiled surface all over with the tines of a fork and oil it as before. Place the tray on a top shelf in the oven and bake for about 10 minutes until brown and semi-risen. Remove the tray from the oven and use a palette knife to invert each circle, pressing down to compress the discs. Cook for a further 5 minutes until flaky and brown.

Give each thoroughly cooked pastry disc a bang with the bottom of a saucepan to flatten it and slip them carefully on to a cake rack to cool. Meanwhile, make the pesto. Heat a small, heavy frying-pan and stir-fry the pine nuts for a couple of minutes until lightly golden. Place the rocket or watercress leaves in the bowl of a food-processor with the pine nuts and the garlic. Blitz. When evenly chopped, with the motor still running, gradually add the olive oil and continue until nicely amalgamated, thick but slack. Transfer to a bowl and stir in the Parmesan to thicken.

To assemble, spread each pastry circle thickly with pesto, going right up to the edge. Cover with a slice of tomato, season with salt and pepper. Garnish with a single basil leaf.

TOMATO TARTE TATIN & VINE-RIPENED CHERRY TOMATO TARTE TATIN

SERVES 4

I had been thinking for some time that an obvious contender for inclusion in this chapter of the book would be a tomato version of Tarte Tatin, the famous upside-down apple tart. It would be important, I was thinking, to use large, very fleshy tomatoes, so that by the time the pastry was cooked their plum-like texture wouldn't have cooked into a mush. They would have to be peeled too, or the skin would spoil the textures. Then, on a visit to Phoenix, at a stylish restaurant (now gone) opened by Rebecca Mascarenhas, the talent behind Sonny's in Barnes, what did I see on the menu? The Phoenix Tomato Tarte Tatin was tiny, scone-size, made with unpeeled cherry tomatoes and pastry rolled so thinly that it cooked before the little tomatoes had had time to burst. To make them like this you need a Yorkshire pudding/cookie tray, or individual tart tins, or to get creative, in a Heath Robinson sort of way, with foil. Peter Goffe Wood, who devised the Phoenix recipe, uses blini pans but I can't imagine anyone having more than one of those at home.

I give two recipes, one for a large tart, made with peeled plum tomatoes, and one for four little tarts, which make a great starter or light snack. Both are simple to make and stunning to look at. They go well with a salad of wild rocket, but to make more of a meal of them, serve them draped with prosciutto and a scattering of black olives.

TOMATO TARTE TATIN

- 4 tbsp olive oil
- 1 heaped tbsp caster sugar
- salt and freshly ground black pepper
- 1 tbsp balsamic vinegar
- 750 g medium tomatoes, cored, peeled and halved through the core
- 150 g puff pastry
- a little flour

TO SERVE

- 25 g freshly grated Parmesan
- about 10 basil leaves

Pre-heat the oven to 400°F/200°C/gas mark 6.

Lightly oil an 18 cm flan tin or ovenproof frying-pan with a smear of the oil. Dissolve the sugar and a little salt and pepper in the vinegar and whisk in 3 tablespoons of the oil. Place the tomato halves, rounded sides down, in the tin, nudging them up close together so they are slightly on their sides. Pour the dressing over the top.

On a floured surface, roll the pastry quite thinly and lay over the top of the tin. Cut round the edge and lightly tuck it down the inside of the tin as if you were tucking in a bed (badly). Use the remaining olive oil to smear the top of the pastry. Place in the oven and cook for about 15 minutes until the pastry is puffed and scorched. Remove from the oven, run a knife round the inside edge of the pastry. Carefully drain most of the liquid into a small jug. Place a large plate over the top of the tart, invert it quickly and set it aside to cool slightly – lukewarm is best for this. Give the dressing a quick whisk and pour it over the top of the tomatoes. Grate over the Parmesan, then snip over the basil and serve, sliced into 4 wedges. This is very good eaten with peas mixed with pesto that has been slackened with a little olive oil.

CHERRY TOMATO TARTE TATIN

SERVES 4

200 g puff pastry

4 tbsp extra-virgin olive oil

approximately 500 g or 64 vine-ripened cherry tomatoes, stalks removed

salt and freshly ground black pepper

4 tbsp aged, thick balsamic vinegar

Pre-heat the oven to 425°F/220°C/gas mark 7.

Divide the puff pastry into 4 balls and roll into 13 cm discs. Pour 1 tablespoon of the oil into the four 10 cm tart tins, swirl it around, then arrange the tomatoes in the pans in a single layer. Season with salt and pepper and pour 1 tablespoon balsamic vinegar over each pan. Cover with a puff pastry disc, tucking the pastry into the pans to form a lip. Bake for approximately 15 minutes until the pastry is puffed and golden. Remove from the oven, run a knife round the inside edge of the tart, place a plate over the top and invert it quickly. Peter Goffe Wood recommends serving the tarts on a rocket and goat's cheese salad.

Also see:
Green Tomato and Apple Pie (page 416)
Green Tomato Tarte Tatin (page 412)
Green Tomato and Zabaglione Tart (page 416)
Pastilla au Poisson (page 332)
Shaker Tomato Cream Pie (page 424)
Fresh Tomato Tarts with Thyme (page 209)

tomato sauces

'Here is a little tip when making tomato coulis/sauce during the months when the tomatoes are not so good. In a frying-pan heat up some extra-virgin olive oil, enough to make a thin film across the base of the frying-pan , until it is very hot – a haze should rise from it. Add some chopped tomatoes and let them sizzle for a few minutes, then fry them until they are soft. Add a tablespoon or so of tomato puree, depending on the redness of the tomatoes, to every 450 g of tomatoes. Season with salt and pepper. Pass through a food mill.

'The act of sizzling the tomatoes brings out the natural sugar in them and slightly caramelizes it, thus sweetening the rather dull tomatoes. The extra-virgin olive oil will impart a wonderful flavour to the sauce.'

Franco Taruschio, *Leaves From the Walnut Tree*, Pavilion, 1993

Salsi de Pomodori, Salsa Marinara, Sugo di Pomodoro, Pizzaiola, Salsa allia Napolitana: in Italy, tomato sauce has any number of names. All versions are similar but they are likely to turn out differently every time they are made. In summer they are put together with fresh tomatoes, in winter with tinned or bottled ones.

The sauces you will find here are not necessarily associated with pasta. Many are, and the selection begins with the Ubiquitous Tomato Sauce, but you will also find roast tomato sauce, tomato sauces flavoured with unusual spices, and fresh tomato ketchup. The reason for including these sauces is because they have many uses apart from being teamed with pasta. There is, of course, an inevitable blurring of the edges. Fresh Tomato Compôte and Roast Tomato Sauce, for example, would be delicious stirred into silky egg pasta, and both could be used to make a layered pasta dish. Equally, some of the sauces that are famously associated with specific types of pasta – Puttanesca with penne and Vongole with spaghetti – could be used in other ways too. Because of this overlap, the Tomatoes and Pasta section follows this one.

In a professional kitchen, one of the tricks of the trade is what is called 'mounting a sauce'. Scraps of ice-cold butter are quickly stirred into a hot sauce just before it is served, to give it a glossy finish, make it thicker and creamier, and to mellow the flavour. This works brilliantly with smooth tomato sauces. Just bring the sauce to the boil, take it off the heat and whisk in the butter. Serve immediately without reheating.

For the sake of convenience, these recipes have been divided into those made with tinned, sun-dried and fresh tomatoes. Despite that, many recipes that specify tinned tomatoes can be made with fresh and vice versa. You just have to use your noddle.

THE UBIQUITOUS TOMATO SAUCE: SALSA DI POMODORO

SERVES 6

Everyone should know how to make a basic tomato sauce that can be varied to suit what is to hand and what the sauce is required for. For example, if ordinary onions aren't available, use spring onions, shallots or red onions. Or leave out onions altogether. And what of garlic? You may like to include one clove or a whole head. You may wish to blanch it first or roast it before it is added to the sauce. Which herbs to use? You may wish to use none. Or perhaps you may want to scent the sauce with, say, tarragon or basil or even to dominate it with chopped coriander, mint or parsley. You may wish to have a thick sauce or a thin sauce, or one that is somewhere in between. Perhaps you want a chunky sauce or a smooth sauce. Perhaps you want to add things to it – chilli, olives or red pepper, for example.

I had planned to offer a basic sauce made with tinned tomatoes that could be fine-tuned to suit all manner of uses. Then, one day, when I was flipping through Alastair Little's *Italian Kitchen*, I discovered that he had been there before me. So, as Alastair has been one of my favourite chefs since his early days at 192 in Kensington Park Road, West London, before he opened Alastair Little in Frith Street, Soho, in 1985, I thought I'd use his. It is quick, easy, the perfect template. I give it as he wrote it, with the cooking stages that define its use.

- 1 kg tinned tomato pieces in their liquid
- 1 tbsp sugar or 2 tbsp tomato ketchup
- 1 tsp oregano (optional)
- 2-4 tbsp good olive oil (more makes it marginally richer)
- 1 garlic clove, minced (optional)
- 4 basil leaves
- 1 bay leaf (optional)
- 2 tsp salt
- 1 tsp pepper

Sauce 1

Place all the ingredients in a pan. Bring to the boil, lower the heat, then simmer for 20 minutes, or until thick and syrupy. Remove the bay leaf. This is now a basic pasta sauce, and pizza topping. Sieve if you wish.

Sauce 2

Simmer for about half an hour until it has reduced and concentrated by about one-third. A good general-purpose tomato sauce.

Sauce 3

Slowly simmer and concentrate. Reduce it by 75 per cent and use it sparingly as a relish or paste when a recipe calls for a rich sauce.

Sauce 4

'Arrabbiata' – internally angry or irritated. This is basically Sauce 2 with the addition of hot chillies to taste.

Sauce 5

As for Sauce 2. With the addition of chopped good anchovies and stoned black olives at the end of the cooking process, it becomes 'Napolitana'.

CHILLI TOMATO SAUCE

SERVES 4

Stewing tinned tomatoes with garlic, chilli and a slug of red wine, until much of the liquid has evaporated, results in an intensely flavoured and subtly seasoned sauce. Once strained and sieved, it is done but when mixed with fresh tomatoes, which is an optional addition, the flavours are lifted and textures become more interesting. It is good with deep-fried foods such as fish cakes and chips, but just the ticket with Mexican burrito, enchilada and other tortilla dishes.

- 400 g tin Italian tomatoes
- 1 red chilli pepper
- 3 garlic cloves, left unpeeled, bashed with a fist to crack them
- 1 tbsp tomato ketchup
- a slug of red wine
- salt and freshly ground black pepper
- a squeeze of lemon juice
- 2 firm, ripe tomatoes, cored, peeled, seeded and chopped

Place the tinned tomatoes, chilli, garlic, ketchup, red wine and a seasoning of salt and pepper in a small saucepan. Boil hard, giving the mixture a couple of good stirs while breaking up the tomatoes at the same time. Cook for around 15 minutes until the liquid is reduced by at least half. Remove the chilli, then pour and push the mixture through a sieve – boil it again if it seems watery. Taste, and adjust the seasoning with salt and pepper and lemon juice. Stir the fresh tomatoes and their juices into the sauce. Transfer to a serving jug. Either allow it to reach room temperature or chill it before serving.

RED PEPPER AND TOMATO SAUCE WITH SAFFRON AND HONEY

SERVES 6

A quick and easy store-cupboard sauce inspired by the Moroccan way of cooking tomatoes with honey and saffron. It ends up thick and fragrant and can be eaten hot as a relish-cum-sauce or cold as a dip.

- 340 g jar red peppers (pimientos)
- 1 tbsp olive oil
- 400 g tin chopped tomatoes
- a generous pinch of saffron stamens, softened in a little boiling water
- 1 tbsp runny honey
- salt and freshly ground black pepper
- 2 cloves garlic, peeled
- a squeeze of lemon juice

Drain the red peppers and place in the bowl of a food-processor with the tomatoes. Add the saffron, honey, salt and pepper, and blitz to a puree.

Pour into a saucepan, add the garlic and simmer for about 30 minutes until very thick and reduced by about half, stirring often. Taste and adjust the seasoning with lemon juice, salt and pepper. Transfer to a bowl to cool.

NIÇOISE SAUCE

SERVES 4-6

Another excellent example of how a tin of tomatoes and a few other choice ingredients can be turned quickly into an unusual pasta sauce. This one is adapted from Linda Collister's exhaustive *Sauce Book* (Conran Octopus, 1997). She suggests serving it with rigatoni or polenta. Also see Provençal Sauce (page 298), made with fresh tomatoes.

- 1 Spanish onion, peeled and finely chopped
- 3 tbsp olive oil
- 3 plump garlic cloves, peeled and finely chopped
- 400 g tin chopped Italian tomatoes
- 50 g anchovies preserved in olive oil, drained
- salt and freshly ground black pepper
- 1 tsp honey or sugar
- 400 g tuna in olive oil, drained
- 100 g good-quality black olives, pitted
- a squeeze of lemon
- 2 tbsp finely snipped basil

Soften the onion in the olive oil, in a medium-sized pan over a medium-low heat. Allow at least 20 minutes for this so that it is juicy and floppy and only lightly coloured when you stir in the garlic. Cook for several more minutes. Liquidize half the tomatoes with the anchovies. Add this with the rest of the tomatoes to the pan, season with pepper and add the honey or sugar. Simmer vigorously for several minutes to incorporate the flavours and thicken the sauce slightly.

Flake the tuna and stir it into the sauce. Heat through, add the olives, taste and adjust the seasoning with salt and lemon juice. Stir in the basil and serve.

OREGANO AND SUN-DRIED TOMATO SAUCE

SERVES 4

I've pinched the idea for this gorgeous posh garnish sauce from Michel Roux (senior) of the Waterside Inn. He serves it tepid or cold with meaty fish, such as tuna or monkfish, and offsets the flavours with a dribble of basil oil made by blitzing fresh basil leaves (5 g) with extra-virgin olive oil (30 ml).

75 g sun-dried tomatoes in olive oil

100 g vine tomatoes

100 ml chicken stock

1 tbsp balsamic vinegar

½ tbsp finely chopped oregano or marjoram leaves

salt and freshly ground black pepper

Place both sorts of tomato, the chicken stock and the vinegar in the bowl of a food processor. Blitz at high speed for 2 minutes. Pour into a bowl and stir in the oregano or marjoram. Taste and season with salt and pepper.

SALSA MARINARA/SUGO DI POMODORO

SERVES 6-8

Alla Marinara usually means sailor's-style and doesn't refer to a particular combination of ingredients. In America, however, it is the universal name for tomato sauce. Even more confusingly, Pizza alla Marinara is the original pizza from Naples, topped only with tomatoes, garlic and oregano. *Sugo* just means sauce.

This, then, is a fresh tomato version of the ubiquitous full-bodied tomato sauce of Italy, thick, dark and full of flavour without being sweet or acid. It is the sauce that might turn up smeared on pizza, and is used in all manner of pasta dishes as well as accompanying meat, fish and vegetable dishes. The concentration of flavour and the combined thickness and dryness of the sauce can be varied by the length of cooking. In this version oregano is the favoured seasoning, but basil, parsley, thyme or celery would be good alternatives.

The unorthodox ingredient is tomato ketchup. You may prefer to leave it out or substitute the more usual tomato puree. I find that the sweetness of the ketchup compensates for any shortcomings in less than perfectly ripe tomatoes. Which, let's be honest, is often the case in the UK.

75 ml olive oil

3 medium onions, peeled and finely chopped

3 plump garlic cloves, peeled and finely chopped

1.4 kg ripe tomatoes, cored, peeled, seeded and chopped

2 tbsp tomato ketchup

2 tbsp chopped oregano leaves

salt and freshly ground black pepper

Warm the oil in a large, deep, heavy-bottomed saucepan over a medium heat. Put in the onion and cook, stirring occasionally, for about 20 minutes until glassy, softened and beginning to colour. Add the garlic and cook until fragrant. Add the tomatoes, ketchup and oregano. Season generously with salt and pepper. Reduce the heat, partially cover the pan and cook at a gentle simmer for about 15 minutes until the tomatoes are soft and merged with the onions into a jammy sauce. Remove the lid and continue cooking until the required consistency is achieved. Taste and adjust the seasoning.

CLASSIC TOMATO COULIS/ TOMATADA

SERVES 4-6

Tomato coulis is a fresh-tasting, light and elegant tomato sauce with the super-smooth, creamy texture of ketchup. It is cooked with the minimum of additional flavourings: merely shallot (or onion) and garlic (or not).

This sauce crops up repeatedly throughout the book. Its uses are legion and it can be served hot or cold. It goes with fish and meat, is wonderful teamed with béchamel to make baked pasta dishes, and is particularly good mixed with fresh, diced tomato and shredded basil, stirred into hot or cold pasta. It is obvious that the better tomatoes you use the better the flavour of the coulis. Michel Roux, for example, uses French Marmande tomatoes in the coulis he serves at the Waterside Inn at Bray. If they aren't available, very ripe plum or beef tomatoes would be a good alternative. Using more olive oil – M. Roux uses 150 ml – makes the sauce softer and more voluptuous. In Spain and Portugal, a rough-and-ready version of this sauce, made with onions and flavoured with parsley, is called Tomatada.

- 3 tbsp olive oil
- 2 garlic cloves, peeled and crushed to a paste with a pinch of salt (optional)
- 60 g shallots, peeled and finely chopped
- bouquet garni, made with several parsley stalks, 1 bay leaf and 3 sprigs thyme bundled in a leek leaf
- 750 g very ripe Marmande, beef or plum tomatoes, cored, peeled, seeded and chopped
- pinch of sugar
- salt and freshly ground black pepper

Warm the olive oil in a heavy-bottomed pan with the garlic, shallot and bouquet garni. After a couple of minutes, add the tomatoes, sugar and a generous seasoning of freshly ground black pepper, and cook very gently, uncovered, for about 1 hour, stirring occasionally with a wooden spoon until all the moisture has evaporated.

Remove the bouquet garni and blitz the contents of the pan to make a smooth puree. Season to taste. The sauce will keep in an airtight container in the fridge for 5 days.

FRESH TOMATO SAUCE

SERVES 4

Quick and rustic. A simple, refreshing sauce to stir into hot or cold pasta. Delicious with cold poached eggs or meatballs.

- 350 g ripe tomatoes
- salt and freshly ground black pepper
- 1 tbsp vinegar, either red wine, sherry or balsamic
- 1 clove garlic, peeled and very finely chopped (optional)
- 4 tbsp olive oil
- about 10 basil leaves, shredded

Cut the tomatoes in half lengthways, then grate them with the cut side of the tomato facing the grater. Discard the skins. Season the pulp with salt, pepper, vinegar and garlic. Beat in the olive oil. Shred the basil over the top. Stir loosely.

FRESH TOMATOES

FAST CHERRY TOMATO SAUCE

SERVES 4-6

- 25 g butter
- 3 tbsp water
- 500 g cherry tomatoes
- salt and freshly ground black pepper
- sugar
- 1 tbsp tender green herbs

Melt half the butter with the water in a frying pan over a high heat. Add the tomatoes and cook for 2-3 minutes, swirling them round the pan, breaking them up with the back of a wooden spoon. As soon as they have split and begun to soften, press them through a food mill or sieve. Taste and adjust the flavour with salt, pepper and sugar. Continue cooking slowly if you want a thicker sauce. Whisk in the remaining butter in lumps to thicken. Stir in the herbs, chopped or whole, and serve hot or cold.

FRESH TOMATO COMPOTE

SERVES 4-6

A cross between a sauce and a salsa. Serve it with simply cooked chicken or cold cuts. Refreshing and delicious, it always goes down well as part of a cold spread.

- 1 tbsp balsamic vinegar
- 5 tbsp olive oil
- 6 ripe plum tomatoes, cored, peeled, seeded and diced
- sea salt and freshly ground black pepper
- a few basil leaves (optional)

Whisk the vinegar in the olive oil and pour over the tomatoes. Season with a crumble of sea-salt flakes and black pepper. Snip the basil leaves over the top, if liked.

ROAST TOMATO SAUCE

MAKES 500 ML

An intensely flavoured, voluptuous, deeply coloured tomato sauce that can be served hot or cold. Halved tomatoes are roasted with garlic and chopped onion, then everything is blitzed and sieved for maximum smoothness. The sauce will keep happily, covered, in the fridge for up to a week. To make Roast Tomato and Roast Red Pepper Sauce include two quartered and seeded red peppers on the roasting-tray.

- 1 kg medium tomatoes, halved
- salt and freshly ground black pepper
- 1-2 tsp caster sugar
- 3-4 tbsp olive oil
- sprigs of thyme (optional)
- 75 g chopped onion
- 4 garlic cloves, left unpeeled, cracked

Pre-heat the oven to 300°F/150°C/gas mark 2.

Lay the tomato halves, cut side up, on a lightly oiled baking-sheet. Sprinkle them with salt, pepper and caster sugar, then dribble with a little olive oil, just a few drops for each tomato. If you wish to flavour the tomatoes with thyme (or another herb), lay the sprigs across the tomatoes.

Bake for 1 hour then scatter the onions over the tomatoes and tuck the garlic round the edge. Cook for a further 30 minutes, checking that the onions don't catch and burn, until the tomatoes have softened and collapsed, and ceased to be very juicy.

Cool slightly. Then either force the contents of the pan through a sieve, or remove the garlic skin then liquidize everything together and pass through a sieve. Taste and adjust the seasoning.

MEXICAN GRILLED TOMATO SAUCE SERVES 4

The ubiquitous chilli-tomato sauce of Mexico.

- 4 medium tomatoes
- 2 green chillies
- ½ small onion
- 8 springs of coriander
- juice of ½ lemon
- salt and freshly ground black pepper

Grill the tomatoes either over coals (ideally), a naked flame or under the grill. Turn as the skin blisters and blackens but keep going until the flesh is soft. Puncture the chillies with a fork, and grill until charred. Grill the onion until the skin and cut edge is charred and the flesh softened.

Scrape the skins off the tomatoes, chillies and onion, then blitz the flesh in the food-processor with the coriander, lemon juice and a generous seasoning of salt and pepper. Alternatively, pound the tomatoes with the roughly chopped chillies; finely chop the onion and coriander and stir both into the tomato-chilli paste. Season with lemon juice, salt and pepper.

TOMATO SAUCE WITH MARSALA SERVES 4

A slug of Marsala warms up this quickly made tomato sauce, which is thickened with scraps of ham. Serve it with rice, couscous, fried polenta or use as a sauce with pasta, meat or fish.

- a knob of butter
- 1 small onion, chopped
- 4 slices prosciutto, shredded
- 450 g tomatoes, cored, peeled, seeded and coarsely chopped
- 1 garlic clove, peeled and chopped
- salt and freshly ground black pepper
- 75 ml Marsala

Melt the butter in a small pan, stir in the onion and cook it until it is soft but uncoloured. Add the prosciutto, cooking until it begins to curl. Put in the tomatoes and garlic, season with salt and pepper and cook briskly for 5 minutes. Add the Marsala and cook for 2 more minutes. Taste, adjust the seasoning and serve.

PIZZAIOLA/NAPOLITANA SAUCE SERVES 3-4

Pizzaiola or Napolitana is a thick tomato sauce flavoured with herbs, traditionally oregano and garlic. Although common throughout Italy, it originates in and is a speciality of Naples, and owes its name to the fact that it tastes remarkably like the standard Napolitana pizza topping. Sometimes it is called Napolitana. It can be made with fresh or canned tomatoes. Use it as a pizza topping or as a cook-in sauce for meat.

2 garlic cloves, peeled and finely chopped

2 tbsp olive oil

350 g ripe tomatoes, cored, peeled, seeded and diced

1 tbsp finely chopped fresh oregano

salt and freshly ground black pepper

Stew the garlic in the olive oil without colouring, add the tomatoes and cook vigorously for 6 minutes. Stir in the oregano, taste and season with salt and pepper. The sauce is now ready to be used as a cook-in sauce.

To use it as a pizza topping, cook it slightly longer, until it is thick and dry with a smearing consistency, before adding the oregano.

FISH FUMET WITH TOMATOES AND BASIL

SERVES 6

Very occasionally, food tastes so drop-dead gorgeous that you never forget it. That happened to me on a visit to the Waterside Inn at Bray where this clear, pale pink tomato nectar was ladled over fillets of steamed fish. Ironically, I don't remember much about the fish it accompanied but I just had to try to replicate that fumet. Fortunately, the recipe is published in *Sauces* by Michel Roux, with stunning photography by Martin Brigdale. It is made by using tomatoes, red pepper, basil and egg white to clarify and flavour fish stock. Although it seems rather a palaver, it is not difficult so do have a go. For the fish stock, simmer 500 g white fish trimmings and bones with chopped leek and onion, mushroom stalks, and a splash of white wine for about 20 minutes. Strain and season.

600 ml fish stock
500 g very ripe tomatoes, chopped
1 small red pepper, finely chopped
50 g basil, chopped
4 egg whites
8 peppercorns, crushed

Pour the fish stock into a saucepan. Mix together all the other ingredients and add to the pan. Bring to the boil over a medium heat, stirring every so often with a wooden spoon. Once the mixture has come to the boil, reduce the heat and simmer very gently for 20 minutes. Do not stir.

All the ingredients will form into a crust that traps any impurities. Try to disturb it as little as possible when you crack a hole in the clarification crust and spoon the fumet through a sieve into a bowl. Taste and season with salt.

TOMATO SAUCE WITH CUMIN MAKES ABOUT 750 ML

Cumin, with its haunting musty flavour, gives a distinctly Arabic flavour to this Spanish recipe, adapted from Janet Mendel's version in *Traditional Spanish Cooking*, for a smooth tomato sauce. Serve with simply cooked fish, such as red mullet, cod or haddock. Also good with lamb kebabs.

- 1 small onion, peeled and chopped
- 1 garlic clove, peeled and chopped
- 3 tbsp olive oil
- 2 kg tomatoes, cored, peeled and chopped
- 1 tsp salt
- ½ tsp ground black pepper
- ¼ tsp ground cumin
- 1 bay leaf
- a small bunch of parsley
- 100 ml white wine, stock or water

Fry the onion and garlic in the olive oil until softened. Add the tomatoes and cook over a high heat for several minutes before adding the salt, pepper, cumin, bay leaf, parsley and white wine, stock or water. Simmer partially covered, stirring occasionally, for 45 minutes.

Sieve or puree the sauce in a blender.

TWO TOMATO SAUCES WITH CINNAMON

SERVES 6

At the River Café, in West London, they are keen on cinnamon. It goes into sweet and savoury dishes, which is customary in several Arab cuisines but not, as far as I know, in Italian cooking. It works well in tomato sauces, adding its haunting fragrance and musty warm flavour to other more Italian ingredients. I am particularly taken with two of these sauces. The first one is cooked for ages, and is made with tinned tomatoes, coriander seeds, chilli and garlic. It is served with grilled lamb and grilled aubergine.

The second sauce is quicker, made with fresh tomatoes and flavoured with oregano and mint as well as fresh and dried chillies and garlic. This is conceived as a sauce in which to bake a whole loin of tuna, but it goes well with other dense-fleshed fish and almost anything else you might serve with a powerfully flavoured tomato sauce. The original (catering size) recipes can be found in *River Café Cook Book 2* (Ebury). My versions of both have been scaled down by approximately half.

TINNED TOMATO SAUCE WITH CINNAMON

- 3 tbsp olive oil
- 2 garlic cloves, peeled and thinly sliced
- 1½ tsp coriander seeds, crushed
- 1 dried red chilli, crumbled
- 1 whole cinnamon stick
- 2 x 400 g tins plum tomatoes, drained of most of their juices
- salt and freshly ground black pepper

Heat the oil in a pan and gently fry the garlic, coriander seeds, chilli and cinnamon. When the garlic is golden brown, add the tomatoes and roughly break them up. Season with salt and pepper, and cook slowly, stirring occasionally, for at least 1½ hours. Taste again for seasoning. Remove the cinnamon sticks before serving. 'The sauce should be thick and sweet with a hint of the chilli, coriander and cinnamon.'

FRESH TOMATO SAUCE WITH CINNAMON

- 3 tbsp olive oil
- 3 garlic cloves, peeled and finely chopped
- 1-2 dried red chillies, crumbled
- ½ cinnamon stick
- ½ tsp dried oregano
- ½ tsp coriander seeds, lightly crushed
- 3 tbsp finely chopped mint
- 1 kg ripe plum tomatoes, cored, skinned, seeded and roughly chopped
- 1 large fresh red chilli, seeded and chopped
- salt and freshly ground black pepper

Heat the oil in a large, thick-bottomed pan. Add the garlic, dried chilli, cinnamon, oregano and coriander, and fry together until the garlic turns golden. Add the mint, tomatoes and fresh chilli. Stir and cook at a high heat for 10-15 minutes until the tomatoes reduce slightly. Taste and season with salt and pepper.

Use as a baking sauce for fillets of red mullet or cod (allow about 15 minutes) or serve cold. Remove the cinnamon before serving.

COLD TOMATO SAUCE 'JEAN YANNE'

SERVES 4

Remember *nouvelle cuisine*? Remember the vegetable terrine with a tomato coulis? That was the dish made famous by the Troisgros brothers and this sauce is the real McCoy coulis that was served with Terrine of Vegetables 'Olympe'. Jean Yanne, incidentally, is a film director and friend of the Troisgros brothers.

- 500 g tomatoes, preferably Marmande or similar Mediterranean variety, cored, peeled and seeded
- 1 tsp tomato puree
- 1 tbsp wine vinegar
- 3 tbsp virgin olive oil
- salt and freshly ground black pepper
- 12 tarragon leaves, coarsely chopped
- 1 sprig of flat-leaf parsley, coarsely chopped

Press the tomato pulp though a sieve with the back of a spoon. Stir the tomato puree into the pulp, then whisk in the vinegar and olive oil, drop by drop, until completely incorporated. Season with salt and pepper, and stir in the parsley and tarragon.

SAUCE AURORE

When a dish is described as '*à l'Aurore*', it means it comes with a thick smooth tomato sauce made by mixing tomato puree into béchamel sauce and finished with cream and/or butter. It is most often teamed with eggs – sliced, sauced, then burnished under the grill – but is good with poached eggs, cauliflower and pasta.

- 250 ml milk
- ½ small onion, chopped
- ½ bay leaf
- 1 clove
- salt and freshly ground black pepper
- 25 g butter
- 25 g flour
- nutmeg
- 50 ml crème fraîche or thick cream
- 100 ml Cooked Tomato Coulis (see page 242)
- a knob of chilled butter

First make the béchamel by placing the milk, onion, bay leaf and clove in a small pan. Add a pinch of salt. Simmer gently for a few minutes, turn off the heat, cover the pan and leave to infuse for 15 minutes.

Melt the butter in a second pan. Stir in the flour and cook very gently for a minute or two without browning. Strain the infused milk into the roux, and bring the sauce to simmer, whisking vigorously. Cook over a very low heat for a few minutes, season with nutmeg, salt and pepper. Add the cream, stirring with a wire whisk, and simmer for a couple of minutes before adding the tomato coulis. Bring back to the boil and simmer for 5 more minutes. Taste and adjust the seasoning with salt, pepper and nutmeg. Whisk in the chilled butter.

CHILLED LIGHT TOMATO SAUCE

SERVES 4

There is a footnote at the end of the recipe for Chilled Light Watercress Puree in Michel Guérard's *Cuisine Gourmande* that suggests substituting tomato concassé and tomato puree for the watercress: 'The result is a beautifully rosy sauce with a refreshing flavour.' It is also rich and luxurious and would be lovely served with a fish terrine or cold fish.

- 2 leaves (25 g) gelatine
- 2 tsp butter
- 1 heaped tbsp chopped shallot
- 3 heaped tbsp tomato concassé (see page 29), drained
- 1 tbsp tomato puree
- 1 level tbsp chopped tarragon
- 1 pinch chopped garlic
- 2 tbsp dry white wine
- 350 ml whipping cream, very cold
- salt and freshly ground black pepper
- 1 tsp lemon juice

Begin by putting the gelatine to soak and swell in cold water. Heat the butter in a saucepan and soften the chopped shallot for 1 minute, stirring with a wooden spatula.

Add the tomato concassé and puree, the tarragon, garlic and white wine, cover and cook for 1 minute. Add 150 ml of the cream, season with salt and pepper and reduce, simmering, for 10 minutes. Remove from the heat and add the drained gelatine, which will dissolve on contact with the heat. Whisk the mixture well. Pour it into the liquidizer, add the lemon juice and blend for 1 minute until you have a smooth red puree. Put the mixture into a bowl and chill.

Take the chilled sauce out of the fridge and, in a second bowl, whip the remaining cream gently with a balloon whisk for 45 seconds. The cream will become light and froth up to one-third more than its original volume. Continue beating faster for 20-30 seconds. It will thicken but should not become as thick as egg whites beaten to a firm snow. Add the whipped cream to the tomato puree, folding the two together using a wooden spatula. Taste for seasoning and chill until needed.

TOMATO HOLLANDAISE WITH BASIL

SERVES 4-6

Creamy Hollandaise stirred with diced, peeled tomatoes and freshly snipped basil. Heaven. Serve it with poached cod, haddock or sea bass. Or try it with hot peeled new potatoes and instead of basil, try chives.

FOR THE HOLLANDAISE

- 150 g unsalted butter
- 2 egg yolks
- salt and freshly ground black pepper
- juice ½ lemon
- 2-3 plum or other fleshy ripe tomatoes, cored, peeled and diced
- a handful of basil leaves, finely snipped

To make the Hollandaise, melt the butter, rest it for a moment then skim off the froth that will have collected on the top. Whisk the two egg yolks with a splash of cold water over a very low heat until thick and creamy. Continue whisking while adding the melted butter, leaving behind the milky residue in the bottom of the pan. Season with salt and pepper and stir in the lemon juice.

Rest the diced tomato on absorbent kitchen paper so that it is as dry as possible. Just before serving, stir it and the basil into the sauce.

SAUCE ANTIBOISE

SERVES 4

In the style of Antibes on the Côte d'Azur: garlic and tomatoes are the key ingredients, the style is fresh and light. Particularly good with grilled fish, such as red mullet and sardines, anchovies or tuna. Some people add black olives. Also see Sauce Vierge, page 333, which is similar but not the same.

- 3 shallots, peeled and finely chopped
- 1 clove garlic, crushed
- 125 ml olive oil
- 300 g tomato concassé (see page 29)
- 10 black olives, quartered (optional)
- 10 large basil leaves, cut into fine strips
- 12 large coriander leaves, finely chopped
- salt and freshly ground black pepper
- lemon juice

Cook the shallot and the garlic very gently in the olive oil, to soften but not colour. Add the diced tomato and olives, if using, tossing so that they just warm through. Then put in the herbs, and gently combine all the ingredients. Remove from the heat, season with salt, pepper and lemon juice. Note: the tomatoes should not be allowed to get too hot or they will soften. Serve immediately.

FRESH TOMATO KETCHUP AND QUICK TOMATO KETCHUP

Neither of these ketchups is designed to keep; both are for making then eating. Neither ends up the colour of Heinz but both have similar texture; Fresh Tomato Ketchup is fluffier and lighter on account of the apple. It is a grown-up ketchup, with a fruity, fresh, well-rounded flavour, a hint of chilli (Tabasco) and cinnamon, which quickly overpowers the sauce, so watch it. Its colour is darker and less vibrant than Heinz and similar to Whole Earth organic tomato ketchup.

The Quick Tomato Ketchup is a deep terracotta colour and is richly flavoured – balsamic vinegar, thyme, garlic – but its taste is less complex. Both sauces go with anything you might want to eat with ketchup, but have a life beyond. You won't feel guilty, for example, spreading them on bread with a fried egg on top. In fact, these ketchups go with most egg dishes – superb, say, with a courgette frittata or cheese soufflé – but are also a good thing to remember when you want a quick sauce to serve with lamb or chicken kebabs.

If necessary, pour them through a funnel into a bottle or jar and store in the fridge. Both will keep longer if you float a layer of olive oil on top each time you put them away.

FRESH TOMATO KETCHUP

MAKES ABOUT 425 ML

- 1 small onion, chopped
- 1 garlic clove
- 2 tbsp olive oil
- salt
- 1 red pepper, cored, seeds and filament discarded, chopped
- 1 stick of celery, chopped
- 700 g very ripe tomatoes, chopped coarsely
- ½ cooking apple, peeled and chopped
- 1 tbsp red wine vinegar
- ¼ tsp ground allspice
- 3 tbsp white sugar
- a few drops of Tabasco
- 5-cm cinnamon stick
- lemon juice

Soften the onion and garlic in the olive oil with a pinch of salt. Add the red pepper and celery. Cover the pan and cook gently for 5 minutes before adding the tomato and apple. Cook uncovered for about 15 minutes until the tomato has cooked into juice with the core and skin floating around in it.

Pass through a sieve (or liquidize), add the vinegar and allspice. Simmer gently until reduced by half and very thick. Stir in the sugar, Tabasco and cinnamon. Cook for 10 minutes. Remove the cinnamon. Taste and adjust with salt and a squeeze of lemon juice. Allow to cool then chill before serving.

QUICK TOMATO KETCHUP

MAKES ABOUT 350 ML

- 350 g medium very ripe tomatoes
- 2 roughly chopped garlic cloves
- 1 sprig thyme
- 1 tbsp balsamic vinegar
- 1 tbsp olive oil
- 1 tbsp brown sugar

Quarter the tomatoes and place in a pan with all the other ingredients. Cover and boil hard for 5 minutes. Remove the lid, boil for a further 5 minutes until syrupy and reduced slightly. Pass through a sieve. If it isn't the consistency of ketchup, simmer until it is. Cool and chill.

GAZPACHO SAUCE

SERVES 4

An undiluted version of the famous cold salad soup (see pages 110-111) from Andalusia. It goes well with simply grilled fish and scallops, with hot new potatoes and chicken kebabs.

- 6 ripe, medium tomatoes
- 1 medium red onion, chopped
- 1 small cucumber, peeled and chopped
- 2 garlic cloves, chopped
- 1 red pepper, seeds and white filament discarded, diced
- 2 shakes Tabasco or another chilli sauce
- 75 g white breadcrumbs
- 1 tbsp sherry vinegar
- 4 tbsp olive oil
- salt and freshly ground black pepper

Place all the ingredients, except the olive oil, in the bowl of a food-processor. Blitz until smooth, then pour through a sieve to catch stray pips and skin. Taste and adjust seasoning. Whisk in the olive oil in a slow trickle.

ROMESCO

SERVES 4-6

The tale of the annual *romescada* at Cambrils near Tarragona, a kind of challenge to fishermen to produce the 'best' Romesco, is told by Patience Gray in *Honey from a Weed*. Paprika, made with local sweet peppers (*pimentòn*), is pounded with tomatoes, almonds, garlic and bread fried in olive oil, to make a rich, luscious sauce to eat with the day's catch.

This voluptuous sauce goes with most foods you might serve with a tomato sauce – it is superb with boiled potatoes and grilled meats – but could be used as a cook-in sauce. Traditionally Romesco is made in a mortar by pounding the ingredients one by one, but an acceptable version can be prepared in a food-processor by adding the olive oil in a slow trickle at the end. Inevitably, there are many recipes for Romesco. This one is based on one of two versions given by Patience Gray.

- olive oil
- a good slice of pain de campagne
- 12 blanched almonds
- 3 cloves garlic
- 4 large tomatoes, grilled on a wood fire (or under the grill), then peeled, cored and seeded
- 1 wine glass full-bodied red wine, 150 ml
- 1 dsp paprika
- generous pinch chilli powder
- 1 tsp wine vinegar

Heat sufficient oil to cover the base of a frying-pan and fry the slice of bread until golden. Add less than a tablespoon of oil to the hot pan and stir-fry the almonds until golden.

Pound the bread in a mortar, adding the garlic, then the tomatoes, then the almonds, working each to a paste before adding the next. Finally, introduce the wine, paprika, chilli powder and wine vinegar, reducing the whole to a fine smooth paste.

SAUCE CATALANE

SERVES 4

Combining tomatoes with oranges is a particularly Spanish idea, but I discovered this sauce, made with bitter Seville oranges, in Elizabeth David's *French Provincial Cooking*: 'From the Perpignan district, to the west of the Languedoc, where the cookery has a distinct Spanish influence, (this sauce) in its native region goes particularly with partridges and with pork. But it is good with other things from chicken and mutton to fried eggs or slices of baked gammon.'

- 2 tbsp olive oil
- 5 garlic cloves, peeled
- 450 g very ripe tomatoes, cored, peeled and roughly cut up
- salt and freshly ground black pepper
- scant tsp sugar
- 6 slices of Seville or bitter oranges, pips but not skin removed

Heat the olive oil in a sauté pan. Stir in the garlic and tomatoes. Season with a little salt and pepper, and add the sugar. Cook for 10 minutes. Now add the orange slices and cook, uncovered, for a further 20 minutes until the sauce is thick. If you like, remove the garlic before serving. 'The bitter orange slices give a curious and interesting flavour to the sauce but do not let them cook in it for more than 20 minutes or it will be too bitter.'

SAUCE AMÉRICAINE

SERVES 6

Although associated with lobster, this luscious, smooth cook-in sauce goes well with other dense-textured seafood, such as monkfish and cod. Its rich flavour comes from fish stock, Cognac and cream, as well as tomatoes, and it is a deep orange colour.

- a knob of butter
- 1 tbsp olive oil
- 1 medium onion, peeled and chopped
- 1 carrot, peeled and diced
- 2 garlic cloves, peeled and chopped
- 750 g tomatoes, cored, peeled and roughly chopped
- 1 glass dry white wine approximately 150 ml
- 3 tbsp Cognac or brandy
- bouquet garni, made with 2 sprigs thyme, 2 sprigs tarragon, 1 bay leaf, piece of leek green and several parsley stalks
- ½ tsp sugar
- 300 ml fish stock
- salt and freshly ground black pepper
- 1 tbsp tomato puree
- 4 tbsp thick cream
- Tabasco

Melt the butter with the oil in a medium-sized saucepan and stir in the onion, carrot and garlic. Cook for several minutes until the onion is beginning to colour and soften. Add the tomatoes, white wine, Cognac or brandy, bouquet garni, sugar and stock. Season well. Bring to the boil and simmer uncovered for about 20 minutes until the sauce has thickened slightly.

Suspend a sieve over another saucepan, discard the bouquet garni and press the sauce ingredients against the side of the sieve to extract all the liquid. Boil the sauce for several minutes until it has thickened. Whisk in the tomato puree and cream. Taste, and adjust the seasoning, adding a few drops of Tabasco if liked. I do.

SAUCE GRELETTE

SERVES 2

This sauce was invented by Roger Verge and the name is a play on the word *aigrelette*, which means slightly tart; the sauce isn't, so he shortened it to *grelette*, which means 'slender'. It's a cross between a salsa and a regular sauce, the finely diced tomato held together with a little cream, mustard, brandy and white wine vinegar, with a few fresh herbs mixed in at the end. It goes particularly well with cauliflower and watercress.

350 g ripe tomatoes, cored, peeled, seeded and diced

3 tbsp double cream

scant tbsp red wine vinegar

½ tbsp Dijon mustard

1 tsp brandy

½ tbsp each chopped chervil, tarragon and flat-leaf parsley

salt and freshly ground black pepper

Mix together all the ingredients in a bowl. Taste and adjust seasoning.

TOMATO CONCASSÉ WITH RED WINE AND THYME SYRUP

SERVES 4

A perky, sweet-sour, chilli-spiked sauce-cum-salsa for oily fish, such as sardines, herring and mackerel. Serve the fish grilled, preferably gutted, beheaded and butterflied.

- 2 glasses dry red wine
- 1 tsp redcurrant jelly
- 1 sprig thyme
- 1 clove garlic, finely chopped
- a pinch of dried crushed chillies
- salt and freshly ground black pepper
- 4 plum tomatoes, cored, peeled, seeded and diced
- ½ tbsp finely chopped flat-leaf parsley

Place the red wine, redcurrant jelly, thyme, garlic and chillies in a small pan and boil rapidly, stirring until the jelly dissolves, until reduced to 3 tablespoons of liquid. Season with salt and pepper, allow to cool slightly then stir in the tomatoes. Toss with the parsley and serve.

TOMATO JAM WITH BALSAMIC VINEGAR AND OLIVE OIL

SERVES 4

I came up with this recipe when I wanted something to improve the appearance of a dull-looking frittata. The dark terracotta sauce worked a treat. With a few well-chosen leaves, the combination makes a stylish starter and would be an excellent dish for a picnic (but transport the jam separately and anoint before you eat).

As the 'jam' is flavoured with balsamic vinegar, thyme, garlic and olive oil, this smooth sauce goes with almost everything. Try it spooned over potatoes and couscous or use it like a vinaigrette with grilled vegetables.

- 350 g very ripe medium tomatoes, quartered
- 2 garlic cloves, peeled and roughly chopped
- 1 tbsp balsamic vinegar
- 1 tbsp olive oil
- 2 tsp pale brown sugar or honey
- salt and freshly ground black pepper

Place all the ingredients in a pan, except the salt and pepper, cover and boil hard for 5 minutes. Remove the lid, continue for a further 5 minutes until syrupy and slightly reduced. Force through a sieve.

If the sauce isn't the consistency of ketchup, simmer it until it is. Taste and adjust the seasonings with salt and pepper.

TOMATO SAUCE WITH SPRING ONION, GARLIC AND CHIVES

SERVES 4

A quick, fresh-tasting, chunky sauce, which is good hot or cold. Shredded rocket or watercress, young spinach or sorrel leaves, parsley or basil could be added in place of the chives. Serve it with pasta, meatballs, sausages, chicken kebabs, or as a dressing for boiled potatoes or green beans.

- a large knob of butter
- 1 bunch spring onions, trimmed and finely sliced
- 2 garlic cloves, peeled and finely chopped
- 500 g ripe tomatoes, cored, peeled and chopped
- 1-2 tbsp tomato ketchup (depending on sweetness of tomatoes)
- salt and freshly ground black pepper
- a bunch of chives or another soft herb, finely snipped

Melt the butter in a frying-pan that can hold all the ingredients. Add the spring onions and garlic and cook over a gentle heat for about 5 minutes until softened. Add the tomatoes, 1 tablespoon of ketchup, raise the heat and boil hard for 5 minutes. Taste and adjust the seasoning with salt, pepper and possibly more ketchup. Cook for a few more minutes, stir in the chives and serve.

If required cold, allow to cool before adding the herbs.

INDIAN MAKHANI TOMATO SAUCE

SERVES 4

Makhan means butter in some Indian dialects, and in this instance it means that the sauce has been cooked in butter. It is a rich, creamy, smooth sauce, delicious on its own with rice or dhal, scooped up with naan or chapati. It can also be used as a cook-in sauce for fried prawns, fish or chicken, but is very good with potatoes.

750 g tomatoes, cored, peeled and chopped

4 green cardamom pods

3 green chillies, seeded and chopped

6 garlic cloves, peeled

5 cm piece fresh ginger, peeled and chopped

3 black peppercorns

1 tsp red chilli powder or cayenne pepper

40 g butter

1 tbsp tomato puree

3 tbsp double cream

salt and freshly ground black pepper

½ tbsp sugar

1 tsp ground fenugreek (optional)

2 tbsp chopped coriander leaves

Place the tomatoes, cardamom, chillies, garlic, ginger and crushed black peppercorns in a suitable saucepan with the chilli powder or cayenne pepper and half of the butter. Bring to the boil, lower the heat and simmer very gently, uncovered, for 1 hour. Pass through a sieve. Stir in the tomato puree, whisk in the remaining butter and cream, taste and adjust the seasoning with salt, pepper and sugar. Add the fenugreek, if liked, stir in the coriander and serve.

Also see:
Tomatoes and Pasta (pages 267-307)
Tomatoes Alone (pages 31-58)
Tomatoes with Other Vegetables (pages 193-219)
Dealing with a Glut (pages 392-406)

tomatoes and pasta

'Well, there's no recipe – it's just tomato sauce, reduced and passed.' Finally, she concluded that she uses 'lots of garlic, more than most people'.

'Herbs?'

'Oh, yes, always *pebre d'ai* (winter savory), it grows just outside the kitchen door.'

'Thyme? Bay? Parsley?'

'No, only *pebre d'ai* . . . of course the tomatoes have to be peeled!'

'Why?' 'Well, I don't want peel in my sauce!'

'But if the sauce is passed . . .'

'When I say that I pass it, I don't mean that I pass it through a sieve or a food mill – that's too much work. I just mix it (with a hand-held electrical immersion blender), which is easier and, besides, that way the seeds stay in the sauce – I like to bite on a tomato seed.'

Lulu Peyraud to Richard Olney, in *A Provençal Table* (Pavilion, 1995).

I always knew it was going to be difficult to keep this section of the book under control. At one point, when my cooking and researches seemed to be spiralling out of control, I contemplated giving up on the rest of the book and concentrating on tomatoes and pasta. However, I settled eventually on favourite recipes that I return to because I love them so much. Many are my interpretation of classic Italian tomato pasta sauces, such as fiery Arrabbiata, intensely tomato Puttanesca, and Spaghetti con Vongole. Others, such as Tomato Lasagne and Grilled Plum Tomatoes with Pesto, are new ideas. Sometimes these recipes have turned out to be classic recipes.

Many of the well-known tomato sauces are inextricably linked with a type of pasta. Penne, fusilli, rigate, spaghetti, tagliatelle and linguine are names you will see repeatedly when it comes to tomato sauce. There is a good reason for this: tomato sauce needs a pasta it can cling to and the short stubby pastas and the long spaghetti family are the best for this. When these pastas are tossed with tomato sauce with chunks of tomato in it, the sauce clings to the pasta, running over it and inside it, so that every mouthful is properly coated. The practicalities of eating pasta with tomato sauce inspire passionate consideration in Italy, particularly in tomato-producing areas. Take Nino Squillacciotti. He is Mr Pomodoro. He lives and breathes tomatoes, working as a chemist and food scientist with responsibility for new-product development for Italian tomato giant Cirio. He told me proudly about a new spaghetti shape he has invented that will be able to take up 40 per cent more sauce. It may be available by the time you read this book. It is a ridged spaghetti and, a it cooks, the ridges increase in volume. When it is added to the tomato sauce, the sauce is trapped inside the pasta; a sort of Venus fly-trap spaghetti.

As a general rule, avoid tomato-flavoured pasta. If you want to make your own, add 2 tablespoons of tomato concentrate to the dough.

PENNE CON SUGO CRUDO

SERVES 6

Raw chopped tomatoes marinated with olive oil and basil, mixed into freshly cooked al dente penne.

- 8 large ripe plum tomatoes, cored, peeled and chopped into 1cm pieces
- salt and freshly ground black pepper
- 8 tbsp top-quality olive oil
- a bunch of fresh, pungent basil
- 500 g penne

Put the tomato pieces and their juices into a bowl. Season generously with salt and pepper and pour over the olive oil. Tear the basil over the top, stir everything together and leave covered for at least 30 minutes.

Put a large pan of water on to boil and salt it lightly. When boiling vigorously, add the pasta and stir immediately. Cook until al dente. Reserve a little cooking water, then drain the penne into a colander placed in the sink. Quickly return the pasta and the reserved cooking water to the pan and stir in the tomato mixture. Serve immediately. This is delicious made with lemon olive oil.

ORECCHIETTE WITH FRESH TOMATOES

SERVES 2

This is one of my favourite quick suppers and something to make with intensely flavoured sun-ripened tomatoes. The tomatoes are diced and stirred into hot pasta, which has been tossed with the very best olive oil. The dish is particularly fine if the tomatoes are peeled and their seeds removed but if you do that it is vital to save the watery-looking juice and pour that into the pasta too. I like it with no other adornment apart from a twist of sea salt and black pepper but an obvious addition would be basil or a finely chopped chilli pepper. Any short, stubby pasta would work well for this dish but it is particularly pleasing made with orecchiette, the round pasta that looks like little ears.

- 200 g orecchiette
- 350 g vine-ripened tomatoes, cored and peeled
- 4 tbsp extra-virgin olive oil
- salt and freshly ground black pepper

Cook the pasta according to the packet instructions. Drain, then toss with one tablespoon of the cooking water.

Meanwhile, quarter the tomatoes lengthways and scrape out their seeds into a sieve over a bowl. Dice the tomato flesh quite chunkily. Whisk the olive oil into the sieved juice, mix in the tomatoes and, when the pasta is ready, stir the two together. Season generously with salt and pepper.

PASTA 'AL SUGO FREDDO'

SERVES 4-6

One of the classic pasta and tomato dishes: cold raw tomato against hot pasta and molten nuggets of mozzarella, all undercut with bursts of zing from raw garlic and chilli. Simple and very effective.

500 g penne or similar stubby pasta

FOR THE SAUCE

- 500 g ripe but firm tomatoes, cored, peeled, seeded and diced
- 1 buffalo mozzarella, diced
- 15 large basil leaves, sliced into strips
- 2 plump garlic cloves, peeled and worked to a paste with a little salt
- ½ tsp dried chilli flakes
- 7 tbsp extra-virgin olive oil
- salt and freshly ground black pepper

Cook the pasta according to the packet instructions. Drain, reserving 2 tablespoons cooking water. Toss the pasta with the reserved water and keep it warm. While the pasta is cooking, mix together all the sauce ingredients. Taste and season with salt and pepper. However, the flavours will be even better if the sauce is made in advance and left to marinate for a couple of hours.

To serve, toss the drained pasta with the sauce. Leave it to stand for a couple of minutes before serving.

CONCHIGLIE PRIMAVERA

SERVES 6

A short essay on the importance of using excellent ingredients accompanies this recipe in Alastair Little's book *Italian Kitchen*. What it requires, he remonstrates, is ripe, flavoursome plum tomatoes, pungent, fresh basil, fresh, creamy ricotta (ideally made from buffalo milk), best-quality olive oil, and pasta cooked al dente. Timing, too, is of crucial importance. Then, and only then, will the dish taste as intended.

- 8 large ripe flavoursome plum tomatoes
- salt and freshly ground black pepper

Begin making this dish 1 hour before you wish to eat it.

Dip the tomatoes for exactly 1 minute into boiling water, then plunge into cold water. Drain and peel, then chop the tomatoes into 1 cm pieces, leaving the seeds intact. Transfer to a bowl and

- top-quality olive oil
- a bunch of very fresh, pungent basil
- 500 g conchiglie
- 150 g fresh ricotta preferably ricotta di bufala

season generously with salt and pepper and a liberal slug of olive oil. Tear the basil into the tomatoes. Leave covered in a cool place for the salt to draw out the tomato juices and form a sauce.

Thirty minutes before serving, put 5 litres of water on to boil, and salt it lightly. When it is boiling vigorously add the pasta and stir immediately to prevent it sticking to the pot. It takes approximately 10 minutes to cook. While it is cooking mix the ricotta into the 'soupy' tomatoes in the bowl.

When the pasta is al dente, reserve half a cup of the cooking water and drain the pasta in a colander – carefully, so much boiling water creates a lot of steam. Working quickly, transfer the drained pasta back to the pan and stir in the reserved cooking water. Tip in the tomato and ricotta mix and thoroughly toss again. Either serve it at table or dish it up in the kitchen. Do *not* add Parmesan.

SPAGHETTINI ALLA CAPRESE

SERVES 4-6

So simple, so quick. Use the best-quality ingredients you can find.

- 400 g plum tomatoes, cored, peeled, seeded and diced
- 12 black olives, pitted and sliced
- 50 g basil leaves, shredded
- 4 tbsp extra-virgin olive oil
- 100 g buffalo mozzarella, finely diced
- salt and freshly ground black pepper
- 500 g spaghettini
- 1 tbsp freshly grated Parmesan cheese

Mix the diced tomato with the sliced black olives and shredded basil, then toss with the olive oil. Add the diced mozzarella and season with salt and pepper.

Cook the spaghettini until al dente. Drain thoroughly, return to the pan and toss with the Parmesan. Stir the sauce ingredients into the pasta. Toss well, then serve in warmed bowls.

CAMPANELLE WITH FETA CHEESE, TOMATOES AND COURGETTES

SERVES 2

The creamy yet sharp, salty tang of feta cheese, sweet acidity of fresh ripe tomatoes and delicate freshness of lightly cooked courgette are effectively offset by the haunting lemon zip of kaffir lime leaves. Quick, easy and delicious, with a good balance of textures: soft, slippery, crumbly and chewy.

- 6 ripe plum tomatoes
- 200 g egg campanelle
- salt and freshly ground black pepper
- 3 dried kaffir lime leaves or 1 fresh
- 2 medium courgettes, trimmed, quartered lengthways and diced
- 5 tbsp crème fraîche
- 100 g Greek feta cheese

Bring a large pan of water to the boil. When it is ready, remove it from the heat and drop the tomatoes into the water. Count 5 seconds then remove them with a spoon. Bring the water back to the boil, add the pasta and ½ teaspoon of salt. Cook according to the packet instructions.

Cut the tomatoes lengthways into quarters, rip off the skins, cut out the cores and pull out the seeds. Chop the flesh and tip it into a bowl. Rub the dried kaffir lime leaves between your hands over the bowl, or finely shred then chop the fresh leaf and add it to the bowl.

Put a second pan of water on to boil, add salt and, when vigorously boiling, add the courgettes. Cook for 30 seconds, drain and tip them into a suitable serving-bowl that can hold all the ingredients. Drain the pasta thoroughly and add to the bowl with the crème fraîche. Stir well. Chop or crumble the feta into small pieces over the bowl, put in the tomatoes and lime leaves, season with black pepper and stir to mix everything. Serve immediately, or allow to cool and serve as a salad.

CHILLI LINGUINE WITH SPINACH AND LEMON COTTAGE CHEESE AND FRESH TOMATO SAUCE

SERVES 2

This is a bright, vibrant summer recipe when fresh tomato sauce is used to lubricate chilli pasta, which adds a gentle but noticeable buzz to the dish that would have been hard to achieve in any other way. In fact, it adds just the right amount of background excitement needed for this subtle, light, healthy sauce-cum-topping. This is a two-part operation: part one is making a quick, fresh tomato sauce, and part two is jazzing-up some cottage cheese.

- 250 g chilli linguine
- 1 garlic clove, worked to a paste with a little salt
- 1 tbsp olive oil
- 450 g tomatoes, cored, peeled, seeded and chopped
- 1 tbsp tomato ketchup
- salt and freshly ground black pepper
- zest (no white) and juice of 1 lemon
- 250 g cottage cheese
- ½ tsp freshly grated nutmeg
- 100 g young leaf spinach
- 1 tbsp finely chopped flat-leaf parsley

Cook the linguine according to the packet instructions.

Briefly fry the garlic in the oil without colouring, then add the tomatoes. Cook briskly for 3 minutes, letting the mixture soften and thicken. Stir in the tomato ketchup and season with pepper.

Chop the lemon zest finely. Tip it into a bowl with the cottage cheese and the nutmeg, then squeeze over the lemon juice. Season with salt and pepper, and stir thoroughly. Shred the spinach and place it in a colander. Rinse it with boiling water, then with cold water. Drain it thoroughly, pressing against the side of the sieve to remove all the water. Add the spinach to the cottage-cheese mixture with half of the parsley.

To serve, divide the linguine between 2 hot bowls. Spoon over most of the tomato sauce, top with the cottage cheese, then a little more tomato, and sprinkle over a share of the reserved parsley.

TOMATO VODKA PASTA

SERVES 6

This delicious tomato sauce is made by cooking a couple of tins of good-quality Italian tomatoes with garlic, a few dried chilli flakes, a small carton of double cream, a slug of olive oil, and a measure (or two) of vodka. This is the sort of sauce that needs fine-tuning to your taste – more chillies, perhaps, or more vodka. The latter isn't immediately obvious but definitely contributes to a lip-smacking tang that sets this tomato sauce apart from others.

This is one of those pasta dishes where the cooked pasta is stirred into the sauce and the two are briefly cooked together before the dish is served. This version is envisaged as a main dish. For an elegant starter, heat 6 tablespoons of sieved concassé for 5 minutes with 4 tablespoons of double cream. Stir in 2 tablespoons of vodka, then season and serve with a spoonful of caviare, preferably Sevruga, and a sprinkling of chives.

- 2 tbsp olive oil
- 2 plump garlic cloves, peeled and finely chopped
- 2 x 400 g tins Italian tomatoes
- ½ tsp dried chilli flakes or hot pepper sauce, or to taste
- 100 ml double cream
- salt and freshly ground black pepper
- 500 g penne
- 2 tbsp vodka, or to taste
- a squeeze of lemon juice
- 3 tbsp finely chopped flat-leaf parsley

Heat the oil in a pan large enough to hold sauce and pasta. Fry the garlic over a medium-low heat for a couple of minutes, stirring to prevent it turning brown. If you own a mouli-legumes, place it over the pan and puree the tomatoes directly into it. If not, blitz the tomatoes and their juice in a food-processor before you start cooking the garlic, and tip it through a sieve to catch some of the phenomenal number of pips. Add the chilli flakes and simmer quite vigorously until the puree thickens slightly. After 10 minutes stir in the cream. Taste and season with salt and pepper.

Meanwhile, cook the pasta according to the packet instructions. Drain very carefully and stir it into the finished tomato sauce. Add the vodka, stir again and simmer for 1 minute. Taste again and, if necessary, adjust the seasoning with lemon juice. Stir the parsley into the sauce. Serve immediately in hot soup bowls and await gasps of wonder.

TAGLIATELLE WITH TOMATO SAUCE AND BUTTER

SERVES 4-6

Fresh tomato sauce, stirred with creamy unsalted butter into the pasta. Eat with a shower of chopped parsley and freshly grated Parmesan.

- 4 tbsp extra-virgin olive oil
- 2 garlic cloves, peeled and finely chopped
- 2 x 350 g Cirio Rustica (page 20) crushed tomatoes or 2 x 400 g tins whole Italian tomatoes
- salt
- 500 g fresh tagliatelle or fetuccine
- 50 g unsalted butter
- 2 tbsp finely chopped flat-leaf parsley
- freshly grated Parmesan

Pour the oil into a large frying-pan and gently cook the garlic, stirring over a low heat until aromatic but without browning. Tip the crushed tomatoes directly into the pan, or if using whole tomatoes, place a food-mill over the pan and puree the tomatoes directly into it. Raise the heat to medium and cook, stirring often, until the sauce is thick, about 15 minutes. Taste, and season during cooking with salt.

Meanwhile, boil the pasta in plenty of salted water until al dente. Drain thoroughly. Transfer the pasta to the frying-pan. Remove it from the heat and toss to blend thoroughly. Rest for a moment or two before serving in warmed shallow bowls. Place a large pat of butter on top of each serving and shower with parsley. Pass the Parmesan for people to help themselves.

SPAGHETTI COLLA SALSA DI POMODORI

SERVES 6

'In Apulia, where I suspect a fresh tomato sauce is made daily in summer in every household,' begins this recipe in Patience Gray's compulsive *Honey from a Weed*, 'there is a perforated tin utensil, rectangular in form, for sieving the sauce, called a *mattareddha*, found in weekly markets.' This is the recipe she gives. It results in a thick, voluptuous sauce, which transforms a simple spaghetti into something truly memorable. Serve with a dusting of freshly grated pecorino.

olive oil

1 sweet white onion, chopped

leaves from a head of celery (sedano, celery grown as a herb, is preferred)

1 tsp dried oregano

a small bunch of flat-leaf parsley, leaves only, chopped

1 kg fresh plum tomatoes, gently squeezed to release some of the pips

1 bay leaf

a few drops red wine vinegar

½ tsp salt

1 tsp sugar

500 g spaghetti

pecorino

Cover the bottom of a pan that will hold all the ingredients with olive oil. Put in the onion, celery, oregano and parsley. Cook for a few minutes without browning, then put in the tomatoes, bay leaf, wine vinegar, the salt and sugar, and cook slowly, covered, over a heat-diffuser pad. After 40 minutes, pass the sauce through a sieve and, if it has not the consistency of a thick sauce, reheat it and cook until it has.

Meanwhile boil the spaghetti in plenty of salted water until al dente. Drain and turn into a warm bowl. Pour the sauce over the spaghetti and serve with grated pecorino.

PENNE ALLA SALSA DOPPIA

SERVES 6

I read about the 'double sauce' in Patience Gray's *Honey from A Weed*. The name refers to a spectacular dish that dates back to the ancient practice of preparing food communally, and is made with equal layers of pasta, grated pecorino and a hot pepper and tomato sauce. The pasta is tossed and served with a second sauce, made by simmering fine ripe plum tomatoes in olive oil with garlic and fresh basil leaves, poured over the top. More grated pecorino crowns the dish. 'I doubt,' says Patience Gray, 'whether this double sauce has ever been recorded, yet it exists, but probably only where the summer fields are gleaming with the new tomato crop.' Here's my version of the dish based on the descriptive prose in her book.

4 tbsp olive oil

a bunch of bulbous salad onions, trimmed and sliced

2 red chilli peppers, seeded and sliced

1 litre La Salsa (see page 276)

3 garlic cloves, peeled and finely sliced in rounds

8 ripe plum tomatoes, cored, peeled and squeezed to remove some of the pips

a handful of fresh basil leaves

500 g penne rigate or orecchiette

pecorino

Heat 2 tablespoons of the olive oil and soften in it the onion and chilli without colouring. Add the salsa and simmer while the pasta boils in plenty of salted water until it is al dente.

Meanwhile, put the remaining olive oil in a second pan and gently cook the garlic until aromatic but uncoloured. Stir in the tomatoes and basil and allow them to stew and soften but without losing their basic shape.

To assemble the dish, drain the pasta and make layers in a large hot dish of pasta, sauce and grated pecorino. When the layering is finished mix everything together. Lay the whole tomatoes over the top, giving the dish a final scattering of grated pecorino.

SPAGHETTI ALLA PUGLIESE

SERVES 4

Spaghetti is part-cooked then finished in the pan with a sauce made of anchovy, chilli, garlic, capers, black olives and tomatoes. Another idea for this sauce is to soften an onion before adding the tomatoes, garlic and anchovy, and serve the capers and black olives, with a handful of basil and flat-leaf parsley leaves, as a garnish. In this case the sauce is spooned over spaghetti and served with lamb meatballs or thick slices of roast loin of lamb, which has been rolled through chopped herbs.

- 400 g spaghetti
- 6 anchovy fillets preserved in olive oil
- 5 tbsp olive oil
- 500 g tomatoes, cored, peeled and chopped
- ½ red chilli (or more to taste), finely chopped
- 1 garlic clove, peeled and finely chopped
- 8 basil leaves
- 1 tbsp finely chopped flat-leaf parsley
- 12 black olives, pitted and halved
- 1 heaped tbsp capers, rinsed and squeezed

Bring a large pan of salted water to the boil, put in the spaghetti and half cook it. Drain.

Roughly chop the anchovies. Heat the olive oil in a deep frying-pan and mash them into it to make a rough paste. Add the tomatoes, chilli and garlic and tear the basil over the top. Cook over a medium heat for about 15 minutes or until the sauce has thickened. Taste and adjust the seasoning. Add the drained spaghetti to the pan. Increase the heat and cook, stirring constantly, until the spaghetti is al dente. Add the parsley, olives and capers. Mix well and serve.

PENNE ALLA PUTTANESCA

SERVES 6

Chilli, black olives and basil combine with tomatoes to make a delicious sauce that translates as 'whore'. Every cook makes it differently, altering the quantities, the length of time it is cooked and sometimes adding other ingredients. In summer, with the sweet, succulent tomatoes, it is one of the finest pasta sauces. In winter, when canned tomatoes are a necessity, it is different altogether. A version of Puttanesca, with raw tomatoes, is made by adding crushed dried chillies to the recipe for Penne con Sugo Crudo (see page 269).

Puttanesca is a rough-and-ready sauce. For a refined version, remove the tomato seeds.

- 500 g penne
- 5 tbsp olive oil
- 1 large onion, peeled, halved and sliced
- 1 red chilli (or more to taste), finely chopped
- 1 garlic clove, peeled and finely chopped
- a handful of basil leaves
- 1 kg ripe tomatoes, cored, peeled and chopped
- 20 plump black olives, pitted and halved

Boil the penne in plenty of salted water until it is al dente. Drain and keep warm.

Heat the oil in a suitable pan over a medium heat and gently cook the onion until floppy but hardly coloured. Add the chilli, garlic and a few basil leaves, and cook for a few more moments before adding the tomatoes. Increase the heat, season with salt and pepper and cook for 10-15 minutes or until thickened. Stir in the olives and the rest of the basil. Serve over or stirred into the drained penne.

SUGO DI POMODORO E MELANZANE

SERVES 4

This sauce is a classic combination of tomatoes and aubergines. Although my quantities are for two as a main course, they are easily scaled up in proportion. Watch out for the chilli, though: the quantity given already packs a hefty punch.

- 1 aubergine, sliced 0.5 cm thick
- 5 tbsp extra-virgin olive oil
- 1 medium onion, peeled, halved and finely sliced
- 1 plump garlic clove, peeled and finely chopped
- 1 green chilli, seeded and finely chopped
- 400 g ripe tomatoes, cored, peeled, seeded and diced
- salt and pepper
- a few basil leaves
- 50 g finely grated pecorino or Parmesan
- 400 g penne, cooked al dente

Place the aubergine slices in a bowl and sprinkle over 3 tablespoons of olive oil, quickly tossing the slices around to cover all of them with a smear of oil. If you are using a frying-pan, get the pan very hot and cover the surface with a film of oil. Reduce the heat immediately to medium-low and fry the aubergine slices in a single layer until soft to the touch and scorched in places. If you are using a griddle, get it very hot and cook the slices quickly until they are tender and beginning to wilt. Lay them out on kitchen paper, then press down to get rid of some of the oil.

Add the remaining oil to the pan and fry the onion and garlic until soft and golden. Add the chilli, then the tomatoes and aubergine slices. Season with salt and pepper, add the basil leaves torn up. Cook for a further 4 minutes. Stir in the cheese and serve with penne.

GRILLED TOMATO CASARECCE WITH PESTO

SERVES 4

When you grill little plum tomatoes, or one of the other small 'grown for flavour' or vine-ripened varieties until their skins burst, the flesh softens slightly and their juices begin to dribble, their flavour intensifies wonderfully. Tossed with olive oil and a little balsamic vinegar they are great as they are stirred into hot pasta but even more delicious with pesto.

- 450 g baby plum or other small tomatoes, stalks removed
- 3 tbsp olive oil
- 350 g casarecce
- 1 tbsp balsamic vinegar
- salt and freshly ground black pepper

FOR THE PESTO

- 3 tbsp pine nuts
- 60 g basil leaves
- 2 garlic cloves, peeled and roughly chopped
- 7 tbsp best-quality olive oil
- 3 tbsp freshly grated Parmesan, plus extra for serving

Pre-heat the grill.

Place the tomatoes in a bowl with the olive oil and toss around gently so that they are all glistening. Tip them into a small oven-dish, place under the hot grill and cook until the skins pop and scorch.

Meanwhile, cook the pasta according to the packet instructions, and make the pesto. Heat a small, heavy frying-pan and stir-fry the pine nuts for a couple of minutes until they are lightly golden. Tip them on to absorbent kitchen paper to drain. Place the basil leaves in the bowl of a food-processor with the pine nuts and garlic. Blitz. When evenly chopped, with the motor still running, gradually add the olive oil and continue until nicely amalgamated, thick but slack. Transfer to a bowl and stir in the Parmesan.

When the pasta is cooked and drained, tip it into a suitable serving-bowl. Add the tomatoes with their juices and the vinegar. Season generously with salt and pepper. Gently stir together and loosely fold in 2 tablespoons of the pesto. Serve the rest separately for people to help themselves, and pass round some extra Parmesan.

CASARECCE WITH SPINACH, ROAST TOMATOES AND GOAT'S CHEESE

SERVES 4

Here's an example of how to use roast tomatoes to transform a simple pasta dish into something very special. Other ingredients include blanched spinach, mascarpone, tiny flecks of red chilli, goat's cheese and a squeeze of lemon juice. In this recipe, incidentally, the tomatoes are peeled; their skin would spoil the texture of the dish.

8 plum tomatoes, cored, peeled and halved through the core

2 tbsp olive oil

salt and freshly ground black pepper

½ tsp sugar

500 g casarecce or another short, chunky pasta

125 g mascarpone

400 g spinach, picked over, tough stalks removed

1 small bird's-eye chilli, seeded and finely chopped

200 g goat's cheese, diced

juice of 1 small lemon

Pre-heat the oven to 350°F/180°C/gas mark 4.

Arrange the tomatoes, cut side up, on a shallow baking-sheet lined with foil. Smear the tomatoes with olive oil, season with salt, pepper and sugar and cook in the oven for 20 minutes. Remove from the oven and cut the tomato halves in half again.

Cook the pasta according to the packet instructions. Tip it into a warm serving bowl and toss it with any remaining olive oil, then mix in the mascarpone, stirring until it has dissolved. Keep it warm.

Meanwhile, put a large pan of salted water on to boil. When the water is boiling, blanch the spinach for 30 seconds. Tip it into a colander and hold the spinach under cold running water for a few seconds, then squeeze it against the sides to get rid of all the water. Chop it roughly.

Stir the spinach into the pasta, mixing well, then stir in the chilli. Season well with pepper. Finally, stir in the lemon juice and loosely toss the mixture with the goat's cheese and tomatoes.

EGG TAGLIATELLE WITH FRESH HERBS AND GRILLED CHERRY TOMATO SALAD

SERVES 3-4

Pasta tossed with lemony olive oil and masses of fresh herbs is a wonderful canvas for grilled cherry tomatoes, served as a garnish.

- 1 tbsp red wine vinegar
- 1 tbsp whipping cream
- 1 tbsp Dijon mustard
- salt and freshly ground black pepper
- 150 ml vegetable oil
- 500 g cherry tomatoes
- 1 tbsp olive oil
- 225 g egg tagliatelle
- 2 tbsp best-quality olive oil
- 1 tbsp lemon juice
- 1 small garlic clove, peeled and chopped
- 1 small shallot, peeled and chopped
- 4 tbsp finely chopped tender green herbs, choosing a mixture of at least 3 of any of the following: chives, flat-leaf parsley, basil, mint, chervil or celery
- 1 tsp chopped thyme or rosemary or tarragon or marjoram
- a handful of either water-cress, rocket, sorrel or nasturtium leaves, chopped finely
- freshly grated Parmesan

First make the vinaigrette. Whisk together the vinegar, cream, mustard, salt and pepper and gradually add the vegetable oil. Set it aside.

Place the tomatoes in a bowl and use your hands to smear them with the tablespoon of olive oil, then lay them in a single layer in a grill-pan. Season with salt and pepper and place under a hot grill until they blister and split. Toss immediately in 4 table-spoons of the vinaigrette (keep the rest in the fridge but use it within a week).

Meanwhile, cook the pasta according to the packet instructions. Mix all the herbs together in a bowl. When the pasta is cooked al dente, drain it carefully, keeping back a couple of tablespoons of cooking liquid. Put the pasta back into the pan with the reserved liquid and toss with the 2 tablespoons of best olive oil, the lemon juice, the garlic and the shallot. Tip the seasoned pasta into a suit-able serving-bowl, sprinkle over the herbs, season with salt and pepper and toss thoroughly. Serve with the tomatoes on top. Hand round the Parmesan separately.

MACARONI WITH GARLIC, TOMATOES, ALMONDS AND BASIL

SERVES 4-6

This sauce is a variation on pesto.

75 g blanched almonds
6 garlic cloves, peeled
6 ripe plum tomatoes, cored, peeled, quartered and seeded
30 g basil leaves
salt and freshly ground black pepper
50 ml olive oil
500 g large macaroni

Heat a heavy frying-pan and stir-fry the almonds until they are evenly golden but not browned. Blitz them with the garlic in a food-processor. Add the tomatoes and basil, season with salt and pepper and process until smooth. With the motor running, or using a whisk if you prefer, beat in the olive oil. Taste and adjust the seasoning.

Cook the macaroni until al dente, then drain and dress with the sauce.

TONNARELLI WITH ROCKET, TOMATOES AND SHAVED PARMESAN

SERVES 4-6

The combination of slippery pasta with silky sweet tomatoes and the peppery tang of rocket, all undercut with salty, creamy Parmesan is a winning combination. The tomatoes could be roasted and the rocket and Parmesan turned into pesto, but in this recipe, from Arancio d'Oro in Rome – which I discovered in Patricia Wells's book *Trattoria* – the tomato is fresh, the rocket torn and the Parmesan shaved. At Arancio d'Oro they use a square pasta called tonnarelli, which is also known as *maccheroni alia chitarra*, and is similar to taccazzette, another square or diamond shape like small lasagne, a speciality of southern Italy.

- 500 g tonnarelli, tagliatelle or fettucine
- salt and freshly ground black pepper
- 50 g chunk of Parmesan
- about 75 g wild rocket or large-leaf watercress, washed, dried and torn
- 4 tbsp extra-virgin olive oil
- 4 large ripe plum tomatoes, cored and coarsely chopped

Bring a large pan of salted water to the boil. Put in the pasta and cook until al dente. Drain, toss with salt and pepper and keep warm.

Meanwhile, use a potato peeler to shave the Parmesan into long slices. Place half of it into a warmed serving-bowl that can accommodate the entire dish. Add the rocket, olive oil and tomatoes and toss to blend. Add the drained, seasoned pasta and toss. Season again and divide between warmed shallow soup bowls. Serve topped with the remaining Parmesan.

PENNE WITH TOMATO AND BALSAMIC VINEGAR

SERVES 6

A classy store-cupboard dish from the River Café in West London; they use syrupy ten-year-old balsamic vinegar, which gives the sauce a wonderful, rich depth of flavour, but supermarket stuff gives pretty good results too. I particularly recommend Belazu.

- 2 tbsp olive oil
- 2 garlic cloves, peeled and cut into slivers
- a handful of fresh basil
- 2 x 400 g tins peeled plum tomatoes
- salt and freshly ground black pepper
- 250 g penne rigate
- 75 g butter, cut into pieces
- 4 tbsp aged balsamic vinegar
- 120 g pecorino, freshly grated

Heat the oil in a large pan and gently fry the garlic until light brown. Add a few of the basil leaves and then the tomatoes. Stir and cook gently for 30-40 minutes, until the mixture has reduced to a thick sauce. Season with salt and pepper and add the remaining basil.

Cook the penne in a generous amount of boiling salted water, drain thoroughly and return it to the saucepan with the butter. When this has melted, add the balsamic vinegar and toss over a gentle heat for a few seconds until the penne are brown. Throw in a handful of the grated pecorino, and finally stir in the tomato sauce. Serve with more pecorino passed separately.

PENNE ALL' AMATRICIANA

SERVES 4

The original version of this sauce was made with pig's cheek. The secret of the dish is to cook the bacon and onions until golden brown, before reducing a little red wine and then adding the tomatoes. The sauce must be thick and almost dry with undercurrents of flavour. Some cooks like to put in rosemary, oregano or basil.

- 175 g pancetta, cut into matchsticks
- 2 tbsp olive oil
- 2 medium onions, peeled and finely chopped
- ½ tsp red chilli flakes or 1-2 dried red chillies, crumbled
- 1 glass red or white wine, 150 ml
- 2 x 400 g tins peeled plum tomatoes
- 1 tsp dried oregano
- 1 garlic clove, peeled and finely chopped
- salt and freshly ground black pepper
- 400 g penne
- 100 g Parmesan, freshly grated

Place the pancetta and the olive oil in a pan and cook, gently at first, then raising the heat as the fat begins to run, until the pancetta is crisp. Add the onions and chilli flakes and continue cooking for 10-15 minutes, until the onions are brown and crisp but not burnt. Pour in the wine – it will seethe and evaporate almost immediately – then the tomatoes, and season with oregano, chopped garlic, salt and pepper. Bring to the boil, lower the heat and simmer for at least 45 minutes, until the sauce is thick and almost dry.

Cook the penne in plenty of boiling salted water. Drain it thoroughly, toss it with half of the Parmesan, add it to the sauce and mix. Serve with extra grated cheese on the side.

PASTA E CECI

SERVES 4-6

The success of this comfort dish relies on soaking, then gently simmering the chickpeas – *ceci* – with rosemary, lots of garlic and olive oil, so that they end up creamy and well flavoured. Fresh tomatoes are then pureed into the chickpeas along with ditalini, or another small tubular pasta. Pasta e Ceci is often served as a soup but with pasta it is more like a vegetable stew. This recipe is based on one given by Anna del Conte in *The Gastronomy of Italy*.

200 g chickpeas
2 large sprigs rosemary
4 garlic cloves, peeled and crushed
75 ml olive oil
salt
500 g tomatoes, cored, peeled and chopped
150 g ditalini or another small tubular pasta
4 tbsp extra virgin olive oil to serve
4 tbsp freshly grated Parmesan, plus extra to serve

Soak the chickpeas in plenty of cold water for 8 hours. Drain and rinse them. Put them in a large, heavy-bottomed pan and add 1.5 litres of water. Add the rosemary, garlic and olive oil. Bring to the boil, turn down the heat, cover the pan tightly and cook at the lowest simmer until the chickpeas are tender, which can take from 2 to 4 hours, sometimes longer. When the chickpeas are ready, season with salt, then cook for a further 10 minutes. Discard the rosemary; the garlic will have melted.

Place a food-mill or sieve over the chickpeas and puree the tomatoes directly into the pan. Simmer for 10 minutes, then taste and adjust the seasoning. Meanwhile, bring a pan of salted water to the boil and cook the pasta until it is just al dente. Drain it and add to the chickpeas and tomatoes.

Ladle the soupy stew into warm bowls. Add a swirl of olive oil and a mound of Parmesan, handing round more separately.

MEATBALLS IN TOMATO SAUCE WITH SPAGHETTI: POLPETTINE CON SALSA DI POMODORO

SERVES 4

I once spent a blissful few days in and around Naples with Susanna Gelmetti and her colleagues from Cirio enjoying some superb tomato-based food. Susanna heads the Cirio Kitchen in Kensington, where she and other Italian cookery writers give demonstrations to show off the Cirio range of tomato products. She also runs Italian cookery weeks at schools on the Amalfi coast, Apulia and Umbria.

This is Susanna's version of the everyday Italian family dish Polpettine con Salsa Di Pomodoro. It is, of course, served with spaghetti. If you prefer, add the meatballs to the tomato sauce before serving. Another idea, which I particularly like, is to double the quantity of tomato sauce and toss sauce, spaghetti and meatballs together before serving with freshly grated Parmesan.

100 g fresh ricotta cheese
100 g Emmenthal, roughly chopped or grated
100 g very lean minced pork
150 g minced veal
1 egg
sunflower oil for frying
salt and freshly ground black pepper

FOR THE TOMATO SAUCE
400 g tin chopped tomatoes
4 tbsp extra-virgin olive oil
½ onion, finely chopped
fresh basil leaves, roughly torn
400 g spaghetti

Begin with the tomato sauce. Heat the olive oil in a pan and sauté the chopped onion for about 4 minutes. When the onion becomes transparent, add the tin of chopped tomatoes and cook for a further 20 minutes. Remove the pan from the heat. Add the roughly torn basil leaves and season. Keep the sauce warm until the meatballs are ready to serve.

To make the meatballs, combine the cheeses, meat and the egg. Season the mixture with salt and freshly ground black pepper and shape into cherry-size balls.

Cook the spaghetti in plenty of boiling salted water until al dente. Drain and keep warm.

Heat the sunflower oil in a frying-pan. When it is very hot, add the meatballs in batches, frying for about 2-3 minutes until crusty and cooked through. Remove and drain on kitchen paper. Serve the warm tomato sauce over the spaghetti and top with the meatballs.

SPAGHETTI WITH MI-CUIT TOMATOES, GARLIC AND CHILLI

SERVES 4

A classy store-cupboard dish, which is ready in the time it takes to boil the spaghetti.

350 g spaghetti

12-14 mi-cuit tomatoes (see page 21), cut into ribbons

3 garlic cloves, finely chopped

large pinch of dried chilli flakes

5 tbsp extra-virgin olive oil

1 tbsp finely chopped flat-leaf parsley

salt and freshly ground black pepper

Boil the spaghetti in plenty of salted water until al dente.

When it is almost ready, mix together the rest of the ingredients in a large frying-pan and heat. Drain the spaghetti and toss it well in the tomato mixture. Season with salt and pepper. Serve at once.

PENNE WITH RED ONIONS, TOMATOES, CHICKEN, FETA AND BASIL

SERVES 4-6

Light, fresh and packed with interest and summer flavours.

- 500 g penne
- 4 tbsp olive oil
- 2 big red onions, peeled, halved and sliced into chunky half-moons
- 1 plump garlic clove, finely chopped
- 700 g tomatoes, cored, peeled and chopped
- 6 skinless chicken thighs, cut into bite-sized pieces
- 3 tbsp balsamic vinegar
- salt and freshly ground black pepper
- 150 g feta cheese, diced in chunks
- a small bunch of basil, leaves only, torn

Cook the penne according to the packet instructions. Drain it and keep it warm.

Heat 2 tablespoons of the oil in a large frying-pan or heavy-based flameproof casserole over a medium heat. Stir-fry the onions until they wilt and soften. Add the garlic and continue to stir-fry for 10 minutes. Add the tomatoes, turn up the heat and boil fiercely for 2 minutes.

Meanwhile, in a separate frying-pan, heat the remaining 2 tablespoons of oil and brown the chicken all over. You may need to do this in batches, the idea being to cook it briskly over a medium heat, letting each surface get crusty, but not stick to the pan, before turning it over. This stage of the cooking should take about 2-3 minutes per batch. When all the chicken is done return it to the pan and pour on the balsamic vinegar. Let it bubble up and over the chicken to colour it, then gradually evaporate – which it does very quickly – and turn syrupy. Tip the mixture into the onions and tomatoes and simmer for 10 minutes to transfer flavours and finish cooking the chicken. Taste and season with salt and pepper. Stir in the feta and the basil, and serve immediately over the penne.

SPAGHETTI CON VONGOLE

SERVES 4

No book on tomatoes would be complete without this famous dish of spaghetti with clams in tomato sauce. It comes from the Amalfi coast. A very good version can be made with tinned tomatoes and clams, but this recipe is for the real thing: a garlicky fresh tomato sauce laced with parsley, plenty of small clams, such as palourdes, and al dente spaghetti. For ease of eating, most of the boiled clams are taken out of their shells but a few remain for the look of the dish.

- 2 kg small clams, scrubbed under running water
- 1 medium onion, peeled and chopped
- 2 garlic cloves, peeled and finely chopped
- 4 tbsp olive oil
- 750 g ripe tomatoes, cored, peeled, seeded and chopped
- 3 tbsp parsley
- salt and freshly ground black pepper
- 400 g thin spaghetti

Discard any clams that refuse to close when tapped against a hard surface. Pour 150 ml water into a pan large enough to hold the clams. Bring swiftly to the boil, add the clams and cover tightly. Cook for a few minutes, giving the pan a couple of firm shakes, until all the clams have opened.

Place a colander over a large bowl and tip in the clams. Discard any that have not opened. Give those that remain a good shake then return the liquid to the pan. Boil hard to reduce by half. Pour the liquid through a fine sieve lined with muslin or a new J-cloth to collect the grit. Set aside 12 clams in their shells and pick the rest out of their shells.

Soften the onion and garlic in 3 tablespoons of the olive oil without colouring. Add the tomatoes and most of the parsley. Season lightly with salt but with plenty of pepper. Pour in the reserved clam juice and boil until the sauce is thick and jammy. Taste and adjust the seasoning.

Meanwhile, boil the spaghetti in plenty of lightly salted water until al dente. Drain and toss it with the remaining olive oil and keep warm in a serving-bowl.

Stir all the clams into the sauce and reheat gently. Pour the sauce over the spaghetti, scatter over the last of the parsley and serve immediately.

LINGUINE WITH FIERY PRAWNS SERVES 3-4

Tinned chopped tomatoes are what you need for this quick, simple and utterly delicious dish made by frying chilli, garlic, spring onions and herbs with prawns and the tomatoes. The sauce is stirred into cooked linguine, scattered with more herbs and eaten with a squeeze of lemon.

- 400 g linguine
- 6 tbsp olive oil
- 400 g raw shell-on giant tiger prawns
- 2 garlic cloves, peeled and very finely chopped
- ½ habanera chilli pepper, seeded and very finely chopped
- a bunch of spring onions, trimmed and finely sliced
- 1 tbsp chopped coriander leaves
- 1 tbsp chopped flat-leaf parsley
- 400 g vine tomatoes, peeled, seeded and diced
- salt and freshly ground black pepper
- 1 large lemon, cut lengthways into 4

Cook the linguine according to the packet instructions. Drain and return it to the pan, then toss it with 1 tablespoon of the olive oil. Cover and keep warm.

If using frozen prawns, slip the prawns into a bowl of warm water for a few minutes, then drain them and remove their shells. Use a small sharp knife almost to split the prawns lengthways so that when cooked they open out butterfly-style.

Heat the rest of the oil in a large frying-pan over a medium-high heat and quickly fry the garlic, chilli, spring onions and half of the coriander and parsley. Then put in the prawns. Cook, stirring all the while, as they change colour from grey to pink, then tip in the tomatoes and heat through. Pour the sauce into the pasta and return the pan to the heat, toss for a few seconds, stir in the remaining herbs, season with salt and pepper and serve with a wedge of lemon, to be squeezed over the pasta just before it's eaten.

ROASTED AND RAW TOMATO SAUCE

SERVES 6

The dense texture of plum tomatoes is what you need for this ambrosial nectar. Some of the tomatoes are halved, seasoned with olive oil and a hint of thyme, then roasted slowly with garlic until their flesh is soft and the flavour intensified. Roasted and fresh tomatoes are pureed together then sieved, which results in a sauce that has a freshness and depth of flavour that beggars belief.

Serve with penne or a similar short, hollow pasta. Also good with dumplings and meatballs, with corned-beef hash and other greasy dishes, and poached chicken or boiled leeks.

12 large ripe plum tomatoes
3 tbsp olive oil
salt and freshly ground black pepper
3 plump garlic cloves
a small bunch of thyme
2 drops Tabasco

Pre-heat the oven to 325°F/170°C/gas mark 3.

Halve 6 of the tomatoes horizontally. Lay them on a sheet of foil on a baking-sheet. Smear them with olive oil and season with salt and pepper. Tuck the garlic cloves between the tomatoes and lay the thyme over the top. Bake for 30 minutes until the tomatoes are soft and the cut surfaces lightly scorched. Turn off the oven and leave the tomatoes in it for 10 minutes. Then take them out, discard the thyme and scrape the gooey tomato flesh and buttery garlic into the bowl of a food-processor.

Core, scald and peel the remaining tomatoes. Tip them into the food-processor. Blitz at high speed, then pass through a sieve. Taste and adjust the seasoning with salt, pepper and Tabasco. Whisk in the remaining olive oil and serve.

ALL' ARRABBIATA

SERVES 2-4

An 'angry' tomato sauce, enraged by chillies. It can be made with entirely fresh ingredients or a mixture of fresh and convenience – say, fresh tomatoes and dried chillies. It could be used as a sort of cook-in sauce for nuggets of poached or fried chicken, for chunks of white fish or prawns, and is delicious with steamed mussels, lamb or veal. It is also very attractive served over pasta with a dollop of mascarpone or crème fraîche with a scattering of basil leaves.

- **2 large red peppers**
- **2 tbsp olive oil**
- **2 red onions, peeled and chopped**
- **500 g ripe tomatoes, cored, peeled and chopped or 400 g tin Italian tomatoes**
- **1 red chilli, seeds discarded, finely chopped, or chilli sauce to taste**
- **20 basil leaves, snipped**
- **salt and freshly ground black pepper**
- **sugar**

Pre-heat the grill.

Rinse the peppers and cook under the grill, turning from time to time, until the skin is blackened and blistered all over. Transfer to a plate, cover with clingfilm and leave for 20 minutes before removing the skin. Halve the peppers lengthways and remove the stalk, seeds and white filament. Slice the peppers into 1cm strips.

Meanwhile, heat the oil in a medium saucepan over a medium-low flame. Fry the onions, stirring occasionally, until floppy but not coloured, about 10 minutes. Add the tomatoes to the onions. Turn up the heat and cook for about 10 minutes until thick. Add the peppers, the chilli and half of the basil and cook for a further couple of minutes. Taste and adjust the seasoning with salt, pepper and sugar (the tomatoes may need sweetening). Serve garnished with the remaining basil.

RED PESTO

SERVES 6

This works best when it is made with sun-dried tomatoes that have been preserved in oil. The great advantage of using oil-preserved tomatoes is that the oil can be used in the recipe. It's a pity that red pesto ends up looking so sludgy – it is nowhere near as attractive or aromatic as its green relative pesto Genovese. In fact, the first time I made it, I added tomato concassé to improve its looks, which turned out to be a very good idea. On another occasion I added a handful of basil, and I've made it with a few finely chopped black olives stirred in. All these additions, incidentally, should be made after the pesto is finished so that they look distinctive and the taste is separate from that of the pesto.

Despite its unappetizing appearance, red pesto tastes terrific. It has an intensely tomato flavour, undercut with a rich, creamy tang from the pine nuts, oil and Parmesan. It is used like regular pesto: a dollop stirred into hot pasta. Mixed with yoghurt or cream, it becomes an instant creamy pasta sauce. Red pesto will keep in the fridge for several days.

best-quality olive oil

75 g pine nuts

100 g sun-dried tomatoes, preserved in oil

3 garlic cloves

100 g fresh grated Parmesan or pecorino cheese

salt and freshly ground black pepper

OPTIONAL EXTRAS

6 good-quality black olives, pitted and chopped

2 tbsp chopped grilled red pepper

a handful of finely chopped basil

a handful of chopped coriander leaves

½ small red chilli, finely chopped

Heat a frying-pan, add a few drops of oil and stir-fry the pine nuts until they are lightly golden. Touch on absorbent kitchen paper to drain.

Place a sieve over a bowl and tip the tomatoes into it. Shake a couple of times. Place the tomatoes, garlic and pine nuts in the bowl of a food-processor and blitz to make a chunky, rough paste. Scrape down the sides of the bowl so that everything is amalgamated. With the motor running, gradually add the drained tomato oil and the olive oil until the mixture emulsifies into a thick, soft, creamy puree. Transfer to a bowl, stir in the Parmesan and season to taste with salt and pepper. If you plan to include one or more of the optional extras, add them now.

CHERRY TOMATO AGRODOLCE WITH BACON

SERVES 8

Imagine, if you will, the sweet, fruity intensity of perfectly ripe cherry tomatoes. Roast half a kilo with olive oil, basil and a splash of balsamic vinegar, then puree the soft flesh with a small quantity of stewed onions, celery and bacon. Mix everything together and you have a luscious, rich sauce. Serve it stirred into pasta, as a poaching sauce for chicken or cod fillets, or use it with béchamel in baked pasta dishes.

1 kg ripe cherry tomatoes
4 tbsp olive oil
1 tbsp balsamic vinegar
1 tbsp snipped basil leaves
1 tsp runny honey
salt and freshly ground black pepper
100 g rindless, thin streaky bacon, sliced into lardons
1 medium onion, peeled and finely chopped
2 sticks celery heart, finely chopped
juice of ½ lemon
Tabasco to taste
Worcestershire sauce

Pre-heat the oven to 325°F/170°C/gas mark 3.

Place the tomatoes, 3 tablespoons of the olive oil, the balsamic vinegar, basil, honey and a pinch of salt in a lidded enamel or earthenware casserole. Cover and cook in the oven for 40 minutes or until the tomatoes are squashy.

Meanwhile, place the bacon in a small saucepan with the remaining olive oil. Cook gently until the fat begins to run and the meat changes colour. Add the onion and celery and cook, stirring every so often, until the vegetables are very soft and golden. Spoon off the excess fat and tip the contents of the pan into the bowl of a food-processor. Add the tomato and blitz at high speed until liquidized. Pour it through a sieve, to catch the pips and skin, into a clean saucepan. Taste, and adjust the seasoning with lemon juice, salt and pepper and a few drops of Tabasco and Worcestershire sauce. Simmer for a few minutes before serving.

PROVENÇAL SAUCE

I'm never quite sure what the exact difference is between a dish called Provençal and one called Niçoise. Both are cooked with tomatoes and garlic, often onions too. Black olives, which are always in dishes called Niçoise, are sometimes in those described as à la Provençale. Anyway, this particular Provençale sauce has the lot: tomatoes, onions, garlic and black olives, and a few other ingredients associated with the South of France. It is delicious with pasta, couscous or potatoes, and makes a delicious cook-in sauce for chicken (see page 358) and cod.

4 tbsp olive oil

2 medium onions, peeled, halved and finely sliced

4 garlic cloves, peeled and sliced in wafer-thin rounds

20 basil leaves, torn

1 sprig of thyme

salt and freshly ground black pepper

6 anchovy fillets, chopped

1 glass white wine, 150 ml

500 g ripe tomatoes, cored, peeled and chopped

18 good-quality black olives, pitted

Choose a heavy-bottomed pan. Place it over a medium heat and add 2 tablespoons of the oil.

Stir in the onions, garlic, basil and thyme. Season with salt and pepper. Cover the pan and sweat everything gently until it is soft, floppy and quite juicy. Stir in the anchovies and the wine. Cook, uncovered, until most of the liquid has disappeared. Add the tomatoes and simmer for 15 minutes until the sauce thickens. Add the olives. Cook for a few minutes, check the seasoning and serve.

SAUSAGES WITH CARAMELIZED ONION AND TOMATO SAGE SAUCE

SERVES 4

A simple, quick way of using tomatoes to transform sausages into an elegant supper dish. Serve over penne or spaghetti. Also good with rice or potatoes.

- **2 tbsp cooking oil**
- **1 large Spanish onion, peeled, halved and sliced into wedges**
- **8 butcher-style, high-meat-content pork sausages**
- **6 sage leaves, shredded**
- **1 tbsp Dijon mustard**
- **8 medium-sized ripe tomatoes, peeled, cored and roughly chopped**
- **a pinch of sugar**
- **salt and freshly ground black pepper**
- **1 tbsp coarsely chopped flat-leaf parsley**

Put the oil in a spacious pan over a medium heat. When it is hot, stir in the onions and cook for about 12 minutes until they brown and turn tender but without burning.

Meanwhile, run a sharp knife down the sausages to slash the skin. Peel it off and discard. Break each sausage into 6 pieces. Drop them into the onions and stir-fry, adding the sage. Cook for 6-8 minutes until firm. Stir in the mustard. Add the chopped tomatoes, season with a pinch of sugar and plenty of salt and pepper. Simmer for about 8 minutes, until the tomatoes make a thick sauce. Toss the parsley over the top and serve.

PAPPARDELLE WITH CHICKEN LIVERS AND TOMATOES

SERVES 4

A favourite, even with people who think they don't like chicken livers.

- approximately 400 g chicken livers
- 2 tbsp olive oil
- 2 plump garlic cloves, peeled and crushed
- 1 small onion, peeled and finely chopped
- 1 tsp rosemary leaves, chopped to dust
- 3 good-sized sage leaves, shredded and finely chopped
- 1 glass red wine, 150 ml
- 400 g tin chopped tomatoes
- salt and freshly ground black pepper
- 500 g pappardelle
- a knob of butter
- freshly grated Parmesan

Rinse the livers and pat them dry with kitchen paper. Remove any stringy membrane or discoloured parts. Cut into 2.5 cm pieces.

Heat the olive oil in a frying-pan over a medium heat. Add the garlic and cook for 2 minutes without letting it brown. Add the onion and cook until soft for about 8 minutes. Add the prepared livers, rosemary and sage, and cook, stirring, until the livers are browned all over, 2-3 minutes. Remove the livers to a plate. Turn up the heat. Add the wine and stir vigorously as it bubbles, allowing it to reduce by half. Add the tomatoes, and cook for 10-15 minutes until the sauce becomes noticeably thick and jammy. Taste and season with salt and pepper.

Meanwhile, cook the pasta in plenty of salted water until al dente. Drain it and toss with the butter in a warmed serving bowl. Return the livers to the pan and heat through for a minute or two. Pour the sauce over the pasta, toss and serve with freshly grated Parmesan.

SALSA ROSSA (COOKED)

SERVES 4

Fresh Salsa Rossa (see page 189), like its relative Salsa Verde, is a relish-cum-sauce served to liven up gently flavoured foods such as poached meats and fish. This cooked version is delicious with pasta and pasta gratins and goes well with poached and fried or barbecued fish and meat. It can be served hot or cold. It is a good sauce to build upon and could be used as a cook-in sauce with, for example, canned clams or nuggets of chicken. Like All' Arrabbiata (see page 295), it is a sauce that can be made entirely with fresh ingredients, with a combination of fresh and convenience, or entirely with convenience.

2 large mild onions, peeled and finely chopped
4 tbsp olive oil
2 red peppers
1 small red chilli, seeded and finely chopped
2 plump garlic cloves, peeled and finely chopped
400 g tin Italian tomatoes
salt and freshly ground black pepper

Gently sauté the onion in the olive oil until it is slippery and tender. Allow at least 20 minutes for this.

Meanwhile, pre-heat the grill and lay under it the peppers, turning as the skins blister black. Transfer to a plate, cover with clingfilm and leave for 20 minutes before removing the skin. Discard stalk, pips and white filament, then dice the flesh. Add the peppers, chilli and garlic to the onions and continue cooking for a further 10 minutes. Add the tomatoes and their juice to the pan, turn up the heat and boil hard for 10 more minutes. Tip the contents of the pan into the bowl of a food-processor and blitz at high speed until pureed. Taste and season with salt and pepper. Salsa Rossa can be kept in a jar in the fridge for up to 2 weeks; a thin layer of olive oil reduces deterioration.

GOLDEN TOMATO LASAGNE WITH BASIL AND VINE TOMATOES

SERVES 4

This is a lovely light summer lasagne made with several different-shaped and sized tomatoes including two golden varieties but regular red tomatoes would be good too. As is usual with baked lasagne, the dish is finished with a topping of sauce but here it's scattered with tiny golden tomatoes, which will scorch, blister and taste divine. Just before serving, the surface is scattered with basil leaves, which immediately release their heady aroma. This is a dish to make and eat: if left around, the tomatoes will weep and make the sauce watery.

- 1 red pepper
- 30 g butter, plus a little extra
- 1 heaped tbsp flour
- 1 tbsp Dijon mustard
- 600 ml milk
- salt and freshly ground black pepper
- 2 egg yolks
- 1 tsp olive oil
- 250 g yellow cherry tomatoes, stalks removed
- 8 orange-yellow vine tomatoes, cored, peeled and sliced thickly
- 3 large beef tomatoes, cored, peeled and sliced thickly
- 8 sheets fresh lasagne
- 1 basil plant, leaves only, 6 reserved for garnish

Pre-heat the oven to 400°F/200°C/gas mark 6.

Turn the grill to high, place the pepper on a baking tray and grill, turning until the skin blackens all over. Transfer to a plate, cover with clingfilm and leave for 20 minutes before removing the skin. Quarter the pepper from base to stalk, opening it like a flower. Remove each segment, trimming away seeds and membrane. Cut into strips.

Make the béchamel by melting the butter, stirring in the flour, then mustard, incorporating the milk, whisking as it comes to the boil to avoid lumps. Establish a simmer, season generously with salt and pepper and cook for 5 minutes. Mix a little of the sauce into the egg yolks, stir it back into the pan and cook without boiling for a couple of minutes.

Place the oil in a bowl, tip in the cherry tomatoes, and roll in the oil.

Butter a 20 cm x 25 cm earthenware or ceramic gratin dish and smear with a couple of tablespoons of béchamel. Cover with sliced tomatoes and red pepper, tear over some basil, season, spoon over more béchamel then lay on 2 sheets of lasagne. Cover with béchamel, tomatoes, red pepper, basil, béchamel, lasagne and tomatoes, ending with enough béchamel to cloak the surface. 'Plant' the cherry tomatoes over the top and bake for 20-30 minutes until they burst and the edges of the lasagne are turning brown. Scatter on the reserved basil and eat.

BANGELLONI

SERVES 2-3

Tomatoes have a crucial role in this dish – so-called because it is best described as bangers meet cannelloni. Fried sausages are bundled with a few baby spinach leaves into fresh lasagne, which has been liberally spread with Dijon mustard. The 'cannelloni' are laid out in a gratin dish on a bed of diced tomatoes, covered with soft, silky, caramelized onions, then cloaked in a thick, creamy mustard béchamel sauce.

An irresistible combination of sweet and silky (the onions), fresh and acidic (the tomatoes and spinach), creamy and tangy (the sauce), firm and chewy (the meaty sausages), and slippery carbohydrate (the pasta).

- 3 tbsp cooking oil
- 2 large onions, peeled, halved and thinly sliced
- salt and freshly ground black pepper
- 10 long slim high-meat-content pork sausages
- 25 g butter, plus a little extra
- 1 heaped tbsp flour
- 2 tbsp Dijon mustard
- 400 ml milk
- 400 g ripe tomatoes, cored, peeled, seeded and diced
- 5 sheets fresh lasagne
- 50 g baby-leaf spinach

Pre-heat the oven to 400°F/200°C/gas mark 6.

Heat 2 tablespoons of the oil in a spacious frying-pan over a medium heat. Add the onions, season with salt and pepper, and cook until they begin to melt. Lower the heat and leave to cook while you prepare everything else: you want the onions soft and brown and this is best done slowly over a low heat.

Smear the sausages with the remaining oil and fry them in a second pan over a medium heat until they are brown, crusty and cooked through, about 15 minutes. Drain on absorbent kitchen paper.

Melt the 25 g butter in a medium pan, stir in the flour, then 1 tablespoon of the mustard. Add the milk, whisking as it comes to the boil to avoid lumps. Establish a simmer, season with salt and pepper and cook for a few minutes.

Butter a 20 cm × 25 cm gratin dish and smear with a couple of tablespoons of sauce. Spread with the diced tomato, season with salt and pepper. Cut the sheets of lasagne in half to make 10 squares. Spread each one with the remaining mustard. Place a sausage on top, divide the spinach between the sheets and roll up in the lasagne. The ends of the sausages and probably some spinach too, will hang out. Place the bangelloni, seam down, on the tomatoes, laying them all out in a single layer, snuggling them up closely. Don't worry if you haven't done a neat job. Place the onions over the top and cover with the sauce. Bake for 20 minutes until the top is blistered and bubbling and any edges poking out are crisp.

FOLDED SPINACH LASAGNE WITH THREE CHEESES AND FRESH TOMATO SAUCE

SERVES 4

This is an elegant and unusual spin on the usual way with lasagne. Rather than using sheets of pasta to layer the ingredients, in this recipe the lasagne is partially cooked then each sheet is cut in half to make two squares, which are stuffed with a mixture of cottage cheese, mozzarella and Parmesan then folded into triangles.

The little 'pocket handkerchiefs' are laid out like Provençal roof tiles and rest on a layer of nutmeg-seasoned béchamel, topped with a quickly made garlic and parsley-flavoured fresh tomato sauce. It looks spectacular, the dark green of the spinach lasagne against the bright red of the tomato sauce and the splash of white from the oozing, wobbly béchamel.

1 tbsp olive oil

8 sheets green lasagne

FOR THE TOMATO SAUCE

1 tbsp olive oil

1 garlic clove, crushed to a paste with a pinch of salt

500 g tomatoes, cored, peeled and roughly chopped

1 tbsp tomato ketchup

salt and freshly ground black pepper

1 tbsp chopped flat-leaf parsley

FOR THE BÉCHAMEL SAUCE

50 g butter

50 g flour

600 ml milk

salt and freshly ground black pepper

3 tbsp freshly grated Parmesan nutmeg

Put a large pan of salted water on to boil. Add the tablespoon of olive oil and the pasta, one sheet at a time. Boil for 6 minutes. Lay out a tea-towel on a work surface then carefully remove the lasagne, one sheet at a time. Spread them on the tea-towel and cut them in half. Overlay any breakages (lift one piece of pasta on top of another) – they glue together.

Now make the tomato sauce. Heat the oil in a pan over a medium-low flame, cook the garlic for 20 seconds then add the tomatoes. Simmer for 6 minutes, stir in the ketchup, a decent seasoning of salt and pepper and the parsley. Boil for 1 minute until thickened.

To make the béchamel, melt the butter in a saucepan, stir in the flour then whisk in the milk, cooking until smooth and boiling. Establish a simmer, season generously with nutmeg, black pepper and half a teaspoon of salt. Cook for 6 minutes. Stir in the Parmesan.

Pre-heat the oven to 400°F/200°C/gas mark 6. Butter a gratin dish, approximately 20 cm x 30 cm. Spread in it a third of the béchamel, then a third of the tomato sauce.

Make the stuffing by stirring together all the ingredients and seasoning with salt and pepper. Place 1 tablespoon of stuffing on each pasta square, fold over from corner to corner. Arrange in the dish – one or more layers – covering

FOR THE STUFFING
450 g cottage cheese
1 mozzarella cheese, grated
3 tbsp freshly grated Parmesan
½ tsp freshly grated nutmeg
2 egg yolks
2 tbsp chopped flat-leaf parsley
salt and freshly ground black pepper
extra Parmesan to finish

with tomato and finishing with béchamel, not worrying that some edges will poke through. Sprinkle with Parmesan and bake for 20 minutes or until the top is blistered and bubbling.

LASAGNE WITH RICOTTA AND TOMATO SAUCE

SERVES 6

An irresistible combination of tomatoes stewed with onion, layered with ricotta mixed with egg, Parmesan and basil, interleaved with lasagne.

4 tbsp olive oil
3 large onions, peeled and finely chopped
3 x 400 g tins peeled plum tomatoes, drained
salt and freshly ground black pepper
2 handfuls basil leaves, shredded
50 g butter
450 g ricotta
1 large egg plus 1 egg yolk
100 g Parmesan, freshly grated
nutmeg
18-20 sheets lasagne, fresh or pre-cooked
4 mozzarella, cut into strips

Pre-heat the oven to 400°F/200°C/gas mark 6.

Heat the oil in a large pan and stir in the onion. Cook gently, stirring occasionally, for 30-40 minutes, until the onions are silky and soft. Place a food mill over the pan and puree the tomatoes directly into it. Season generously with salt and pepper and add half the basil. Simmer steadily, uncovered, stirring occasionally, for about 30 minutes until the sauce is thick and reduced. Taste and check the seasoning and then, off the heat, whisk 15 g of the butter, cut into chunks, into the sauce. Leave to cool slightly.

Put the ricotta, whole egg and yolk into a bowl with half the grated Parmesan, the rest of the basil, a generous seasoning of salt and pepper, and a cautious grating of nutmeg. Stir to mix thoroughly.

Use the rest of the butter to smear a suitable gratin-style dish, approximately 23 cm x 28 cm. Spread 2-3 tablespoons of tomato sauce over the bottom of the dish and lay out 3-4 slices of lasagne, slightly overlapping, to cover. Spoon more tomato over the pasta, then cover with some of the ricotta mixture and then with more tomato. Sprinkle some of the mozzarella over the top and continue with more layers as before, finishing with the bulk of the mozzarella and the last of the Parmesan.

Bake the lasagne for 20-30 minutes until the top is crusted and the tomato sauce is bubbling round the sides.

LAMB AND SPINACH EGG PAPPARDELLE WITH DOUBLE TOMATO SAUCE

SERVES 4-5

It was about three forty-five on a weekday afternoon when my sister and I crawled into the Chalet Restaurant in Grosvenor Street, weary and starving after hours of tramping round London's West End. The twin sisters (Italian, I should think) who run what appears to be a café-cum-sandwich-bar, welcomed us like long-lost friends and ushered us down to their spotless basement restaurant. Before long, we were tucking into a plate of excellent home-made pasta. It was my sister's lasagne – its meat and separate tomato sauce oozing through the creamy white sauce – that inspired this recipe.

Like the Chalet Restaurant, I used wide strips of pasta instead of sheets of lasagne for this old favourite.

- 1 small onion, peeled and chopped
- 500 ml milk
- 2 cloves
- 1 bay leaf
- salt and freshly ground black pepper
- 400 g tin Italian tomatoes
- 2 tbsp tomato ketchup
- 400 g tin cherry tomatoes
- a knob of butter
- 1 large onion, peeled, halved and finely sliced
- 1 tbsp chopped thyme leaves
- 500 g minced lamb
- 1 tbsp flour
- ½ glass white wine, 75 ml
- 50 ml stock or water
- 225 g tender young spinach
- 15 g basil leaves
- squeeze of lemon juice

Pre-heat the oven to 350°F/180°C/gas mark 4.

Place the small onion in a pan with the milk, the cloves, the bay leaf and a seasoning of salt and pepper. Simmer gently for 10 minutes, remove from the heat, cover and leave for at least 15 minutes.

Meanwhile, puree and sieve the tinned Italian tomatoes and simmer briskly with the ketchup for 10 minutes until reduced and thickened. Stir in the strained cherry tomatoes and turn off the heat.

Melt the knob of butter in a decent-sized pan over a medium-low heat, cook the onions with the thyme for about 10 minutes until tender but uncoloured. Stir in the lamb, raising the heat slightly, and stir-fry until uniformly brown. Stir in the tablespoon of flour, add the wine and the stock, mixing thoroughly. Simmer gently for 10 minutes. Turn off the heat, stir in the spinach and basil. Taste and adjust seasoning with salt, pepper and lemon juice.

Meanwhile, cook the pappardelle according to the packet instructions. Make the white sauce by melting the butter, stirring in the flour and whisking in the strained flavoured milk while it comes up to the boil. Add plenty of nutmeg and simmer gently for 5 minutes.

To assemble the dish, make two layers with the meat, pappardelle, tomato sauce and a scant share of the white sauce,

225 g egg pappardelle
50 g butter
2 heaped tbsp flour
freshly grated nutmeg
2 mozzarella

leaving most of the sauce for the topping. Cover with slices of mozzarella and bake for 20 minutes until the cheese has melted and turned golden, and the sauce is bubbling round the edges.

Also see:
Tomato Sauces (pages 234-266)
Tomatoes Alone (pages 31-58)

tomatoes & rice, grains & pulses

'Viola had not offered any help, except that of arranging a few tulips and narcissi on the table. Dulcie had asked her advice about the food, but she had not seemed interested and only remarked that Aylwin had once said that he didn't like tomatoes. Dulcie, therefore, had been careful to avoid any dish containing these 'love apples', as she now called them to herself, saying over the phrase 'Alywin can't take love apples' with a good deal of enjoyment. But she had not repeated it to Viola, who did not seem to be amused by such trivialities.'

Barbara Pym, *No Fond Return of Love*

Tomatoes and rice might not seem an obvious combination but it turns up in most tomato-growing countries. In Mexico, Portugal, Spain, Turkey, Greece, France and Italy, there is tradition of cooking tomatoes with long-grain rice. This might be as simple as stirring tomato concentrate into the cooking water for rice, or building up a Sofrito (see page 201) with garlic, onion, and flavouring from lard or bacon dripping. Spices, such as cinnamon or saffron, and herbs, like basil and parsley, might be added too. In place of water, stock might be used. The tomato 'water' collected after seeding tomatoes to make concassé would be an ideal addition to a vegetarian tomato-rice dish.

The most complicated version of rice with tomatoes is possibly Jambalaya. This seafood, rice and tomato dish from Louisiana resembles the paella of Spain, but relies on tomato to a far greater extent. In Italy tomatoes are also cooked with round arborio rice in risotto, either on their own or with other compatible ingredients such as spinach, basil, saffron and mushrooms.

Tomatoes also combine well with leftover rice, either cooked up together or separately by 'revitalizing' the rice with other ingredients, then serving it with a well-flavoured tomato sauce.

Tomatoes go particularly well with grilled polenta. Use it, for a change, instead of bread in any of the bruschetta recipes given on pages 91 to 94. Grilled cherry tomatoes, for example, dressed with olive oil and balsamic vinegar, piled on to crusty grilled polenta with a few shavings of Parmesan and a handful of rocket, would make a satisfying light meal. Thin slices of grilled polenta can be used like lasagne, layered with roasted tomatoes and red peppers, then covered with a creamy béchamel sauce before the dish is finished in the oven. I keep a pack of ready-made polenta, sold in a slab that resembles a chunk of Cheddar cheese, especially for such impromptu meals.

Cracked bulgar wheat and couscous are even more convenient and both work brilliantly with tomatoes. Bulgar is a key ingredient with tomatoes in the Lebanese parsley salad Tabbouleh (see page 323), and there is a bottomless pit of variations on that theme, with prawns, for example, other herbs and flavourings that go well with tomatoes. Lentils are most often combined with tomatoes in soups (see pages 76 and 360) but remember them together for healthy, satisfying vegetable stews with spinach and fresh coriander. I came up with just one recipe using tomatoes with barley, but it's a good one!

RED RICE

SERVES 4

Rice with a haunting tomato flavour and brick red colour.

225 g basmati rice
6 tbsp concentrated tomato puree or sun-dried puree
2 tbsp olive oil

Rinse the rice in a colander under running water. Tip it into a heavy saucepan with the 350 ml water, tomato puree and olive oil. Place on a high heat and bring to the boil, stirring a couple of times to dissolve the puree. Turn the heat to very low, clamp on a tight-fitting lid and cook for 10 minutes without peeking. Switch off the heat and leave the rice for 10 minutes to finish cooking in its own steam.

TURKISH PILAF WITH TOMATOES AND CINNAMON

SERVES 4

Serve with lamb or chicken kebabs or enjoy it on its own.

250 g basmati rice
20 g butter
500 ml tomato juice
pinch of salt
pinch of sugar
small cinnamon stick

Place the rice in a medium saucepan and cover it with boiling water. Stir and leave to stand until the water cools. Drain the rice and rinse it under running water.

Wipe out the pan, add the butter and tomato juice and generous pinches of salt and sugar, and the cinnamon. Bring to the boil. Add the rice, stir, and bring to the boil. Reduce the heat immediately, cover the pan and cook gently for 10 minutes. Remove from the heat and leave the rice to stand for 10 minutes. Remove the cinnamon before serving.

PILAF WITH TOMATOES

SERVES 6

Richard Olney is the author of several of my favourite cookbooks. This recipe comes from *A Provençal Table* which Olney, an American, wrote after he had lived in France for more than forty years. The book chronicles the recipes of his friend Lulu Peyraud, who, with the help of Lucien and her large family, runs the famous family vineyard Domaine Tempier, near Bandol in the South of France. Of this particular recipe Mr Olney writes, 'This pilaf is specially intended to accompany grilled lamb skewers (also given in the book), but it is delicious as an accompaniment to almost any grilled or pan-fried meat or poultry. Served by itself, a handful of torn-up fresh basil leaves sautéd with the tomatoes, will do wonders.' This is very similar to Portuguese Tomato Rice, which is made with chicken stock instead of water, and doubles the quantity of onion.

- 500 g tomatoes, cored, seeded and finely chopped
- salt and freshly ground black pepper
- 3 tbsp olive oil
- 1 onion, peeled and finely chopped
- 400 g long-grain rice
- 1 litre boiling water
- 2 garlic cloves, lightly crushed, peeled and finely chopped
- 4 tbsp cold butter, diced

Spread out the diced tomato and sprinkle it with a little salt. Scoop up and place in a colander. Leave to drain for 1 hour.

Warm 1 tablespoon of the olive oil in an earthenware casserole, protected from direct heat by a heat-diffusing mat. Add the onion and sweat, covered, over a low heat until it is soft but not coloured. Add the rice and a large pinch of salt. Stir regularly with a wooden spoon for a couple of minutes, or until the rice turns milky and is well coated with oil. Pour in the boiling water, stir once, and leave, tightly covered, to barely simmer for 20 minutes.

Heat the remaining olive oil in a large frying-pan, add the chopped garlic, and as soon as it begins to sizzle add the tomatoes and toss repeatedly over a high heat for a couple of minutes, or until their liquid has evaporated but before they begin to fall apart. Add the tomatoes and the diced butter to the rice and toss lightly together with two forks. Serve immediately.

LEMON TOMATOES WITH RICE

SERVES 4

An idea from Constance Spry, from her formidable *The Constance Spry Cookery Book*, for using up cold leftover rice. With a lemon-flavoured tomato sauce, it becomes a useful recipe to have up your sleeve.

- 200 g boiled rice
- 175 ml milk
- 2 bay leaves
- salt and freshly ground black pepper
- 1 egg
- 40 g butter
- 1 garlic clove, peeled and crushed to a paste with a little salt
- 1 small onion, peeled and finely chopped
- 750 g tomatoes, cored, peeled, seeded and chopped
- a pinch of sugar
- 1 tbsp tomato puree
- 2 heaped tbsp finely chopped mixed herbs, such as basil, watercress, mint, tarragon, etc.
- zest of 1 small lemon, finely chopped
- a squeeze of lemon juice

Put the rice, milk, bay leaves and a little salt into a pan and simmer for about 5 minutes until the milk has been absorbed. Beat the egg and stir it into the rice. Use a little of the butter to grease a ring mould or other suitable dish. Pack the rice mixture into the buttered mould or dish and set it aside in a warm place.

Melt the remaining butter and cook the garlic and onion for about 10 minutes over a medium flame until softened and pale gold in colour. Add the tomatoes, salt, pepper and sugar, and simmer briskly for 10 minutes. Add the tomato puree, half the herbs, the lemon zest and juice, and cook for a few more minutes. Turn out the rice on to a warm plate. Pour the tomato mixture into the middle and garnish with the reserved herbs.

GIULIA'S TOMATO SAUCE AND DRY RICE

SERVES 6

One of my 'new' favourite books, and a companion to *An Omelette and a Glass of Wine*, is *South Wind Through the Kitchen: The Best of Elizabeth David*, edited by Jill Norman. It was in the latter that I found Giulia's Tomato Sauce and Dry Rice and a description of it by Derek Hill that immediately made me want to cook it: 'Riso secco may sound dull, but the contrast of the hard hot rice and the cold tomato "salad" is absolutely delectable. It's most important, I remember, that the rice should not be shaken about or disturbed.'

FOR THE 'SALAD'

- 750 g ripe Marmande or other excellent tomatoes, cored, peeled and sliced
- 6 tbsp olive oil
- 2 tbsp red wine vinegar
- ½ small shallot, finely chopped
- salt and freshly ground black pepper
- a pinch of sugar

FOR THE RICE

- ½ small onion, peeled and finely chopped
- 1 tbsp olive oil
- about 40 g butter
- 500 g long grain rice
- 4 tbsp freshly grated Parmesan or pecorino

Mix the tomatoes with the olive oil, wine vinegar, shallot and season with salt and pepper. Leave the mixture to steep for 2 hours, and immediately before serving stir in the sugar.

Put the onion in a deep saucepan or casserole with the olive oil and a knob of the butter. Sauté until it is golden, throw in the rice and cook until it turns 'a pale blond colour'. Now pour in around 750 ml salted water or broth, and cook, covered, for 20 minutes. 'Take care that the rice is not too liquid; it is sufficient for the water to cover it by one finger's depth or less; when cooked turn it on to a serving dish and on top put, here and there, some flakes of butter and some grated cheese.'

The tomato sauce is served separately.

FRESH TOMATO RISOTTO WITH PARMESAN

SERVES 6-8

Choose the strongest-flavoured, ripest tomatoes you can lay your hands on for this wonderful summer risotto. It is based on a recipe from Patricia Wells's *Trattoria*, which comes from 'chef Walter Tripodi of the restored monastery-inn La Frateria di Padre Eligio, in Cetona, in Tuscany'.

- **1 litre vegetable, chicken or tomato stock (sees page 61)**
- **500 ml tomato coulis or fondue (see pages 242 and 44) or another well-flavoured smooth tomato sauce**
- **50 g unsalted butter**
- **2 tbsp extra-virgin olive oil**
- **1 shallot, peeled and very finely chopped**
- **2 bay leaves**
- **salt and freshly ground black pepper**
- **350 g arborio rice**
- **50 g freshly grated Parmesan, plus extra for the table**

In a large saucepan, combine the stock and tomato sauce and bring to a simmer. Keep the liquid simmering, very gently, while you prepare the risotto.

In a large heavy-bottomed saucepan, combine 25 g of the butter, the oil, shallot, bay leaves and a generous pinch of salt over moderate heat. Cook, stirring, until the shallot is soft and translucent, but not browned, for about 3 minutes. Add the rice and stir until it is well coated with the fats, glistening and semi-translucent, about 5 minutes. As soon as the rice turns shiny and even more translucent, add a ladleful of the simmering liquid. Stir constantly, as it sizzles, for a couple of minutes until the rice has absorbed most of the liquid. Add a second ladleful of liquid and stir constantly until all the liquid is absorbed, adjusting the heat to maintain a gentle simmer. Continue adding ladlefuls of hot stock, stirring constantly, until the rice is almost tender but firm to the bite, about 17 minutes in total. The risotto should have a creamy, porridge-like consistency.

Remove the saucepan from the heat and stir in the remaining butter and the cheese. Cover and leave it to stand off the heat for 5 minutes, to allow the flavours to blend and the rice to finish cooking. Taste for seasoning. Discard the bay leaves.

Serve in warmed shallow soup bowls, passing the additional cheese.

CHEAT'S TOMATO AND BASIL RISOTTO

SERVES 4

It's a relief that supermarkets have dropped the term 'grown for flavour'. The short-hand for a decent tomato these days is 'vine'. You'll need some for this tomato risotto. It's a simple recipe made with a stock cube but there are two points of faff; one is that the tomatoes must be peeled and seeded, and the other is sieving the seeds to save the juice. This juice is packed with flavour and too good to waste. Serve the risotto on its own with grated Parmesan or make it while a chicken roasts for a mid-week treat with asparagus. I served the risotto with roast quails wrapped in sheets of Parma ham and vine leaves.

- 2 shallots
- 1 garlic clove
- 400 g vine tomatoes
- 25 g butter plus an extra knob
- ½ glass white wine
- 250 g risotto rice
- 12 basil leaves
- 800 ml boiling water
- 1 chicken or vegetable stock cube
- grated Parmesan to serve (optional)

Boil the kettle. Peel and finely chop the shallot. Peel and chop the garlic. Sprinkle the garlic with a pinch of salt and crush to a paste. Immerse the tomatoes in boiling water from the kettle and count to 30. Drain and splash with cold water. Cut out the core in a pointed plug shape, quarter the tomatoes and remove the skin. Place a sieve over a bowl. Scrape the tomato seeds into the sieve. Crush with the back of a wooden spoon to extract maximum juice. Slice the tomatoes into strips then into dice. In a pan over a low heat, dissolve the stock cube in 800 ml boiling water from the kettle. Melt the butter in a spacious sauté pan and gently soften the shallot, adding the garlic after about 10 minutes. Cook for a further couple of minutes then stir in the unwashed rice, tossing it around for 2-3 minutes. Add the wine and stir as it bubbles away into the rice. Repeat with the tomato juice then add a ladleful of stock, continuing thus until a third of the stock remains. Stir in a third of the chopped tomatoes and continue adding stock as before. When the rice is tender, stir in the remaining tomatoes and season with salt and pepper. Shred the basil over the top and add the knob of butter. Stir, cover and leave for 5 minutes before giving a final stir. Serve with Parmesan if liked.

TOMATO RISOTTO WITH ROAST TOMATOES

SERVES 6

This is a lovely tomato risotto made with fresh tomato concassé (see page 29) and roast tomatoes. The fresh tomatoes and their juices melt into the rice before it is cooked with stock and then right at the end the roast tomatoes are stirred in.

- 750 g ripe tomatoes, preferably plum, cored and peeled
- 1 tsp sugar
- salt and freshly ground black pepper
- 60 g butter
- 2 shallots or small onions, peeled and chopped
- 350 g arborio rice
- 1 litre hot chicken stock or vegetable bouillon
- 12 roast or slow-roast tomatoes (see page 34)

OPTIONAL EXTRAS

- basil leaves
- freshly grated Parmesan

Place a sieve over a bowl. Quarter the tomatoes lengthways and remove the seeds, scooping them and their juices into the sieve. Sprinkle with the sugar and season generously with salt and pepper. Leave to drip while you chop the tomato flesh then press the debris against the side of the sieve into the bowl to catch all the juices.

Melt three-quarters of the butter in a heavy-bottomed, medium-sized saucepan and add the shallots or onions. Cook gently until soft and translucent. Stir in the rice and the diced tomato, and cook for I minute before adding the seasoned tomato juices. Cook until the liquid has almost entirely evaporated. Pour a couple of ladles of hot stock into the rice, let it come to the boil, then simmer very gently until almost all the stock has been absorbed. Pour on more stock, just enough to cover the rice and tomatoes, and continue cooking, adding more stock until the rice is swollen and tender but retains a slight bite. This will take about 25 minutes. Slip the roast tomatoes off their skins and cut them into 2 or 3 pieces. Stir them and their juices into the risotto with the last of the butter and, if liked, a few torn basil leaves. Serve immediately, with or without Parmesan.

SUN-DRIED TOMATO RISOTTO

SERVES 4

I learned this unorthodox way of making risotto from Simon Hopkinson, who perfected the technique in the kitchens of Bibendum. It effectively eliminates all the hassle of making risotto because almost all the stock is added in one go right at the beginning. It is cooked briefly, and left for 30 minutes off the heat with a tight-fitting lid clamped into position, and the risotto is virtually done. This restaurant trick means the dish can be prepared to this stage in advance; it takes only minutes to finish it off with extra stock, cream and butter. The amount of extra stock required to complete cooking the rice is hard to quantify; and the amount of extra butter, and possibly cream, which is just to make the risotto richer and creamier, is up to you. Look out for superfino rice as opposed to arborio for this way of cooking risotto.

This version is made with dried rather than oil-soaked sun-dried tomatoes, and the intense flavour is reinforced with a splash of balsamic vinegar and wine.

- 20 sun-dried tomatoes (see page 395)
- 450 ml boiling chicken stock or vegetable bouillon
- 30 g butter
- 8 small pink Thai shallots or 4 ordinary shallots, peeled and finely chopped
- 3 tbsp olive oil
- 1 small garlic clove, peeled and finely chopped
- 200 g superfino rice
- 2 tbsp balsamic vinegar
- 1 glass red wine, approximately 150 ml
- knob of butter
- 50 g freshly grated Parmesan cheese, plus extra for serving

Place the sun-dried tomatoes in a bowl and cover with some of the boiling stock. Leave for about 20 minutes until the tomatoes are soft. Scoop them out of the bowl, reserving the liquid. Slice into chunky ribbons.

Choose a heavy-bottomed medium saucepan with a tight-fitting lid. Melt the 30 g butter in the pan and gently soften the shallots without browning. Add the garlic, stir in the rice, coating it thoroughly with butter, then add the vinegar and red wine, and cook until the liquid has almost evaporated. Stir in the tomato strips and pour on their soaking liquid with three-quarters of the hot stock. Bring gently to the boil, stirring from time to time. When the liquid is boiling evenly, put a tight-fitting lid on the pan, take it off the heat and leave it for 30 minutes without removing the lid.

When the 30 minutes is up, lift the lid off the risotto: it will have absorbed all the liquid and look unpromising. Return it to a low heat and gradually stir in the remaining hot stock, the knob of butter, and the Parmesan, stirring as it transforms into a perfect, molten state. It is ready when the rice is moist but not wet and the grains of rice have slopped together but retain a slight bite at their centre. Serve the risotto with plenty of freshly grated Parmesan.

JAMBALAYA

SERVES 3-4

Jambalaya is a rice, meat and seafood stew from Louisiana. Traditionally the cooking starts with the so-called 'trinity' of onion, green pepper and celery that begins many dishes from the Deep South but thereafter, according to Paul McIlhenny (Mr Tabasco and author of *The Tabasco Cookbook*), almost anything goes. The name is a jumble of *jambon*, the French word for ham, and *alaya*, which means rice in an African dialect, and the dish usually includes a spicy pork sausage of some sort, although it often ends up with ham. Whatever the ingredients, a good Jambalaya is always spiked with plenty of chilli.

My version of this easy-going dish is even more colourful, made with red onions and red peppers. I have purposely restrained the chilli-heat by using cayenne at the beginning of the cooking and adding Tabasco towards the end, while serving Tabasco and a wedge of lemon alongside so that people can adjust their own heat threshold. Chunks of chicken are almost lost in the vegetables and a can of peeled tomatoes colours the rice. Right at the end of cooking, peeled prawns doused in Tabasco are stirred into the swollen tomato rice. Jambalaya can simmer away gently on top of the stove but to avoid any risk of a crusty bottom (although some people claim that's part of its charm) and ensure even cooking without soupiness, it is best done in the oven. You need a good supply of ice-cold beer to drink with this.

2 tbsp cooking oil

2 medium red onions, approximately 265 g, peeled and chopped

2 plump garlic cloves, peeled and finely chopped

1 red pepper, seeded and chopped

1 celery heart, finely sliced, leaves reserved

1 bay leaf

salt and freshly ground black pepper

½ tsp cayenne pepper

2 organic chicken legs or 4 organic thighs

2 pepperoni sausages (optional)

200 g headless, raw, shell-on giant tiger prawns

½ tsp Tabasco

250 g basmati rice

400 g tin whole Italian tomatoes

Heat the oil in a 2.2 litre cast-iron casserole dish and stir in the onion and garlic. Cook for about 5 minutes, then add the red pepper, celery and bay leaf. Season with salt and pepper and cayenne and cook for about 10 minutes while you prepare everything else.

Pre-heat the oven to 375°F/190°C/gas mark 5.

Remove the skin from the chicken and cut the meat from the bone in chunks. Slice the pepperoni, if using. If the prawns are frozen, slip into warm water for a few minutes to defrost, then remove the shells. Place the prawns in a bowl and toss with the Tabasco.

Stir the chicken into the vegetables and when it's changed colour, add the pepperoni, if using, rice and tinned tomatoes with their juice. Add the stock. Bring to a simmer, cover the pan and cook in the oven for 20 minutes.

By now the rice will have absorbed most of the liquid but the Jambalaya should be nicely moist. If it isn't, add a little more stock and return to the oven for 5 more min-

- 1 chicken stock cube, dissolved in 500 ml water
- 1 tbsp finely chopped parsley
- lemon wedges, to serve

utes. Stir in the prawns, cover again and cook for 10 more minutes. Sprinkle the reserved celery leaves and parsley over the top, and serve with lemon wedges and the Tabasco bottle.

POLENTA, TOMATO AND MOZZARELLA LASAGNE

SERVES 3-4

This is one of those quick and delicious supper dishes that can almost be made from the store cupboard. Rather than use ready-set polenta, make your own by stirring 1 tsp salt, 200 g quick-cook polenta and 1 tsp chopped thyme into 900 ml vigorously boiling water. Stir thoroughly whilst turning the heat very low. Stir regularly for about 5 minutes until very thick and tender and shrinking from the walls of the pan. Pour the lava-like polenta onto a large chopping board or plate, using a metal spatula to smooth approximately 1.5 cm thick. Leave to go cold.

- 3 tbsp olive oil
- 1 medium red onion, peeled, halved and finely chopped
- 1 tbsp balsamic vinegar
- 1 garlic clove, peeled and finely chopped
- a small basil plant, leaves only
- 400 g tin chopped tomatoes
- 350g jar piquillo red peppers, split and sliced
- salt and freshly ground black pepper
- ½ tsp sugar
- a shake of Tabasco
- 350 g prepared polenta
- a knob of butter
- 6 tbsp freshly grated Parmesan
- 2 mozzarella cheeses
- 16 cherry tomatoes, stalks removed

Pre-heat the oven to 425°F/220°C/gas mark 7.

Heat 2 tablespoons of the oil in a frying-pan over a medium heat. Cook the onion, tossing it around every now and again, for about 8 minutes until floppy and browned at the edges. Add the balsamic vinegar and let it bubble away. Put in the garlic and stir it until it is aromatic. Then add 6 basil leaves, the chopped tomatoes and the sliced pepper. Season with salt, pepper and the sugar. Add a shake or two of Tabasco. Bring to the boil, then turn down the heat so that the sauce cooks at a steady simmer until thick. This will take 10-15 minutes.

Remove the polenta from its packet and cut 20 thin slices, approximately 0.5 cm thick. Smear a suitable gratin-type dish with butter and lay out half the polenta. Top with the sauce. Strew a few of the basil leaves over the top and sprinkle over a couple of tablespoons of Parmesan. Arrange the rest of the polenta over the top. Slice the mozzarella thinly and lay it over the middle section of the dish. Sprinkle with the remaining Parmesan. Place the cherry tomatoes in a bowl with the remaining olive oil and toss. 'Plant' the tomatoes on top of the gratin.

Cook for 15-20 minutes until the tomatoes are very soft and juicy, the mozzarella melted, the Parmesan lightly crusted and the edges of the polenta gorgeously scorched in places. Tear the remaining basil over the top and serve.

BORANI AND ROCKET SALAD

SERVES 4 AS A MAIN DISH, 8 AS A STARTER

Borani is an ancient Persian word that translates as tomatoes with rice. It's a wonderfully versatile dish that cooks up like a cake and can be sliced like a terrine. It is good, for example, as a starter, served with some sprigs of flat-leaf parsley and black olives, but is interesting and filling enough to be served as a main dish with, say, baked potatoes. It is best, I think, served warm or chilled and is perfect for buffets, picnics and lunch boxes.

400 g onions, peeled and finely chopped
1 red pepper, cored, seeded and diced
2 tbsp vegetable oil
4 large garlic cloves, peeled and finely chopped
2 heaped tsp paprika
600 g ripe tomatoes, cored, peeled, seeded and chopped
200 g round-grain rice
1 tsp salt
1 tsp freshly ground black pepper
3 tbsp finely chopped flat-leaf parsley
½ tbsp thyme leaves
1 tbsp finely chopped mint
a little extra vegetable oil
juice of ½ lemon
a pinch of salt
a pinch of sugar
½ tbsp balsamic vinegar
2 tbsp olive oil
2 shallots, very finely chopped
150 g rocket, washed and drained

Pre-heat the oven to 375°F/190°C/gas mark 5.

Place the chopped onion and pepper in a heavy-based pan with the vegetable oil. Cover and leave to cook slowly, for 10-15 minutes, stirring a couple of times, until the onions are softened but not browned. Stir in the garlic and the paprika, cook for a couple of minutes, then add the tomatoes and cook, uncovered, for 5 minutes. Add the rice and 250 ml water. Cover the pan and cook on the lowest possible heat (a heat-diffuser pad is useful here) for about 35 minutes until all the liquid is absorbed, the mixture is thick and the rice tender. Stir in the salt, pepper, herbs, a little more vegetable oil and the lemon juice, and taste for seasoning.

Transfer the mixture to a lightly oiled non-stick 18 cm square cake tin and smooth the top. Position a piece of baking paper to fit exactly and bake for 20 minutes. Discard the paper and cook for a further 15 minutes. Remove from the oven, leave for at least 15 minutes, then run a knife round the inside edge of the tin, cover the tin with a plate and invert quickly. Leave it to cool and firm up before cutting into slices.

To make the salad, dissolve a generous pinch of salt and sugar in the balsamic vinegar, whisk in the olive oil. Stir in the diced shallot, add the rocket and toss.

Serve a slice of borani with the salad on the side.

BULGAR PILAF WITH TOMATOES

SERVES 4

I offer two versions of this, one a traditional Lebanese recipe flavoured with cinnamon and allspice, and a second of my own, with saffron, honey and a hint of fresh mint, lemon zest and garlic. Both are good eaten with yoghurt and toasted pitta. They also go well with fish, eggs or barbecued meat and poultry.

LEBANESE TOMATO PILAF

- 1 tbsp olive oil
- 1 small onion, peeled and finely chopped
- 350 g ripe tomatoes, cored, peeled and chopped
- 300 ml water
- 200 g bulgar wheat
- ½ tsp cinnamon
- ¼ tsp allspice
- ½ tsp salt

Heat the oil in a medium pan and cook the onion until pale and transparent. Add the tomatoes, stirring a couple of times, then add the water. Bring to the boil over a medium heat, cover the pan and cook for 5 minutes. Add the bulgar, cinnamon, allspice and salt. Stir thoroughly, reduce the heat to medium-low, cover the pan and cook for about 10 minutes until the bulgar is soft and all the liquid absorbed.

SAFFRON AND LEMON TOMATO PILAF

- 1 onion, chopped
- 5 tbsp olive oil
- 6 plum tomatoes, cored and peeled
- a pinch of saffron steeped in 1 tbsp hot water
- 1 tsp honey
- 200 g bulgar wheat
- salt and freshly ground black pepper
- 300 ml light vegetable or chicken stock or water
- 5 cm strip lemon zest (no white), finely chopped
- 1 garlic clove, peeled and finely chopped
- about 25 fresh mint leaves, shredded
- Greek yoghurt to serve

Fry the onion in 2 tablespoons of the olive oil until soft and floppy. Place a sieve over a bowl, halve the tomatoes and scrape out their seeds into the sieve. Press the seeds against the side of the sieve to extract all the juice. Chop the tomato flesh. Tip the tomato juice and diced flesh into the onion, add the saffron and honey and cook for a couple of minutes before stirring in the bulgar. Season with salt and pepper. Add the stock, bring to the boil, immediately turn down the heat as low as possible, cover the pan and cook for about 15 minutes until all the liquid is absorbed.

Meanwhile, mix the lemon zest with the garlic and most of the shredded mint. Chop all three together. Stir the remaining oil into the pilaf, add the mint and garlic mixture. Give a final stir, check the seasoning and serve hot with the remaining mint sprinkled over the yoghurt.

CRACKED WHEAT WITH TOMATOES

SERVES 8

'Kurdish Jews,' writes Claudia Roden in her *Book of Jewish Food*, 'use cracked wheat bulgar more than any other community does.' This recipe is one after my own heart, and is her adaptation of one of their everyday foods. It is best made with fresh tomatoes, but tinned ones will do.

- 1 kg tomatoes, cored and peeled
- 6 tbsp olive oil
- 1 tsp sugar
- salt and freshly ground black pepper
- 325 g coarse or medium bulgar wheat

Place the tomatoes in the bowl of a food-processor and blitz. Leave them as they are or pass them through a sieve. You should end up with about a litre of liquid. Pour the tomato into a large pan with 3 tablespoons of the oil, the sugar, a scant teaspoon of salt and plenty of black pepper. Bring to the boil, stir in the bulgar and simmer, covered, for 10 minutes. Remove from the heat. Leave covered for 10 minutes until the wheat has absorbed the tomato juice and is plump and tender. Stir in the rest of the oil and serve. Good hot or cold.

GREEN COUSCOUS WITH PRAWNS AND TOMATO CONCASSÉ

SERVES 3

Here's an excellent example of how diced tomato can be used as a garnish to provide an essential fresh, lively flavour that makes the dish. Warm couscous and peas are mixed with finely chopped spinach and mint, then poached prawns are stirred in. The crowning glory is a cascade of diced tomato.

- 200 g headless, raw, shell-on giant tiger prawns
- 500 ml stock, or 1 chicken stock cube and 500 ml water
- 4 kaffir lime leaves
- 225 g couscous
- 200 g frozen petit pois
- 150 g young spinach leaves
- 25 mint leaves, plus ½ tbsp finely chopped mint
- salt and freshly ground black pepper
- juice of ½ lemon
- lemon wedges

If the prawns are frozen slip them into a bowl of warm water for a few minutes to defrost. Then place them in a saucepan with the stock and kaffir lime leaves, and bring slowly to the boil. Establish a gentle simmer and cook for about 3 minutes until the prawns are uniformly pink and cooked through. Strain the liquid into a spacious china serving bowl and stir in the couscous with a fork to help prevent lumps forming; do this a couple of times, then cover the dish. Tip the prawns on to a plate to cool then remove their shells.

Meanwhile cook the frozen petit pois in boiling salted water, according to the packet instructions. Drain.

Place the spinach, washed and shaken dry, if necessary, in the bowl of a food-processor with the mint leaves. Blitz until finely chopped. By now the couscous will be tender and have absorbed all the stock. Fork it again, then stir in the chopped mint and spinach. Season generously with salt and black pepper, taste and adjust the

- 350 g ripe tomatoes, cored, seeded and diced (see page 29)

seasoning (couscous needs plenty of salt), pointing up the flavours with lemon juice. Fork up the couscous again. Stir in the petit pois and the prawns. Tip the tomato concassé over the top, sprinkle on the tablespoon of chopped mint and serve with lemon wedges.

LEBANESE TABBOULEH

SERVES 4

I am absolutely addicted to this attractive salad. I first discovered it at the Phoenicia, a Lebanese restaurant in Kensington, where I also met my hero Elizabeth David (her sister, it turned out, lived next door). It is something that every Lebanese restaurant makes well. The main ingredient is flat-leaf parsley, chopped very finely and mixed with diced tomato, a little bulgar and spring onion, the whole seasoned with lemon juice, olive oil and mint. It is refreshing and satisfying and goes with just about everything. It looks very pretty served nestled inside crisp salad leaves and decorated with a garnish of tomato concassé (see page 29), which tumbles down the mound of tabbouleh like jewels. Serve it as part of a cold spread, or with hummus and other dips, or alongside kebabs. Traditionally it is eaten scooped up in a lettuce leaf.

I often bulk up the quantity of bulgar – the ingredients here can take up to 200 g, although you might also wish to increase the quantity of onion – to make more of a meal of the Tabbouleh. If you do so, make up the quantity of liquid with water or stock so that it is just under double the volume of the bulgar.

- 6 ripe medium tomatoes, preferably plum, cored and peeled
- 75 g bulgar
- 2 medium spring onions, trimmed and finely chopped
- salt and freshly ground black pepper
- 3 tbsp olive oil
- juice of ½ lemon
- 1 very large bunch vigorous flat-leaf parsley, leaves only, finely chopped
- 1 small bunch fresh mint, leaves only, finely chopped
- curls of crisp lettuce

Place a sieve over a bowl. Quarter the tomatoes lengthways. Scrape the seeds and juices into the sieve. Finely chop the flesh and set aside the dice from one tomato. Using the back of a spoon, press the seeds and their juices against the side of the sieve to extract maximum juice. Tip the main quantity of diced tomato together with the juices into a bowl with the bulgar. Stir in the spring onions and season generously with salt and pepper. Leave to allow the tomato juices to rehydrate the bulgar.

When the bulgar is ready – it will remain slightly nutty but be tender – whisk the olive oil into the lemon juice and stir it into the bulgar along with the parsley and mint. Stir well, taste and adjust the seasonings. Line a bowl with several layers of lettuce, spoon in the Tabbouleh and tumble the reserved diced tomato over the top.

LENTILS IN WINE AND TOMATO

SERVES 4

Delicious on its own, or serve topped with a poached egg, with roast poultry, game or lamb.

- 1 small onion, peeled and finely chopped
- 1 medium carrot, peeled and finely chopped
- 4 rashers rindless, thin-cut, streaky bacon or pancetta, chopped
- 2 tbsp olive oil
- 300 g Puy lentils
- 150 ml white wine
- 175 g Cooked Tomato Coulis (see page 242)
- 175 ml chicken stock (a cube is fine)
- salt and freshly ground black pepper
- 4 sage leaves, shredded
- a squeeze of lemon juice

In a heavy pan, fry the onion, carrot and bacon in the oil over a medium-low heat until the onions are golden. Put in the lentils and stir-fry for a few minutes, then pour in the wine. Allow it to bubble up then add the tomato coulis and enough stock just to cover the lentils. Add the sage. Bring to the boil, then reduce the heat to a simmer, cover the pan and cook, stirring occasionally, until the lentils are tender and the dish is juicy, rather than soupy. If the lentils are drying out before they are tender, add more stock. Taste and adjust the seasoning with salt, plenty of pepper and a squeeze of lemon juice. The flavours are improved if the dish is left overnight then reheated.

FARRO ALL' AMATRICIANA

SERVES 4

Almost risotto, but this time made with barley.

- 200 g pearl barley
- 700 ml water
- 2 tsp salt
- 3 tbsp olive oil
- 2 tsp finely chopped red chilli or ½ tsp dried chilli flakes
- 75 g pancetta or rindless streaky bacon, chopped into small pieces
- 1 medium onion, peeled and finely sliced
- 1 glass red wine, approximately 150 ml
- 2 x 400g tins chopped tomatoes, drained
- 4 tbsp freshly grated Parmesan or pecorino cheese

Partially cook the barley by placing it in a pan with the water and the salt. Bring to the boil, reduce the heat to a gentle simmer, cover the pan and cook for 40 minutes. Drain.

Meanwhile, heat the oil in a frying-pan and add the chilli, then the pancetta or bacon, and the onion. Cook until the onion is limp and the fat from the pancetta or bacon has run free. Pour on the wine and cook until it evaporates. Add the tomatoes and the drained cooked barley. Simmer gently for about 30 minutes. Add a little more water if the mixture seems dry. Serve topped with the grated cheese.

tomatoes with fish and seafood

'Herrings baked with rice and tomatoes is a dish that might be tried for luncheon one day.

Take some herring fillets and cut them in half crosswise. Also skin some tomatoes, and have ready some boiled and well-drained rice. Now put a layer of the fillets in a buttered fireproof dish, and over them a layer of tomato slices. Sprinkle over this salt and pepper and a little lemon juice, or vinegar if you prefer it. Cover with the rest of the fillets, on these spread the rice and, lastly, the remaining tomato slices. Dot with butter and bake for about three-quarters of an hour in a moderate oven.'

Ambrose Heath, *Good Food* (1934)

Tomatoes and fish, as a combination, doesn't immediately fire the imagination – well, not until you start thinking about it. My first thoughts take me back to my mother's fish pies, the mashed potato covered with slices of tomato that looked pretty but had little connection with the fish. In tomato-producing countries, throughout the Mediterranean, in parts of Africa, Asia, particularly India, in Mexico and the American Deep South, there is a tradition of cooking fish in tomatoes. The sauce might be simple, with little more than tomatoes and some fresh herbs, or it might contain spices, such as cinnamon, saffron and coriander, and herbs as diverse as fennel, savory, chervil, celery and parsley. Some such sauces are almost a meal in themselves, with additions such as anchovies, olives, capers, chillies, onion and garlic, or cheese.

The exactitude of the sauce will, of course, depend on the fish or shellfish: it would be pointless to match a highly complex sauce with a delicately flavoured fish. Nevertheless, I have come across recipes for cooking fish in tomatoes with just about any fish and shellfish you care to mention, including salmon, sturgeon, red mullet, sardines, cod, haddock, plaice, trout and swordfish, as well as prawns and mussels. In fact, any fish or shellfish that swims near a tomato plant risks its life.

The more delicate fish, such as sole and trout, suit a gently flavoured smooth tomato sauce, with just enough acidity to offset the sweet, bland taste of the fish. The stronger-flavoured fish and shellfish, salt cod, mussels and sardines, are a match for almost any tomato sauce you care to throw at them.

Raw tomatoes can work well with seafood too. The acidity in tomatoes makes them suitable as a marinade, and slices of fresh tomato will counteract the oiliness of sardines and mackerel. Think, too, of diced raw tomato as a garnish for simply cooked fish, such as a fine piece of roast cod, served over mashed potato. Which more or less brings me back to where I started. Have you tried fish pie made with tomatoes?

BAKED HADDOCK WITH TOMATOES AND SAFFRON

SERVES 4

A very tasty idea from Kiwi chef Anna Hansen (now at the Modern Kitchen), served by Peter Gordon when at the Sugar Club in Notting Hill, London, and simple to whip up at home. Plum tomatoes would be best for this slightly adapted version but any medium-sized very ripe tomato will do.

- 4 x 200 g haddock, pollack or cod fillet cut from the middle, bones removed
- salt and freshly ground black pepper
- 3 tbsp olive oil
- 6 medium ripe tomatoes, cored, peeled, halved and cut into thin slices
- a generous pinch of saffron stamens, soaked in 1 tbsp boiling water
- 400 ml white wine
- 4 tbsp extra-virgin olive oil

Season the fish with salt and pepper. Heat a large pan that can hold the fillets comfortably without crowding, add the olive oil and, when it is hot, lay in the fish, skin side down, then fry for 2 minutes. Turn the fish and add the tomatoes, saffron and wine. Turn the heat up to full and cover the pan with foil or a tight-fitting lid. Length of cooking will depend on the thickness of the fillet but check after 4 minutes.

Remove the fillets carefully to hot serving plates (Peter served them atop mashed potato) and keep warm. With the sauce on full boil, add the extra-virgin olive oil and reduce for a minute or two until the sauce thickens, then spoon it over the fish and eat immediately.

MORUE AUX TOMATES

SERVES 4-6

'Skin 5 or 6 large tomatoes; remove the pips as much as possible; chop the tomatoes small. Melt a chopped onion in warmed olive oil; add the tomatoes and stir until most of their moisture has evaporated, add a tablespoon of flour, moisten with half a pint of stock or water; add a bouquet of herbs, 2 cloves of garlic, salt and pepper, and continue cooking while the salt cod is prepared.

'Take your soaked cod, scale it, cut into square pieces, roll them in flour, and fry them in a deep pan of olive oil. When they are golden on both sides, remove and drain them on paper. Put them into the tomato sauce; simmer another 10 minutes before serving.'

Elizabeth David, *French Provincial Cooking*

Note: you need 900 g salt cod, middle section, and it must be soaked in cold water for 12-24 hours and rinsed before proceeding with the recipe. 'Salt cod,' writes Mrs David, 'should always be soaked and cooked in porcelain, glazed earthenware, or enamelled vessels. Metal tends to discolour it.'

COD AND TOMATO PLAKI

SERVES 4

Plaki is a Greek word, which translates roughly as a way of braising fish with vegetables. It's an imprecise dish, not something to get in a twist about having measurements exact. This version is made with a thick, garlicky tomato and parsley sauce, which is poured over cod fillets then cooked quickly in a relatively hot oven. The only important point about the sauce is to cook the onion and garlic until it is soft and slippery before adding the tomatoes. This is because you are aiming for gentle flavours that come from thoroughly cooked onion, yet the chunks of tomato need to remain, well, chunky. In that way, when the dish emerges from the oven, the sauce will have depth of flavour yet will have kept its freshness. It should not cook down into a watery slop.

When I cooked this Plaki, I was using up a glut of over-ripe tomatoes and made far too much. It turned out to be a useful sauce to have in the fridge – I've eaten it with pasta and new potatoes. It makes a delicious garden supper with hot cauliflower florets, runner beans and a few flakes of Parmesan.

3 tbsp olive oil

1 large red onion, peeled and roughly chopped

2 plump garlic cloves, peeled and roughly chopped

1 tsp freshly chopped marjoram or thyme leaves

1 bay leaf

salt and freshly ground black pepper

500 g ripe tomatoes, cored, peeled, skinned and roughly chopped

a squirt of tomato ketchup (optional)

2½ tbsp roughly chopped flat-leaf parsley

4 x 200 g fillets cod, pollack or haddock, skinned

Pre-heat the oven to 350°F/180°C/gas mark 4.

Smear a suitable earthenware or ceramic gratin dish with a little of the oil and pour the rest into a medium saucepan. Add the onion, garlic, marjoram or thyme and the bay leaf to the saucepan. Season generously with salt and a little pepper, and cook for about 15 minutes over a medium-low heat stirring every now and again until the onion is slippery and tender. Add the tomatoes, turn up the heat and cook vigorously for 5-6 minutes so that some of the liquid is boiled away. Taste and adjust the seasoning, adding the tomato ketchup if the sauce isn't sweet enough. Remove from the heat and stir in 2 tablespoons of the parsley.

Run your index finger over the fish fillets to locate any bones and tug them out with tweezers. Slice each fillet into 2 and lay out the pieces in the oiled dish. Season with salt and pepper. Pour over the hot tomato sauce and bake for 15 minutes.

Serve garnished with the reserved parsley and, if liked, a dribble of your fruitiest olive oil over the top.

LIBYAN FISH TAGINE WITH TOMATOES

SERVES 4

The 'tagine' is the ubiquitous, witch's hat-style earthenware cooking dish of North Africa and has given its name to the stews often cooked in it, which usually involve fish, chicken, mutton or goat. However, you don't need to own a tagine to cook this dish. In fact, this recipe, adapted from Alastair Little and Richard Whittington's second book together, *Food of the Sun*, is made in two large frying-pans.

What makes this cumin-flavoured tagine of fish and potatoes Libyan I don't know, but it is a light yet satisfying and very aromatic dish with an intriguing tomato sauce.

- 4 medium large potatoes, approximately 700 g, peeled
- 5 tbsp olive oil
- 2 medium-large onions, approximately 300 g, peeled, halved and finely sliced
- 1 celery stalk, trimmed and finely sliced
- 4 tsp cumin seeds
- 2 garlic cloves, peeled and finely chopped
- 2 red chillies, seeded and finely chopped
- 2 tsp paprika
- 2 tsp turmeric
- salt and freshly ground black pepper
- 4 cod steaks, approximately 175 g each
- 600 ml passata or crushed tomatoes (see page 28)
- a large handful of coriander leaves

Quarter the potatoes lengthways and slice them chunkily. Rinse and drain. Choose a non-stick lidded pan that can hold all the ingredients. Warm half the oil over a medium-low heat and put in the potatoes. Fry gently, tossing and turning from time to time, so that they become tender but not crisp or uniformly coloured. This takes about 20 minutes.

Cook the onions in the remaining oil in a spacious frying-pan over a medium heat. Toss frequently until they are beginning to flop then add the celery. Cook, adjusting the heat so that the mixture softens without drying and burning, until tender. This should take about the same time as the potatoes.

Toast the cumin seeds in a dry pan over a low heat for a minute or two then grind to a powder. Stir it with the garlic, chillies, paprika and turmeric into the cooked onions. Season lightly with salt and pepper and cook for a further couple of minutes.

Season the potatoes thoroughly with salt and pepper. Season the fish lightly and place it on top of the potatoes. Spoon over the aromatic onion mixture, then pour on the passata. Bring to a bubble, immediately lower the heat, put on the lid and cook gently for 6 minutes or until the fish is just done. Serve in large warmed bowls, scattered with the coriander leaves.

MONKFISH WITH GARLIC AND TOMATO-WINE SAUCE

SERVES 4

Don't be alarmed by the vast quantity of garlic in this dish. Not, that is, if you use sweet, juicy new-season garlic. Some of its pungency and any harshness is removed by boiling it briefly in water before it is fried until golden together with fillets of monkfish. A delicious, quick, simple and very impressive dish, I discovered it in Ann and Franco Taruschio's book *Franco and Friends: Food From the Walnut Tree*, and I have cooked it so often that it feels as if it has become my own.

24 cloves new-season garlic, peeled

2 tbsp olive oil

4 pieces boneless monkfish, each weighing 200 g

150 ml dry white wine

750 ml passata or crushed tomatoes (see page 28)

4 sprigs fresh rosemary

salt and freshly ground black pepper

Drop the garlic into a pan of boiling water and cook until it is al dente. Drain. Heat the olive oil in a large frying-pan and fry the monkfish with the garlic until golden. Add the wine and reduce until it has evaporated. Add the passata and rosemary. Season with salt and pepper.

Simmer gently over a moderately low heat for about 10 minutes or until it is cooked – take care because monkfish has very dense flesh. Serve the fish with the sauce and the garlic cloves.

PASTILLA AU POISSON

SERVES 6

Pastilla is a large pie made with paper-thin pancakes called briouats and a pigeon and chicken filling. It is a great Moroccan party dish. The less common fish filling, explains Claudia Roden, in her exhaustive *The Book of Jewish Food*, is especially favoured by Jews. Mass-produced briouats, also known as warka, are widely available in France but unless you shop in a Middle Eastern store, as I can, in West London, here we have to make do with filo pastry.

- 1 large onion, peeled and coarsely chopped
- peanut or light vegetable oil
- 3 garlic cloves, crushed
- 750 g ripe tomatoes
- 2 tsp sugar
- ¼-½ tsp ground cloves
- salt and freshly ground black pepper
- 750 g firm white fish fillet, such as cod or haddock, skinned
- 100 g small button mushrooms, quartered
- 1 large bunch of coriander, leaves only, chopped
- 4 eggs, lightly beaten
- 12 sheets filo pastry
- 1 egg yolk

Pre-heat the oven to 375°F/190°C/gas mark 5.

In a large frying-pan, sauté the onion in 2 tablespoons of oil until soft. Add the garlic and fry until slightly coloured. Put the tomatoes in the blender and reduce them to a liquid. Pass them through a sieve then pour them into the pan. Add the sugar, the cloves and a seasoning of salt and pepper. Simmer for 5 minutes. Put the fish into the tomato sauce and simmer for 5 minutes, turning it once: it should be slightly underdone. Lift the fish out of the pan and set it aside to cool.

Add the mushrooms to the sauce and simmer for 8 minutes. Stir in the chopped coriander and the lightly beaten eggs. Cook very gently, stirring occasionally, until the sauce sets to a thick cream. Break up the fish into small pieces, discarding any bones. Fold it into the tomato cream. Remove from the heat.

A word of warning: filo pastry dries out very quickly and becomes brittle. Don't open the packet until the last moment, work with one sheet at a time and keep the rest covered with a damp tea-towel. Brush a large round pie-or baking-dish with oil. Fit into it a sheet of filo, letting the edges hang over the sides of the dish. Brush it with oil and repeat with 3 or 4 sheets, brushing each with oil and overlapping them so that there are no gaps. Spread half of the filling on top and cover it with 5 sheets of filo, brushing each with oil as you go. Spread the remaining filling over these. Bring the edges of the filo up over the filling. Cover with the remaining sheets, brushing with oil. Cut off the corners and tuck in the edges around the side of the dish. Paint the top with the egg yolk mixed with a little water.

Bake for about 40 minutes, or until crisp and golden.

POACHED SEA BASS WITH SAUCE VIERGE

SERVES 6

Vierge means virgin, and is a term for the best-quality olive oil made from the first pressing of olives. In this sauce, which, I think, originates from Michel Guérard's seminal *Cuisine Gourmande*, olive oil is flavoured with slivers of new-season garlic, basil and a little red wine, and mixed with peeled, diced tomatoes. It is one of the classiest dressings I know, and is a superb alternative to mayonnaise or aïoli to serve with fish such as sea bass, cod or haddock. The original recipe includes coriander seed but this simplified version doesn't, and the basil could be replaced with chives or coriander leaf. There is also more tomato in my recipe. It is also very good made with quartered cherry tomatoes. The fish, incidentally, could also be steamed, grilled or baked in the oven.

FOR THE SAUCE VIERGE

- 1 tbsp red wine vinegar
- salt and freshly ground black pepper
- 2 plump new-season garlic cloves, sliced in wafer-thin rounds
- 6 very ripe plum tomatoes, cored, peeled, seeded and diced
- 200 ml best possible olive oil
- a handful of basil leaves

FOR THE COURT-BOUILLON

- 1 onion, finely chopped
- 1 stick celery, peeled and thinly sliced
- 1 carrot, finely chopped
- 6 fillets sea bass, cod or haddock, cut from the middle of the fish, each weighing about 175 g
- 1 bay leaf
- 1 tsp salt
- 1 litre cold water
- 1 tbsp white wine vinegar

Make the Sauce Vierge by mixing together the vinegar, some salt, several grindings of pepper and the garlic in a large bowl. Stir in the tomatoes and leave to macerate for 30 minutes. Stir the olive oil into the salad and tear or snip the basil over the top. Stir again and serve.

Make the court-bouillon by placing all the ingredients in a saucepan, bring to the boil and simmer for 20 minutes. Then slip the fish fillets into the boiling court-bouillon. Simmer gently for 10 minutes, turn off the heat and leave for 10 minutes. Take the fish out of the pan and remove the skin.

To serve, place a fish fillet on a warm dinner plate, spoon over the sauce and serve with mashed or new potatoes and, perhaps, green beans. It looks stunning served over green beans with new potatoes served separately.

TURBOT WITH TOMATOES

SERVES 4 AS A STARTER

A sort of ceviche, made by marinating slivers of turbot in tomatoes mixed with sherry vinegar and walnut oil. A simple and effective dish, that I once ate at a dinner party given by Jeremy Round, from his book, *The Independent Cook*.

- 500 g turbot, skinned and filleted
- 6 tomatoes, roughly chopped, plus extra peeled tomato for garnish
- salt and freshly ground black pepper
- 3 tbsp walnut oil
- 1 tbsp sherry vinegar
- tarragon leaves for garnish

Slice the turbot fillets straight across the grain into thin slivers. Liquidize the tomatoes with lavish seasoning, plus the walnut oil and vinegar. Pass the puree through a sieve, to get rid of the skin and pips.

Marinate the fish pieces in the tomato mixture for 6-12 hours, then lift them out, shaking off excess marinade.

Arrange on serving plates with a teaspoon of the marinade splodged on top decoratively (you may need to beat it first if it has separated), plus a sprinkling of tarragon leaves and a neat strip or two of peeled tomato flesh to garnish.

MACKEREL WITH PEAS IN WINE AND TOMATO

SERVES 4

The rich, meaty flesh of mackerel is delicious cooked with tomato. In this unusual recipe fillets, carefully boned, are rolled and held in place with a cocktail stick. Then, covered with a highly seasoned tomato coulis, they are cooked with peas. With the little sticks removed, the mackerel are eaten from soup bowls with garlicky bruschetta on the side. A wonderful dish sometimes to be found on the menu at the Walnut Tree Inn at Abergavenny in Franco Taruschio's days.

- 1 onion, peeled and finely chopped
- 4 garlic cloves, peeled and chopped
- 2 tbsp olive oil
- 150 ml white wine
- 600 ml Cooked Tomato Coulis (see page 242)
- 2 tbsp finely chopped flat-leaf parsley
- 1 sprig of thyme
- a generous pinch of red chilli flakes or 1 red chilli, seeded but left whole
- salt and freshly ground black pepper
- 4 fresh mackerel, each weighing 450 g, filleted
- 450 g shelled peas or frozen petit pois
- you will also need 8 cocktail sticks

In a pan that can accommodate all the ingredients, fry the onion and garlic in the olive oil until tender and golden. Add the wine and reduce by two-thirds. Add the tomato coulis and parsley, thyme and chilli. Season with salt and pepper.

Roll up the mackerel fillets and skewer with a cocktail stick. Put them in the tomato sauce, add the peas and cook gently for about 10 minutes. Carefully remove the cocktail sticks.

Serve in shallow soup bowls with bruschetta – thick slices of sourdough bread or *pain de campagne*, toasted then seasoned with extra-virgin olive oil, crushed garlic and a twist of salt.

SALMON PAILLARD WITH GINGER TOMATO SAUCE AND FRESH CORIANDER

SERVES 2

This is a smart, clever dish devised in the early eighties by Jeremiah Tower for the opening of Stars in San Francisco. In the original, super-thin slices of fish are laid out on a hot butter-smeared plate and almost immediately turned and dressed with a very quick tomato-sauce-cum-salsa flavoured with ginger and garlic. 'By the time you garnish the plates with cilantro (coriander), the fish will be done.' Rather than serving one slice of fish as a starter, my version is envisaged as a main course so the fish is cut in slightly thicker slices and cooked briefly (for no more than a minute) under a hot grill.

New potatoes and extra-thin French beans are a good accompaniment.

350 g salmon fillet, cut from the middle, skinned

50 g butter

salt and freshly ground black pepper

150 ml fish stock

50 g fresh ginger, peeled and finely chopped

3 garlic cloves, peeled and finely chopped

4 medium 'grown-for-flavour' tomatoes, cored, peeled, seeded and diced

1 tbsp coarsely chopped coriander leaves

Run your index finger over the fish to locate any bones and remove with tweezers. Use a sharp knife to cut the salmon into 6 x 0.5 cm slices, cutting on the slant to the skin side, angling your knife at about 45° to get wider slices.

Melt half the butter. Lay a sheet of foil on the grill-pan, brush generously with some of the melted butter and lay out the pieces of salmon. Brush with butter and season with salt and pepper. Preheat the grill.

Meanwhile, make the sauce by placing the fish stock, ginger, garlic and tomatoes in a small pan. Season with salt and pepper. Bring to the boil and cook for 2 minutes. Cut the remaining butter into pieces and whisk them one by one into the pan to thicken the sauce magically. Turn off the heat.

Grill the salmon for 1 minute without turning. Carefully lift it on to hot plates, arranging 3 pieces on each plate. Pour over the sauce, scatter over with the coriander and serve.

MAQUEREAUX AU VIN BLANC

SERVES 2-4

An interesting way to serve mackerel, either as a main dish with new potatoes or as a dinner party starter with a slick of your finest olive oil.

- 4 mackerel fillets
- 4 medium-large tomatoes, approximately 300 g, peeled, cored and cut in half
- a knob of butter
- 1 shallot or small onion, peeled and finely chopped
- 3 tbsp finely chopped parsley
- 1 glass dry white wine, 150 ml
- salt and freshly ground black pepper
- a squeeze of lemon juice
- 1 tbsp finely snipped chives

Pre-heat the oven to 350°F/180°C/gas mark 4.

Using sharp scissors, trim away the gills and flabby edges of the mackerel fillets. Cut each fillet in half running a sharp knife down either side of the ridge of bones and discard. Run your index finger over the flesh to locate any other bones and pull them out.

Place a sieve over a bowl. Quarter the tomatoes lengthways and scrape the seeds and juices into the sieve. Press the seeds against the sides of the sieve to extract maximum juice. Pour the juice into a small saucepan. Chop the tomatoes into small dice.

Butter a glass or ceramic gratin-style dish that can hold 1 litre of liquid; I used an 18 cm x 28 cm oval dish. Mix the chopped tomatoes, shallot and 1 tablespoon of parsley in the dish. Smooth it out and place the mackerel fillets over the top, pushing them up close together, flesh side up. Add the wine to the tomato juice and bring quickly to the boil. Pour over the mackerel, helping the liquid between the fillets with a knife. Season the fish generously with salt and pepper.

Cook in the middle of the oven for 25 minutes, then take out the dish. Without disturbing the fish, spoon the juices from either end of the dish back into the small saucepan. Tilt the dish and carefully pour the remaining juice into the pan. Reduce the liquid by slightly more than half. Pour it over the fish again and leave to cool. Sprinkle over the lemon juice, then scatter over the remaining parsley and the chives. Serve without breaking up the fillets too much, with a share of tomatoes and juice.

SARDINES IN A MOORISH TOMATO SAUCE

SERVES 4

A useful quick way to add interest to tinned sardines.

- **3 x 120 g tins sardine fillets, packed in olive oil**
- **450 g tomatoes, cored and peeled, or 400 g tin chopped tomatoes**
- **1 small red pepper, seeds and white filament discarded, finely chopped**
- **1 small onion, finely chopped**
- **2 garlic cloves, peeled and chopped**
- **25 g chopped flat-leaf parsley**
- **1 small red chilli pepper, seeded and finely chopped, or ½ tsp red chilli flakes**
- **¼ tsp saffron, soaked in 1 tbsp hot water**
- **¼ tsp ground cumin**
- **a pinch of paprika**
- **a splash of white wine or white wine vinegar**
- **salt and freshly ground black pepper**
- **1 lemon, cut into wedges**

Drain the sardines, reserving the olive oil. Place the tomatoes, pepper, onion, garlic and 2 tablespoons of the parsley in the bowl of a food-processor and blitz. Heat 3 tablespoons of the reserved oil in a frying-pan and cook the tomato mixture for about 10 minutes or until it thickens. Add the chilli, the saffron and its water, the cumin, paprika, vinegar and a generous seasoning of salt and pepper. Simmer vigorously for a further 5 minutes. Add the drained sardines to the sauce and cook for 5 more minutes. Serve the sardines hot or cold garnished with the remaining parsley and lemon wedges to squeeze over the top.

SARDINE GRATIN WITH TOMATOES, BASIL AND AUBERGINE

SERVES 4-6

Sardines are butterflied, their backbones removed, and sandwiched with tomato and aubergine. Basil and garlic are the flavourings, and the gratin is finished with a layer of grated Gruyère.

I find that the simplest way to cook a large quantity of aubergines is in the oven. If you prefer, they can be fried then drained on absorbent kitchen paper to remove some of the oil, or oiled then cooked on a hot griddle.

- 1 kg, approximately, aubergines, trimmed and sliced lengthways
- approximately 8 tbsp olive oil
- 1.5 kg ripe but firm tomatoes cored, peeled, seeded and chopped
- salt and freshly ground black pepper
- a large bunch of basil, leaves only
- 3 garlic cloves, peeled and chopped
- 100 g grated Gruyère
- 12 sardines, heads and scales removed, opened out and the spine removed
- 1 tbsp lemon juice
- lemon wedges to serve

Pre-heat the oven to 400°F/200°C/gas mark 6.

Disgorge the slices of aubergine with salt for 20 minutes. Rinse and pat dry then lay out the slices in a single layer on a lightly oiled baking-sheet. Smear the top of the slices with a little olive oil. Cook for 10 minutes, then turn them and cook for another 5 minutes. The aubergine should be tender and lightly scorched in places.

Cover the base of a frying-pan with a film of oil and quickly fry the tomatoes. Season with salt and pepper.

Chop the basil leaves, then chop the basil and garlic together to make a green paste. Mix with 3 tablespoons of olive oil.

Smear a gratin dish that can hold all the sardines in a single layer with olive oil. Lay in it half of the aubergine slices. Season with salt and pepper. Add half of the tomatoes and half of the basil and garlic paste. Sprinkle over half of the Gruyère, then arrange the sardines over the top. Season with salt and pepper, squeeze over a little lemon juice. Cover with the remaining aubergines, tomatoes, basil and garlic and, finally, the last of the cheese.

Cook in the oven for 30 minutes. Serve with lemon wedges.

SARDINES WITH TOMATO AND ROCKET

SERVES 2

This recipe is a classic example of what happens when you eat something delicious in a restaurant then re-create it at home. This time the idea came from when Ian Bates, late of Bibendum, was cooking at the Chiswick, (a long-gone restaurant started by Adam Robinson when he ran the Brackenbury in Shepherd's Bush).

The dish is simple and effective. Grilled sardines are laid over sliced tomatoes, spread with a fresh herb sauce, inspired by salsa verde, then almost hidden under a mound of lightly dressed green leaves. On one visit, coriander dominated the flavours, but another time, it was mint, but rocket works particularly well, with its interesting peppery tang. It is also good on toast made with sardines from a can.

FOR THE GREEN SAUCE

- 2 garlic cloves, peeled
- 90 g wild rocket or watercress
- a few mint leaves
- 4 anchovy fillets
- 1 tbsp capers, drained
- scant tbsp Dijon mustard
- 7-10 tbsp olive oil
- salt and freshly ground black pepper

FOR THE SALAD

- 4 ripe, full-flavoured tomatoes, cored and sliced
- 2 tbsp vinaigrette
- 1 medium shallot, finely chopped
- 90 g rocket
- 4 fresh sardines, gutted but with heads on
- 2 tbsp olive oil
- salt and freshly ground black pepper

Begin by making the green sauce – you are certain to have too much but it's not worth making any less and the leftovers are delicious dribbled over any tomato salad you care to make or with hot roast tomatoes. It would also be good served with hot pasta and cold diced tomatoes. Anyway, put the garlic, rocket leaves, mint, anchovies, capers and mustard into the bowl of the food-processor with a couple of tablespoons of the olive oil. Blitz, scraping down what's thrown against the side of the bowl and, with the machine running, add the rest of the oil in a thin stream; you're aiming for the consistency of a lumpy mayonnaise. Season with salt and pepper.

Lay the tomatoes in the middle of 2 dinner plates. Cover them with about 2 tablespoons of sauce.

Make the salad: the vinaigrette with the shallot, then add the rocket.

Rinse the sardine inside and out and pat dry with absorbent kitchen paper. Smear them with olive oil and season thoroughly with salt and pepper. Pre-heat a ridged griddle (or barbecue – make sure that the racks are really hot) and cook the sardines quickly over a fierce heat. This should take a couple of minutes a side.

Lay the sardines over the sliced tomatoes and top with a mound of rocket and shallot salad. Serve with crusty bread.

RED MULLET WITH TOMATOES

SERVES 4

Triglie alla Livornese is the Italian name for this dish, from Livorno, the Tuscan seaport. It is famous for its fish dishes, many of which are of Jewish origin, as Claudia Roden explains in 'The Sephardi World' section of her comprehensive *The Book of Jewish Food*.

> 'The port city was once predominantly Jewish. The community was formed in the seventeenth century by Marranos from Spain and Portugal who were invited to settle by the Grand Duke Ferdinando I de Medici and allowed to revert to their old religion. These Marranos were among the first to introduce tomatoes to Italy – which was the second country after Spain to adopt the New World vegetable. They did so through their contacts with the Marranos of South America, who had emigrated as New Christians to escape the pressures of the Inquisition. The New Christians had been among the first who sailed with Christopher Columbus, and they became involved in the early trade of New World vegetables. That may be why some old classics with tomatoes – like this one – were called alla mosaica (referring to the prophet Moses and meaning Jewish).'

So there you are. This is Claudia's recipe.

- 4 garlic cloves, peeled and chopped
- 4 tbsp extra-virgin olive oil
- 500 g ripe tomatoes, cored, peeled and chopped
- salt and freshly ground black pepper
- 1 tsp sugar
- 4 red mullet, each about 250 g, cleaned and scaled, heads on, liver intact
- 3 tbsp chopped flat-leaf parsley

In a large frying-pan that can hold the fish in one layer, sauté the garlic in the oil until it is aromatic and lightly coloured. Add the tomatoes, salt, pepper and sugar, and simmer for 10 minutes. Arrange the fish in the sauce, and cook at a steady simmer, turning once, for about 7 minutes, or until done. Add the parsley before serving.

MALTESE TINNED TUNA STEW

SERVES 4

Wonderful tomatoes are grown in Malta and I found many interesting things to do with them, and other ingredients, in Anne and Helen Caruana Galizia's charming book, *The Food and Cookery of Malta* (Prospect Books). This recipe isn't exactly traditional but brings together tomatoes, tuna, olives, capers and fresh herbs with the authors' excellent potato dish called Patata Fgata. The result is one of those wonderful meals-in-a-pot, when fresh tomatoes cook into a delicious fruity goo with a hint of acidity.

- 6 medium-sized potatoes, peeled
- 3 tbsp olive oil
- 2 Spanish onions, peeled and sliced
- 2 garlic cloves, peeled and crushed
- 2 tbsp chopped flat-leaf parsley, marjoram, basil or mint
- 2 bay leaves
- 1 tbsp white wine
- 500 g ripe tomatoes, cored, peeled, and chopped
- 1 tsp sugar
- salt and freshly ground black pepper
- 200 g tin sustainable tuna in brine, drained
- a handful of pitted black olives
- a handful of capers, drained
- 2 tbsp chopped flat-leaf parsley or coriander
- ½ tbsp chopped mint

Chop the potatoes into large, even-sized chunks. Heat 2 tablespoons of the oil in a large non-stick pan over a medium heat and stir in the onion and garlic. Cook for a couple of minutes then add the potatoes, the parsley (or marjoram, basil or mint), the bay leaves, wine, tomatoes and sugar. Add a little water if the potatoes are not quite covered and season with ½ teaspoon of salt and several grinds of black pepper. Bring to the boil, cover and simmer gently until the potatoes are tender.

Stir in the drained tuna, broken into chunks, the olives, capers and the parsley or coriander with the mint. Dribble over the last of the olive oil and serve immediately with crusty bread and a green vegetable or salad.

TUNA WITH TOMATOES AND LEMON

SERVES 4

This is an old Marseillaise recipe, which I came across in Paul Strang's fascinating book about food fairs and markets in south-west France. It is one of the few fish stews that is actually better eaten warm or cold with a splash of olive oil and a crust of good bread. The tomatoes tenderize the dense flesh of the tuna while impregnating it with a wonderful flavour. The recipe is an authentic original contributed by Erick Vedel to Strang's *Take 5000 Eggs*.

3 tbsp extra-virgin olive oil, plus extra for serving

200 g onion, peeled, halved and sliced

700 g fresh tuna, skinned, boned and cut into 2.5 cm thick slices

500 g ripe, plum tomatoes, cored, peeled and each cut into 8 segments

½ lemon, thinly sliced

2 bay leaves

salt and freshly ground black pepper

1 small chilli, halved and seeded

200 ml dry white wine

Pre-heat the oven to 350°F/180°C/gas mark 4.

Coat the bottom of a casserole with the oil and spread over it a third of the onions, followed by slices of tuna, some of the tomatoes, more onions, some of the lemon slices and the bay leaves. Season with salt and pepper, add a second layer of tuna and the rest of the tomatoes, lemon slices and chilli. Pour in the white wine and top up with enough water to just cover the fish.

Cover the casserole and bring it to the boil over a medium heat, then either reduce the heat to a simmer, or transfer the casserole to the oven for about 1 hour. Allow to cool and serve with a splash of olive oil.

PAN-SEARED TUNA AND TOMATO WATER

SERVES 4

A simple idea from an engaging book called *Recipes 1–2–3* by Rozanne Gold, which includes only recipes with three ingredients – apart from salt and pepper. The tomato, in my view, is the star here, coming up trumps in two different ways. The dish is described as a chic version of Salade Niçoise, with tomato juice as a dressing and slices of tomato mixed with olives to go with a piece of seared fresh tuna. Good additions would be finely chopped hard-boiled egg, slices of potato and boiled green beans.

6 large ripe tomatoes, cored and peeled

36 oil-cured black olives, halved and pitted

4 fresh tuna steaks, 175 g each

salt and freshly ground black pepper

An hour or so before serving, trim off the outer wall of the tomatoes with a small sharp knife. Remove the seed pulp and reserve (see page 27). Cut the tomato flesh into strips approximately 3 mm wide x 4 cm long. Put the tomato julienne and the olives in a small bowl with ½ teaspoon of salt. Leave for 30 minutes.

Coarsely chop the reserved pulp of the tomatoes and press it through a sieve or blitz in the food-processor.

Sprinkle the tuna lightly with salt and pepper. Heat a large non-stick frying-pan or griddle and sear it on both sides until browned but still pink inside.

Spoon the tomato liquid over 4 plates. Place the cooked fish over the sauce, and top with the tomato-olive mixture.

GRILLED MUSSELS WITH TOMATOES, ALMONDS AND FENNEL

SERVES 4

Pre-cooked mussels are left on the half shell and topped with a mixture that could be described as fresh tomato pesto. Once assembled, the mussels are grilled until the topping is crisp, golden and aromatic. It is an idea to play around with by using different herbs but is a speciality from Trapani in Sicily. At Belgo, the London chain of Belgian restaurants that specializes in mussels, they serve something similar called mussel pizza – the half-shells are laid out on round metal trays and served as a main dish. This way of preparing mussels is also an excellent canapé but must be eaten hot.

- 1.4 kg cleaned mussels
- 2 slices bread, crusts removed, cubed
- olive oil
- 25 g blanched almonds
- 3 garlic cloves, peeled
- salt and freshly ground black pepper
- 500 g plum tomatoes, cored, peeled, seeded and finely diced
- bunch fennel fronds, finely chopped

Discard any mussels with cracked shells and those that don't close when tapped, then place them in a large, lidded pan and set on a high heat. Cook, shaking the pan occasionally, until all the shells open. Throw away any that don't. Keep the mussels on the half-shell, discarding the top shells, and arrange on a baking tray.

Fry the bread cubes in olive oil, tossing until they are evenly golden. Set aside. Add a little more oil to the pan and fry the almonds until pale golden. Place the croutons, almonds and garlic in the bowl of a food-processor. Blitz until processed to a fine dust. Mix the breadcrumbs, tomatoes and fennel fronds together with a decent seasoning of salt and pepper. Spoon the mixture over the individual mussels, covering them well. Dribble with olive oil.

Pre-heat the grill. Cook the mussels until golden brown and crisp. Serve hot.

STEAMED MUSSELS WITH TOMATO, CUMIN AND HERBS

SERVES 4-6

Scraps of bright red tomato and green herbs caught among a huge mound of inky black steamed mussels look spectacular. At the Sugar Club in Notting Hill, London, Peter Gordon refined this combination to perfection and underpins the fruity acidity of ripe tomatoes, which goes so well with the creaminess of mussels, with white wine, olive oil and spring onions, but the dish is dominated by cumin. This colourful take on Moules Marinière is a great dish for sharing with friends but be sure to serve it with finger bowls – hands-on is the best way to eat it.

Paul Merrony, of Merrony's in Sydney, Australia, makes a similar dish, called Mussels with Tomato and Herbs. He uses 500 ml of tomato concassé, a bunch of chopped chives, the chopped leaves of a small bunch of flat-leaf parsley and from a small bunch of tarragon, with 250 g of butter. He suggests placing 1.4 kg cleaned mussels in a pan with the tomato concassé and the butter. Cover and cook over a high heat, shaking the pan every now and again. After 6-12 minutes, when all the mussels have opened, mix in the herbs. 'Serve with a bib, a finger-bowl, and plenty of crusty bread. And big spoons.' Cheers.

600 ml dry white wine
1 kg ripe tomatoes, cored, seeded and cut into 1 cm dice
6 tsp cumin seeds, toasted
1 large handful fresh basil leaves
1 large handful fresh flat-leaf parsley leaves
2 bunches spring onions, sliced
100 ml olive oil
2 tsp cracked black pepper
2 kg cleaned mussels
extra chopped parsley

Bring the wine to the boil in a large pot with a tight-fitting lid.

Place the tomato in a bowl and mix it with the cumin, basil, parsley, spring onions, olive oil and pepper. Add half of this to the boiling wine and tip all the mussels on top. Pour on the remaining tomato mixture and give it all a stir. Bring back to a full boil with the lid on and don't look for 5 minutes. Tip the mussels into bowls, but discard any that refuse to open. Sprinkle with the extra parsley.

TOMATO MOUCLADE

SERVES 4-6

Mouclade is an elegant, saffron-flavoured creamy mussel and onion soup-cum-stew. In this tomato version, the mussels are cooked in white wine and garlic, then combined with a chunky tomato and onion sauce let down with fish stock and the intensely flavoured juices from the mussels. It looks spectacular served with a scattering of chopped parsley and needs some crusty bread to mop up the indescribably good tomato sauce.

- 75 g butter
- 2 Spanish onions, peeled and chopped
- 900 g ripe tomatoes, cored, peeled and roughly chopped
- 1 tbsp tomato ketchup or sun-dried tomato puree
- 2 tbsp finely chopped flat-leaf parsley
- salt and freshly ground black pepper
- 1 shallot, peeled and finely chopped
- 2 plump garlic cloves, finely chopped
- a small bunch of thyme
- 300 ml dry white wine
- 1.8 kg cleaned mussels
- crème fraîche (optional)

Melt 50 g of the butter in a large, heavy-bottomed pan that can hold the finished soup, stir in the onions, cover the pan and cook until they are soft but uncoloured. Add the tomatoes, tomato ketchup and half the parsley. Season well with salt and pepper and cook, uncovered, for 15 minutes.

Meanwhile, melt the remaining butter in a lidded pan that can hold the mussels, and cook the shallot and garlic with the bunch of thyme for several minutes before adding the wine. Bring to the boil, then add the mussels. Clamp on the lid, bring the liquid quickly back to the boil and cook for a few minutes until the mussels open. Discard any that don't. Tip the mussels into a colander held inside a bowl and shake to catch all the juices. Strain the juices through muslin or a J-cloth (to catch the shell grit) into the tomatoes.

Pick over the mussels, extracting about half from their shells and leaving the rest intact or on the half-shell. Add the mussels and as much of the shallot and garlic as you can collect to the tomatoes. Heat through, taste and adjust the seasoning (mussels tend to be quite salty), sprinkle on the last of the parsley and serve with a bowl of crème fraîche for people to help themselves.

FRAGRANT PRAWN CURRY WITH TAMARIND AND SPINACH

SERVES 4

Bottled spicy tomato sauce and fresh tomatoes are vital to the success of this interesting curry. It has no particular cultural associations but uses flavourings that appear throughout Asia. Tamarind gives the curry a sour, fruity flavour, which goes well with prawns and tomatoes, and is a seasoning often used in Thai hot and sour soups.

More haunting flavour, this time sweet yet pungent, and very aromatic, comes from ground coriander seed, while turmeric gives the curry a rich golden colour and gentle flavour. Coconut cream unites the dish, and ginger complements the fresh tomato with a vibrant blast of flavour. Spinach, flung in at the last moment, looks suitably dramatic against the tomatoes and prawns.

- 400 g raw headless tiger prawns or good-quality cooked prawns, with shells
- a bunch of large-bulb spring onions or 2 small white onions
- 1 tbsp cooking oil
- 2 garlic cloves, peeled and finely chopped
- 5-cm piece fresh ginger, peeled and thinly sliced
- 1 tsp ground turmeric
- 1 tsp ground coriander seed
- 1 tbsp tamarind pulp
- 2 tbsp of Chilli Tomato Sauce (see page 237) or 2 tbsp tomato ketchup mixed with 2 shakes of Tabasco
- 100 g creamed coconut salt and freshly ground black pepper
- 8 plum tomatoes, cored, peeled, quartered and seeded
- 225 g fresh leaf spinach, rinsed and shaken dry
- a handful of coriander leaves

If using frozen prawns slip them into a bowl of warm water and leave for a couple of minutes. Peel off their shells and place the shells in a pan. Cover with water. Trim and finely slice the onions, adding the trimmings to the prawn shells. Bring slowly to the boil and simmer for 10 minutes.

Warm a wok over a medium heat, add the cooking oil and stir-fry the spring onion. As it softens add the garlic and ginger and, after a minute or two, add the turmeric and ground coriander, then the tamarind and the Spicy Tomato Sauce. Crumble in the creamed coconut and 150 ml of strained prawn stock (or 150 ml water and ¼ chicken stock cube), stir until smooth then taste and adjust the seasoning with salt and pepper. Add the prawns, and cook until they change colour (if making this dish with cooked prawns, just heat them through) then add the tomato. Cook for 1 minute, stir in the spinach, allow it to wilt, then serve sprinkled with coriander leaves.

PRAWNS AND GREEN BEANS IN A FRESH TOMATO SAUCE

SERVES 3-4

There isn't much cooking involved in this simple summer supper. It is one of those recipes that is easy to scale up or down to suit however many mouths you have to feed, and is served cold. It goes particularly well with hot new potatoes, but if you prefer, serve it over couscous stirred with extra mint and edged with shredded cos lettuce.

- 200 g peas, shelled or frozen weight
- 300 g green beans or runner beans
- 500 g squashy ripe tomatoes
- salt and freshly ground black pepper
- a pinch of sugar
- a few drops of wine vinegar or lemon juice
- Tabasco
- a few mint leaves
- 160 g peeled and cooked king prawns

Put two medium-sized pans of water on to boil. Add ½ teaspoon of salt to both pans.

Meanwhile, if necessary, shell the peas. Remove the ends of the beans and cut them in half unless they are very small. If using runner beans, top, tail and string them, then cut them on the diagonal into thin slices. Drop the peas into one pan of boiling water and the beans into another. Bring back to the boil, cook for 1-2 minutes until just tender. Drain.

Place the tomatoes in the bowl of a food-processor and blitz briefly, using the pulse button, until roughly chopped and juicy like salsa. Do not over-process them into a puree. Tip the chopped tomato into a suitable serving bowl. Season with salt, pepper, sugar, wine vinegar or lemon juice, and a few drops of Tabasco to perk up the flavours. Stir in the prawns, peas and beans, taste and adjust the seasoning as necessary. Tear the mint over the top.

PRAWNS WITH PARSLEY AND ALMOND TOMATO SAUCE

SERVES 4

In Spain, nuts are often used to thicken sauces, and here they effect the balance between the sweetness of the tomatoes and the prawns, the fiery cayenne and the sharpness of the lemon.

- 3 tbsp olive oil
- 1 Spanish onion, peeled and finely chopped
- 700 g ripe tomatoes, cored, peeled, seeded and chopped
- salt and freshly ground black pepper
- ½ tsp sugar
- 100 g blanched almonds
- 100 g pine kernels
- 4 garlic cloves, peeled and chopped
- a small bunch of flat-leaf parsley, leaves only
- ¼ tsp cayenne pepper
- juice of ½ lemon
- 400 g shelled cooked prawns or shrimps

Heat the oil and cook the onion until soft and golden. Add the tomatoes. Season with salt, pepper and sugar. Cook uncovered for 10 minutes, stirring often, until the sauce is thick but juicy.

Meanwhile, place the almonds, pine kernels, garlic and parsley leaves in the food-processor bowl. Add 3 tablespoons of water and process the mixture to a thick paste. Scrape the paste into the tomatoes and cook for a few minutes, adding a little more water if the sauce is very thick. Stir in the cayenne. Taste and season with salt, pepper and lemon juice. Fold in the prawns. Heat through and serve with boiled rice.

SHRIMPS OREO LIMANI

SERVES 2-3

This is my approximation of a dish served at the bougainvillea-clad beach taverna of the Istron Bay Hotel in Crete. Tiny shrimps are scorched in Cognac, then simmered in the oven in an intensely flavoured lemon and parsley tomato sauce speckled with chunks of feta cheese. In Crete the dish is served as an appetizer with crusty bread. Back home I've replaced shrimps with good-quality prawns and would suggest eating the dish with rice or piled on to a crisp tortilla.

- 1 small lemon
- 4 tbsp olive oil
- 1 small onion or shallot, peeled and finely chopped
- 2 garlic cloves, peeled and finely chopped
- 2 tbsp finely chopped flat-leaf parsley
- 350 g Cirio Rustica or 400 g tin chopped tomatoes
- ½ tsp soft brown sugar
- salt and freshly ground black pepper
- 200 g raw, headless tiger prawns or good-quality cooked prawns
- 3 tbsp Cognac or brandy
- 50 g feta cheese

OPTIONAL EXTRAS

- 2-3 tortillas
- 1 tbsp cooking oil
- 4 scoops Greek yoghurt
- ½ tbsp finely chopped flat-leaf parsley

Remove the zest from half the lemon and chop it finely to dust.

Warm 3 tablespoons of the oil in a pan that can hold all the ingredients over a medium heat. Add the onion and garlic and cook for 5 minutes, stirring a couple of times, before adding 1 tablespoon of the parsley and the lemon zest. Cook, stirring once, for 2 minutes before adding the tomatoes, sugar and a generous seasoning of salt and pepper. Adjust the heat so that the mixture is bubbling gently and leave it to cook for 10 minutes.

If using frozen prawns, slip them into a bowl of warm water to defrost for a couple of minutes then remove the shells.

Heat the last tablespoon of olive oil in a small frying-pan, then add the prawns, tossing them around for a minute until they are pink all over. Pour on the Cognac and squeeze over the juice from the lemon. Let everything sizzle up. Strike a match and light the liquid, allowing the flames to die down of their own accord. Cook for about 30 seconds more, just until the prawns are thoroughly coated and before the liquids have evaporated. Tip the contents of the pan into the tomato and simmer for 5 minutes before adding the feta, broken into small chunks. Simmer together for 3 minutes, then add the remaining parsley.

To cook the tortilla, get a frying pan very hot. Add half the cooking oil, swirl it round the pan and toast the tortilla for 1 minute a side until crisp. Repeat with the second tortilla. Pile the prawn mixture in the centre of the tortillas, rolling them up if you wish. Accompany with a scoop of Greek yoghurt dusted with the parsley.

SQUID WITH TOMATOES AND GREEN PEAS

SERVES 4

Many people dislike the thought of squid so much that they refuse even to try it. This is a pity because the snowy white body tube of this excellent mollusc is tender and sweet, and comes without a shell.

One of my favourite ways of cooking squid is with tomatoes and peas, and the idea comes from Marcella Hazan's *Classic Italian Cookbook* (Macmillan, 1988). The dish more or less cooks itself. It is best eaten with plenty of crusty bread to scoop up the wonderful juices.

- 1 medium onion, peeled and finely chopped
- 3 tbsp olive oil
- 2 garlic cloves, peeled and finely chopped
- 2 tbsp finely chopped flat-leaf parsley
- 450 g ripe tomatoes, cored, peeled, seeded and chopped, or 400 g tin chopped Italian tomatoes
- 900 g smallest possible squid, fresh or frozen, cleaned by the fishmonger
- salt and pepper
- 350 g fresh or frozen peas

Put the onion in a flameproof casserole with the olive oil and sauté it over a medium heat, stirring occasionally, for about 10 minutes until it begins to soften and turn golden. Add the garlic and cook for a couple of minutes before adding half of the parsley and the tomatoes. Cook at a gentle simmer for 15 minutes until the tomatoes begin to thicken with the onions.

Slice the squid sacs (its body) into 1.5 cm rings. Cut off the tentacles. Squeeze out the hard mouth from the centre of the tentacles – it will pop out easily – and discard everything else. Divide the tentacle clusters in half.

Add rings and tentacles to the casserole. Season with salt and pepper, stir well, cover and cook at a gentle simmer for 20-30 minutes until the squid is tender. Stir in the peas, season again and cook for a few more minutes until they are done. Stir in the remaining parsley and serve.

Also see:
Gazpacho Andaluz with Crab (page 110)
Jambalaya (page 318)
Linguine with Fiery Prawns (page 293)
Lobster Bisque (page 72)
Manhattan Clam Chowder (page 73)
Niçoise Sauce (page 239)
Spaghetti con Vongole (page 292)

tomatoes with poultry, game & meat

'In the dish Chicken in Onion Tomato Gravy (Murgh Masala), the cinnamon, cardamom and cloves aromatize; the turmeric lends yellow colour; the onions, garlic and ginger root and tomatoes act as thickeners as well as imparting flavour and colour to the dish. The tomatoes also function as tenderizing and souring agents.'

Julie Sahni, *Classic Indian Cookery* (Grub Street, 1997)

There are few cuts of meat and types of poultry that don't go with tomatoes. When a stew seems dry, and no stock is available, who hasn't added a few tomatoes to the pot? It would seem that just about every cook since tomatoes made their mark on our culinary map has done just that, and some of the recipes have become classic combinations. Tomatoes with red peppers, for example, often with a little chilli too, turn up in the cuisines of France, Italy, Greece, Turkey, Spain and Portugal. And probably in the cooking of some other countries too. However, it is with meat that tomato sauces or gravies are most complex. Here we can see the scale of variety in the way that tomatoes can be used and flavoured. Diverse combinations, such as tomatoes and meat with cumin and saffron, cinnamon and ginger, or with almonds and pine kernels, coriander, mint and flat-leaf parsley, lemon and tamarind, various wines and vinegars, are just the tip of the iceberg. These layers of flavour can be found in the aromatic tomato and meat stews and tagines of Morocco and Algeria, the curries of India and Mauritius, the chilli-hot stews from Portugal, Spain and Mexico.

Many more recipes use smaller quantities of tomato, but its inclusion is vital to the success of the dish. Chicken Chasseur, for example, a creamy mushroom and chicken casserole, is lifted by the last-minute addition of tomato concassé, and is one of many recipes that didn't make it into these pages. I hope my selection does justice to the possibilities that tomatoes offer as an integral ingredient with meat.

BALSAMIC TOMATO CHICKEN WITH BASIL

SERVES 4

One of my favourite ways to inject fresh flavour and vivacity to lacklustre chicken and tomatoes. Foolproof, quick and tasty.

- 50 g butter
- 1 tbsp cooking oil
- 1 garlic clove, crushed to a paste with a pinch of salt
- 400 g chicken thigh fillet, cut in strips 5 cm long x 1 cm wide
- 2-3 tbsp aged balsamic vinegar
- 500 g tomato concassé (see page 29)
- salt and freshly ground black pepper
- sugar
- a squeeze of lemon juice
- a knob of butter
- a handful of basil leaves

Melt half of the butter in a frying-pan over a medium heat. Add the oil and garlic, and cook until aromatic. Put in the chicken, turn up the heat and fry briskly until it is plump and springy. Pour over the balsamic vinegar, quickly stirring everything around until it evaporates – a few seconds. Add the rest of the butter and the tomatoes. Season with salt and pepper, and simmer for about 15 minutes until the tomatoes have turned into a sauce and the chicken is completely cooked. Taste, and adjust the seasoning with salt, sugar and a squeeze of lemon juice. Stir in the knob of butter until it has dissolved. Shred the basil leaves over the top and serve.

CHICKEN WITH TOMATOES AND CORIANDER

SERVES 4-6

A hint of tamarind complements the lemony tang of fresh coriander in this wonderfully rustic chicken and tomato stew. It is easy to make and everybody seems to like it: the pieces of chicken are imbued with a fresh tomato sauce thickened with red onions and garlic, and stirred with masses of chopped coriander leaves, garlic and a little mint. Serve it with almost anything: potatoes, pasta, rice, polenta, a chunk of bread or over bruschetta.

- 3 tbsp olive oil
- 750 g chicken thigh fillet, sliced into thick strips
- large knob of butter
- 3 medium red onions, peeled, halved and sliced in wedges
- 1 tbsp tamarind paste
- 1 bay leaf
- 750 g ripe tomatoes, cored, peeled and chopped
- salt and freshly ground black pepper
- a large bunch of coriander, chopped
- a small bunch of mint, leaves only, chopped
- 3 garlic cloves, peeled and finely chopped

Heat 2 tablespoons of the oil in a pan that can accommodate all the ingredients. When the oil is very hot, fry the chicken, cooking for a couple of minutes a side, turning as the chicken browns and goes crusty. Remove it from the pan. Add the butter and as soon as it has sizzled, stir in the onions. Cook briskly, stirring every now and again, until the onion is wilted and scorched in places. Stir in the tamarind, the bay leaf and the tomatoes. Cook for 10-15 minutes, until the tomatoes have broken down somewhat, then return the chicken. Cook at a gentle simmer for about 30 minutes until the chicken is tender. Taste, and adjust the seasoning. Stir in the herbs and garlic, then serve.

CHICKEN CACCIATORA

SERVES 4

Cacciatora means 'hunter-style'; throw the fowl in the pot with herbs and tomatoes, and maybe a few mushrooms.

- 8 portions good-quality chicken
- salt and freshly ground black pepper
- 3 tbsp olive oil
- large knob of butter
- 1 small onion, finely chopped
- 2 stalks celery heart with leaves, finely sliced
- a generous pinch of dried red chilli flakes
- 600 g tomato concassé (see page 29) or 2 x 400 g tins crushed or chopped tomatoes, preferably Cirio Rustica
- a herb bundle, made with 2 bay leaves, 4 sprigs parsley, 2 sprigs rosemary and several celery leaves

Season the chicken all over with salt and pepper. Place a large frying-pan over a high heat, put in the oil and butter, and when the butter has melted, lay in the chicken, skin side down, without crowding it. Cook until the skin is crisp and brown. Turn and cook for 5 more minutes. Transfer to a plate.

Stir the onion, celery and chilli into the hot juices left in the pan, adjusting the heat so that everything cooks gently for 5-6 minutes. Add the tomato concassé, or the tomatoes. Add the herb bundle. Stir well, season with salt and pepper and simmer briskly for 5 minutes before burying the chicken pieces in the sauce. Return to a simmer, partially cover the pan and cook for about 25 minutes until the chicken is tender. Taste, and adjust the seasoning. Discard the herb bundle, and serve.

CHICKEN PROVENÇALE

SERVES 4

When a dish is described as à la Niçoise or à la Provençale, it is made with a chunky tomato sauce cooked with garlic, often with onions, and sometimes with olives, anchovies and aubergine. The Niçoise version tends to be the more elaborate of the two and might also include capers, artichokes and courgettes. Basil is likely to appear in both, and tarragon, too, might be included. Both sauces are a celebration of local vegetables and flavourings and are liberally interpreted according to what is available. Black olives always appear in Niçoise sauces but come and go in Provençale. Tuna, often tinned, is sometimes a key ingredient of Niçoise Sauce (see page 239, for a version made with tinned tomatoes). Anyway, it is a combination of ingredients that travels well, and in the summer, when British pot basil is going mad, throwing out the hugest, most pungent leaves possible, and tomatoes are full of flavour, the dish will be a close approximation of the real thing.

It will be all the better if you splash out on an organic chicken – a whole one cut into quarters – although pre-prepared thighs would be the more convenient option. What is unusual about the preparation of this good-natured dish is that the chicken flesh is slashed, in the way that you might with beef or lamb, and pasted with an aromatic mixture of herbs and chopped garlic. It is then washed with lemon juice and fried in olive oil before it's buried in a luscious, fruity, piquantly spiced tomato sauce. The surprisingly savoury depth of flavour comes from a few anchovies, which don't taste the least bit fishy and melt away entirely.

Rice is the traditional accompaniment to Chicken à la Provençale but new potatoes or green beans and a chunk of bread to mop up the wonderful tomato sauce go well too.

1.4 kg organic chicken, cut into 8 pieces, or 8 plump chicken thighs, skinned

juice of 1 lemon

2 garlic cloves, peeled and worked to a paste with a little salt

1 tbsp finely chopped thyme leaves

salt and freshly ground black pepper

1 quantity Provençal Sauce (see page 298)

Pre-heat the oven to 400°F/200°C/gas mark 6.

Make several small slits in each chicken piece. Place in a bowl, squeeze over the lemon juice and roll the pieces around to season thoroughly. Mix the garlic paste with the thyme and smear it into the cracks, helping it in with the end of a teaspoon or similar. Season with salt and pepper. It will look messy.

Heat the remaining oil in a frying-pan and brown the chicken pieces all over. Season again. Tip the Provençal Sauce into a spacious heavy-bottomed flameproof casserole and heat it through. Bury the pieces of chicken in the sauce, cover the pan and cook for 20-30 minutes until the chicken is done.

GINGER AND GARLIC CHICKEN IN A CHILLI TOMATO SAUCE

SERVES 4

This is a good example of how tinned tomatoes can be used to make a tasty, well seasoned cook-in sauce for meat or fish.

The long, slow stewing, which is how the sauce is made, has a two-fold effect: first the liquid and juice in the tomatoes is reduced and concentrated, and second, the flavourings – in this case garlic, chilli and bay – are absorbed into the very fabric of the sauce. Once the cooking is done, the contents of the pan are forced through a sieve, leaving behind all the pips and skin, to emerge luscious and thick, yet still with a pouring consistency. This puree will turn into a sort of thick jam if it's left to cook even longer. Then it is the perfect thing to serve as a dipping sauce for deep-fried foods, particularly small pieces of fish, chicken or vegetables, which have been egg-and-bread crumbed or dipped in batter.

In this recipe, chicken is stir-fried briefly with ginger, garlic and lemon juice before it is poached in the tomato sauce. The dish goes very well with potato pancakes and a crisp green vegetable, but would also make a good pasta sauce.

FOR THE CHICKEN

6 organic chicken legs or 12 thighs

2 garlic cloves, peeled and worked into a paste with a little salt

juice of 1 lemon

5-cm piece fresh ginger, peeled and very finely diced

4 tbsp olive oil

salt and freshly ground black pepper

FOR THE SAUCE

2 x 400 g tins peeled Italian tomatoes

2 garlic cloves, lightly crushed

1 bay leaf

1 fresh red chilli

salt and freshly ground black pepper

1 tbsp tomato ketchup

a squeeze of lemon juice

Joint the chicken legs and remove the skin. Cut the meat off the bones and into bite-sized chunks. Place the garlic paste in a mixing bowl and stir it with the lemon juice. Add the ginger and stir in 2 tablespoons of the olive oil. Season generously with pepper. Put in the chicken, and use your hands to mulch everything together. Leave to marinate while the sauce is prepared.

Force the tomatoes through a sieve, or blitz them in a food-processor, then pass through a sieve. Put the tomato juice, garlic, bay leaf, chilli and a pinch of salt into a medium-sized saucepan. Establish a gentle simmer and cook for about 40 minutes or until the tomatoes have disintegrated into a thick sauce. Pass the sauce through a sieve into a pan that can also accommodate the chicken. Taste, and adjust seasonings with ketchup, lemon juice, salt and pepper.

Place a wok or large frying pan over a high heat, add the remaining oil and swirl it round the pan. Tip the chicken mixture into the wok, adjust the heat, season with salt and stir-fry for a few minutes while the meat turns white and some edges are crusted. Transfer the contents of the pan into the tomato sauce and simmer gently for 10-15 minutes until the chicken is cooked.

HARIRA

SERVES 6-8

This recipe is based on Alastair Little and Richard Whittington's version of a famous Moroccan chick-pea and tomato soup that is normally *flavoured* with lamb or chicken. Their Harira is a complete meal, and is one of those wonderful soupy stews that gets better after a day or two. Every mouthful seems different, underpinned, as it is, with interesting flavours – ginger, saffron, garlic, coriander, lemon, and flat-leaf parsley – which are infused into the tomato and chicken broth. For convenience of eating, the chicken is part-cooked then taken off the bone. If you prefer, leave the meat on the bone.

- 200 g dried chickpeas, soaked overnight
- 6 tbsp olive oil, plus a little extra
- salt and freshly ground black pepper
- 1.3 kg chicken or 6 chicken legs, jointed
- 2 tbsp sunflower oil
- 700 g onions, peeled and chopped
- 2 garlic cloves, peeled and chopped
- 1.75 litres chicken stock
- 2 tbsp white wine vinegar
- 100 g brown lentils
- 900 g ripe plum tomatoes, cored, peeled, seeded and chopped
- 100 g basmati rice
- a pinch of saffron, soaked in 1 tbsp boiling water
- 2.5-cm piece root ginger, peeled
- 1 lemon
- a large bunch of coriander, leaves only, coarsely chopped
- a bunch of flat-leaf parsley, leaves only, coarsely chopped
- extra-virgin olive oil to serve

Drain the chickpeas, cover them with fresh water and bring to the boil. Drain again. Cover with fresh water to a depth of about 2.5 cm and bring to the boil. Lower the heat, film the surface with olive oil and cook at a bare simmer for 1 hour, or until tender but still with a slight crunch, checking every 10 minutes. Add more water as necessary to keep the chick-peas immersed. When the chickpeas are ready, add 1 tea-spoon of salt, cook for a few more minutes then drain.

Joint the chicken, discarding wing-tips, parson's nose, excess skin and any flaps of fat. Brown it, skin side down, in a little sunflower oil and reserve. In a large pan, fry the onions in 2 tablespoons of olive oil until translucent. Add the garlic and cook for a further minute. Add the chicken pieces, reserving the breast, and pour over the stock, vinegar and 700 ml of water. Bring to the boil, lower the heat to a gentle simmer and skim. Poach the chicken for 10 minutes or until it is just resilient when pressed. Remove with a slotted spoon and transfer to a chopping-board.

Add the lentils and tomatoes to the stock and simmer for 20 minutes, then add the rice and continue to bubble gently until both lentils and rice are cooked. Stir in the chickpeas.

Cut the meat from the chicken joints. Slice each breast into four pieces and put all the chicken into the pot with the saf-fron and its soaking water. Simmer for 5 minutes. Taste and season with salt and pepper.

Remove the pan from the heat. Grate in the ginger and squeeze in the juice of the lemon, through a sieve to catch pips. Add the herbs to the pan and stir with the remaining olive oil. Serve in large soup bowls with your finest olive oil for people to add more if they wish. Plenty of bread is essential.

MEDITERRANEAN CHICKEN

SERVES 2-3

I have taken to keeping a stash of sun-dried tomatoes and sun-dried red peppers in my food cupboard, invaluable for the times when I crave the intense flavours of summer at the wrong time of year. In this dish, both tomatoes and peppers are stewed in red wine with balsamic-vinegar-glazed chicken, whole garlic cloves and onions.

The quantity of garlic in this intensely flavoured stew sounds alarming but cooked in this way it ends up tender, buttery and sweet, while holding its form. The harshness is softened into a rich, mellow flavour that won't linger on the breath. Serve the stew over pasta, with buttered noodles or potatoes.

- 75 g Italian sun-dried tomatoes
- 50 g Italian sun-dried red peppers
- 16 garlic cloves
- 2 tbsp olive oil
- 1 Spanish onion, approximately 225 g, peeled, halved and cut into thick wedges
- 225 g chicken thigh fillet cut into kebab-sized pieces
- 2 tbsp balsamic vinegar
- 1 glass red wine, approximately 150 ml
- freshly ground black pepper

Place the dried tomatoes and peppers in a bowl and cover with 150 ml warm water. Lay out the garlic on a chopping-board and press down on them with the flat of a heavy knife until you hear a crack: the skins will now flake away easily.

Heat the olive oil in a flameproof casserole and stir-fry the onions over a medium heat until lightly browned and starting to wilt. Add the garlic and stir-fry for a couple of minutes, then add the chicken. Continue stir-frying until the meat has changed from pink to white, then add the balsamic vinegar. Let it bubble away while you fish the dried peppers out of the bowl. Slice them in thick bands, and when the balsamic vinegar is syrupy, add them, the tomatoes and the soaking water with the wine to the pan. Establish a gentle simmer, cover the pan and leave to cook for 20 minutes.

Remove the lid and cook for a further 10 minutes to reduce the liquid slightly. Taste, and adjust the seasoning with black pepper – the dried tomatoes and peppers are salty.

MOROCCAN CHICKEN TAGINE

SERVES 6-8

Early on in my search for unusual tomato recipes, I came across Djej Matish Mesla, or Chickens Cooked with Sweet Tomato Jam, in Paula Wolfert's marvellous book *Couscous and Other Food From Morocco* (Harper and Row, 1973). This was the first time I had come across tomatoes cooked with honey. When combined with saffron, toasted sesame seeds, coriander, cinnamon and ginger, it sounded like overkill. But this tagine, which I have adapted slightly, is most definitely worth the expense of 2.25 kilos of tomatoes. Do save the tomato water (see page 28). A word of warning: you will need to start this recipe 24 hours in advance.

- a pinch of powdered saffron
- 1/4 tsp ground ginger
- salt and freshly ground black pepper
- 1 tsp chopped garlic
- 50 ml vegetable or olive oil
- 2 chickens, approximately 1.5 kg each, quartered and skinned or 12 organic thigh fillets
- 70 g grated onion
- 4 tbsp chopped coriander leaves
- 2 tsp ground cinnamon
- 2.25 kg ripe tomatoes, cored, peeled, seeded and roughly chopped
- 2 tbsp tomato puree
- 4 tbsp thick dark honey, such as Greek Mount Hymettus
- 2 tbsp toasted sesame seeds

The day before you plan to eat the tagine, make a paste with the saffron, ginger, half a teaspoon of pepper, the garlic and oil, and rub it into the flesh of the chickens. Leave, covered in the fridge, overnight.

The next day, place the chickens, with the marinade, in a large casserole. Add 500 ml water, the grated onion, coriander, a generous pinch of salt, and one teaspoon of the cinnamon. Bring to the boil, reduce the heat, and simmer, uncovered, for 20 minutes.

Add the tomatoes, the tomato puree, and a little sprinkle of salt. Cook over a brisk heat, turning the chicken often in the sauce, until it is very tender. Remove the chicken and keep warm while finishing the sauce.

Let the tomatoes cook down rapidly until all the water has evaporated – about 1 hour over high heat, stirring occasionally to avoid scorching, and continuously for the last 15 minutes. When all the water has gone, the oil from the marinade will have been released, the tomatoes will begin to fry in it and the sauce will start to thicken considerably. Add the honey and the remaining teaspoon of cinnamon, and cook for a few minutes to bring out their flavours. Reheat the chicken quarters in the sauce for 5 minutes, rolling them around to coat them evenly. Transfer to the warm serving-dish, sprinkle with sesame seeds, and serve hot or warm.

MURGH MASALA

SERVES 8

In this subtle curry, pieces of chicken are stewed in an aromatic, highly spiced tomato sauce. Turmeric – or Indian saffron, as it is sometimes called – stains the onions yellow, and roasted cumin, cinnamon and cardamom combine with cayenne and garlic to provide an interesting spicy flavour. Fresh coriander is stirred in at the end, 'to provide a nice colour contrast to the reddish brown gravy', says Julie Sahni in *Classic Indian Cookery* (Grub Street, 1997) whence this wonderful recipe comes. Serve it with rice and hot naan bread for scooping up the delicious juices.

10 tbsp light vegetable oil

2 x 1.5 kg chickens, skinned and cut into 8-10 pieces, or use skinned legs and thighs in any combination

600 g onions, peeled, halved and thinly sliced

2 tbsp finely chopped garlic

3 tbsp finely chopped fresh ginger

1 tbsp turmeric

1 tsp cayenne

2 cinnamon sticks, 7.5 cm long

4 cardamom pods

1 tbsp roasted cumin seeds, ground

700 g ripe tomatoes, cored, peeled and finely chopped

salt

4 tbsp coarsely chopped coriander leaves

Heat 2 tablespoons of the oil in a large heavy-bottomed pan, preferably with a non-stick surface, over a high heat. When it is very hot add the chicken pieces, a few at a time. Sear and brown them all over. Remove them with a slotted spoon and set aside.

Add the remaining oil, reduce the heat to medium-high, and add the onions. Fry for about 30 minutes until light brown, stirring constantly to prevent burning. Add the garlic and ginger and cook for a further 5 minutes. Add the turmeric and cayenne, and stir rapidly for 10 seconds. Add the cinnamon, cardamom and cumin, then the tomatoes, along with the chicken, one tablespoon of salt, and 450 ml of boiling water. Stir to mix, reduce the heat and simmer, covered, until the chicken is cooked and very tender, and the tomato gravy thickened. This takes about 45 minutes. If necessary, remove the lid, increase the heat and boil rapidly until the sauce thickens. If, on the other hand, the evaporation is too fast, add a little water. Let the dish rest, covered, for at least 1 hour, preferably two. Reheat, stir in the coriander and serve.

POLLO AL CHILLINDRON

SERVES 6

In this colourful Spanish summer chicken stew fresh tomatoes become a thick sauce, which is flecked with chunks of pepper, onion, garlic and Serrano ham. Serve it with rice and thinly sliced, quickly boiled spring greens.

- 8 chicken legs, jointed
- salt and freshly ground black pepper
- 3 tbsp olive oil
- 1 Spanish onion, peeled and finely chopped
- 4 plump garlic cloves, peeled and finely chopped
- 200 g Serrano ham, sliced thinly
- 400 g tin roast pimientos, sliced, or 4 sun-dried red peppers, soaked, or 3 red peppers, grilled, peeled, seeded and sliced (see page 199)
- 1 kg tomatoes, preferably 'grown-for-flavour', cored, peeled and chopped

Rub the chicken pieces with salt and pepper. Heat the oil in a heavy-bottomed casserole over a medium heat, lay out the chicken so the dish isn't crowded, and brown it all over. When it is ready set it aside on a plate.

Add the onion to the pan. Reduce the heat slightly and fry for a few minutes until it starts to turn glassy. Add the garlic and ham and toss together, cooking for a few minutes before you return the chicken to the pan. Add the sliced pimientos or the peppers with the tomatoes and their juices. Season with salt and pepper. Partially cover the pan and cook for about 35 minutes, or until the chicken is tender. Remove the lid and cook for a further 10 minutes or until the sauce is reduced and thickened.

POULET MINERVA

SERVES 4

Cinnamon, cloves and lemon go well with tomatoes, flattering their sweetness. Here they combine initially to season pieces of chicken, then to flavour a thick tomato sauce for cooking chicken. The idea comes from a delightful book, *Cooking à la Pym* by Hilary Pym and Honor Wyatt, which gives recipes for some of the dishes mentioned in Barbara Pym's novels. This one, named after a brindled tortoiseshell cat that loved tomato skins, comes from *Quartet in Autumn*. Mine is a free interpretation, which is good served with lemon-flavoured couscous and is easy to scale up or down.

- 8 chicken thighs, skinned
- juice of 1 lemon
- 1 flat tsp ground cinnamon
- 1 flat tsp ground cloves
- 2 tbsp cooking oil
- 50 g butter
- 10 medium ripe tomatoes, cored and peeled
- approximately 150 ml white wine (optional)
- 2 tbsp tomato puree

Make several little slits in the chicken with the point of a small, sharp knife. Mix the lemon juice, cinnamon and cloves with half the oil. Rub this mixture all over the chicken. Now heat the remaining oil and butter in a frying-pan, and when the butter has melted brown the pieces of chicken all over. Remove them to a heavy-bottomed pan.

Meanwhile, place a sieve over a bowl and quarter the tomatoes over it, scraping the seeds and juices into the sieve. Roughly chop the tomato flesh and add it to the frying pan. Squash the seeds against the side of the sieve to extract maximum juice. Make it up to 300 ml with water or white wine, stir in the tomato puree, and add to the pan with any juices from the chicken marinade. Let it bubble up, scraping up any bits sticking to the bottom of the pan. Cook over a moderate heat until the tomatoes have merged into a thickish sauce. Season well with salt and pepper and pour over the chicken. Cook, partially covered, for about 25 minutes until the chicken is tender. Rest the stew for 10 minutes before serving.

TOMATO CHICKEN WITH ROSEMARY, CELERY AND CARROTS

SERVES 4

When inspiration flags, one combination that always turns out well is chicken and a tin, bottle or carton of tomatoes. We're talking here about the comforting chicken stews that everyone loves and are virtually impossible to ruin. In this one I used creamed tomato, the silky puree sold in a carton, but you could use chopped or crushed tomatoes or, indeed, fresh tomato concassé, for the thick, luscious, rosemary-scented tomato gravy. The stew is served garnished with crisp scraps of bacon and a scattering of fresh parsley. It would be just as good made with thyme or *herbes de Provence* instead of rosemary.

- 8 chicken thighs or drumsticks, skinned
- 3 tbsp vegetable oil
- 6 rashers rindless streaky bacon, cut into lardons
- 2 large onions, peeled, halved and thinly sliced
- 2 celery hearts, sliced unfurled together with leaves
- 3 sprigs of rosemary, leaves only
- salt and freshly ground black pepper
- 2 tbsp flour
- 1 glass red or white wine, approximately 150 ml
- 250 ml creamed tomato
- 8 small carrots, trimmed and scraped
- 2 tbsp chopped parsley

Cut the flesh off the chicken bones, slice it into 3 cm nuggets and place them in a bowl.

Warm 1 tablespoon of the oil in a heavy-bottomed casserole over a medium heat and fry the bacon crisp. Remove it and set it aside.

Add the onions, celery and rosemary to the pan, season with salt and pepper, cover and adjust the heat so that the vegetables sweat without colouring. Cook for 10 minutes, stirring occasionally. Remove to a plate.

Dust the chicken with the flour, tossing to coat evenly. Add more oil to the pan and cook the chicken briefly in batches over a medium-low flame until it is golden all over. Return all the chicken to the pan and pour in the wine, stirring to make a thick, smooth sauce. Add the tomato, stirring as it comes up to simmer, then the onions, celery and carrots. Season thoroughly, establish a gentle simmer, cover the pan and cook, stirring once or twice, for 20-30 minutes until the chicken and carrots are tender. Taste and adjust the seasoning. Stir in the parsley and bacon just before serving.

RABBIT POTACCHIO

SERVES 4-6

Potacchio is the name of a tomato sauce flavoured with rosemary, lemon zest, onion and chilli. The flavourings are chopped together very finely, in the style of gremolata (see page 374), then fried briefly. Once the tomatoes are put in, the sauce is cooked for a few minutes before the rabbit is added. This lovely recipe comes from Anna del Conte, who writes so clearly and well about her native Italian food.

2 small rabbits, each jointed into 6 pieces

1 lemon

3 tbsp olive oil

50 g butter

150 ml dry white wine

FOR THE POTACCHIO SAUCE

1 unwaxed lemon

1 small onion or 3 shallots, peeled and finely chopped

1 tbsp finely chopped rosemary

1 small red chilli, seeded and finely chopped

1 onion, peeled and finely chopped

2 garlic cloves, peeled and finely chopped

salt and freshly ground black pepper

3 tbsp extra-virgin olive oil

450 g tomatoes, cored, peeled and chopped

salt and freshly ground black pepper

Wash and dry the rabbit pieces. Place in a bowl and squeeze over the juice from the lemon. Heat the oil and butter in a large saucepan, and when the butter is foaming, add the rabbit and fry on all sides until it is nicely browned. Add the wine, let it bubble up and almost evaporate, then put in the onion and garlic. Season with salt and pepper, cover the pan and cook for 20 minutes.

While the rabbit is cooking, prepare the sauce. Use a zester or potato peeler to remove the zest from the lemon, then chop it finely. Make a pile of the onion, the rosemary, the lemon zest and the chilli, and chop it together. Put the oil in a frying-pan and when it is hot add the chopped ingredients. Sauté gently for 5 minutes or so, then add the tomatoes and a little salt. Cook over a lively heat for about 15 minutes, stirring frequently.

Tip the Potacchio into the sauté pan with the rabbit and mix it with all the lovely cooking juices at the bottom of the pan. Cook for a further 15 minutes. Check that the rabbit is tender, correct the seasoning and serve.

DUCK AND TOMATO MOLE WITH PEAS

SERVES 4

It seems implausible that chocolate might go well with tomatoes until you remember that both plants – chillies, too – originated in South America. The Aztecs matched these ingredients successfully with game and poultry. It is stretching it a bit far to call this dish a *mole*, but it is in the Aztec style, as in the famous Mole Poblano, and a small quantity of dark chocolate gives the sauce its rich, glossy sheen, and a surprising depth of flavour that isn't noticeably chocolaty. Try it.

500 g tomatoes, peeled

2-3 tbsp olive oil

4 duck legs, jointed, skin scored lightly in a close cross-hatch

1 red onion, peeled, halved and cut lengthways into chunky slices

2 red peppers, peeled with a potato peeler, seeded and white filament discarded, sliced into chunky strips

½ tsp dried red chilli flakes

2 garlic cloves, peeled and finely chopped

15 g dark bitter chocolate

salt and freshly ground black pepper

150 g frozen petit pois

Halve the tomatoes and scrape the seeds into a sieve over a bowl. Press them against the sides of the sieve to release the tomato 'water' – you should get about 150 ml. Roughly chop the tomato flesh.

Heat 2 tablespoons of the oil in a large frying-pan and, when very hot, brown the duck pieces. Set aside in a medium-sized heavy-bottomed pan. Reduce the heat to medium, and cook the onion for 5 minutes. Add the peppers and continue to cook, stirring occasionally, until they are tender. Add the extra tablespoon of oil if necessary. Stir in the chilli flakes, the garlic, the tomatoes and the tomato water. Cook briskly, stirring to break down the tomatoes, for 5 minutes. Tip the tomato sauce over the duck. Place the pan over a low heat, partially cover it, and simmer for 30-40 minutes until the duck is tender. Stir in the chocolate and when it has completely dissolved, taste and adjust the seasoning with salt and pepper. Add the peas, increase the heat and simmer for a couple of minutes. Serve with rice.

ANCHOVY BEEF WITH CARAMELIZED ONIONS, SUN-DRIED TOMATOES AND SERRANO HAM

SERVES 2

The wonderful thing about sun-dried tomatoes is that after a few minutes' soaking and gentle stewing they hold the rich, deep flavour of the finest vine-ripened, sun-drenched Mediterranean tomatoes. In this quick supper dish, they are combined with other Mediterranean foods – anchovy fillets, Serrano ham, garlic and Spanish onions – and thin strips of British beef, to make a luscious, intensely savoury stew.

It is a one-pot dish, which leaves no doubt that a packet of those unpromising-looking, leathery rust-coloured scraps is worth its high price tag.

- 8 sun-dried tomatoes (see page 21)
- 200 ml boiling water
- 2 medium-large onions, peeled and halved
- 2 tbsp cooking oil
- salt and freshly ground black pepper
- 4 anchovy fillets, chopped
- 1 large garlic clove, peeled and chopped
- 6 thin slices beef steak, sliced into chunky ribbons
- 2 slices Serrano ham, sliced into chunky ribbons
- 1 tbsp tomato ketchup
- juice of ½ lemon, and zest, finely chopped
- 100 g frozen peas
- 1 tbsp freshly shredded basil

Place the tomatoes in a bowl and pour over the boiling water. Cover and leave to soak.

Slice the onions down rather than across. Heat a spacious pan that can hold all the ingredients over a medium-high flame. Add the oil and stir in the onions. There will seem to be an awful lot of them but within 10 minutes they will have started to brown, give up their juice and soften. Keep them moving so that they don't burn, then lower the heat and let them cook, adding a little salt and pepper, for a further 10 minutes.

Add the anchovies, the garlic and the steak to the pan, stirring until the meat has changed colour. Stir in the tomatoes, their liquid, the ham, the ketchup, the lemon zest and juice. Bring the contents of the pan back to the boil, establish a gentle simmer, partially cover, and leave to cook for 30 minutes until the meat and tomatoes are tender and the liquid reduced and thickened. Five minutes before the end of cooking, add the peas. Taste, and adjust the seasoning. Stir in the basil, and serve with boiled new potatoes.

MEAT-STUFFED TOMATOES

SERVES 4

One of my earliest 'foreign' food memories dates back to south-west France when I was twelve or thirteen. I *know* I wasn't particularly interested in food at the time but I was very taken with the trays of stuffed tomatoes that were laid out each day in the shop at the campsite where we were staying. They were craggy, misshapen and very red. A dome of meat burst up from inside them and, perched on the top like a pixie's hat, was a little lid complete with stalk. I saw these exotic tomatoes every day when I collected the bread for breakfast. I never once ate one.

There have been many occasions since when I have eaten tomatoes stuffed with meat and they have always been a disappointment. It is important, I think, to take care in making the stuffing so that it doesn't end up hard and dull. The version here comes from the hand of a master, and the inclusion of chicken livers with minced beef and sausagemeat, egg, cream and masses of parsley is what makes Simon Hopkinson's stuffed tomatoes so good. You need the biggest tomatoes you can find for this recipe. If Marmande or another craggy variety is available, use it: they will give better results than your average beef tomato.

If, and it happened when I made this recipe, you have some mixture left over, bag it up and put it in the freezer for another time. Courgettes, incidentally, or slices of hollowed out marrow, would be good stuffed with this mixture.

8 large ripe beef tomatoes
4 tbsp fresh white breadcrumbs
4 tbsp milk
2 medium onions, peeled and finely chopped
75 g butter
3 celery stalks, peeled and finely chopped
2 garlic cloves, peeled and chopped
1 tbsp tomato puree
225 g minced beef
100 g good-quality sausage-meat
100 g chicken livers, chopped
150 ml dry white wine
freshly grated nutmeg
salt and freshly ground black pepper

Pre-heat the oven to 350°F/180°C/gas mark 4.

Cut the tops off the tomatoes and scoop out the insides with a teaspoon, leaving a 1 cm wall of flesh. Arrange the tomatoes in a lightly oiled baking-dish. Roughly chop the scooped-out flesh and set it aside. Soak the breadcrumbs in the milk.

Using a heavy-bottomed medium-sized pan, fry the onions in the butter until soft. Add the celery and garlic, and fry for a few more minutes until everything is pale golden. Stir in the tomato puree and the reserved tomato flesh, and cook briskly until the mixture is rusty-looking and devoid of moisture. Add the minced beef and sausagemeat, turn up the heat a little and fry it carefully, breaking up the meats with a wooden spoon as you go. Tip in the livers, stir them around for a moment and add the wine, a little at a time with the heat turned up full. Allow it to bubble away to almost nothing before adding more. Season with nutmeg, salt and pepper. Add the cream and, stirring briskly, cook for 5 more minutes until it has been fully absorbed and the mixture is good and thick. Check the seasoning, stir in the parsley and leave it to cool for 10 minutes before stirring in the beaten egg together with the milk-soaked breadcrumbs.

Spoon the mixture into the tomatoes and put on the lids

- 100 ml thick cream
- 2 tbsp finely chopped flat-leaf parsley
- 1 large egg beaten
- 2-3 tbsp olive oil

firmly. As with my campsite tomatoes, the meat should push up the hats as they cook. Spoon the olive oil over the tomatoes and bake in the middle of the oven for ahout 40 minutes or until the tomatoes are soft and wrinkled. They are at their best when eaten warm, with crisp, very hot French fries.

STEAK ROLLS WITH TOMATO SAUCE

SERVES 4

This is a variation on Beef Olives, made by stuffing thin slices of steak with bacon, parsley, garlic, grated Parmesan and pine kernels, and cooking them with tomatoes and white wine. A sort of osmosis occurs while the dish cooks away slowly for about 2 hours: you end up with meltingly soft meat and a richly flavoured, thick tomato sauce. Traditionally, the rolls are served on tagliatelle but they are excellent with mashed potato.

- 1 large bunch flat-leaf parsley
- 1 stick celery, trimmed and cut in half
- 1 bay leaf
- 12 thin slices steak, weighing about 75 g each
- 12 thin rashers rindless, streaky bacon
- 2 tbsp dried oregano
- 3 garlic cloves, peeled and finely chopped
- 50 g toasted pine kernels
- 75 g Parmesan, finely grated
- salt and freshly ground black pepper
- 2 tbsp olive oil
- 1.2 kg plum tomatoes, cored, peeled and finely chopped
- 300 ml white wine
- 4 tbsp tomato puree, diluted with 4 tbsp hot water
- you will also need 12 cocktail sticks

Pick the leaves off the parsley stalks, then bundle the stalks with the bay leaf and celery and tie together with cotton thread. Finely chop the parsley leaves.

Lay a slice of beef between 2 sheets of greaseproof paper and pound lightly all over. Repeat with the other slices. Cut the bacon rashers in halves or thirds, depending on their size, and lay them out to cover the beef. Sprinkle on some of the parsley, season with oregano and garlic, then divide the pine kernels and Parmesan equally between the pieces of meat. Season with salt and pepper, then roll up, tucking in the sides so that no filling escapes, and secure with a cocktail stick. Heat the oil in a heavy casserole over a medium heat and fry the rolls until they are brown all over. Add the tomatoes, the wine and the tomato puree, then tuck the celery bundle between the rolls. Season lightly with salt and pepper, and if the rolls are not completely immersed, add a little boiling water. Reduce the heat, partially cover the pan and cook very gently – a heat-diffuser pad would be handy here – for 2 hours or until the meat is very tender and the sauce is thick and clinging to the rolls. Remove the cocktail sticks, discard the celery bundle, check the seasoning and serve.

TOMATICAN

SERVES 6

In this spicy beef stew from Chile the gravy is made from tomatoes flavoured with paprika and oregano. Sweetcorn, onions and garlic thicken it and the end result is all at once rich and fresh. Serve Tomatican with potatoes and hot tortilla for wiping the plate clean.

- 4 tbsp vegetable oil
- 500 g beef sirloin, diced
- 3 onions, finely sliced
- 2 garlic cloves, crushed
- 2 tbsp paprika
- 3 fresh corn-on-the-cob
- 6 ripe beef tomatoes, cored, peeled and chopped
- salt and freshly ground black pepper
- ½ tsp dried oregano

Heat the oil in a lidded pan that can accommodate all the ingredients. Sauté the beef, onions, garlic and paprika until the meat is browned and the onions tender.

Meanwhile, cut off the tip of the corn-on-the-cob. Stand each on the flattened end and use a large, heavy knife to slice off the kernels.

Add the tomatoes, their juices and the corn kernels to the stew, and season well with salt and pepper. Stir in the oregano. Cover the pan and leave to cook, very slowly, for about 1½ hours, or until the meat is tender and surrounded by a luscious thick sauce. Adjust the seasoning and serve.

ROGNONS DE VEAU AUX TOMATES

SERVES 4-6

'Skin the kidneys and soak them in warm salted water to clean them. Put them into a pan with good dripping, and ¼ lb of bacon for 2 lb of veal kidneys. Let them roast very gently for about 20 minutes.

'In the meantime brown a dozen or so chopped shallots in bacon fat or beef dripping; add 1 lb of tomatoes, chopped, seasoning of salt, pepper, basil or marjoram, a lump of sugar and a glass of port, or sweet white wine, or cider. When this has cooked for 10 minutes, add ½ lb mushrooms, and the kidneys and bacon. Cook for another 10 minutes.

'This dish can be served quite alone, or with a galette of potatoes.'

Elizabeth David, *French Country Cooking*

ESCALOPE OF VEAL WITH GARLIC AND TOMATOES

SERVES 4

An elegant, clever dish from Elizabeth David.

Serve it with mashed or boiled potatoes. If you object to veal, pork escalope works very well in this dish.

- 4 veal escalopes ('cut from the leg')
- salt and freshly ground black pepper
- olive oil
- 450 g tomatoes, cored, peeled and chopped
- a handful of dried bread-crumbs
- 4-5 garlic cloves, peeled and chopped finely
- 1 large bunch parsley, leaves only, finely chopped

Season the escalopes on both sides with salt and pepper.

Cover the bottom of a thick sauté pan with olive oil. When it is hot (but not boiling) put in the seasoned escalopes. Cook them gently so that they are just golden on both sides. When they are ready, add the tomatoes and, as soon as they have melted, the breadcrumbs, the chopped garlic and parsley. Cook for another 8-9 minutes, after which most of the oil should have been absorbed, and the tomatoes turned to a thick sauce.

OSSO BUCO ALLA MILANESE

SERVES 4

People get very steamed up about Osso Buco. The name refers to a classic veal stew and to the cut of meat used for it. 'Ossobuchi,' writes Anna del Conte, in her seminal work *The Gastronomy of Italy*, 'are about 9 cm in diameter and should be 4 or 5 cm thick. Inside the circle of meat is the bone, and inside the bone the marrow, this being the essence of the dish.' The contentious ingredient is tomatoes –some say yes, and others, including Anna del Conte, say no: 'I find these jar with the gremolata, a mixture of lemon rind, parsley and garlic, and also with the delicacy of a well-made risotto Milanese, the traditional accompaniment.' My version, however, is made with fresh tomatoes. I often make a relatively quick hybrid version of Osso Buco with 750 g diced shoulder or breast veal. It is cooked in exactly the same way (sometimes I don't bother to put in the carrots, onion and celery) but it is ready within 45 minutes. This strictly unorthodox recipe, which I like to serve with new potatoes, would probably have me hounded out of Milan – but it is delicious.

- 1 tbsp olive oil
- 50 g butter
- 1 garlic clove, split
- 6 ossobuchi, securely tied round with string
- 2-3 tbsp flour for dusting
- 1 onion, finely chopped
- 1 carrot, finely chopped
- 1 stick celery, strings removed and finely chopped
- 150 ml white wine
- 500 g tomatoes, cored, peeled, seeded and chopped
- 250 ml chicken, veal or vegetable stock
- 2 branches thyme
- salt and freshly ground black pepper

FOR THE GREMOLATA

- zest of 1 unwaxed lemon, finely chopped
- 2 garlic cloves, peeled and finely chopped
- 2 tbsp finely chopped flat-leaf parsley

Heat the oil and butter in a spacious pan over a gentle heat. Add the garlic and cook for a few minutes until it is aromatic – don't let it brown – then discard it. Dust the veal with flour. Raise the heat and brown the meat. Lift it from the pan and set it aside. Add the onion, the carrot and the celery, and sauté for about 10 minutes, stirring frequently. Return the meat to the pan and add the wine. Boil vigorously for 3 minutes, turning the veal over and over. Add the tomatoes, the stock and the thyme. Season generously with salt and pepper. Bring to a gentle simmer. Cover the pan with a tight-fitting lid and leave to cook very gently for 1½–2 hours, or until the meat is very tender.

The sauce is supposed to be thick and fragrant. If it seems too watery, remove the ossobuchi and boil briskly to reduce. Taste and adjust the seasoning.

Mix together the lemon zest, garlic and parsley, and chop them again together. Remove the string from the ossobuchi. Place them on a heated dish and sprinkle with the gremolata. Spoon over the sauce and serve with risotto Milanese, in which the rice is cooked in chicken stock or beef broth and flavoured with saffron, white wine and Parmesan.

ROMAZAVA

SERVES 6

The national dish of Madagascar is a mixed meat and tomato stew, freshly flavoured with ginger and garlic. Additional vivacity and colour come from the last-minute addition of spinach. According to Keith Floyd, who cooked it on his TV series *Floyd on Africa*, the meat is boiled, then stewed with a vast quantity of tomatoes. The onions, garlic and ginger remain al dente and the garlic pungent. The spinach merely melts. I have adapted the recipe slightly because I loathe undercooked onion. If you wish to be authentic, add the onion with all the garlic and ginger when I add the second lot of garlic and ginger.

- 5-7 tbsp groundnut oil
- 450 g braising steak, cut into 5 cm pieces
- 450 g leg or shoulder of pork, cut into 5 cm pieces
- 6 chicken drumsticks
- 2 onions, peeled, halved and finely sliced
- 1 kg ripe tomatoes, cored, peeled and roughly chopped
- 8-10 garlic cloves, peeled and very finely chopped
- 50 g fresh ginger, peeled and sliced into thin batons
- salt and freshly ground black pepper
- 450 g young spinach leaves, or shredded mature spinach leaves

Warm a spacious heavy-based saucepan over a medium heat. Cover the base with a film of oil. When the oil is hot, sauté the meats and chicken separately in uncrowded batches, pouring in more oil as necessary, and cook briefly to seal without browning. Set aside the meat on a plate, keeping it in separate piles. When all the meat is cooked, use 2 tablespoons of oil and sauté the onions until they are glassy and beginning to soften.

Return the beef to the pan with the onions, tomatoes, half of the garlic, a quarter of the ginger, and 150 ml water. Season with salt and pepper. Bring to the boil, turn down the heat immediately, establish a gentle simmer and cover the pan. Cook for 30 minutes. Stir in the pork and simmer for a further 30 minutes. Add the chicken and simmer for 10 minutes. Add the remaining garlic and ginger. Cook for 10 minutes, then add the spinach. Stir it into the tomato gravy, cooking until the leaves are beginning to wilt. Check the seasoning and serve.

AUBERGINE GRATIN WITH LAMB, SPINACH AND TOMATO

SERVES 3

Long, thin slices of griddled or roasted aubergine are used like lasagne to sandwich a well-flavoured lamb sauce with blanched spinach. The dish is finished with slices of mozzarella and a dusting of Parmesan to melt all over the top and create a thin, crisp crust.

- **2 plump aubergines, trimmed and cut length-ways into 0.5 cm thick slices**
- **4 tbsp olive oil**
- **150 g young spinach**
- **1 medium red onion, peeled, halved and sliced into wedges**
- **2 garlic cloves, peeled and chopped**
- **salt and freshly ground black pepper**
- **200 g minced lamb**
- **400 g tin Italian whole tomatoes**
- **1 mozzarella**
- **2 tbsp freshly grated Parmesan**

Pre-heat the oven to its highest setting.

Disgorge the aubergine slices with 1 tbsp salt for 20 minutes, rinse and pat dry. Smear a large baking-sheet with a little of the olive oil and lay out the aubergine slices, nudged up close. Paint them with more of the olive oil, reserving 1 tablespoon. Bake for 10 minutes, then turn the slices and cook for a further 5 minutes until they are tender and smelling richly of olive oil. Remove the aubergine from the oven and reduce the temperature to 400°F/200°C/gas mark 6.

Bring a large pan of salted water to the boil. Add the spinach, cook for 30 seconds, drain, rinse with cold water, drain again, then squeeze out the moisture and chop roughly. Put the remaining tablespoon of olive oil into a frying pan, add the onion and garlic, a generous seasoning of salt and pepper, and cook for a few minutes until the onion is softening. Stir in the meat, a little more salt and pepper, and cook until it is brown and juicy. Open the tin of tomatoes and slice through them a few times with a sharp knife, then tip them into a sieve held over the meat. Leave the meat, onions and tomato juice to bubble away for 10-15 minutes until moist and cohesive, with most of the liquid absorbed or evaporated. Stir in the spinach and turn off the heat.

Lay out half the aubergine slices in a suitable gratin dish. Season with salt and pepper, then spoon over the meat mixture. Cover with half of the tomatoes and top with the remaining aubergine slices. Spread the remains of the tomatoes on top. Slice the mozzarella and lay it in overlapping slices in the middle of the gratin. Dust with the Parmesan. Cook in the oven for about 15 minutes, or until the mozzarella has melted, the Parmesan has formed into a thin crust and the filling is sizzling between the aubergines.

LAMB WITH FENNEL, TOMATOES AND SPINACH

SERVES 4

A rather wonderful chemical reaction seems to take place when lamb is stewed with tomatoes. The acidity in the tomatoes liberates the fat in the meat and results in a particularly luscious sauce. And when the succulent sweetness of slowly cooked onions is added to the equation, this simple combination is sublime. In Greece they've got this sort of dish down to a fine art and it lends itself well to the addition of fennel, its aniseed flavour pointed up with ouzo. In this version of a typical Greek lamb and tomato stew, buttered spinach is served as a sort of top-knot garnish. Plainly boiled potatoes, that can be squashed into the wonderful tomato gravy, go well with it.

- 4 large, meaty lamb shoulder chops
- salt and freshly ground black pepper
- 2 tbsp flour
- 3 tbsp olive oil
- 2 tbsp ouzo, Pernod, Ricard or pastis
- 2 medium onions, peeled, halved and sliced
- 2 large fennel bulbs, trimmed, halved through the root and sliced
- juice of 1 small lemon
- 1 tbsp oregano or marjoram leaves
- 400 g tin Italian tomatoes
- 225 g young leaf spinach
- 25 g butter

Spread out the chops on a plate, season with salt and pepper and dust both sides with the flour. Heat 1 tablespoon of the oil in a cast-iron casserole and fry the chops briefly over a medium heat, turning after a couple of minutes. Turn up the heat, pour over the alcohol, then let it bubble up and evaporate. Transfer the chops and their juices to a plate.

Add the remaining oil to the dish, reduce the heat to medium-low and add the onions. Cook, stirring a couple of times, for about 10 minutes until they are beginning to soften but not colour, then add the fennel. Season with salt and pepper, cover the dish with a lid and leave it to sweat for a few minutes. Now switch on the oven and leave it to heat to 350°F/180°C/gas mark 4.

Bury the chops in the onions and fennel, squeeze over the lemon juice and shower in the oregano. Pour the tomatoes over the top, season again and replace the lid. Cook in the oven for 30 minutes. When the stew is ready, rinse and drain the spinach and squash it into a saucepan placed over a low heat. Cook, covered, stirring every few minutes until the spinach is floppy and tender. Tip it into a colander, squeeze out the excess liquid and chop it against the side. Return the spinach to the saucepan with the butter and heat it through. Spoon a share of spinach over each serving of stew.

LAMB RAGÙ

SERVES 4-6

'And you've put basil in it, like I told you,' said Sophia. 'Yes, and I used a tin of tomatoes, and cooked it very slowly for hours and hours.'

Barbara Pym, on spaghetti Bolognese, in *An Unsuitable Attachment.*

Ragù, which is the proper name for the meat sauce in spaghetti Bolognese and in countless stuffed-pasta dishes such as cannelloni and lasagne, is one of those recipes that varies from cook to cook. Usually it is made with minced veal or beef, although sometimes with a mixture of minced meats. The objective, however, is always the same. What you're after is a thick, dark, reddish-brown lotion, when the meat and tomato merge into a sauce with no distinctive characteristics. Ragù cannot be hurried. Marcella Hazan, the godmother of Italian recipe-writing, suggests 3½ hours, although 5, she says, would be better. Made with lamb, as in this somewhat unorthodox recipe, the desired texture, colour and rich flavour can be achieved within an hour, probably less.

1 tbsp olive oil

40 g butter

50 g pancetta or thin rashers of rindless, streaky bacon, sliced into lardons

1 medium onion, peeled and finely diced

2 medium carrots, peeled and finely diced

2 sticks celery, peeled and finely chopped

450 g good quality minced lamb

salt and freshly ground black pepper

250 ml dry red wine

150 ml milk

¼ tsp nutmeg

400 g tin Italian tomatoes or 350 ml passata or 350 g crushed tomatoes

a squeeze of lemon juice

Heat the oil and butter in a heavy-bottomed saucepan or flameproof casserole and cook the bacon gently until it is beginning to crisp. Add the onion to the pan and fry for a couple of minutes before adding the carrot and celery. Two minutes later add the lamb and stir it around until all the meat has changed colour. Season generously with salt and pepper, and add the wine. Turn up the heat to medium-high and cook, stirring constantly, until it has evaporated. Add the milk and nutmeg, and continue to cook, stirring frequently, until the milk has almost entirely disappeared, about 10 minutes. Now add the tomatoes. Bring the sauce to the boil and immediately turn down the heat as low as possible and cook at a gentle simmer, uncovered, for up to 35 minutes, until the sauce is thick and homogeneous. Taste the Ragù, and adjust the seasoning with salt, pepper and a squeeze of lemon juice.

SLOW-BRAISED LAMB WITH FLAGEOLET BEANS

SERVES 6

Meltingly soft, rich lamb with herby tomato juices. This is one of those wonderful recipes that really does cook itself: everything is piled into one dish, then placed in a low oven, leaving you free to come back hours later to a house full of delectable aromas and a meal ready and waiting. The only possible drawback is that you need to start twenty-four hours ahead so that the flageolet beans can soak overnight. (I experimented with a 'quick' method – boil the beans for 5 minutes, cover the pan and soak for an hour – it isn't foolproof: even after 5 hours' cooking the beans were still tough.) I wouldn't recommend canned beans here, because they'll collapse without absorbing the juices.

- 12 shallots
- 450 g flageolet beans, soaked overnight in plenty of water
- 2 large onions, peeled, halved and sliced
- 12 garlic cloves, peeled
- 2 bay leaves
- 4 sprigs rosemary or 1 small bunch thyme
- 2 sprigs sage
- salt and freshly ground black pepper
- 300 ml red wine, or half wine-half water mixed
- 2 x 400 g tins Italian tomatoes
- juice of 1 lemon
- 1 shoulder of lamb, about 1.8 kg
- 2 tbsp anchovy essence

Trim the root end of the shallots, peel and separate the sections leaving the shoot-end intact.

Rinse the flageolet beans under running water and drain. Tip them into a large casserole or ovenproof dish. Push the sliced onions among the beans with the shallots and herbs and all but two of the garlic cloves. Season very generously with pepper but lightly with salt. Pour over the wine, the tomatoes and their juice, breaking up the tomatoes a bit, then squeeze over the lemon juice.

Trim away any flaps of fat from the joint and make several incisions in the fleshy parts with a small sharp knife. Slice the two remaining garlic cloves and post the slivers into the gashes in the lamb. Smear the anchovy essence over it (this adds a subtle, salty pungency) and push the joint into the beans. Cover the casserole or use foil to make a lid and cook for 4 hours in the lower part of the oven at 275°F/140°C/gas mark 1. Remove the lid, increase the oven temperature to 425°F/220°C/gas mark 7, and cook for another hour. If the joint is very fatty, skim away surface fat before you serve directly from the dish.

TAVA

SERVES 6

Adamou & Sons in Chiswick was an excellent if idiosyncratic Cypriot greengrocer. This home-from-home was stuffed to the gills with Greek and Cypriot foodstuffs and could always be counted on to provide many different types of tomato and wonderful Cyprus potatoes until it closed, finally, early in 2011. This is a family recipe: one of those excellent stick-it-in-the-oven-come-back-two-hours-later dishes. Cumin and bay scent the tomato sauce that tenderizes the lamb and seeps into the gorgeous potatoes.

An Italian version of this, flavoured with rosemary and chilli, is made in exactly the same way. Use shoulder, rather than leg, omit the onion, cumin, bay leaves and tomato puree, and include 6 whole garlic cloves, 2 sprigs of fresh rosemary and 1 chopped chilli. In place of the Cyprus potatoes, use 450 g peeled new potatoes cut into 4 cm wedges. These are added when the meat is tender; then the stew will need to be cooked for about another 30 minutes.

- 1.4 kg Cyprus potatoes, peeled and cut into large pieces
- 1.4 kg boned leg of lamb, cut into large pieces
- 1 large onion, peeled and chopped
- 450 g tomatoes, cored, peeled and chopped
- 50 g cumin seeds, lightly crushed
- 2 tbsp tomato puree
- approximately 350 ml chicken or vegetable stock
- salt and freshly ground black pepper

Pre-heat the oven to 400°F/200°C/gas mark 6.

Mix together the potatoes, lamb, onion, tomatoes and cumin seeds, and place in a deep baking-dish.

Stir the tomato puree into just enough stock to cover the meat and vegetables. Add the bay leaves and season with salt and pepper.

Cover the dish with foil and bake for 2 hours. Uncover and serve hot.

TOMATO BREDIE

SERVES 4

A lamb and tomato stew from South Africa – and something to remember when autumn days turn chilly but tomatoes are still plentiful. The tomatoes and onions melt into a garlic-scented sauce, which permeates the potatoes and flavours the lamb.

- 2 Spanish onions, peeled and thinly sliced
- 40 g butter or cooking oil
- 900 g boned lamb shoulder, scrag end of neck or chump chops
- juice of 1 small lemon
- salt and freshly ground black pepper
- 1 plump garlic clove, worked to a paste with a pinch of salt
- 1 bay leaf
- 1 scant tbsp sugar
- 900 g ripe tomatoes, cored, peeled, seeded and chopped
- 6 medium-sized potatoes, peeled and halved

Pre-heat the oven to 300°F/150°C/gas mark 2.

Cook the onions in the butter or cooking oil in a spacious, heavy-bottomed casserole until tender and beginning to brown. Meanwhile, trim the meat and cut it into chunky kebab-size pieces.

Scoop the onions out of the pan and quickly brown the meat. Squeeze the lemon juice over the meat, return the onions and season well with salt and pepper. Add the garlic, bay leaf, sugar and tomatoes. Cover the dish and cook for 1½ hours. Then tuck the potatoes into the casserole, cover it again and cook for a further 40 minutes or until the potatoes are tender.

LAMB STEW WITH TOMATOES AND POTATOES

SERVES 4

A marvellous recipe from Lulu Peyraud, in collaboration with Richard Olney, from *A Provençal Table*.

- 1 lamb shoulder, approximately 2 kg, surface fat removed, boned and cut into 5 cm cubes
- salt and freshly ground black pepper
- flour
- 3 tbsp olive oil
- 1 large onion, peeled and coarsely chopped
- 4 garlic cloves, crushed and peeled
- 1 glass white wine, approximately 150 ml
- bouquet garni, made with 1 bay leaf and a small bunch of thyme
- 500 g tomatoes, cored, peeled, seeded and chopped
- 150 ml Tomato Coulis (see page 242)
- 450 g small, waxy potatoes (ratte, cornichon, Nicola or similar)

Season the meat and dredge it with flour. Choose a heavy sauté pan of a size to hold the pieces without crowding. Warm the olive oil, brown the meat on all sides over a medium heat, add the onion and garlic, turn down the heat and shuffle the contents of the pan around until the onions are softened and lightly coloured. Turn up the heat again and deglaze the pan with the white wine, stirring and scraping the bottom and sides with a wooden spatula or spoon. Add the bouquet garni, the tomatoes, and the tomato coulis and potatoes, bring to the boil, and adjust the heat to maintain a gentle simmer, covered, for 1½ hours in all.

TAGINE OF LAMB WITH RAISINS, ALMONDS AND SWEETENED TOMATOES

SERVES 8

In Morocco tomatoes are sometimes sweetened with honey and cooked in meat stews, or tagines, with various spices and herbs. These dishes make a magnificent meal for a large group of people and adapt easily and well. Green beans, for example, or sliced courgettes or aubergines can be added, although potatoes, which can be mashed into the gorgeous tomato juices, are perfect. Roasted almonds, slivers of pickled lemon and handfuls of coriander leaves, sometimes boiled eggs too, are the traditional garnishes. The combination of soft, succulent, tomato-imbued lamb, the heady, scented smells, the fresh green herbs and crunch of roasted almonds is outstanding. This particularly full-flavoured version is suggested by Antony Worrall Thompson, in *Great British Chefs 2* by Kit Chapman (Mitchell Beazley, 1995).

8 lamb shanks, piqued with garlic and anchovies
2 tsp saffron stamens
3 tsp ground ginger
3 tsp paprika
1½ tsp freshly ground black pepper
1 tbsp ground cinnamon
oil for frying
10 garlic cloves, peeled and chopped
500 g grated onion
2 cinnamon sticks
900 ml tomato juice
900 ml chicken stock
1.5 kg tomatoes, cored, seeded and roughly chopped
100 g raisins
4 tbsp clear honey
500 g small new potatoes, peeled but left whole
6 tbsp chopped fresh coriander
2 pickled lemons, peel only cut into strips
225 g blanched whole almonds, toasted
a handful of coriander leaves

Trim the fat from the lamb then toss it with the saffron, ginger, paprika, pepper and ground cinnamon, and leave overnight. Heat the oil in a large pan and fry the lamb until brown all over. Add the garlic, grated onion and cinnamon sticks, then cover with the tomato juice and the chicken stock. Bring to the boil, turn down the heat and simmer for 1½ hours.

Remove the meat and set it aside. Add the tomatoes, the raisins, honey and potatoes to the pan. Cook until the tomatoes break down, the sauce thickens and the potatoes are tender. Remove the cinnamon sticks. Return the lamb to the sauce, taste, and adjust the seasoning. Stir in the chopped coriander.

Serve in soup plates garnished with the pickled lemon peel fried in oil, toasted almonds and coriander. Tabbouleh (see page 323) and aubergine puree are Antony's preferred accompaniments.

ALGERIAN LAHM LHALOU WITH COUSCOUS

SERVES 4-6

Canned tomatoes are crucial to the heady mix of sweet and sour flavours and tender lamb in this exotic Algerian tagine served with quickly made couscous.

- 750 g boneless leg of lamb
- 2 tbsp olive oil
- 2 red onions
- 25 g ginger
- 2 garlic cloves
- 1 heaped tsp each ground cumin and coriander
- 1 flat tsp chilli flakes
- generous pinch saffron stamens
- 1 cinnamon stick
- 1 bay leaf
- 1 lemon
- 1 dsp honey
- 400 g can chopped tomatoes
- 1 chicken stock cube
- 80 g bunch coriander
- 200 g ready to eat prunes
- 1 tbsp balsamic vinegar
- 200 g couscous

Cut the lamb into 5 cm strips, slicing away any fat. Season lavishly with salt and pepper. Heat 1 tbsp oil in a spacious frying-pan and quickly brown the meat in ucrowded batches, transferring to a heavy-bottomed, lidded casserole. Peel, halve and finely slice the onions. Peel and thinly slice the ginger in small scraps. Chop the garlic. Finely chop the coriander. When the meat is done, add the remaining oil to the pan and gently soften the onion, adding the garlic after a few minutes. Add cumin and ground coriander, chilli, cinnamon and bay, stirring to cook the spices. Squeeze lemon juice into the pan, add saffron, honey, tomatoes and the stalk half of the coriander. Dissolve the stock cube in 600 ml boiling water and add that too. Simmer uncovered for 5 minutes then stir into the meat. Bring to the boil, reduce the heat to low, cover and simmer for 45 minutes. Stir in the prunes and balsamic. Simmer, uncovered, for a further 30 minutes or so, until the meat is tender and the juices thickened. Serve over couscous (you will need 200 g hydrated in 500 ml chicken stock with a splash of olive oil and squeeze of lemon).

DELHI LAMB WITH TOMATOES AND POTATOES

SERVES 6

Madhur Jaffrey gave me the confidence to cook Indian dishes, and this is one of my absolute favourites. Serve it with green beans, rice, naan and lime pickle.

- 7 tbsp vegetable oil
- approximately 200 g peeled and finely chopped onion
- 1 green chilli, seeded and finely chopped
- 5 garlic cloves, peeled and finely chopped
- 1 kg boned lamb shoulder, cut into 2.5 cm chunks
- 1 tbsp ground cumin
- 2 tsp ground coriander
- ½ tsp ground turmeric
- ¼ tsp cayenne pepper
- 1½ tsp salt
- 350 g tomatoes, cored, peeled and chopped
- 450 g medium-sized waxy potatoes, peeled and cut in half
- 425-700 ml water
- a squeeze of lemon
- coriander leaves (optional)

Put the oil in a large, heavy pan and set it over a high heat. When hot, put in the onion, green chilli and garlic. Stir-fry until the onions have browned slightly. Add the meat and stir it about vigorously for 5 minutes. Put in the cumin, coriander, turmeric, cayenne and 1½ teaspoons of salt. Cook for a moment or two then add the tomatoes. Continue cooking on a high heat for 10-15 minutes, or until the sauce is thick and the oil seems to separate from it. Add the potatoes and 425 ml of water. Stir well, bring to the boil, then establish a steady simmer. Partially cover the pan and cook for about an hour until the meat is very tender. If the sauce seems to be getting too thick, add extra water. Taste, adjust the seasoning with lemon juice, and serve with coriander, if liked.

PORK WITH TOMATOES

SERVES 4 AS A MAIN DISH, 8 AS A TAPA

This simple dish – little chunks of pork fried in olive oil with garlic then stewed in tomatoes flavoured with bay – appears on every tapas menu, often served lukewarm, spooned into split bread rolls. That's the way I like it, but it's lovely hot, too, spooned into a chunk of crusty baguette or ciabatta: supper on the hoof.

- 3 tbsp olive oil
- 3 large garlic cloves, peeled and finely chopped
- 500 g lean pork, cut into sugar-lump size cubes
- salt and freshly ground black pepper
- 1 kg ripe tomatoes, cored, peeled and chopped
- 1 bay leaf
- ¼ tsp sugar
- 4 x 20 cm chunks baguette or 2 ciabatta, split
- butter (optional)

Put the oil in a large frying-pan, preferably non-stick, over a medium-high heat. When it is hot, fling in the garlic and stir it once round the pan then add the pork. Cook briskly until it is browned all over. Season with about ½ teaspoon of salt and plenty of black pepper, then add the tomatoes, bay leaf and sugar. Simmer for about 20 minutes, possibly longer, until the meat is tender and the tomatoes have reduced to a thick, rich sauce that clings to the meat. Taste, adjust the seasoning, remove the bay leaf and spoon into the bread, which you will have buttered if you are greedy like me. Eat immediately.

CHICKPEAS, TOMATOES AND SPINACH WITH SPICY GARLIC PORK

SERVES 4

A useful recipe that can be made almost entirely with store-cupboard ingredients and which doesn't involve much work. That is not to say it is a 'cheat's' dish. Rather, it utilizes two excellent convenience products that are never a waste of space in the kitchen cupboard: canned Italian tomatoes and chickpeas. With them, and initially cooked separately with masses of finely chopped garlic, are chunks of pork fillet. This hearty, full flavoured meal-in-a-bowl is great as it is with a hunk of crusty bread and butter.

- 2 tbsp olive oil
- 3 large garlic cloves, worked into a paste with ½ tsp salt
- 350-450 g pork fillet, cut into kebab-size pieces
- 400 g tin Italian peeled tomatoes
- 400 g tin chickpeas
- 1 tsp West Indian Hot Pepper Sauce or ½ tsp dried chilli flakes
- salt and freshly ground black pepper
- a squeeze of lemon juice
- 350 g young leaf spinach, rinsed and shaken dry
- a handful of coriander leaves, chopped

Use your hands to smear 1 tablespoon of the olive oil and the garlic paste all over the meat. Open the tomatoes and slice through them a couple of times while still in the tin. Tip the chick-peas into a colander and rinse well in cold running water.

Choose a heavy-bottomed pan and get it very hot over a medium heat. Put in the remaining oil and tip it backwards and forwards to cover the base of the pan. Lay in the meat in a single layer, allowing it to form a crust, and thus not stick, before turning it. You may have to do this in batches. Return all the meat to the pan, add the tomatoes, chickpeas and pepper sauce. Stir well and adjust the heat to simmer, then cook for about 20 minutes or until the meat is tender and the tomatoes have formed a thick sauce, but with pieces of tomato still visible. Taste and adjust the seasoning with pepper and lemon juice.

Stir the spinach into the sauce and, as soon as it begins to wilt, add the coriander. Serve immediately. If you think you will need to keep it waiting, don't add the spinach and coriander until you are about to dish up.

PICADILLO

SERVES 6

Picadillo is the name of the ubiquitous minced-meat sauce that crops up in Mexican cooking, rather like the Italian Ragù. It is made with a mixture of minced beef and pork and is lavishly flavoured with tomato, celery, chilli, garlic, red pepper, olives and raisins. It is served either rolled up in tortilla or over rice.

- 200 g minced beef
- 200 g minced pork
- 2 tsp malt vinegar
- salt and freshly ground black pepper
- ¼ tsp sugar
- 2 tbsp cooking oil
- 1 onion, peeled and finely chopped
- 1 garlic clove, peeled and finely chopped
- 1 green chilli, seeded and finely chopped
- 1 red pepper, seeded, white filament discarded and finely chopped
- 3 celery sticks, peeled and finely sliced
- 1 medium potato, peeled, rinsed and cut into small dice
- 9 stuffed green olives
- 1 tbsp raisins
- 2 tbsp blanched almonds, toasted
- 400 g tinned tomatoes
- 2 tbsp tomato puree

Mix the meats together with the vinegar, a good seasoning of salt, pepper and sugar. Heat the oil in a large frying-pan or flameproof casserole and cook the onion briskly with the garlic and the chilli, for a couple of minutes. Add the red pepper and the celery, and cook for a further 5 minutes. Increase the heat and stir in the meat and potato. Cook until the meat is thoroughly browned and the liquid given off by the vegetables has been absorbed. Stir in all the other ingredients. Bring to the boil, turn down to a simmer and cook for 20 minutes. Check the seasoning, and simmer until the Picadillo has cooked into a thick sauce.

ANDALUSIAN HASH

SERVES 4

Since I discovered this recipe in Janet Mendel's inspirational *Traditional Spanish Cooking* I've cooked it repeatedly. The combination of salty scraps of bacon and nuggets of fried pork cooked in a tomato sauce flavoured with cinnamon, saffron and white wine is exceptional. When you add fried almonds, chopped parsley, triangles of fried bread and hard-boiled eggs, it becomes a feast. If you prefer, use lamb or beef.

- 2 tbsp olive oil
- 75 g blanched almonds
- 100 g salt pork or streaky bacon or pancetta, diced
- 500 g pork, cut into small dice
- 1 onion, finely chopped
- 400 g tomatoes, cored, peeled and chopped
- ½ tsp ground cinnamon
- a grating of fresh nutmeg
- ¼ tsp saffron stamens, crushed
- ½ tsp freshly ground black pepper
- ½ tsp salt
- 6 tbsp white wine
- 6 tbsp water
- 2 hard-boiled eggs, quartered lengthways
- 1 tbsp chopped parsley
- triangles of fried bread

Heat the oil in a frying-pan over a medium heat and stir-fry the almonds until they are golden. Scoop them out of the pan and rest on absorbent kitchen paper to drain. In the same oil, fry the salt pork, bacon or pancetta with the pork. When it has browned, stir in the onion. Cook until the onion is beginning to soften and brown, then add the tomatoes. Fry for a couple of minutes then put in the cinnamon, nutmeg, saffron, ½ teaspoon of pepper and about ½ teaspoon of salt. Pour in the wine and water. Cover the pan and cook until the meat is tender and the liquid absorbed. Garnish with the fried almonds, the quartered eggs, the chopped parsley and the fried bread.

OREGANO AND LEMON PORK MEATBALLS IN A GARLICKY TOMATO SAUCE

SERVES 4

A quick, unusual meatball recipe.

1 tbsp butter
1 small onion, peeled and finely chopped
1 small, unwaxed lemon
1 tbsp chopped oregano or marjoram leaves
50 g fresh breadcrumbs
1 heaped tbsp crème fraîche
350 g organic minced pork
1 egg yolk
salt and freshly ground black pepper

FOR THE TOMATO SAUCE

4 garlic cloves, peeled and crushed
2 tbsp olive oil
approximately 700 g ripe tomatoes
1 glass red wine, 150 ml
salt and freshly ground black pepper
¼ tsp sugar

Melt the butter in a deep frying-pan or shallow saucepan over a medium-low heat and cook the onion until it is soft but hardly coloured. Meanwhile, remove the paper-thin zest from the lemon and chop it very finely. When the onion is ready, squeeze the lemon juice over the onion: it will seethe and splutter. Continue cooking until the onion is syrupy and merely moist. Stir in the oregano and turn off the heat. Tip the contents of the pan into a mixing bowl and leave to cool. Place the breadcrumbs in a small bowl and stir in the crème fraîche until thoroughly amalgamated.

Make the sauce. Put the garlic in the frying-pan with the 2 tablespoons of olive oil. Cook very gently, tossing every now and again, until it is aromatic, beginning to soften but not brown.

Meanwhile, blitz the tomatoes into a chunky puree in the food-processor. Add tomatoes, red wine, a generous seasoning of salt and pepper and ¼ teaspoon sugar to the frying pan. Mix everything together and simmer, stirring occasionally until thick. Taste and adjust the seasoning.

Finish making the meatballs by adding the pork, breadcrumb mixture and the egg yolk to the onions. Work together, mixing thoroughly, with your hands. Form it into a ball, then pinch off small pieces and roll between your hands into marble-sized balls. My mixture made 36. Drop them into the simmering sauce – they will fit snugly – return to a simmer and cook until firm, testing one after 15 minutes. Serve immediately or reheat as required.

Also see:
Tomatoes and Pasta (pages 267-307)
Tomatoes and Rice, Grains and Pulses (pages 308-325)

dealing with a glut

STUFFED DRIED TOMATOES

'I have followed Patience Gray's directions for folding leathery dried tomatoes around bits of anchovies, capers, and fennel seeds like tiny sandwiches, tucking them tightly together in small jars, topping with a bay leaf, and then covering with olive oil before putting the lid on. I spend a good deal of my year finding the most beautiful half-pint jars in which to give these as gifts. They're received with wild acclaim – the perfect antipasto as well as that sublime mouthful you seek sometimes. If you make them, too, use one very small piece of anchovy, no bigger than half a dime, per tomato, one very large caper, two fennel seeds, and the very best olive oil you can find. Add to this a scattering of the best oil-cured olives that have been crushed by the side of a cleaver to pit them, perhaps a crumb of dried hot red pepper, as well as a curl of lemon or orange peel (zest). Put the tops on the jars and refrigerate. Let them marinate in a cool place if you have a reliable one, or under refrigeration, for at least two weeks before tasting. You will find them mouthfuls of the most flagrantly exciting tastes. Give them as gifts, but be sure to keep a little jar for yourself. Gray advises, "Eat them with a glass of wine in winter."'

Sharon Nimtz and Ruth Cousineau, *Tomato Imperative*, Little, Brown and Company

DEALING WITH A GLUT

In Britain, the gardener's solution to a glut of tomatoes is to make chutney. In Germany, it is traditional to pickle green tomatoes – the last of the crop that refuse to ripen. In Italy, where the tomato dominates the cuisine, they grow tomatoes especially to make sufficient sauce to last through the winter. Whole tomatoes, tomato fillets and cherry tomatoes are all bottled. Other tomatoes are dried in the sun, left outside until all the moisture has evaporated and they harden like bits of old leather to be rehydrated when fresh tomatoes aren't available. These same sun-dried tomatoes are packed in olive oil flavoured with garlic and herbs, thus rendered succulent and ready to eat from the jar. In the land of the *pomodoro*, they even grow special varieties of tomato for preserving as they are on the vine – *da serbo*. They are bunched up and hung in a sheltered place to dry like grapes. Months later they are eaten on bread, in soups and oven dishes, in fact in any dish that requires tomatoes.

In Greece, where the tomatoes are big, gnarled and often predominantly green, they don't generally preserve them. When tomatoes are available they eat them, when they aren't, they don't. The exception is that the tiniest, unripe fruit are used to make syrupy spoon sweets – *glyka tau koutaliou* – called *domataki*, which are kept for special occasions.

This section of the book is devoted to preserving a glut of tomatoes. Most recipes are for the traditional solutions – bottling or making chutneys, sauces and ketchup – but there are a few surprises too. Although green tomatoes are often an inevitable result of growing tomatoes at home and are often preserved in pickles and chutneys, I found so many other interesting recipes for them that I decided to award them their own section. Many more recipes for preserving a glut of tomatoes, together with a comprehensive guide to preserving technique, can be found in *Preserving* by Oded Schwartz (Kyle Cathie, 1996).

FREEZING TOMATOES

Freezing is the simplest solution to a tomato glut. To avoid possible contamination, rinse and dry the fruit, remove the calyx (it's the first part to go mouldy) and cut into wedges. Either leave the seeds intact or remove entirely (save the juice by pressing the seeds through a sieve for vinaigrette, Bloody Mary and tomato Martini), weigh, bag up, squeeze out excess air from the bag, tie and label. Peeled and seeded tomato halves or diced fruit can be frozen flat and then bagged up, so they freeze separately like peas. This is useful if you envisage using a few tomatoes at a time. Either way, frozen tomatoes keep without spoiling for a year but are only suitable for cooked dishes.

TO STERILIZE JARS AND BOTTLES

The simplest way to do this is to place clean, open jars on a paper-towel-lined tray and place in the oven which has been pre-heated to 325°F/170°C/gas mark 3 for 10 minutes. Or, if you have a dishwasher, run the jars and lids through the cycle, after which they will be ready for use. Allow to cool slightly before filling with hot jam, pickle or preserve. Seal immediately; turn jars upside down to avoid condensation.

PRESERVING WITH HEAT

Jams with a low sugar content, ketchups, tomato sauces and other tomato preserves risk contamination by moulds and bacteria if they are not heat-treated. This is not difficult or complicated. Always use sterilized jars or bottles, seal them carefully when they have been filled, and then immerse them in water. Heat the water to boiling point, and simmer for 25 minutes (500 g jars) to 45 minutes (1 litre jars), depending on size. To protect the jars, so that they don't knock into each other and crack, wrap them in newspaper and place them on a metal rack or on folded newspaper. It is also important to leave the jars to cool in the water before storing.

Always use new seals and corks. Corks must be tied on with string during cooking. Note: always check that the seals have made a vacuum before storing, by trying to lift the lids.

SETTING POINT FOR JAMS

Jams need sugar, acid and pectin to set. Tomatoes are high in pectin and most, particularly green tomatoes, contain quite a bit of acid. Consequently, tomato jams and conserves don't require artificial pectin or preserving sugar to achieve a firm set.

Setting point is reached by rapid boiling. Test for setting after 15 minutes, and every 5 minutes thereafter: pour a little hot jam on to a cold saucer. Leave for a couple of minutes, then push the jam with a finger. If it wrinkles it has reached setting point.

PATIENCE GRAY'S CONSERVE OF PLUM TOMATOES/POMODORI PELATI

One of the most attractive sights in the store-cupboard is a bottle of preserved tomatoes. At Carluccio's, in Covent Garden, London, they sell tiny cherry tomatoes in bulbous jars with little handles and tall, wide jars of plum tomato halves with their seeds intact. These sun-ripened tomatoes taste like fresh ones, and are far more 'pure' in flavour than the finest tinned tomatoes. They will transform winter sauces.

Should you face a tomato glut, bottling is a lovely way to preserve the best fruit. The only time I have ever bottled tomatoes was using Patience Gray's method described in *Honey From A Weed, Fasting and Feasting in Tuscany, Catalonia, The Cyclades and Apulia*. She recalls the annual ritual of picking their own San Marzano tomatoes, ripening them to the darkest red, and bottling them in 1 litre preserving jars. It is difficult to be precise with this sort of recipe because you could use any sort of glass jar, and should be warned that whatever its size, it will hold far more fruit than you could imagine possible. The tomatoes are peeled, gently squeezed to remove some seeds and juice, but kept whole. They are then packed into sterilized jars, layered with a little sliced onion, a sprig of basil, thyme, a bay leaf, some peeled garlic and green chilli peppers. A little salt is added. No water. The jars are sealed with rubber rings, and securely closed.

The jars are simmered for between 25 and 45 minutes depending on their size (as described on page 393) and left to cool in the water. They can then be stored for the winter. Before using, pour off their liquor, which will have turned acidic, and heat the pelati in olive oil. 'They will taste like fresh tomatoes.'

TO PRESERVE FRESH TOMATOES IN OIL

'Choose ripe tomatoes, medium size, absolutely whole, perfect, and without the slightest crack or bruise. If the tomato has a hole where the stalk is, drop a little wax on it. Roll the tomatoes in a clean cloth and dry well.

'Put them carefully into jars with a large mouth, fill the jars with nut oil (*huile d'arachide*) without taste so that the tomatoes are covered with a layer of oil an inch deep. On the oil pour a layer of eau-de-vie (to prevent the oil from going rancid) half an inch deep. Seal hermetically.

'The oil can be used afterwards as it will remain quite tasteless.'

Elizabeth David, *A Book of Mediterranean Food*

'SUN-DRIED' TOMATOES PRESERVED IN OLIVE OIL

While I was researching this book, someone told me that a very famous chef, with three Michelin stars, once said he would never allow a sun-dried tomato in his kitchen. He reckoned they were a hype, he said, a nonsense and a fashion ingredient. There are, of course, plenty who would disagree with him. The sun-dried tomato has been so wholeheartedly embraced because it tastes like the very essence of ripe tomato and is a convenient product.

Delia Smith popularized the idea of making 'sun-dried' tomatoes in the oven and it is worth considering if you have a glut of truly wonderful, ripe plum tomatoes, preferably of a long, skinny Italian variety. After drying, the tomatoes look unpromising, but if you pack them in olive oil, with or without other seasonings such as garlic and herb, you will end up not only with dried tomatoes that will keep safely for several months, but with the most exquisite oil.

900 g, or more, ripe plum tomatoes

salt

a small bunch of fresh rosemary or thyme

5 garlic cloves, peeled

1 bay leaf

olive oil, approximately 75 ml

Pre-heat the oven to its lowest setting, less than 275°F/140°C/gas mark 1, if possible – an Aga or cooling wood-fired oven is ideal for this.

Cut the tomatoes in half lengthways, leaving a hinge so that they can close like a book. Use your finger or the end of a teaspoon to gouge out the seeds, catching them in a sieve over a bowl (save the juices: see pages 27-28). Place the tomatoes on a wire rack set over a baking-tray and sprinkle the cut surfaces with a little salt. Turn them over and leave them to drain for about 30 minutes. Then turn them so that they lie, cut side up, close together but not touching, on a wire rack set on a dry baking-sheet. Leave in the oven for 10-14 hours, checking that the tomatoes aren't actually cooking, and changing around the trays as necessary, until they have lost almost all their moisture and are wrinkled, shrunken, yet still soft and pliable.

In a large sterilized jar (see page 393), arrange the tomatoes with the rosemary or thyme, garlic cloves and bay leaf. Pour in enough olive oil to cover. Seal the jar and store in a cool, dark place. They will be ready to eat after 2 weeks.

Another idea is to sandwich the tomatoes with a scrap of salted anchovy (soaked, boned, cleaned, rinsed, dried), 2 rinsed and dried salted capers, and a few fennel seeds before bottling. Pack the sandwiches in small lidded jars, add a bay leaf and fill with olive oil. Cover and store to serve as a winter aperitif treat. See also Stuffed Dried Tomatoes (page 391).

TOMATO CONFIT

Picture, if you will, the intense flavour and molten texture of whole baby tomatoes that have been poached very gently in olive oil seasoned with whole garlic cloves, thyme and balsamic vinegar. The skin of the little tomatoes will probably have split and patches of its flesh will be stained dark brown, but as the tomato bursts in your mouth there will be an explosion of flavour. They will keep in a jar for several weeks in the fridge and are served, brought back to room temperature, with some of the vinaigrette. They are very good with cold cuts of meat, pork pie, or British and Irish hard cheeses, particularly Cheddar. Any leftover vinaigrette makes a fine dressing for a tomato (or other) salad.

- 10 new-season garlic cloves, peeled
- 2 flourishing sprigs of thyme
- 1 tbsp brown sugar
- 6 tbsp olive oil
- 2 tbsp balsamic vinegar
- 500 g cherry or baby plum tomatoes

Place everything except the tomatoes in a small, stainless-steel saucepan and simmer gently for 10 minutes. Add the tomatoes – I sometimes prick each one to avoid bursting – which should be more or less submerged, cover the pan and leave to simmer very gently – a heat-diffuser pad is useful – for 30 minutes. The garlic and tomatoes should be tender. Leave to cool then pour into sterilized jars (see page 393) and seal. The tomatoes look very pretty served from a Kilner jar.

TOMATO SAUCE FOR THE WINTER

When Simon Hopkinson wrote of the therapeutic and enjoyable pleasures of making a great vat of tomato sauce with over-ripe end-of-season tomatoes, he hit a chord with me. Home-made tomato sauce, with ripe, good-flavoured tomatoes, generously seasoned, and prepared without preservatives, is always better than all but the very best commercial products. And a fresh tasting, full-flavoured tomato sauce is one of the most useful things you can have in the cupboard. Come the winter, when you can't buy a decent fresh tomato, a real tomato sauce with meatballs or lasagne will be a treat indeed.

- 5 kg very ripe tomatoes, cored, peeled and roughly chopped
- 200 ml olive oil
- 1 whole head garlic, broken into cloves, then bruised with the flat of a knife and peeled
- 1 rounded tbsp salt
- ½ tbsp freshly ground black pepper
- thinly pared zest (no pith) of 3 lemons
- 2 large handfuls of basil leaves, torn into pieces

Put everything into a very large pan with a thick, heavy base. Bring to a very gentle simmer and leave to cook for 2-3 hours, stirring fairly often, until thick and jammy. (A heat-diffuser pad will prevent the sauce catching.) Decant into sterilized, rubber-sealed glass preserving jars (see page 393) and allow to cool. Keep in the fridge until needed.

To preserve indefinitely, see page 393.

Another, more rustic, approach is documented in Patience Gray's *Honey From a Weed*, at the end of a wonderful essay on the making of 'la salsa':

> *'The sauce that many Apulian householders prepare for winter is made on a large scale, involving the whole family and at least a hundred kilos of Leccesi tomatoes grown for this purpose, but often far more.*
>
> *'Using a funnel and some kind of jug, you fill each bottle leaving a little space at the top, the space being filled afterwards with a sprig of basil and a covering of olive oil. But first you have to "bump" the bottles to get the air bubbles out. You then with a clean white rag clean the inside neck of each bottle, and line them up on a table, insert the leaf of basil, fill up with olive oil, and put in the corks. After two or three days you drive them in.'*

TOMATO CATSUP/KETCHUP

ABOUT 10 X 500 ML JARS

'No matter how carefully she flavoured the stews or spiced the puddings, the piglets always squealed for tomato ketchup. She used to try and stop them having it, and make one bottle last a week, but it was always gobbled up by Monday and then the piglets would grumble until she went out again to do the big shop.

'"But things will be different soon," thought Mother Pig happily. She reached down one of the big jars and emptied it into a huge soup tureen.'

Mary Rayner, *Mrs Pig's Bulk Buy* (Piccolo Books)

The day after I published a recipe for Red Flannel Hash in my *Evening Standard* column, my friend Roger de Freitas rang to say that it had inspired him to make the tomato ketchup from *The Joy of Cooking* by Irma S. Rombauer and Marion Rombauer Becker. 'It was wonderful, bright red like Heinz and very thick and creamy,' he enthused. 'You absolutely must include the recipe in your tomato book.'

Catsup, as ketchup is still known in America, originated in Malaysia, and its name derives from the local word for 'taste'. According to Annie Bell, writing in the *Independent* after wading through *Pure Ketchup: A History of America's National Condiment*, ketchup 'first dripped out of a bottle in New England in the 1830s and trickled across the Atlantic some fifty years later'. By 1915, there were over 8,900 catsups marketed, with names like Beefsteak and Eagle Tomato Ketchup, but Heinz has conquered all.

Everyone loves it and it has no equal. It is a secret weapon in professional kitchens: Alastair Little, Michel Guérard and countless others add it to tomato soups and sauces, Anton Edelmann used to smear it under Savoy canapés, and Simon Hopkinson adds it to toad-in-the-hole. At home small children are introduced to it with fish fingers, and it is the one condiment that most people can't do without. Shepherd's pie and fish and chips would be unthinkable without it. I'm sure it's addictive: you should read the cautionary tale of Mrs Pig and how she cured her little ones of their ketchup-with-everything addiction.

So, if Heinz (The Original, 1886) tomato ketchup is so good, and free from artificial colour and preservatives, why bother to make it at home? I won't attempt to answer that, except to say that ketchup is no trouble to make because it is no more than spiced, pureed tomato seasoned with sweet and sour flavourings.

This recipe, from the revised edition of *Joy* – as we aficionados call it – *The All New All Purpose Joy of Cooking* by Irma Rombauer, Marion Rombauer Becker and Ethan Becker (Scribner), is for making ketchup in mega quantities. It is very good indeed and is worth the minimal effort. It looks wonderful bottled in sterilized (see page 393) Grolsch beer bottles, which have sprung stoppers, and makes a lovely present. My own experimentations (see page 257) were made with domestic quantities and the delicious results were gone within twenty-four hours. Roast Tomato Sauce (page 245) is also a lovely 'ketchup' and very, very undemanding to make.

- 6.3 kg ripe tomatoes, chopped
- 8 medium onions, peeled, halved and sliced
- 2 red peppers, seeds and white filament removed, chopped
- 175 g soft brown sugar
- ½ tsp dry mustard
- 7.5 cm piece of cinnamon stick
- 1 tbsp whole allspice
- 1 tbsp whole cloves
- 1 tbsp ground mace
- 1 tbsp celery seeds
- 1 tbsp black peppercorns
- 2 bay leaves
- 1 garlic clove, peeled
- 500 ml cider vinegar
- salt
- paprika to taste (optional)

Combine the tomatoes, onion and peppers in a large pot over a medium heat and simmer, stirring occasionally, until very soft. Push through a coarse-mesh sieve and return to the pot with the sugar and mustard. Tie the cinnamon, allspice, cloves, mace, celery seeds, black peppercorns, bay leaves and garlic in a square of muslin and dangle it into the stew. Bring the mixture to a rolling boil, then reduce to a simmer. Continue to cook, stirring often and carefully – it blips over the edge – until the sauce is reduced by half. Remove and discard the spice bag. Stir in the cider, salt and paprika to taste. Reduce the heat and simmer, stirring almost continually, for 10 minutes.

Cool, then pour through a funnel into sterilized bottles (see page 393). Preserve as instructed on page 393, or store in the fridge and use within a month.

MRS RUNDELL'S FRESH TOMATO SAUCE

'This is an excellent sauce to make when tomatoes, either home-grown or imported, are plentiful and cheap', wrote Elizabeth David in *Spices, Salt and Aromatics* of Mrs Rundell's sauce given in *A New System of Domestic Cookery* published in 1806.

It hardly needs a recipe:

'Put from 900 g-1.4 kg or more, of very ripe tomatoes, whole and unskinned, into an earthenware or other oven pot. Add nothing whatsoever. Cover the pot. Put into a moderate oven (325°F/170°C/gas mark 3), and leave it for almost an hour, or until the tomatoes are soft and squashy. Press them through a sieve or a mouli.

'Heat the resulting puree in a thick saucepan, adding, for every 450 g of tomatoes, a teaspoon each of salt and sugar, and optionally, a little ground ginger or cinnamon, dried or fresh basil or marjoram, and crushed garlic if you like. A tablespoon of port per 450 g of tomatoes has a wonderfully mellowing effect on the sauce. For immediate use, cook the sauce as little as possible so that it retains its freshness of flavour and bright colour.'

Use immediately or store in fridge or freezer. It can be preserved in the usual way (see page 393).

RED ONION MARMALADE WITH SUN-DRIED TOMATOES

A versatile sweet-sour onion and tomato jam-cum-relish for piling on to bruschetta, serving with cheese, terrines and char-grilled calves' liver.

- 2 tbsp olive oil
- 2 large red onions, peeled, halved and finely sliced
- ½ tsp salt
- freshly ground black pepper
- 2 tbsp caster sugar
- 6 sun-dried tomatoes, soaked in boiling water for 10 minutes, then chopped
- 2 tbsp red wine vinegar
- 150 ml coarse red wine

Heat the oil, throw in the onion, season and add the sugar. Cook very slowly for 30 minutes or until the onions are soft and slippery. Add the sun-dried tomatoes, vinegar and red wine, and cook for a further 30 minutes or until jam-like.

Cool and store in a sterilized screw-top jar (see page 393). It will keep in the fridge for a couple of weeks.

LEMON TOMATO JAM/ CONFITURA DE TOMAQUET

Lemons and tomatoes are often teamed together: a salad, for example, of peeled, sliced tomatoes interspersed with wafer-thin slivers of unpeeled lemon is extremely refreshing. Here, ripe tomato concassé and the juice from the tomato seeds, which helps to set the jam, are stewed with lemon juice then sweetened with sugar. It is eaten at room temperature and preserves beautifully (see page 393). Natalie Hambro, in *Particular Delights*, makes a similar jam that she aptly describes as, 'a beautiful, translucent red, like stained glass'. She adds cardamom with tomatoes and lemons (1 teaspoon with 2 kg red tomatoes, 2 kg sugar, the juice and rind of 3 lemons) and suggests quartering the peeled, seeded tomatoes and leaving them in layers with the sugar overnight. Then, when the tomatoes have melted with the sugar into a syrupy juice, the whole lot is boiled with the lemon rind, juice and spice.

These intriguing jams can be eaten on bread or scones or whatever, or served as a dessert with Greek or set yoghurt or ice cream. They are also delicious as a relish with soft cheeses and poultry. Natalie Hambro serves hers with steamed grey mullet.

750 g ripe tomatoes, cored and peeled

OPTIONAL EXTRAS

1 bay leaf

2 cloves

2 tbsp lemon juice

300 g caster sugar

2 green cardamom pods

Place a sieve over a bowl. Halve the tomatoes over the sieve and scrape out the seeds and their juices. Chop the flesh.

Place the tomato flesh, the bay leaf, cloves or cardamom if using, strained juices and lemon juice in a saucepan and bring slowly to the boil. Reduce the heat and simmer gently, stirring occasionally, for about 20 minutes until thick and jammy. Put in the sugar and stir continuously until it has dissolved. Boil to setting point, 105°C. Test for set, then stir for a few minutes to mix in the scum, which need not be removed. Lift out the cardamom, bay and cloves if used. Allow to cool slightly then pot into sterilized, heated jars (see page 393). Seal immediately.

TOMATO JELLY/DULCE DE TOMATE

MAKES 5 X 250 ML JARS

Dulce de Tomate, to give it its Spanish name, is a delicate tomato jelly-cum-jam. The recipe will work with green tomatoes, too, although you may need to add extra sugar. It comes from Janet Mendel's book, *Traditional Spanish Cooking*, and she suggests spooning it over ice-cream, serving it with cream cheese or with croissants for breakfast.

- approximately 4 kg tomatoes, cored, peeled, seeded and chopped
- approximately 2 kg sugar
- 1 vanilla pod
- 5 cloves
- zest of 1 small lemon, coarsely chopped

First weigh the prepared tomatoes. Place in a pan with the same weight of sugar, the vanilla pod, cloves and lemon zest. Bring to the boil, then cook on a medium heat for about an hour until the jelly is thick. It will have approximately halved in quantity. Spoon into sterilized jars (page 393) and preserve in the usual way (see page 393).

RED TOMATO MARMALADE

Flavoured with lemon juice and coriander, this is an intriguing combination dreamed up by Oded Schwartz for his book, *Preserving*.

- 1 kg firm, ripe tomatoes, cored, seeded and coarsely chopped
- 1 kg preserving or granulated sugar
- zest, finely sliced, and juice of 2 lemons
- 1½ tbsp coriander seeds, coarsely crushed

Put the tomatoes in the preserving-pan with the sugar, lemon zest and juice. Bring slowly to the boil, stirring as the sugar dissolves, then simmer for 5 minutes. Skim, then add the coriander seeds.

Return the mixture to the boil, then, stirring frequently, boil for 30 minutes, until setting point is reached. Remove the pan from the heat and leave the fruit to settle for a few minutes. Ladle the marmalade into the hot sterilized jars (see page 393), then seal.

YELLOW TOMATO PRESERVE

You could, of course, use red tomatoes for this preserve, but it seems appropriate to combine yellow tomatoes with lemongrass. The idea comes from Oded Schwartz's *Preserving*, and the preserve is thick and chunky. Certainly something different to serve for tea.

- 1 kg yellow tomatoes, cored
- 2 lemons, thinly sliced into semi-circles
- 1 lemongrass stalk, bruised
- 75 ml water
- 750 g preserving or granulated sugar
- 250 g soft light brown sugar

Put all the ingredients in the preserving pan (there is no need to chop the tomatoes). Bring slowly to the boil, then simmer gently for 15 minutes. Return to the boil and, stirring frequently, boil steadily for 25 minutes, or until setting point is reached.

Remove from the heat and leave the tomatoes to settle for a few minutes. Remove the lemongrass. Ladle the preserve into hot sterilized jars (see page 393), then seal.

TOMATO AND APPLE BUTTER

This recipe comes from Felicity and Roald Dahl's *Memories with Food at Gipsy House* (Penguin, 1991). It is a wonderful book, a good read and great recipes, which give a fascinating insight into the life of a man we *know* to have been obsessed with chocolate and peaches. Recipes come from various members of the family, and cooks who have lived *en famille* with the Dahls. Phoebe, it would seem, is the jam queen and this is her recipe.

- 500 g tomatoes, quartered
- 500 g apples, peeled, cored and sliced
- 900 g sugar
- zest, grated, and juice of 1 orange
- passata or sieved concassé (see page 29; optional)

Put the tomatoes and apples in a pan with just enough water to stop them from sticking to the bottom. Cook over a moderate heat, stirring occasionally, until they are tender.

Rub the cooked fruit through a sieve. Measure the puree. Each 500 g of fruit should produce 450 ml puree; if necessary, use passata or sieved concassé to make up this quantity. Combine the fruit puree with the sugar and add the juice and grated rind of the orange.

Boil carefully and slowly until it thickens, for about 30-45 minutes, stirring occasionally. Pour into sterilized hot jars (see page 393), allow to cool and seal.

PICKLED SUN-DRIED TOMATOES

Serve as a relish with cheese on toast or with chunks of strong-flavoured cheese, some good crusty bread and a salad of peppery leaves such as watercress or rocket.

- 20 pieces sun-dried or mi-cuit tomato (see page 21)
- 75 ml balsamic vinegar
- 75 ml white wine vinegar
- 40 g Demerara sugar
- 4 sprigs thyme
- 2 sprigs rosemary
- 2 garlic cloves, peeled and sliced
- 1 bay leaf
- 50 ml olive oil

If using dried sun-dried tomatoes (i.e., not preserved in olive oil or freshly made), soak them in boiling water for 2 hours. Place the two vinegars, the sugar, herbs and garlic in a small saucepan and bring quickly to the boil. Whisk in the olive oil. Place the tomatoes in a sterilized jar (see page 393), pour over the vinegar, cover and leave for at least 1 week before using.

ROAST TOMATO AND FRESH BASIL CHUTNEY

Rich and gorgeous. Serve it with roast or grilled meats, cheesy pastries and egg dishes.

- 10 ripe plum tomatoes, cored and peeled
- 1 onion, halved through the core, skin left intact
- the cloves of 1 head of garlic
- 100 ml olive oil
- salt and freshly ground black pepper
- 1 tbsp brown sugar or runny honey
- 1 small bunch of basil, leaves only

Pre-heat the oven to 350°F/180°C/gas mark 4.

Lightly smear a roasting-tin with olive oil and arrange in it the tomatoes with the onion halves, cut side down. Tuck the garlic among the tomatoes. Drizzle with the remaining oil. Bake for 30 minutes. Remove from the oven and allow to cool slightly. Peel and discard the skin and root of the onion and slice finely. Peel the garlic and chop it coarsely. Cut the tomatoes into quarters. Tip everything, tomatoes, garlic, onions and their juices, into a pan, season with salt, pepper, and sugar, and simmer gently until the chutney is thick and the onion tender. Cool slightly, stir in the torn basil and spoon into sterilized jars (see page 393). Serve cold; this chutney improves after 24 hours and keeps, covered, in the fridge for a couple of weeks.

RATATOUILLE CHUTNEY

The perfect chutney to make with a glut of over-ripe tomatoes. The combination was inspired by the Mediterranean Chutney served at one of my all-time favourite restaurants: Joyce Molyneux's Carved Angel at Dartmouth in Devon (sadly no longer in business).

- 900 g ripe tomatoes, cored, peeled and chopped
- 450 g onions, peeled and diced
- 450 g courgettes, trimmed and cut into 1 cm cubes
- 450 g aubergines, trimmed and cut into 1 cm cubes
- 450 g red pepper, seeded, white filament removed and cut into 1 cm cubes
- 4 garlic cloves, peeled and crushed
- 1 tbsp salt
- 1 tbsp coriander seeds, lightly crushed
- ½ tsp cayenne pepper
- 1 tbsp paprika, preferably Noble Sweet
- 1 bay leaf
- 2 sprigs thyme
- 350 g caster sugar
- 275 ml red wine vinegar

Place all the vegetables in a large saucepan. Add the garlic, salt, coriander, cayenne, paprika, bay leaf and thyme, and simmer, covered, on a low heat for 20 minutes. Remove the lid and simmer for a further 20-30 minutes until most of the liquid has evaporated. Add the sugar and stir until it has dissolved, then pour in the vinegar. Simmer until the mixture thickens and most of the vinegar has evaporated.

Ladle into hot, sterilized jars (see page 393), allow to cool slightly and cover. Leave to mature for at least 1 month.

TWO-TOMATO CHUTNEY

A thick dark red chutney with a fruity sweet-sour background flavour. Good with British and Irish hard cheeses and cold cuts of meat.

750 g medium red onions, peeled
15 Thai shallots or small shallots
1 medium onion, peeled and finely chopped
750 g ripe tomatoes, cored, peeled and chopped
8 garlic cloves, sliced in wafer-thin rounds
225 g brown sugar
10 oil-preserved sun-dried tomatoes
150 g sultanas
2 tbsp balsamic vinegar
150 ml red wine vinegar
1 tsp salt
2.5 cm piece fresh ginger, peeled and finely chopped
¼ tsp paprika
¼ tsp ground cloves
¼ tsp ground mace
¼ tsp ground cardamom

Finely chop 450 g of the red onions; cut the rest into quarters and then into thin half-moons. Drop the shallots into boiling water, establish a simmer and cook for 5 minutes. Rinse them in cold water, then peel them. Put the red onions, the medium onion, the tomatoes and garlic into a pan together and boil until they have reduced to a thick, pulpy mass. Stir in the sugar until it is dissolved, then add the shallots, the sun-dried tomatoes and all the other ingredients. Establish a steady simmer and cook until the chutney is thick and the shallots tender to the point of a sharp knife.

Pour into hot, sterilized jars (see page 393), cool and seal. It will keep for several months.

Also see:
Tomato Stock (page 61)
Green Tomato Chutney (page 413)
Green Tomato Jam (page 415)
Pickled Green Tomatoes (page 414)

green tomatoes

'After lunch Rose tidied the kitchen completely, and began to prepare the twins' supper. She had made a pink blancmange, of which anachronistic confection the twins were very fond. It was shaped like a cowering rabbit and quivered oleaginously on a green Wedgwood plate. She had put fresh raspberries in little glass bowls decorated with damask rose petals, and washed nasturtium leaves and wild sorrel to put in their salad. Now she began to make their stew. She cut a long slice from a shoulder of lamb and chopped it into neat little squares. These she put in to brown in some green gold olive oil in a heavy pan. She quartered three green tomatoes and sliced three courgettes, and chopped up a bunch of green spring onions, adding a clove of garlic for its stomachic properties and its efficacy against evil. These she added to the oil and meat in the pan, together with a chopped green pepper. She stirred it once and put on the lid. Later she would drop in ten tiny new potatoes. Five each. Lastly she took some spinach leaves and a handful of watercress and minced them up finely, saving all the juice. At the last minute she would add this, and the whole thing would turn a marvellous faery green. With it she would serve bright buttered carrots. Sometimes she made them an episcopally gorgeous beetroot stew with rosy cubes of chicken and green peas, but green stew was their favourite.'

Alice Thomas Ellis, *The Sin Eater*

Most people think of green tomatoes as being the ones that appear too late in the season to stand a chance of ripening. Many can be brought on, inside in the warm, and their skins will gradually turn red, but they never develop the fruity sweetness of a fully ripened fruit. There is also a limited number of green varieties with names such as green grape (a grape-shaped, small cherry), green zebra (stripy and medium-sized) and evergreen (lobe-shaped fruit). Green tomatoes, of either type, rarely go on sale and remain the domain of the gardener. As such, they have rarity value, and when they crop up in dishes normally reserved for red tomatoes they aren't immediately recognizable.

Their fresh acidity and firm, almost crisp, texture, which, when cooked, holds its shape better than that of a ripe tomato, means that green tomatoes tend to turn up in chutneys and pickles, often teamed with apples. Cooking apples and green tomatoes have much in common: they are both mouth-puckeringly sour when eaten raw but are transformed when cooked with plenty of sugar. Unlike ripe tomatoes, which strike most of us as being a bit odd for pudding, green tomatoes work just as well in sweet dishes as they do in savoury ones. They go well with creamy foods and eggs, with bacon and leeks, and ideas for using them turn up in the cuisine of every tomato-growing country. Hence, Green Tomato Raita, Green Tabbouleh, Green Tomato Risotto, Green Tomato Salsa, and Green Tomato Gratin. It isn't very often, though, that they are seen on restaurant menus – with the notable exception of fried green tomatoes.

The limited availability of green tomatoes means that their potential has yet to be fully explored. Should you develop a taste for them, I recommend ordering a copy of Sharon Nimtz and Ruth Cousineau's *Tomato Imperative* (see Bibliography).

FRIED GREEN TOMATOES

SERVES 2-4

This is probably the most familiar way of cooking green tomatoes. They are good eaten hot from the pan as a snack, but can be served as a vegetable with grilled meat or fish.

- 750 g green tomatoes
- 50 g flour
- approximately 100 g fine, dry breadcrumbs
- ½ tsp chilli powder
- salt
- 2 eggs
- olive oil for frying

Slice the tomatoes quite thickly and touch them on absorbent kitchen paper to drain. Sift the flour in a cereal bowl. Place the breadcrumbs in a second bowl, season with the chilli powder and plenty of salt, then toss. Crack the eggs into a third bowl and whisk. Dip the tomato slices first in flour, then in the egg, and finally press them into the breadcrumbs so that they are thoroughly coated.

Quarter-fill a frying pan with oil. Place it over a medium heat and, when it is hot, fry the tomatoes until they are crisp and golden on both sides. Drain on kitchen paper and serve hot.

GREEN TOMATO COMPOTE WITH CHILLIES AND CORIANDER

SERVES 2-3

Mexican in origin, this sweet-sour sauce could be served in place of salsa and is at its best eaten tepid or cold. It is also very good rolled in a hot tortilla with a scoop of Greek yoghurt or soured cream. Its success relies on the onions being cooked until they are silky and sweet before the tomatoes are added to provide a good contrast of acidity. Chilli and masses of fresh coriander balance the flavours.

- 2 tbsp olive oil
- 1 Spanish onion, peeled, halved and sliced
- 1 garlic clove, peeled and sliced in thin rounds
- 450 g green tomatoes, cored and peeled
- 1 red chilli, seeded and finely chopped
- juice of 1 lime
- salt and freshly ground black pepper
- 25 g coriander, chopped coarsely

Heat the olive oil in a frying-pan over a medium heat. Add the onion, stir constantly as it begins to wilt, then add the garlic. Cook for at least 20 minutes until it is floppy and beginning to colour.

Meanwhile, halve the tomatoes then slice them into chunky wedges. Add the chilli to the onions, stir a couple of times, then put in the tomatoes and the lime juice. Season with salt and pepper and simmer until the tomatoes are soft and jammy. Stir in the coriander. Serve warm or cold.

GREEN TOMATO OMELETTE

SERVES 1

Green tomatoes have a different sort of alchemy with eggs from that of red ones. Their fresh acidity cuts through the richness of the eggs and cheese combined in this omelette. This is one of those omelettes that defy categorization: it isn't exactly a frittata or tortilla – a chunky omelette sliced like a cake – and it doesn't lend itself to being rolled up in the French style. It is cooked quickly over a fierce heat until the edges are crisp, the middle gooey. The top is firmed under a pre-heated grill. It can be eaten hot, tepid or cold.

- 3 medium green tomatoes, cored and cut in 1 cm thick slices
- approximately 3 tbsp polenta or flour
- 50 g butter
- 3 spring onions, sliced
- 3 fresh eggs
- 1 tbsp crème fraîche or Greek yoghurt
- 50 g Parmesan
- 3 drops Tabasco
- salt and freshly ground black pepper

Dip the tomato slices in the polenta or flour and shake off the excess. Melt half the butter in a frying-pan and sauté the tomatoes until they are coloured but hardly softened. Add the spring onions to the pan with a little of the remaining butter and cook until soft. Tip on to a plate.

Whisk the eggs with the crème fraîche or yoghurt, half the Parmesan, the Tabasco and the spring onions. Season with salt and pepper.

Pre-heat the grill.

Return the pan to the heat, turned up high, and add the remaining butter, swirling it round so the entire base is smeared. Tip in the egg mixture and quickly lay the tomato and onions on top. Cook for about 30 seconds, pushing the edges towards the middle in a few places and tilting the pan to let the uncooked egg run into the gaps. As soon as the bottom is set, hold the pan very close to the grill to cook the top quickly. Slip the omelette on to a warm plate. Sprinkle over the remaining Parmesan.

LEMON AND GREEN TOMATO SAUCE WITH CRÈME FRAÎCHE

SERVES 4

A refreshing sauce for pasta or poached chicken.

- 25 g butter
- 1 garlic clove, pounded to a paste with a pinch of salt
- 450 g green tomatoes, cored, peeled and chopped
- zest of 1 unwaxed lemon, finely chopped
- 1 tbsp caster sugar
- 150 g Greek yoghurt or crème fraîche
- salt

Melt the butter in a small saucepan over a medium heat. Add the garlic, cook it briefly until it is aromatic, then add the tomatoes. Put in the lemon zest and sugar, then cook briskly for a few minutes until the tomatoes soften. Tip the contents of the pan into a food-processor with the yoghurt or crème fraîche and blitz. Pass the sauce through a sieve. Taste and adjust the seasoning with salt.

GREEN TOMATO GRATIN

SERVES 6

'The mild acidity of green tomatoes blends perfectly with onions that have been roasted to bring out their sweetness,' says Paula Wolfert of this Turkish recipe, in her book *Mediterranean Cooking*. Serve it warm with poached chicken or on its own with thin shavings of feta cheese and some crusty bread to scoop up the delicious sweet-sour juices.

- 3 tbsp olive oil
- 5 medium onions, chopped
- 1.4 kg green tomatoes, halved
- salt and freshly ground black pepper
- a pinch of cayenne pepper
- 250 ml vegetable, poultry or meat stock
- 150 g feta cheese

Pre-heat the oven to 400°F/200°C/gas mark 6.

Heat 2 tablespoons of the oil in a saucepan over a moderate heat, add the onions and cook until tender. Transfer them to a round, shallow baking-dish. Place the tomato halves on top. Add the remaining olive oil, season with salt and pepper, cayenne, and pour over the stock. Cover the dish with foil and cook in the oven until the tomatoes are completely tender and all the moisture has been absorbed – check after 40 minutes.

Remove the foil, crush the tomatoes into the onions with a potato masher or a fork. Correct the seasoning and serve warm, covered with very thin slices of feta cheese.

GREEN TOMATO TARTE TATIN

SERVES 2

This is Gary Rhodes' recipe – you could use red or yellow tomatoes but they must be under-ripe and of a firm variety or they will collapse. Also see pages 232-233 for other Tarte Tatins.

- olive oil
- 6 green tomatoes, halved through the middle
- salt and freshly ground black pepper
- a knob of butter
- 1 tsp demerara sugar
- 100-175 g puff pastry

Pre-heat the oven to 450°F/230°/gas mark 8.

Heat an ovenproof frying-pan with a trickle of olive oil. Season the cut surface of the tomato halves with salt and pepper and place, cut side down, in a circular pattern, filling the pan. Increase the heat so that the tomatoes are frying, not stewing. After 1 minute, add the butter and sprinkle with the sugar. Continue to fry for a minute or two, shaking the pan occasionally so that the tomatoes are evenly coated with butter. They will have started to caramelize. Remove the pan from the stove and leave to cool.

Roll out the pastry into a 20 cm circle. Put it on top of the cooled tomatoes, pressing lightly to help it take on the shape of the tomato border. Bake the tart for 15-20 minutes until the pastry is crisp and golden. Take it out of the oven, put a plate over the pastry and invert to turn out the tart. If liked, brush the tomatoes with more butter, sprinkle with extra sugar and flash under the grill until it is bubbling.

Cut the tart in half and eat immediately. Gary reckons 'it eats well' with a dressing made with 4 tbsp olive oil, 1 tbsp balsamic vinegar, 4 tbsp soured cream and a squeeze of lemon or lime juice, plus a few torn basil leaves, slices of red onion and Parmesan shavings.

GREEN TOMATO RAITA

SERVES 4

Serve with curry or over rice with dhal.

- 4 green tomatoes, cored and chopped
- 2 spring onions, trimmed and very finely sliced
- 2 tbsp finely chopped coriander
- 1 green chilli, seeded and finely chopped
- a generous pinch of cumin
- 200 g plain yoghurt
- salt and a pinch of cayenne pepper

Place all the ingredients except the salt and cayenne pepper in a bowl. Stir, then season with salt and cayenne. Mix and chill.

GREEN TOMATO CHUTNEY

This might just as well be called gardeners' chutney. The recipe is by Gary Rhodes and is taken from the 1998 edition of *Picnic Recipes* (Council for the Protection of Rural England), published to celebrate National Picnic Weekend each June.

- 1.25 kg green tomatoes, cut into 8
- 600 ml malt vinegar
- 5 large onions, peeled and finely chopped
- 225 g raisins
- 450 g sultanas
- 350 g demerara sugar
- 25 g salt
- 4 tsp ground mixed spice
- 4 tsp ground cinnamon
- 2 tsp ground ginger

Place the tomatoes in a preserving-pan, add the vinegar and simmer over a low heat for 30 minutes. Add the onions, raisins and sultanas, and continue to cook for a further 30 minutes. Add the sugar, salt and spices, and simmer gently for 1½-2 hours until thick. Stir occasionally.

Leave to cool slightly, then spoon into hot, sterile jars (see page 393).

PICKLED GREEN TOMATOES

Second to pickled onions, this is my all-time favourite pickle. If you don't already grow your own tomatoes, plant some now so that you can try it! Whole green tomatoes are bottled with your favourite herbs or spices – garlic, bay, dill, vanilla or cinnamon would all be good choices – in sweetened vinegar water. Two months later, or longer if you can wait, you are in for a treat. Versions of this recipe are popular in Germany, throughout Eastern Europe and North America. The pickle goes with terrines, cheese and cold meat pies. This version comes from Joyce Molyneux's *The Carved Angel Cookery Book* but I first discovered it in Caroline Conran and Susan Campbell's 1971 *Poor Cook*, a book long overdue a reprint.

1.4 kg small green tomatoes, rinsed

100 g salt

900 g granulated sugar

300 ml white wine vinegar

1 vanilla pod or 1 cinnamon stick

Place the tomatoes in a saucepan. Add the salt to 2.25 litres of cold water in a separate pan and stir until it dissolves completely, then bring the water to the boil. Pour enough over the tomatoes to cover. Simmer for 10 minutes, then drain and peel the tomatoes.

Place the sugar, vinegar, vanilla pod or cinnamon stick and 150 ml cold water in a pan large enough to take the tomatoes too. Stir over a medium heat until the sugar has dissolved, then bring to the boil. Add the tomatoes and simmer very gently for 5 minutes. Remove from the heat and leave to cool in the syrup for 8 hours or overnight.

Strain off the syrup into a separate pan and bring it to the boil again. Boil for 10 minutes, and add the tomatoes. Simmer for a further 5 minutes, then remove from the heat. Pack into hot sterilized jars (see page 393) and seal while still hot. Store in a cool, dark place for at least a month before using.

GREEN TOMATO JAM

This recipe was clipped from the *Daily Mail* on 26 September 1996 by an eagle-eyed friend. It was first published in a turn-of-the-century part-work called *Isobel's Home Cookery* put out by C.Arthur Pearson (1886-1901). I didn't get a chance to make it but my friend says, 'The jam is nice, not as sharp as the red one, maybe coriander seeds would give it an edge.' Serve like marmalade, for breakfast.

- **1.5 kg green tomatoes, cored, peeled and chopped**
- **1.5-2 kg sugar**
- **1 tsp ground ginger**
- **1 tsp salt**
- **a pinch of cayenne pepper**
- **juice and peel of 2 lemons**

Blitz the tomatoes in a food-processor and pass through a sieve into a saucepan. To each 600 ml of tomato pulp add 450 g sugar. Cover over a medium heat, stirring frequently until the sugar dissolves, then add the rest of the ingredients.

Boil briskly to setting point, stirring occasionally. Remove the lemon peel. Cool slightly then stir into sterilized jars (see page 393). Cool, cover, then seal.

GREEN TOMATO AND ZABAGLIONE TART

SERVES 4

Darren Simpson was the chef at Sartoria in London's Savile Row before he settled in Australia. He's a classy modern chef, his style informed by his years under Simon Hopkinson at Bibendum in Chelsea, and with Rose Gray and Ruthie Rogers at the River Café in Hammersmith. This simple, clever recipe was on his first menu when Sartoria opened in June 1998, made with Italian green tomatoes from www.andreasveg.co.uk. I've made it so often, it feels like my recipe.

150 g all-butter puff pastry

4 beef-size Italian green tomatoes, halved through their middles

100 g caster sugar, plus a little extra

1 vanilla pod

splash of Italian brandy, plus a little extra

FOR THE ALMOND CREAM

100 g butter

100 g caster sugar

1 egg, beaten

100 g ground almonds

FOR THE ZABAGLIONE

1 egg yolk

1 tbsp caster sugar

4 tbsp Marsala

Pre-heat the oven to 400°F/200°C/gas mark 6.

Roll out the puff pastry into a rough circle about ½ cm thick, prick all over with a fork and leave in the fridge to rest.

Use a finger to remove some of the tomato seeds. In a frying-pan over a very low heat gently melt the sugar with the vanilla pod and the brandy, then add the tomatoes and stew together for a couple of minutes.

Make the almond cream by beating the butter and sugar together until light and fluffy. Then slowly add the egg and the ground almonds.

Spread a thin layer of the almond cream over the pastry, leaving a 1 cm border. Place the stewed tomatoes on top. Sprinkle with some more caster sugar and another splash of brandy. Place the tart in the oven and bake for about 15 minutes until golden brown and crisp.

Meanwhile, whisk the egg yolk, sugar and Marsala over a bain-marie, until it becomes a thick, warm cream. Serve the tart with the zabaglione on warm plates.

GREEN TOMATO AND APPLE PIE

SERVES 6

Bite into this pie and initially you will think you are eating a regular American-style double-crust apple pie. Gradually, after another bite or two, you will isolate a sour but noticeably tomato flavour,

which seems to highlight the fruity acidity of sweetened cooking apples. The hint of lemon juice and zest, which go so well with both cooking apples and green tomatoes, creates a curiously addictive and different interpretation of sweet-sour. This combination of fruit works particularly well with the almost-puff pastry, which is light and flaky but also quite substantial.

FOR THE PASTRY

- 450 g strong plain flour
- salt
- 150 g lard, placed in the freezer for 1 hour
- 150 g butter, placed in the freezer for 1 hour, plus an extra knob
- ice-cold water to mix
- 1 egg yolk, mixed with 1 tbsp milk, for egg wash

FOR THE FILLING

- juice of 1 lemon, and zest, finely shredded
- 2 Bramley cooking apples
- 500 g green tomatoes, cored, peeled and quartered
- nutmeg
- 25 g butter, plus an extra knob
- 4 tbsp sugar

TO SERVE

- crème fraîche or ice cream
- caster sugar

Sift the flour and a pinch of salt in a mixing-bowl. Take the lard or butter out of the freezer. Peel back the paper, dip the fat into the flour and grate it into the bowl, dipping back into the flour every now and again to make the grating easier. Repeat with the other fat. Now, mix the lard and butter evenly into the flour by making sweeping scoops with a palette knife until it resembles heavy breadcrumbs. Stir in 1 tablespoon of water at a time until the dough clings together, and form it into a ball. Put it in a polythene bag and chill in the fridge for 30 minutes.

Pre-heat the oven to 400°F/200°C/gas mark 6.

Make the filling. Put the lemon juice into a bowl. Peel, core and quarter the apples. Slice very thinly across the quarters and immediately toss in the lemon juice. Add the tomatoes and lemon zest and use your hands to mix the ingredients together. Season lightly with freshly grated nutmeg.

Use the knob of butter to grease a large pie-dish. Dust with flour and shake out the excess. Cut the pastry in half and roll out 1 piece to fit the pie-dish. Tuck the pastry into position, trimming away the overhang and using the scraps to plug any tears or cracks. Spoon the filling into the pastry case. Sprinkle over the sugar. Cut up the 25 g butter and scatter all over the surface. Roll the other piece of pastry and cut it to make a lid. Brush round the rim with the egg wash and fit the lid, pressing together the edges to seal. Brush the pastry gently with egg wash. Cut out shapes – leaves, apples, tomatoes, etc. – and use them to decorate the top. With the point of a knife, etch the surface with a few swirls and make a couple of slits, or prick in a few places with a fork, for the steam to escape.

Bake for 15 minutes. Then lower the oven temperature to 300°F/150°C/gas mark 2, and cook for a further 30 minutes or until the pastry is golden, lightly puffed and thoroughly cooked. Dust with caster sugar and serve hot with ice cream, cold with crème fraîche. Place a bowl of caster sugar on the table.

GREEN TOMATO FOOL

SERVES 6-8

This looks very pretty, rather like a greengage fool, with the pale green puree swirled into whipped cream. A marginally healthier version could be made with a mixture of Greek yoghurt and cream. Usually the mixture is turned into a uniform cream but it looks far prettier if it is left streaked, rather like raspberry ripple ice cream.

There is absolutely no reason why this shouldn't be made with red tomatoes: flavour it with a hint of lemon, or cardamom, vanilla or fresh basil. If there is a shortage of green tomatoes, halve the quantity and serve the fool with sponge fingers and extra caster sugar.

900 g green tomatoes, cored, peeled and chopped

1/4 tsp freshly grated nutmeg or a handful of fresh basil leaves

300-450 g sugar

300 ml whipping cream or 150 ml Greek yoghurt and 150 ml whipping cream

Place the tomatoes in a suitable pan with the nutmeg or basil and cook until soft and thick. Tip them into a sieve placed over a bowl. Wash the pan, then pass the tomatoes through the sieve back into the pan. Simmer until the puree is very thick and dry. Stir in 300 g of the sugar and cook over a gentle heat until it has dissolved. Taste and add more sugar if you think it necessary. Cool the puree.

Whip the cream (if you are using a mixture of yoghurt and cream, fold the yoghurt into the whipped cream) in a large, chilled serving-bowl until the whisk forms ribbons but the cream isn't stiff. Either fold all of the chilled tomato puree into the cream or reserve a little. Serve the fool in scoops in chilled glasses, topped with a dollop of the reserved puree.

GREEN TOMATO UPSIDE-DOWN CAKE

SERVES 8-10

Soon after I began work on this book a friend brought me a copy of *Tomato Imperative* by Sharon Nimtz and Ruth Cousineau (Little, Brown, 1994) from Los Angeles. I read it from cover to cover and promptly hid the book, fearful that I might use it as a template for my own book. When my book was more or less finished, I felt able to read it again and this recipe particularly took my fancy. It evolved out of a failed attempt to make Tomato Tarte Tatin (see page 232): 'Ruth distractedly grated lemon rind directly over the brown sugar in the baking pan instead of into the cake ingredients, and we decided to keep it that way.' Serve it warm as a dessert with crème fraîche.

- **8 tbsp butter, softened**
- **75 g dark brown sugar**
- **1 lemon**
- **750 g small green tomatoes, cut in thin wedges**
- **300 g flour**
- **50 g sugar**
- **1¼ tsp baking powder**
- **½ tsp baking soda**
- **¼ tsp salt**
- **350 ml buttermilk**

Pre-heat the oven to 375°F/190°C/gas mark 5.

Spread 2 tablespoons of the butter on the bottom and sides of a 25 cm x 5 cm deep round cake tin. Sprinkle the brown sugar evenly over the bottom. Grate the lemon zest evenly over the sugar. Then overlap the wedges of tomato in concentric circles over the zest and sugar.

Stir the flour, sugar, baking powder, baking soda and salt together, and work in the remaining butter with your fingertips until the mixture resembles coarse breadcrumbs. Stir in the buttermilk. Pour the batter into the pan over the tomatoes. Bake until golden brown and a toothpick inserted in the centre comes out dry, about 45 minutes.

Leave to cool for 20 minutes before inverting the cake on to a serving platter.

sweet tomatoes

'The tomate confite farcie aux douze saveurs is one of the few dishes in the Michelin red guide whose place on the menu has to be clarified with a parenthesis (dessert), indicating that though it sounds like a veggie, it eats like a sweet. It is a speciality of the kitchen of the great chef Alain Passard, which a lot of people think is the best and most poetic in Paris, and probably all France; it requires a hair-raising amount of work by the commis, the kitchen cabin-boy; and many people who care about French cooking believe that it is a kind of hopeful portent – a sign that the creative superiority of French cooking may not yet be extended indefinitely. Normally, a braised tomato becomes a tomato sauce. ("The limitations of this insight," one of Passard's admirers noted gravely, "describe the limitations of Italian cuisine.") To make a tomato get sweeter without falling apart not only is technically demanding but demonstrates, with a stubborn, sublime logic, an extremely abstract botanical point. Tomatoes are not vegetables; they are fruit.'

Adam Gopnik, 'Is There A Crisis in French Cooking?', *New Yorker,* spring 1997

Okay, everyone knows that tomatoes are a fruit – but we rarely eat them as one. It is curious that even the sweetest, ripest and most luscious tomatoes appeal to us as a savoury food rather than as something to serve with custard or ice cream – or in a fruit salad where they look stunning and might even be confused with pomegranate, glistening like glassy red jewels in the bowl.

Every now and again, since the early days of tomato cookery, people have experimented with using the tomato as a fruit. Some ideas are more successful than others but one or two, such as Green Tomato Fool (see page 418) and Shaker Tomato Cream Pie (see page 424), are enduringly popular. In the 1990s a minor fashion for *haute cuisine* sweet tomato dishes has been inspired by Alain Passard's *Tomate Confite Farcie aux Douze Saveurs*. The plum tomatoes are cut open, the middles scooped out, and stuffed with a farce made of finely chopped orange and lemon zest, sugar, ginger, mint, pistachios, star anise, and cloves. They are then poached in a constantly moving vanilla-scented caramel for 45 minutes and the result leaves you in no doubt that a tomato is a fruit, and that it can be delicious treated like one. Darren Simpson, chef of Sartoria, Sir Terence Conran's tenth restaurant, chose a Green Tomato and Zabaglione Tart (see page 416) for his opening menu.

The choice of recipes here rejoices in the old and new ways of using tomatoes as a fruit. I hope you will be tempted, but the first time you make one, I wouldn't mention that the fruit involved is tomato. Curiously people often find the thought of sweet tomato dishes offputting. Until, that is, they taste them.

A word of warning. Always use a dense-textured plum tomato for these recipes, unless specifically stated otherwise, or when the tomatoes are poached or roasted, which most of the recipes require, with sugar and other sweet, aromatic flavourings, they will cook into a puree.

While I am not convinced that the tomato treated as a fruit will catch on in a big way, its relative the tamarillo, which has a very sour flavour and denser texture, is another matter altogether.

A WORD ABOUT TAMARILLOS

The tamarillo, or tree tomato, looks spectacular, like a red egg, or perhaps a cross between a Victoria plum and a plum tomato. Its particular shade of red, and we're talking skin rather than flesh, is post-box meet ruby underpinned with yellow. Beneath the skin, which is far darker and thicker than that of a regular tomato, the flesh is paler and more orange; the seeds are black and glossy. To eat raw, which I wouldn't recommend because the flesh is eerily smooth and mouth-puckeringly tart, the skin is tough and indigestible. When cooked, however, the skin softens and is quite acceptable, although many recipes require that it is removed or that the cooked flesh is scraped off the skin. As it cooks, the flesh of a tamarillo turns a deep red and its texture remains denser than that of the firmest tomato, similar to a very firm plum yet almost slimy like papaya or mango. The seeds are edible.

Tamarillos, like tomatoes, come originally from South America. These days, they are grown in a number of tropical and subtropical countries. Although they feature in savoury recipes, in pickles and jams or as a tart sauce to serve with chicken, they are most often treated as a fruit. They are very popular, for example, in cooked desserts in Australia and New Zealand, and highly prized for their fruity, sour flavour, which contrasts well with very sweet sauces. They are particularly good poached whole in flavoured sugary liquids but they look very attractive, even more like a tomato, when split in half to show the seed cavity and tomato shape.

Do not confuse tamarillos with tomatillos, which resemble the Cape gooseberry or physalis: they look like yellow cherries and are hidden under a green leaf-like casing, which eventually splits and dries into flaky wings. The tomatillo, which features widely in Mexican cooking, is not a member of the tomato family.

MOROCCAN TOMATO SWEETMEATS

SERVES 6

In *Moorish Food* by Sarah Woodward (Kyle Cathie, 1998), I discovered that these are a speciality of the splendid Mamounia hotel in Marrakesh. Large plum tomatoes are halved, their seeds squeezed out and the cavities seasoned with an exotic combination of flavourings then baked until the sugar caramelizes with the spiced juices and the flesh achieves a succulent melting consistency. They taste more sweet than savoury, but they could be served either way. They would be a colourful garnish to a tender tagine of lamb, for example, but also splendid with a creamy rice pudding eaten with sheep's milk yoghurt. I like to serve them as part of a mezze-style buffet.

- 1 kg large plum tomatoes, cored and peeled
- 1 tsp ground cinnamon
- ¼ tsp saffron stamens
- 1 tbsp orange flower water
- 2-3 tbsp groundnut oil
- 150 g caster sugar
- 100 g blanched almonds
- 15 g butter

Pre-heat the oven to 275°F/140°C/gas mark 1, preferably lower.

Halve the tomatoes, cutting through their length, then use the end of a teaspoon or your finger to dig out the seeds. Arrange the tomatoes on a lightly oiled baking-tray and sprinkle the cinnamon and saffron over them evenly. Do the same with the orange flower water, the oil, and finally the sugar.

Place the tray in the bottom of the oven. Cook for 2-3 hours until the tomatoes are of melting consistency. Turn off the oven and leave to cool. Meanwhile, melt the butter in a frying-pan and stir-fry the almonds until lightly golden. Decorate the cooled tomatoes with the nuts.

POACHED PLUM TOMATOES WITH VANILLA ICE CREAM

SERVES 4

I really do believe that I was overtaken with tomato fever while I was researching this book. One boiling hot day when every surface in my kitchen was covered with tomatoes, I decided to make a tomato lunch. We started with Gazpacho and Tomato Spoon Bread (see pages 110 and 106) and followed that with Meat-stuffed Tomatoes (see page 370). Most people thought I was joking when I put a dish of poached tomatoes on the table for pudding. 'They're plums, aren't they?' they said. I admitted the truth – but before you could say Jack Robinson, they were all gone.

- 150 ml white wine
- 150 ml fresh orange juice
- 4 tbsp unrefined brown sugar
- 2 cardamon pods, lightly crushed
- 2 cloves
- 450 g ripe plum tomatoes, cored, peeled and quartered lengthways
- vanilla ice cream

Place the wine, the orange juice, the sugar, the cardamom pods and the cloves in a small saucepan. Heat through gently, shaking the pan as the sugar dissolves. Leave to simmer for 10 minutes, then remove the pan from the heat and cover. Bring the liquid back to a simmer and add the tomatoes. Cook at a very low simmer for 3-5 minutes until tender.

Use a slotted spoon to transfer the tomatoes to a serving-dish. Let them settle for a minute, then strain their juices back into the poaching liquid. Bring the poaching liquid back to a simmer and cook for several minutes until reduced by about a quarter and turning very syrupy. Pour over the tomatoes and leave to cool. Serve with a scoop of vanilla ice cream and crisp, thin dessert biscuits. Or, if you want to be really controversial, with a wedge of Tomato Spice Tea Bread.

SHAKER TOMATO CREAM PIE

SERVES 6

'When tomatoes made their appearance in American cookery books, in the mid-nineteenth century,' writes Norma MacMillan, in her book *In A Shaker Kitchen*, 'the instructions were to cook them for several hours to make sauces and catsups, but not to eat them raw.' Shakers, she goes on, were growing tomatoes as early as 1823, and enjoyed them raw, fried and baked in a sweet pie.

You need nice ripe tomatoes for this, and they should be peeled so that the skin doesn't interfere with the soft texture of fruit and shortcrust pastry. In order to soak up some of the copious juices from the tomatoes, it is a good idea to sprinkle breadcrumbs or polenta between the slices.

The pie looks delicate and pretty made with yellow tomatoes.

FOR THE PASTRY

- 300 g plain flour, plus a little extra
- a pinch of salt
- 150 g cold butter, cut into pieces
- 1 egg yolk, lightly beaten with 4 tbsp cold water

FOR THE FILLING

- approximately 4 tbsp polenta or fresh breadcrumbs
- 700 g firm, well-flavoured tomatoes, cored, peeled and thickly sliced
- 2 tbsp light soft brown sugar
- freshly grated nutmeg
- 150 ml whipping cream, plus 2-3 tbsp extra
- 1 large egg
- 1 egg yolk

Pre-heat the oven to 375°F/190°C/gas mark 5.

To make the pastry, sift together the flour and salt. Add the butter, rubbing it quickly into the flour until the mixture resembles coarse breadcrumbs. Add the egg and water, a little at a time, to bind, and use a knife to stir the dough into a clump. Knead it a couple of times, pat it into a ball, cover and set aside in a cool place for 30 minutes.

Cut the pastry into 2 pieces, one slightly larger than the other. Dust a work surface lightly with flour and roll the larger of the two pieces to fit a 23 cm flan tin. Smear the tin with oil or butter, then wrap the dough round the rolling pin and loosely drape it over the tin, lifting the edge of the dough with one hand and pressing it into the base and up the sides with the other to prevent shrinkage. Trim off the excess dough and use the scraps to plug any tears or cracks.

Now fill the pie. Sprinkle the entire surface with some of the polenta or breadcrumbs and arrange the tomatoes on top, sprinkling them with sugar, a little nutmeg and more polenta or breadcrumbs as you go. Lightly beat the 150 ml of cream with the whole egg and the egg yolk, and pour it over the tomatoes, nudging aside the slices so that the mixture settles.

Roll out the remaining pastry dough for the top crust, brush the rim of the filled pie and fit the lid, crimping the edges together to seal. Decorate the top of the pie with shapes – leaves, tomatoes, etc. – cut from any pastry trimmings, then paint it with the reserved cream, thinning it with a little milk if necessary. Make a few small holes or slits in the lid for the steam to escape. Bake the pie for 35-40 minutes or until the pastry is golden brown and quite cooked. Dust the surface with caster sugar and serve hot, lukewarm or cold. It is delicious with either crème fraîche, Greek yoghurt, or ice cream. But custard is good too.

SWEET CONFIT OF TOMATOES WITH A VANILLA CREAM

SERVES 4

When Coast opened in London's West End in the mid-nineties, this was the dish that everyone talked about. Love it or hate it, the idea of cooking tomatoes like plums and baking them in a glaze of citrus fruit, then arranging the cooled tomato 'petals' inside individual moulds, to make a lid for a firm vanilla cream, helped put the restaurant on the map. When the moulds are upturned to reveal the tomato, the dish looks spectacular. It is finished with a little of the warmed citrus juices. The texture and flavour are unexpected – something that you will have to judge for yourself. This dish was most probably inspired by Alain Passard's *Tomate Confite Farcie aux Douze Saveurs* (see page 420), and is similar to Bruno Loubet's Tomato Confit with Honey, Pepper and Rosemary, which is served with vanilla ice cream, but as far as I know this dish is the invention of Steve Terry.

4 ripe plum tomatoes, cored, peeled, halved and seeded
150 g caster sugar
juice of 1 orange
juice of 1 lemon
butter

FOR THE VANILLA CREAM
600 ml thick cream
2½ vanilla pods, split
60 g caster sugar
2½ leaves gelatine, soaked in cold water

Pre-heat the oven to 350°F/180°C/gas mark 4.

Cut the tomatoes lengthways into quarters and lay them on a baking dish Put the caster sugar, orange and lemon juices in a saucepan and cook over a medium heat until the mixture begins to caramelize. Pour the citrus caramel over the tomato quarters and bake the tomatoes for approximately 30 minutes. Remove the tomato 'petals' from the caramel when firm and set aside to cool. Reserve the caramel.

To make the vanilla cream, put the cream in a saucepan. Scrape the seeds out of the vanilla pods and add both seeds and pods to the cream together with the caster sugar. Bring slowly to the boil, then remove from the heat. Discard the vanilla pods and stir in the softened gelatine. Allow the mixture to cool, stirring occasionally, until it starts to thicken.

Arrange 4 tomato 'petals' in the bottom of 4 buttered individual moulds, overlapping to form a single layer. Pour the vanilla cream into each mould. Cover and chill in the refrigerator to set.

To serve, heat the reserved citrus caramel and set aside. Slightly warm the moulds by dipping the base into hot water and turn out on to individual plates. Serve with a little warm citrus caramel poured over.

TOMATO SOUP CAKE

SERVES 6-8

M. F. K. Fisher is to American cookery writing what Elizabeth David is to British. Tucked away in *The Art of Eating* (Collier Books, 1990), is an essay about using spare space in the oven when you are cooking other things. I read: 'This is a pleasant cake, which keeps well and puzzles people who ask what kind it is.' Here's the recipe.

- 3 tbsp butter
- 250 g caster sugar
- 1 tsp baking soda
- 1 can tomato soup
- 300 g flour
- 1 tsp cinnamon
- 1 tsp nutmeg, ginger, cloves mixed
- 175 g raisins, nuts, chopped figs, what you will (sun-dried tomatoes?)

Cream the butter until it is pale and light. Add the sugar, and blend thoroughly. Add the soda to the soup, stirring well, and add this alternately to the first mixture with the flour and spices sifted together. Stir well, incorporate the raisins, nuts etc. and bake in an oiled pan or loaf-tin at 325°F/170°C/gas mark 3, checking that the cake is done (a skewer inserted in the middle should come away dry) after 35 minutes.

GRILLED TAMARILLOS WITH HONEY AND MARSALA

SERVES 4

The first time I ever ate a tamarillo was at Kensington Place in London. There, they are split in half, dredged with icing sugar and placed under a very hot grill until the sugar begins to caramelize. Extra sweetness comes from a fresh raspberry puree, which is served, coulis-style, under the tamarillo and served with vanilla ice cream.

In this similarly simple recipe, the tamarillos are split and the cut sides painted with Marsala, white wine and honey before they are grilled or cooked in a hot oven until the cut side is burnished and the side of the fruit begins to wrinkle and feels soft to the prod.

4 tamarillos
150 ml Marsala
150 ml white wine
4 tbsp runny honey
40 g butter

Pre-heat the grill to its highest setting or the oven to 450°F/230°C/ gas mark 8.

Halve the tamarillos, aiming to cut through their stalks so that each half has a tail. Lay them in the grill-pan or on a shallow oven-dish. Make a few slashes in the flesh and dribble each half with a little Marsala, then with white wine, and finally spread with a thin layer of honey. Cover each with thin slices of butter, using about half the given quantity. Grill, or cook near the top of the oven, for 10-15 minutes until the top is burnished and the fruit feels soft to the touch. Allow to rest for a few minutes before transferring to a serving bowl or plates.

Tip the juices into a small saucepan and briefly boil up with the remaining wines, the honey and butter to make a small quantity of sauce. Spoon the sauce over the fruit and serve with vanilla ice cream.

POACHED TAMARILLOS WITH CINNAMON AND MARSALA

SERVES 6

2 cinnamon sticks
200 g soft brown sugar
1 glass Marsala, 150 ml
2 glasses white wine, 300 ml
6 tamarillos

Place the cinnamon sticks, sugar, Marsala and white wine in a non-reactive saucepan that can hold the submerged tamarillos. Bring to the boil, swirling the pan as the sugar melts, reduce the heat and simmer for 3 minutes. Meanwhile, lightly score the pointed end of the tamarillos with an X. Put them in the boiling syrup, bring it back to the boil, then reduce the heat. Cover with a circle of greaseproof paper and simmer for 10 minutes or until the fruit is just cooked. Leave to cool submerged.

Ease the pulp off the skin and serve warm with crème fraîche and some of the juices.

TAMARILLO AND ANGOSTURA ICE CREAM WITH POACHED TAMARILLOS

SERVES 6

Joan Campbell is someone I've grown to admire over years of subscribing to *Australian Vogue Entertaining*. In Sydney, I am reliably informed, she is a legend in her own lunchtime: her magazine once described her tongue as being as sharp as her palate, her bark as impressive as her bite. Anyway, she and her daughter, Sue Fairlie-Cunninghame, who is also with *Vogue Entertaining*, have impeccable taste in food with a style that manages to be simple yet classy and always with a clever twist.

Take this recipe. Tamarillos are poached in sugar water then half are pulped with a little of the poaching water and a splash of Angostura bitters before being mixed into soft vanilla ice cream. Smart, or what? It is an idea that would work equally well with peaches, pears or plums.

- 450 g caster sugar
- 450 ml water
- 12 tamarillos
- 2 tbsp Angostura bitters
- 1 litre good-quality vanilla ice-cream, softened slightly

Put the sugar and water in a saucepan and bring to a simmer, stirring until the sugar dissolves. Add the tamarillos and simmer until the flesh is tender and has turned a deep red. Transfer the fruit and the syrup to a bowl and set aside to cool, then cover and chill in the refrigerator.

To make the ice cream, skin 6 of the tamarillos and remove their stems. Place in a blender and puree. Pass through a sieve to remove the seeds, then mix the puree with the Angostura. Mix the tamarillo puree with the ice cream, then transfer to a covered container and store in the freezer until you wish to serve it. Slice the remaining chilled tamarillos in half lengthways, leaving the stems intact. Serve them in individual dishes with a scoop of ice cream and some of the juices.

Also see:
Tomato Clafoutis (page 147)

tomato juices & cocktails

'The tomatoes that are the most intensely sweet and concentrated seem to be those that ripen at the very end of the season, sometimes after the foliage has been killed by the first frost. Inside they are practically jam. They make a wonderful base for soups using onions and wild mushrooms.'

Deborah Madison, *The Savoury Way* (Bantam, 1990)

There are some pretty good tinned tomato juices around. My advice would be to experiment until you find one you like and stick with it. If, however, you decide to make your own, and it is worth doing every now and then, you can tailor the juice exactly to your taste. It brings a whole new lease of life to cocktails. How about, for example, a pink gin made with essence of tomato? Or vodka cappuccino with frothy fresh tomato juice? Or a tomato juice cocktail flavoured with a background hint of, say, garlic, or onion, and scented with basil? Or what about a fruit tomato cocktail, with fresh peaches, melon or pineapple?

Things become even more interesting when you cook the tomatoes. Flavours will be markedly different depending on the type of tomato you use and whether they are fresh or tinned. Onions, of course, garlic perhaps, celery, maybe, and herbs, such as parsley, mint and basil, can be used singly or all together. Dill, rosemary or coriander would be interesting too. And there are other equally pervasive flavours, such as cucumber, orange juice and plums. Or even cream.

There is little difference between making a juice and making a sauce or soup. Don't forget, however, that the texture must be thin enough to drink comfortably, and the flavours must be sufficiently fine-tuned so that the juice will taste good chilled.

FRESH TOMATO JUICE MAKES APPROXIMATELY 500 ML

This can be made quickly and easily in a food-processor or liquidizer. Should you ever become fanatical about your tomato juice, you might prefer to peel and core the tomatoes, reserving the tomato water, then blitz that with the tomato flesh and additional ingredients. The advantage of doing that is that there is no risk of bitterness from either skin or pips and you won't need to sieve the juice. Either way, chill thoroughly before serving over ice. This juice is delicious infused with a sprig of mint.

- 8 ripe tomatoes, cored and peeled
- 5 cm piece celery, grated
- 1 tsp grated onion
- a squeeze of lemon
- 3 drops Tabasco
- a pinch of sugar
- 150 ml water
- salt and freshly ground black pepper

Either place all the ingredients in the bowl of a food-processor and blitz until smooth, then pass the juice through a sieve, pressing down on pips and skin to get the maximum pulp. Or quarter the tomatoes over a sieve rested on a bowl then scrape the pips and juice into the sieve. Press on the debris to extract the maximum juice. Then put the juice, with the tomato pulp and all the other ingredients in the food-processor and blitz. Taste and fine-tune seasonings with sugar, salt, black pepper and lemon juice. Add extra water, whisking it in, until the thickness is to your liking.

COOKED TOMATO JUICE MAKES APPROXIMATELY 500 ML

This is the universal favourite combination. Half a red pepper is a very good addition, but vary as you wish.

- 8 ripe tomatoes, roughly chopped, or 400 g tin chopped plum tomatoes
- 1 small onion, chopped
- 2 sticks celery heart with leaves
- 4 parsley stalks, chopped
- 4 basil leaves, torn
- salt and freshly ground black pepper
- 3 drops Tabasco
- a squeeze of lemon juice
- 1 tbsp tomato ketchup, for added sweetness (optional)

Place the tomatoes, onion, celery, parsley and basil in a medium pan with 150 ml water. Season with salt and pepper and simmer, covered, for 30 minutes. Pass through a sieve, pressing down on the ingredients to extract maximum juice. Taste and adjust the seasonings with Tabasco, lemon juice, and ketchup if needed. Whisk in extra water if the juice seems too thick.

IMPROVING TINNED TOMATO JUICE

MAKES APPROXIMATELY 400 ML

- 2.5 cm piece lemon zest (no pith)
- 400 g carton tomato juice
- ½ tsp onion juice
- a pinch of celery salt
- ½ tsp horseradish
- a squeeze of lemon juice
- 3 drops Tabasco
- salt and freshly ground black pepper

Twist the lemon zest over a cocktail shaker. Place it and all the other ingredients in the shaker. Shake well, taste and adjust seasoning with salt, pepper and Tabasco. Discard the lemon twist and pour over cracked ice.

CLEAR TOMATO EXTRACT

MAKES APPROXIMATELY 500 ML

Every time you seed tomatoes it is worth tipping the seeds and their juices into a sieve and collecting the 'water'. You can either be patient and end up with unclouded liquid or you can hurry things along by pressing the seeds against the side of the sieve and risk having sediment in the liquid. This recipe is the real McCoy, an haute-cuisine answer to drawing the liquid from very ripe tomatoes. The result is clear orange-tinted tomato nectar. This essence of tomato makes a mean vodka martini.

Michel Bras, at his restaurant at Laguiole in south-west France, whisks superior olive oil into this nectar and serves a tiny glass of it alongside privileged dishes. I use it to make a tomato vinaigrette (see page 179). It would be just the thing to use in a tomato risotto or tomato aspic. Ideally, the tomatoes should be so ripe, and so full of flavour, that their sweet-sour balance will need no fine-tuning. Some people, however, season the pulp with salt, pepper and sugar, which might speed up the extraction but might also spoil the flavour: it is best to season at the end. The pulp isn't good for much after it has been drained in this way. If you can't bear to throw it away, use it in stock, or as the basis for a tomato sauce.

2 kg very ripe tomatoes

Roughly chop the tomatoes, place them in a food-processor and blitz. Line a sieve with muslin or a clean J-cloth and place it over a bowl. Pour in the tomato pulp, cover, and stand in a cool, fly-free place overnight. The extract can be stored in the fridge for several days; you may find it has jellied. It can also be frozen.

FROTHY TOMATO JUICE

MAKES APPROXIMATELY 250 ML

The skin helps to improve the colour of this juice, which keeps its cappuccino-like froth for long enough to spritz those cocktails. For maximum flavour choose perfectly ripe tomatoes that need minimal seasoning.

6 very ripe, squashy tomatoes
salt and freshly ground black pepper

Blitz whole or halved tomatoes until frothy and smooth. Pass through a sieve, taste and adjust seasoning if necessary. Blitz again if not frothy enough.

TOMATO, CUCUMBER AND YOGHURT JUICE

MAKES APPROXIMATELY 550 ML

A refreshing combination, popular in Eastern Europe and the Middle East.

- 300 ml tomato juice
- ½ small cucumber, peeled, seeded and chopped
- ½ small garlic clove, crushed with a pinch of salt
- 4 drops Tabasco
- 6 mint leaves
- 150 ml plain yoghurt
- salt and freshly ground black pepper
- lemon juice

Blitz all the ingredients with 150 ml water or light chicken stock. Taste, and adjust the seasoning with salt, pepper and lemon juice. Pass through a sieve. Add extra water if the juice seems too thick. Chill.

TOMATO, CARROT AND ORANGE JUICE WITH CORIANDER

MAKES APPROXIMATELY 700 ML

Excellent with vodka.

- 225 g young carrots, peeled and grated
- 100 ml orange juice
- 450 g ripe tomatoes, halved
- ½ tsp sugar
- salt and freshly ground black pepper
- a squeeze of lemon juice
- 1 tbsp coriander leaves (optional)

Mix the grated carrots into the orange juice

Place the tomatoes and sugar in a pan and simmer for about 15 minutes until the tomatoes are very soft. Pass through a sieve, pressing down on the debris to extract as much juice as possible. Season with salt and pepper. Blitz the carrots and orange juice and, when smooth, add the tomato, continuing until well amalgamated. Taste and adjust seasoning, adding a little lemon juice if necessary. If liked, add the coriander leaves and blitz again. Serve very chilled with ice.

COCKTAILS

BLOODY MARY AND VIRGIN MARY SERVES 1

The secret, I think, of a top-notch Bloody Mary is rinsing out the glass with sherry. Other people like a smidgen of horseradish or mustard. Thereafter it's a matter of balancing the flavours of Tabasco, Worcestershire sauce, lemon juice, celery salt and black pepper with tomato juice and vodka. It's a very personal thing and my recipe should be regarded as a guideline: you may prefer more or less Tabasco, and want to miss out on the celery salt.

The drink was invented at Harry's New York Bar in Paris in 1921 by Fernand 'Pete' Petiot, who was inspired by the Hollywood actress Mary Pickford. The celery garnish came much later: legend has it that a 1960s guest at the Ambassador East Hotel, Chicago, was served a Bloody Mary without the customary swizzle-stick. She improvised by dipping into a nearby garnish tray and used a stick of celery to stir her drink.

Like most cocktails made with tomato juice, the Bloody Mary is a reviver or pick-me-up. Some people might call it a restorative. Its original name was Red Snapper. When it's made with gin it becomes a Red Lion, with tequila, a Sangre. The Virgin Mary omits the vodka – and sherry.

½ tsp sherry
50 ml vodka
2 dashes Worcestershire sauce
a squeeze of lemon juice
a pinch of celery salt
2-3 dashes Tabasco
150 ml tomato juice
black pepper
a stick of celery

Rinse out a tall glass with the sherry. One-third fill it with ice. Add vodka, Worcestershire sauce, lemon juice, celery salt and Tabasco. Pour on the tomato juice, stir, then season with black pepper. Taste and adjust the seasonings. Serve with a cocktail stirrer or stick of celery.

BLOOD TRANSFUSION

SERVES 1

A do-or-die hangover cure.

- 25 ml vodka
- 25 ml dry sherry
- juice of 1 lime
- 350 ml tomato juice
- 1-2 dashes Worcestershire sauce
- a pinch of celery salt
- 25 ml Fernet Branca

Three-quarters fill a tall glass with ice cubes and pour in the vodka and sherry. Add the lime and tomato juice. Season with Worcestershire sauce and celery salt and stir. Float the Fernet Branca over the top in a layer. Drink the spicy tomato juice through the Fernet Branca, or cream off the Fernet Branca and sip the faux Bloody Mary.

GAZPACHO COCKTAIL

SERVES 2

Make this at the height of summer when sun-ripened, heavy tomatoes are available. Merely blitz the tomatoes in the food-processor with other salad vegetables such as cucumber, red or yellow peppers, boiled beetroot and young carrots. Fresh herbs, such as basil, mint and parsley, are another good addition. To catch pips and skin, pour the cocktail through a fine sieve then adjust the flavours with runny honey, Tabasco and lemon juice. Try it with a shot of vodka or gin.

- 1 small red pepper, seeded, white filament removed, and sliced
- 6 medium vine-ripened tomatoes, halved
- 10 cm length cucumber, peeled and roughly sliced
- ½ garlic clove, peeled
- 3 drops Tabasco
- 1 tbsp tomato ketchup
- ½ tsp sea-salt flakes
- 1 tbsp olive oil
- salt and freshly ground black pepper
- a squeeze of lemon juice
- vodka or gin to taste (optional)

Place all the ingredients, except the lemon juice and the vodka, in the bowl of a food-processor. Blitz at high speed until pureed. Pass through a sieve. Taste and adjust seasoning with lemon juice, more salt and maybe more Tabasco. Stir in the vodka. Serve over ice with a sprig of mint.

PARSLEY AND GIN 'SOUP'

SERVES 2

'The greenish mush is both cooler and inflamer – best eaten in very small portions on hot, humid days by the pool,' wrote Jeremy Round of this cocktail-cum-soup, which was inspired by his search for the perfect Bloody Mary.

- 225 ml good-quality tinned tomato juice
- 50 g celery heart, chopped
- 75 g onion, chopped
- 50 g sweet green pepper, seeded, white filament removed, and chopped
- 4 tbsp chopped flat-leaf parsley leaves
- 50 ml gin

Liquidize. Chill. Sip and savour.

PRAIRIE OYSTER

SERVES 1

Tomato ketchup is the sweetener in this ancient hangover cure. The olive oil makes sure everything slips smoothly out of the glass. The egg yolk must not break.

- 1 tsp olive oil
- 1-2 tbsp tomato ketchup
- 1 very fresh egg yolk
- a dash of Worcestershire sauce
- a dash of Tabasco
- salt and freshly ground black pepper

Rinse the glass with olive oil and throw away the oil. Add the tomato ketchup and the egg yolk, and season with Worcestershire sauce, Tabasco, salt and pepper. Close your eyes and swallow in one gulp. Serve a small glass of iced water on the side.

Also see:
Tomato Stock (page 61)

conversion charts

Metric units are used throughout this book. The approximate equivalents are as follows:

Dry weights	
15 g	½ oz
25 g	1 oz
50 g	2 oz
75 g	3 oz
100 g	4 oz
150 g	5 oz
175 g	6 oz
200 g	7 oz
225 g	8 oz
250 g	9 oz
275 g	10 oz
310 g	11 oz
350 g	12 oz
375 g	13 oz
400 g	14 oz
425 g	15 oz
450 g	1 lb
550 g	1¼ lb
700 g	1½ lb
900 g	2 lb
1.4 kg	3 lb
1.8 kg	4 lb
2.3 kg	5 lb

Liquid measures	
25 ml	1 fl oz
50 ml	2 fl oz
75 ml	3 fl oz
150 ml	5 fl oz (¼ pint)
275 ml	10 fl oz (½ pint)
400 ml	15 fl oz (¾ pint)
700 ml	1 pint
750 ml	1¼ pints
900 ml	1½ pints
1 litre	1¾ pints
1.1 litres	2 pints
1.3 litres	2¼ pints
1.4 litres	2½ pints
1.75 litres	3 pints
1.8 litres	3¼ pints
2 litres	3½ pints
2.1 litres	3¾ pints
2.3 litres	4 pints
2.8 litres	5 pints
3.4 litres	6 pints
4 litres	7 pints
4.5 litres	8 pints

AMERICAN CUP

For solid ingredients that can be measured in tablespoons, such as flour, sugar, herbs and chopped nuts, ¼ cup is the equivalent of 2 tablespoons. 1 cup is equal to 250 ml or 8 fl oz.

OVEN TEMPERATURES

250F	120C	Gas Mark ½	Cool
275F	140C	Gas Mark 1	Very Slow
300F	150C	Gas Mark 2	
325F	170C	Gas Mark 3	Slow
350F	180C	Gas Mark 4	Moderate
375F	190C	Gas Mark 5	
400F	200C	Gas Mark 6	Moderately Hot
425F	220C	Gas Mark 7	Fairly Hot
450F	230C	Gas Mark 8	Hot
475F	240C	Gas Mark 9	Very Hot

LENGTH

0.5 cm	¼ inch	18 cm	7 inches
1 cm	½ inch	20.5 cm	8 inches
2.5 cm	1 inch	23 cm	9 inches
5 cm	2 inches	23.5 cm	10 inches
7.5 cm	3 inches	28 cm	11 inches
10 cm	4 inches	30.5 cm	12 inches (1 foot)

AVERAGE WEIGHTS OF TOMATOES

Cherry tomato: 5 g
average 13 = 100 g, 34 = 250 g
Medium tomato: 60 g
average 4 = 250 g, 7 = 500 g
Plum tomato: 80 g
average 3 = 250 g, 6 = 500 g
Large tomato: 145 g
average 3 = 500 g
Beef-type tomato: 250 g

A 250 g whole tomato is equal to 130 g seeded and peeled tomato or tomato concassé.

500 g of medium-sized tomatoes, gives about 350 ml of cooked tomatoes.

1 American cup of tinned chopped or fresh, peeled, seeded and chopped tomatoes is equal to 250 g or 8 oz.

bibliography

Books – like this one – that aim to be definitive, rely on exhaustive research. I consulted hundreds of books to build up my insight into tomatoes and this bibliography lists the ones I found most useful. Many are in my own cookery library, or borrowed from friends, or consulted at various libraries. Some are out of print, and might be available by mail order through specialist book dealers like Janet Clarke, 3 Woodside Cottages, Freshford, Bath BA3 6EJ (tel. 01225 723186/ www.janetclarke.com). Old and international cookbooks are also available by mail order from Books For Cooks, 4 Blenheim Crescent, London W11 1NN (tel. 020 7221 1992/wwwbooksforcooks.com).

Andrews, Colman: *Catalan Cuisine*, Grub Street, 1997

Bailey, Lee: *Tomatoes*, Clarkson Potter, 1992

Bareham, Lindsey: *In Praise of the Potato*, Michael Joseph 1989/Penguin 1995; *A Celebration of Soup*, Michael Joseph 1993/Penguin 1994; *Onions Without Tears*, Michael Joseph 1995/Penguin 1996; *Supper Won't Take Long*, Penguin, 1997; with Hopkinson, Simon, *The Prawn Cocktail Years*, Macmillan, 1997

Blythman, Joanna: *The Food We Eat*, Michael Joseph, 1996

Boxer, Arabella: *Garden Cookbook*, Weidenfeld & Nicolson, 1974

Brown, Lynda, *The Shopper's Guide to Organic Food*, Fourth Estate, 1998

Carluccio, Antonio: *Italian Feast*, BBC, 1997; Southern Italian Feast, BBC, 1998

Carrier, Robert: *New Great Dishes of the World*, Macmillan, 1997

Caruana Galizia, Anne and Helen: *The Food and Cookery of Malta*, Prospect Books, 1997

Chapman, Kit: *Great British Chefs 2*, Mitchell Beazley, 1995

Child, Julia: *From Julia Child's Kitchen*, Jonathan Cape, 1970

Collister, Linda: *The Sauce Book*, Conran Octopus, 1997

Cost, Bruce: *Foods From the Far East*, Random Century, 1988

Costa, Margaret: *Four Seasons Cookery Book*, Thomas Nelson, 1970/Grub Street, 1996

Cradock, Fanny and Johnnie: *The Cook Hostess' Book*, Collins, 1970

Dahl, Roald: *Memories with Food at Gipsy House*, Viking, 1991, republished as *Roald Dahl's Cookbook*, Penguin, 1996

David, Elizabeth: *French Country Cooking*, Penguin, 1951; *French Provincial Cooking*, Penguin, 1960/ Michael Joseph, 1965; *Spices, Salt and Aromatics in the English Kitchen*, Penguin, 1970; *An Omelette*

and a Glass of Wine, Michael Joseph, 1984; *South Wind Through the Kitchen: The Best of Elizabeth David*, edited by Jill Norman, 1997 [all books now republished by Grub Street]
del Conte, Anna: *The Gastronomy of Italy*, Bantam, 1987
Dimbleby, Josceline: *The Almost Vegetarian Cookbook*, Sainsbury, 1994
Ferrigno, Ursula and Treuille, Eric: *Bread: The Ultimate Visual Guide to the Art of Making Bread*, Dorling Kindersley, 1998
Fisher, M. F. K.: *The Art of Eating*, Collier Books, 1990
Gill, A. A.: *The Ivy, The Restaurant and Its Recipes*, Hodder and Stoughton, 1997
Gold, Rozanne: *Recipes 1–2–3*, Grub Street, 1997
Gray, Patience: *Honey From a Weed*, Prospect Books, 1997
Gray, Rose and Rogers, Ruth: *The River Café Cook Book*, Ebury Press, 1995; *The River Café Cook Book 2*, Ebury Press, 1997
Grigson, Sophie: *Taste of the Times*, Channel 4, 1997
Guérard, Michel, edited by Conran, Caroline: *Cuisine Minceur*, Macmillan, 1976; *Cuisine Gourmande*, Macmillan, 1997
Hambro, Natalie: *Particular Delights*, Jill Norman & Hobhouse, 1981
Hazan, Marcella: *Classic Italian Cookbook*, Macmillan, 1988; *Marcella Cucina*, Macmillan, 1997
Hom, Ken: *Illustrated Chinese Cookery*, BBC Books, 1996
Jaffrey, Madhur: *Illustrated Indian Cookery*, BBC Books, 1996
Johnson, Maria: *The Melting Pot*, Prospect Books, 1995
Kaneva-Judelson, Sasha, editor: *East West Food*, Hamlyn, 1997
Kehayan, Nina: *Essentially Aubergines*, Grub Street, 1995
Little, Alastair, with Whittington, Richard: *Keep It Simple*, Ebury, 1993; *Food of the Sun*, Quadrille, 1996
Little, Alastair: *Italian Kitchen*, Ebury, 1996
McMillan, Norma: *In A Shaker Kitchen*, Pavilion, 1996
Madison, Deborah with Edward Espe Brown: *The Greens Cook Book*, Bantam, 1987/Grub Street 2010
Madison, Deborah, *The Savoury Way*, Bantam, 1990
Mendel, Janet: *Traditional Spanish Cooking*, Garnet, 1996
Molyneux, Joyce: *The Carved Angel Cookery Book*, Collins, 1990
Mosimann, Anton: *Naturally*, Channel4/Ebury, 1991
Nimtz, Sharon and Cousineau, Ruth: *Tomato Imperative*, Little Brown, 1994
Olney, Richard: *The French Menu Cookbook*, Dorling Kindersley, 1985; *A Provençal Table*, Pavilion, 1995
Paterson, Jennifer: *Feast Days*, Grafton, 1992
Pininska, Mary: *The Polish Kitchen*, Papermac, 1990 /Grub Street 2000

Pym, Hilary, and Wyatt, Honor: *Cooking à la Pym*, Prospect Books, 1996
Ramsay, Gordon: *Passion for Flavour*, Conran Octopus, 1996
Rhodes, Gary: *Fabulous Food*, BBC, 1997
Ripe, Cherry, and Pascoe, Elise: *Australia the Beautiful Cookbook*, Cumulus, 1995
Roden, Claudia: *Book of Jewish Food*, Viking, 1997
Rombauer, Irma S., Marion R. Becker, and Ethan Becker: *The All New All Purpose Joy of Cooking*, Scribner, 1997
Round, Jeremy: *The Independent Cook*, Barrie & Jenkins, 1988
Roux, Albert and Michel: *French Country Cooking*, Sidgwick & Jackson, 1989
Roux, Michel: *Sauces*, Quadrille, 1996
Sahni, Julie: *Classic Indian Cookery*, Grub Street, 1997
Sampson, Sally: *Chic Simple Cooking*, Thames & Hudson, 1995
Schwartz, Oded: *Preserving*, Kyle Cathie, 1996
Somerville, Annie: *Fields of Greens*, Bantam, 1993
Spry, Constance and Rosemary Hume: *The Constance Spry Cookery book*, Dent, 1956/1990/Grub Street 2011
Strang, Paul: *Take 5000 Eggs*, Kyle Cathie, 1997
Taruschio, Ann and Franco: *Franco and Friends: Leaves from the Walnut Tree*, Pavilion, 1993/BBC Books, 1997; *Bruschetta, Crostoni and Crostini*, Pavilion, 1995
Toklas, Alice B.: *The Alice B. Toklas Cook Book*, Michael Joseph, 1954/Serif, 1994
Troisgros, Jean and Pierre: *The Nouvelle Cuisine of Jean and Pierre Troisgros*, ed. Caroline Conran, Macmillan, 1980
Verge, Roger: *Cuisine of the Sun*, 1979; *Cuisine Provençale*, Papermac, 1993
Waltenspiels, Ronald, Ruth and Linda: *The Sonoma Dried Tomato Cookbook*, Timber Crest Farms, 1992.
Wells, Patricia: *Trattoria*, Kyle Cathie, 1993; *At Home In Provence*, Kyle Cathie, 1997
Whittington, Richard: *Cutting Edge*, Conran Octopus, 1996
Willan, Anne: *Chateau Cuisine*, Conran Octopus, 1992, 1995
Wolfert, Paula: *Cous Cous and Other Food From Morocco*, Harper and Row, 1973, republished as *Moroccan Cuisine*, Grub Street, 1998; *Mediterranean Cooking*, HarperCollins, 1996
Woodward, Sarah: *Moorish Food*, Kyle Cathie, 1998
Wyatt, Honor: *A La Pym*, Prospect Books, 1995

index

v indicates vegetarian recipe
f indicates fish/shellfish recipe